AF774088

Serverless Distributed Systems in Modern .NET and Azure

Building Resilient Event-Driven Applications

Patrick Kearns

Apress®

Serverless Distributed Systems in Modern .NET and Azure: Building Resilient Event-Driven Applications

Patrick Kearns
Dublin, Ireland

ISBN-13 (pbk): 979-8-8688-2838-6 ISBN-13 (electronic): 979-8-8688-2839-3
https://doi.org/10.1007/979-8-8688-2839-3

Copyright © 2026 by Patrick Kearns

This work is subject to copyright. All rights are reserved by the Publisher, whether the whole or part of the material is concerned, specifically the rights of translation, reprinting, reuse of illustrations, recitation, broadcasting, reproduction on microfilms or in any other physical way, and transmission or information storage and retrieval, electronic adaptation, computer software, or by similar or dissimilar methodology now known or hereafter developed.

Trademarked names, logos, and images may appear in this book. Rather than use a trademark symbol with every occurrence of a trademarked name, logo, or image we use the names, logos, and images only in an editorial fashion and to the benefit of the trademark owner, with no intention of infringement of the trademark.

The use in this publication of trade names, trademarks, service marks, and similar terms, even if they are not identified as such, is not to be taken as an expression of opinion as to whether or not they are subject to proprietary rights.

While the advice and information in this book are believed to be true and accurate at the date of publication, neither the authors nor the editors nor the publisher can accept any legal responsibility for any errors or omissions that may be made. The publisher makes no warranty, express or implied, with respect to the material contained herein.

Managing Director, Apress Media LLC: Welmoed Spahr
Acquisitions Editor: Smriti Srivastava
Development Editor: Laura Berendson
Editorial Assistant: Marina Engler

Cover designed by eStudioCalamar

Distributed to the book trade worldwide by Springer Science+Business Media New York, 1 New York Plaza, New York, NY 10004. Phone 1-800-SPRINGER, fax (201) 348-4505, e-mail orders-ny@springer-sbm.com, or visit www.springeronline.com. Apress Media, LLC is a Delaware LLC and the sole member (owner) is Springer Science + Business Media Finance Inc (SSBM Finance Inc). SSBM Finance Inc is a **Delaware** corporation.

For information on translations, please e-mail booktranslations@springernature.com; for reprint, paperback, or audio rights, please e-mail bookpermissions@springernature.com.

Apress titles may be purchased in bulk for academic, corporate, or promotional use. eBook versions and licenses are also available for most titles. For more information, reference our Print and eBook Bulk Sales web page at http://www.apress.com/bulk-sales.

Any source code or other supplementary material referenced by the author in this book is available to readers on GitHub. For more detailed information, please visit https://www.apress.com/gp/services/source-code.

If disposing of this product, please recycle the paper

Dedicated to my partner Julie and our daughter Clodagh, for their love, support, and understanding.

Table of Contents

About the Author

Patrick Kearns is a senior software engineer, architect, and DevOps practitioner with more than three decades of professional experience, including more than 20 years working with .NET. He has worked across e-commerce, finance, insurance, and enterprise SaaS, helping teams design, build, and operate distributed systems where reliability and scalability are critical. Patrick began his career building monolithic systems using early versions of ASP.NET and WCF. As the industry shifted toward microservices and event-driven architectures, he gained hands-on experience with the practical challenges of distributed systems, including latency, partial failure, and operational complexity. His work spans high-throughput e-commerce platforms and compliance-driven insurance systems, where architectural decisions had direct business impact.

Patrick lives in Ireland, where he balances his work in technology with family life, writing, and creative projects. He continues to experiment, learn, and share knowledge, believing that the best way to master complex systems is to explain them clearly to others. His hope is that this book will help .NET developers feel confident tackling distributed, event-driven systems and that it will provide both the technical guards and the mental models needed to succeed.

About the Technical Reviewer

Sourabh Mishra is an entrepreneur, developer, speaker, author, corporate trainer, and animator. He is a Microsoft guy—passionate about Microsoft technologies and a true .NET warrior. Sourabh started his career when he was just 15 years old. He has loved computers since childhood. His programming experience includes C/C++, ASP.NET, C#, VB.NET, WCF, SQL Server, Entity Framework, MVC, Web API, Azure, jQuery, Highcharts, DevOps, Power Platform, Power Automate, and Angular. Sourabh is a solution architect and has been awarded the Most Valuable Professional (MVP) status. He has the zeal to learn new technologies, sharing his knowledge on several online community forums.

He is a founder of "IECE Digital" and "Sourabh Mishra Notes" (an online knowledge-sharing platform where one can learn new technologies easily and comfortably).

Acknowledgments

My thanks go to my partner Julie and my daughter Clodagh for their patience, support, and understanding throughout the writing of this book. Writing a book takes far more time and energy than most people realize, and I could not have finished it without their support.

I am also grateful to everyone at Apress who helped bring this book to life, especially my editor, reviewers, and the wider publishing team for their guidance, feedback, and patience throughout the process.

My thanks also go to the colleagues, mentors, and peers who helped shape my thinking over the years through conversations, challenges, and shared experience. I would particularly like to thank Philip Hopkins, who acted as an early reviewer and advisor.

Finally, I want to remember my mother, Beverley, who bought me that Toshiba MSX HX-10 in the 1980s and whose encouragement first set me on this path.

Introduction

Distributed systems are everywhere. When you order groceries online, your request travels across services that check inventory, process payments, coordinate logistics, and send confirmation emails. When you stream a movie, a chain of caches, APIs, and delivery networks spring into action. Even when you log in to your company's intranet, you're authenticating against globally distributed identity services. The problem? Distributed systems are hard. They introduce latency, partial failures, and consistency challenges that monoliths never had to face. They also require operational tooling, logs, metrics, and tracing just to understand what happened to a single request. This book exists because serverless on Azure, combined with .NET, offers a practical way to embrace distribution without drowning in complexity. With Azure Functions, Durable Functions, Event Grid, Service Bus, and Cosmos DB, you can build systems that scale elastically, recover from failures, and remain affordable. As a .NET developer, you don't have to learn a new language or abandon your existing skills. You get to bring C#, async/await, dependency injection, and NuGet with you.

Who This Book Is For

This book is written for **.NET developers** who want to take the leap from monoliths to distributed, event-driven systems. You should already be comfortable writing C# and building APIs with ASP.NET (`http://asp.net/`) Core or similar frameworks. You should know the basics of Azure, deploying resources, and managing storage accounts, but you don't need to be a cloud expert.

If you're a cloud architect or DevOps engineer, you'll find the architectural patterns valuable, how to design resilient workflows, when to choose queues versus events, and how to monitor costs at scale. If you're a student or early-career developer, you'll find practical guidance on the trade-offs of distributed systems, knowledge that will serve you for decades.

What You'll Learn

By the end of this book, you'll know how to

- Build Functions that respond to HTTP, queues, blobs, timers, and events
- Orchestrate workflows with Durable Functions, fan-out/fan-in, sagas, and approvals
- Connect services with Event Grid and Service Bus for resilient messaging
- Manage data with Cosmos DB and SQL in a serverless context
- Add observability with structured logging, distributed tracing, and metrics
- Secure endpoints with Azure AD and B2C, including handling tokens and API gateways
- Deploy and operate serverless solutions with CI/CD, IaC, and cost governance
- Avoid risks like runaway bills, hidden bottlenecks, or inconsistent state

In short, you'll be able to design and deliver production-level distributed systems in .NET without reinventing infrastructure.

How the Book Is Structured

The book is organized in three parts:

1. Foundations

- Chapter 1 introduces distributed systems and serverless.
- Chapter 2 dives deep into Azure Functions, triggers, bindings, and execution model.

- Chapter 3 explores event-driven architectures with Event Grid and Service Bus.
- Chapter 4 covers data in distributed systems, including Cosmos DB and event sourcing.

2. Patterns

- Chapter 5 introduces Durable Functions for workflows and orchestration.
- Chapter 6 applies integration patterns, external APIs, human workflows, and hybrid systems.
- Chapter 7 adds observability, tracing, logging, telemetry, and cost monitoring.
- Chapter 8 addresses security and identity, Azure AD, B2C, and API gateways.

3. Operations and Advanced Cases

- Chapter 9 covers deployment, IaC, CI/CD, and zero-downtime strategies.
- Chapter 10 walks through case studies, file streaming, orchestration across services, and multi-tenancy.
- Chapter 11 ties everything together with a reference architecture, risks, and a look ahead.
- Chapter 12 looks at the future of serverless in .NET.

How to Read This Book

You can read the book cover to cover or dip into chapters that matter most for your project. Each chapter ends with exercises that move you from theory to practice. Some are short coding labs; others are thought experiments. Don't skip them; they build intuition. If you're new to Azure, start from the beginning. If you already use Functions, you might skip ahead to Chapters 5–7 to explore orchestration, patterns, and observability.

Running Examples

Throughout the book, we'll build a sample project, a distributed order-processing system. It begins with a single Function in Chapter 2 and evolves chapter by chapter:

- Ingestion via HTTP and queues
- Orchestration with Durable Functions
- Events flowing through Event Grid
- Data managed in Cosmos DB
- Observability with Application Insights
- Deployment pipelines with IaC

By the end, you'll have a reference architecture that resembles real-world systems like e-commerce checkouts, insurance claims processing, or financial workflows.

Code and Tools

All code samples will run on **.NET 8 or later**. You'll need

- Visual Studio 2022–2026 or VS Code
- Azure Functions Core Tools
- An Azure account (free tier is enough for most exercises)

The book avoids unnecessary setup complexity. You can run everything locally and only deploy to Azure when you're ready.

About the Code Examples

Most examples in this book are intentionally simplified to teach concepts, not to model every production concern. You'll see patterns like creating HttpClient inline, minimal error handling, or direct bindings without full DI setup, for example. That's on purpose, so you can focus on the serverless and distributed systems ideas first.

What This Means for Production Use

The code in this book teaches you how to think about distributed systems, when to orchestrate vs. choreograph, how to handle eventual consistency, where circuit breakers matter, and how to design for resilience. These patterns and architectural principles are production-level. The simplified code demonstrations are not. Before deploying any example to production, you'll need to add

- **Security Hardening:** Replace `AuthorizationLevel.Anonymous` with proper Azure AD authentication, store secrets in Key Vault, implement RBAC, and validate all inputs. The Security chapter (Chapter 8) covers this in depth.
- **Error Handling**: Add comprehensive try-catch blocks, distinguish transient from permanent failures, implement proper retry policies with backoff, and handle timeouts. Examples show happy paths; production needs unhappy paths too.
- **Observability**: Include structured logging with correlation IDs, distributed tracing, custom metrics, and alerts. Chapter 7 explores this, but examples throughout are terse to maintain focus on core concepts.
- **Resource Management**: Use `IHttpClientFactory` instead of static `HttpClient` instances, properly dispose of connections, implement cancellation tokens, and handle connection pooling. These details are omitted from examples for brevity.
- **Testing**: Write unit tests for services, integration tests for workflows, and load tests for scale assumptions. The book shows testing patterns, but comprehensive test coverage is your responsibility.

- **Compliance:** Add data retention policies, audit logging, proper tagging for cost allocation, and data residency controls. Chapter 11 discusses risks; your production code must address them.

Think of the Examples as Architectural Sketches, not Blueprints

They demonstrate the what and why of distributed systems patterns. Adding the how of production-grade implementation, with all its error handling, logging, security, and edge case management, is where your engineering judgment comes in. The gap between "teaching example" and "production system" is intentional. This book gives you the foundation and mental models. Building robustly on that foundation, with appropriate testing, security reviews, and operational excellence, is your job as a professional engineer.

Why Now?

The rise of serverless is not hype. Systems are growing more complex. Users demand instant responsiveness. Businesses demand cost efficiency. Teams are smaller, deadlines are tighter, and no one wants to babysit servers. At the same time, .NET has matured. Async/await is now a natural fit for concurrency. Dependency injection is built in. The environment has NuGet packages for almost everything. Azure itself has invested heavily in Functions, Durable Functions, and messaging. The moment is right; .NET and serverless belong together.

Final Thought Before We Begin

Distributed systems will always be challenging. You can't wish away latency, failure, or inconsistency. But you *can* embrace them with tools that give you safety. That's what serverless on Azure provides, a platform that makes resilience, scaling, and observability the defaults. This book is your guide to that platform, not just the APIs but also the mindset, patterns, and practices that make distributed systems survivable.

So grab your keyboard. Let's write our first Function.

PART I

Foundations

CHAPTER 1

Introduction to Distributed Systems and Serverless Systems

Why Distributed Systems

Distributed systems are no longer exotic. Every application you use daily, from banking to food delivery, is powered by services spread across machines, regions, and sometimes continents. As developers, this is the water we swim in. Even small projects today tend to involve APIs, queues, and cloud storage spread across boundaries. This first chapter is about building the right mindset. We'll look squarely at the challenges that come with distribution, trace how software architecture has evolved, and then introduce serverless as a practical way to handle complexity. By the end of the chapter, you'll not only understand why serverless is important, but you'll also have a Function running on your own machine.

Distributed by Default

When you write code on your laptop, it's tempting to think of systems as single, neat processes. In production, that illusion quickly disappears. Services talk to each other over the network. Data lives in different places. Some components scale elastically, and others are fragile. What feels like a simple user action, "place an order," might touch half a dozen services before it completes. That's the baseline reality of modern software. The question isn't whether your system is distributed, but how gracefully it behaves under the realities of distribution, latency, partial failures, and eventual consistency.

© Patrick Kearns 2026
P. Kearns, *Serverless Distributed Systems in Modern .NET and Azure*,
https://doi.org/10.1007/979-8-8688-2839-3_1

Why Serverless Is Relevant

Traditional solutions to distributed problems involve heavy lifting, servers, load balancers, clusters, retry logic, and monitoring dashboards. You can solve them yourself, but it takes time and expertise. Serverless platforms change the trade-off. With Azure Functions, you write small units of code that run in response to events, such as an HTTP request, a message in a queue, or a file upload. The platform takes care of scaling, resilience, and telemetry. You still need to design with distribution in mind, but the infrastructure burden is lighter. For .NET developers, everything is familiar. Functions are written in C#, use dependency injection, support async/await, and consume NuGet packages. They look and feel like the code you already write, just running in a different execution model.

Your First Function

Let's begin with the simplest possible Function:

```
using System.Net;
using Microsoft.Azure.Functions.Worker;
using Microsoft.Azure.Functions.Worker.Http;
using Microsoft.Extensions.Logging;

namespace OrderProcessor;

public sealed class HelloFunction(ILogger<HelloFunction> logger)
{
    [Function("HelloHttp")]
    public async Task<HttpResponseData> Run(
        [HttpTrigger(AuthorizationLevel.Function, "get", "post")]
        HttpRequestData req,
        CancellationToken stopToken)
    {
        logger.LogInformation("Hello function processed a request.");

        var response = req.CreateResponse(HttpStatusCode.OK);
        await response.WriteStringAsync("Hello, serverless .NET!",
        stopToken);
```

```
        return response;
    }
}
```

If you've written ASP.NET Core controllers, this should feel familiar. Instead of `[HttpGet]`, you declare a trigger. Instead of `IActionResult`, you return `HttpResponseData`. Everything else, dependency injection, logging, async/await, works the same.

Run this locally using the Azure Functions Core Tools:

```
func start
```

Then open your browser to http://localhost:7071/api/HelloHttp.

You'll see the greeting. Behind the scenes, the Functions runtime handled the host, routing, and scaling logic. (Obviously, the port number may be different here, so make sure to check which one you are using in the config settings.)

The Journey Ahead

This Function is trivial, but it illustrates two things:

1. **Serverless feels familiar.** It's just .NET code with a different entry point.

2. **The platform is doing more than you see**. Scaling, retries, telemetry, and billing are baked in.

From here, we'll widen the lens. The rest of this chapter explores the nature of distributed systems, why they're difficult, how past architectures tried to cope, and why serverless represents the next logical step. By the end of Chapter 1, you'll have seen not just code, but patterns, case studies, and exercises that shape the way you think about distributed software.

The Challenges of Distribution

When you first encounter distributed systems, it is easy to underestimate just how different they are from single-process applications. On the surface, the ingredients look reassuringly familiar. You still write C# methods, you still persist data, and you still expose and call APIs. That familiarity can create a false sense of continuity, as if scaling out is simply a matter of running the same code in more places. In reality, the moment you move beyond a single server, many of the assumptions that quietly held your system together begin to fall apart.

Once a network is involved, it becomes a first-class concern rather than an implementation detail. Calls that were previously just method invocations now cross process and machine boundaries, bringing latency, partial failure, and timeouts into the picture. Services do not always respond, and when they fail, they often fail in ways that are slow, intermittent, or difficult to reproduce. Data that once lived in a single database now exists in multiple stores, caches, or replicas, and it no longer stays perfectly in sync. Even the act of debugging changes fundamentally. Instead of opening a single log file or attaching a debugger to one process, you are tracing requests across services, correlating logs, and trying to reconstruct a story from events that happened in different places at different times.

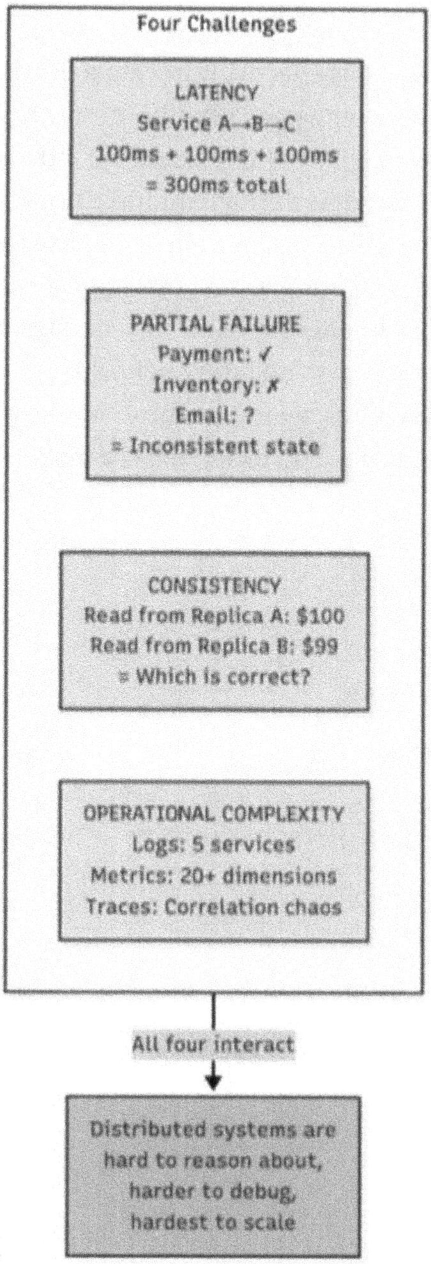

Figure 1-1. *The Four Challenges of Distribution*

These issues manifest in four fundamental ways: latency, partial failure, consistency, and operational complexity (see Figure 1-1). Let's explore each in turn, with .NET examples to show how they surface in practice.

Latency: The Invisible Tax

Inside a monolith, a method call is effectively free. In a distributed system, the same logical operation may involve a network call with a cost measured in milliseconds or seconds. That cost is easy to ignore when looking at individual services, but it compounds quickly as requests flow through multiple hops.

The small example below illustrates this effect. It makes a single HTTP call that waits for two seconds before returning. Even in this trivial case, the latency dominates the execution time. In a real serverless system, each additional service call adds its own network overhead, serialization cost, and retry behavior.

This is why distributed systems favor asynchronous messaging, batching, and orchestration. Latency is not a bug you fix later; it is a tax you pay every time you cross a service boundary.

```
using System;
using System.Diagnostics;
using System.Net.Http;
using System.Threading.Tasks;

public static class LatencyDemo
{
    private static readonly HttpClient Http = new();

    public static async Task Main()
    {
        var stopwatch = Stopwatch.StartNew();

        var response = await Http.GetAsync("https://httpbin.org/delay/2");

        stopwatch.Stop();


        Console.WriteLine(
            $"Status: {response.StatusCode}, Time: {stopwatch.
            ElapsedMilliseconds} ms");
    }
}
```

Here we're calling an endpoint that deliberately delays for two seconds. Locally, the code executes instantly, but over the network, you pay the latency cost.

Now imagine Service A calls B, which calls C. Each hop adds latency. A single request balloons into hundreds of milliseconds or more. For user-facing applications, those extra seconds count. Amazon famously found that every 100ms of added latency cost them 1% in sales.

Serverless systems encourage designs that minimize synchronous chains. Instead of waiting for Service B and C, Service A might publish an event to Event Grid, and each downstream service processes it asynchronously. This trades synchronous latency for eventual consistency.

Partial Failure: When Half the System Works

In a monolith, failures tend to be all-or-nothing. In distributed systems, failures are partial. A payment may succeed while the confirmation email fails. A queue may accept a message while the consumer is down. Users are left in an ambiguous state.

Let's simulate this in a Function:

```
using System.Net;
using Microsoft.Azure.Functions.Worker;
using Microsoft.Azure.Functions.Worker.Http;
using Microsoft.Extensions.Logging;

namespace OrderProcessor;

public sealed class PartialFailureDemo(ILogger<PartialFailureDemo> logger)
{
    private static readonly Random Rng = new();

    [Function("RandomFailure")]
    public async Task<HttpResponseData> Run(
        [HttpTrigger(AuthorizationLevel.Function, "get")]
        HttpRequestData req,
        CancellationToken stopToken)
    {
        // Simulate an unreliable downstream dependency (1 in 3
        requests fails)
        if (Rng.Next(0, 3) == 0)
        {
```

```
            logger.LogError("Simulated downstream failure occurred.");

            var fail = req.CreateResponse(HttpStatusCode.Service
            Unavailable);
            await fail.WriteAsJsonAsync(new { error = "Random failure" },
            stopToken);
            return fail;
        }

        logger.LogInformation("Operation succeeded.");

        var ok = req.CreateResponse(HttpStatusCode.OK);
        await ok.WriteAsJsonAsync(new { time = DateTime.UtcNow },
        stopToken);
        return ok;
    }
}
```

Call this function repeatedly and you'll see intermittent failures. In reality, they aren't "random"; they come from transient network issues, throttling, or downstream crashes. But the effect is the same; sometimes things fail while the rest of the system continues.

Azure Functions provide built-in retry policies. If this function were triggered by Service Bus instead of HTTP, Azure could automatically retry a few times before moving the message to a poison queue. The lesson: design every interaction as if partial failure is inevitable, because it is.

Consistency: The CAP Theorem in Action

Consistency is one of the hardest distributed systems concepts to internalize because a monolith hides it. With one SQL database, you can often assume strong consistency: once a transaction commits, subsequent reads see the same state. When data is split across services, regions, or read models, that assumption breaks down. Updates propagate, and propagation takes time.

A practical demo makes this visible. The functions below simulate a common pattern in distributed systems: a write model and a read model. UpdateProfileA writes to Store A immediately, then replicates the update to Store B after a short delay. If you call

UpdateProfileA and then immediately call ReadProfileB, you may not see the update yet. After a moment, the read catches up. That is eventual consistency in its simplest form: the system becomes consistent over time, not instantly.

Real systems expose this trade-off explicitly. Cosmos DB offers multiple consistency models, from strong consistency (up-to-date reads, higher latency, and lower availability across regions) through to eventual consistency (maximum availability and throughput, but stale reads are possible). The CAP theorem summarizes the constraint: under a network partition, a distributed system must choose between strict consistency and availability. Most production systems choose availability and partition tolerance, then design around the resulting consistency model.

```
using System.Net;
using Microsoft.Azure.Functions.Worker;
using Microsoft.Azure.Functions.Worker.Http;
using Microsoft.Extensions.Logging;

namespace OrderProcessor;

public sealed record UserProfile(string Id, string Name, string Email);

public sealed class ConsistencyDemo(ILogger<ConsistencyDemo> logger)
{
    private static readonly Dictionary<string, UserProfile> StoreA = new();
    private static readonly Dictionary<string, UserProfile> StoreB = new();

    [Function("UpdateProfileA")]
    public async Task<HttpResponseData> UpdateA(
        [HttpTrigger(AuthorizationLevel.Function, "post")]
        HttpRequestData req,
        CancellationToken stopToken)
    {
        var profile = await req.ReadFromJsonAsync<UserProfile>(cancellation
        Token: stopToken)
                      ?? new UserProfile("123", "Alice", "alice@
                      example.com");

        StoreA[profile.Id] = profile;
```

```
        logger.LogInformation("Updated profile {Id} in StoreA",
        profile.Id);

        // Simulate async replication / projection delay to StoreB
        _ = Task.Run(async () =>
        {
            await Task.Delay(TimeSpan.FromSeconds(2),
            CancellationToken.None);
            StoreB[profile.Id] = profile;
            logger.LogInformation("Replicated profile {Id} to StoreB",
            profile.Id);
        });

        var response = req.CreateResponse(HttpStatusCode.Accepted);
        await response.WriteAsJsonAsync(new { profile.Id, Status = "Updated
        in StoreA, replication pending" }, stopToken);
        return response;
    }

    [Function("ReadProfileB")]
    public async Task<HttpResponseData> ReadB(
        [HttpTrigger(AuthorizationLevel.Function, "get")]
        HttpRequestData req,
        CancellationToken stopToken)
    {
        var id = "123";

        var response = req.CreateResponse(HttpStatusCode.OK);

        if (StoreB.TryGetValue(id, out var profile))
        {
            await response.WriteAsJsonAsync(profile, stopToken);
            return response;
        }

        response.StatusCode = HttpStatusCode.NotFound;
```

```
        await response.WriteStringAsync("Not yet updated in StoreB",
        stopToken);
        return response;
    }
}
```

This demo only works while the Functions host stays running. If the host restarts or scales out, the in-memory stores reset. The point is the timing window, not persistence.

Call UpdateProfileA and then immediately ReadProfileB. You'll often see stale data because the two stores aren't synchronized instantly. This toy example mirrors real distributed databases: writes propagate eventually, not immediately. Cosmos DB exposes this trade-off openly with five consistency models. Strong consistency ensures up-to-date reads, but at the cost of throughput and latency. Eventual consistency delivers maximum availability, but clients must tolerate stale reads. The CAP theorem says you can't have consistency, availability, and partition tolerance all at once. Distributed systems live in that trade-off space.

Operational Complexity: The Human Factor

The last challenge is often underestimated. Running a distributed system is complicated because the evidence you need is scattered. Logs, metrics, and traces live across multiple components, and debugging a single user request often means stitching together timelines from different services and triggers.

We already introduced a correlation ID at ingress and flowed it through our messages. That helps you connect work across asynchronous boundaries. At the runtime level, Azure Functions also participates in distributed tracing using the W3C trace context. In the isolated worker model, middleware can capture a trace identifier for each invocation and attach it to log scopes so every log line includes the same identifier. This makes it far easier to follow a single execution through noisy, concurrent logs.

```
using Microsoft.Azure.Functions.Worker;
using Microsoft.Azure.Functions.Worker.Middleware;
using Microsoft.Extensions.Logging;

namespace OorderProcessor;
```

```
public sealed class CorrelationMiddleware(ILogger<CorrelationMiddleware>
logger)
    : IFunctionsWorkerMiddleware
{
    public async Task Invoke(FunctionContext context, Function
    ExecutionDelegate next)
    {
        var traceId = context.TraceContext.TraceParent ?? Guid.NewGuid().
        ToString("N");

        context.Items["TraceId"] = traceId;

        using (logger.BeginScope(new Dictionary<string, object>
        {
            ["TraceId"] = traceId
        }))
        {
            logger.LogInformation("Invocation started");
            await next(context);
            logger.LogInformation("Invocation finished");
        }
    }
}
```

middleware...

```
.ConfigureFunctionsWorkerDefaults(worker =>
{
    worker.UseMiddleware<CorrelationMiddleware>();
})
```

Middleware helps correlate logs within a single invocation. To correlate across multiple functions, you still need to carry an application correlation ID through messages, which is why we added `CorrelationId` to the order.

The Cumulative Effect

Latency, partial failure, consistency, and operational complexity don't strike in isolation. They interact. Latency makes failures look like timeouts. Partial failures cause inconsistent states. Inconsistent state makes debugging harder. Operational sprawl turns every outage into a treasure hunt. This is why distributed systems have a reputation for difficulty. But by recognizing these challenges up front, you can design for them. Serverless provides safety, retries, poison queues, built-in telemetry, and abstractions that encourage event-driven design. It doesn't erase the problems, but it helps manage them.

A Historical Perspective

Distributed systems didn't appear out of nowhere. The problems we face today, latency, partial failures, consistency, and operational sprawl, are the result of decades of evolution (see Figure 1-2) in computing. To understand why serverless feels like the "next step," it helps to look back at where we've come from.

The Mainframe Era: Everything in One Box

Early enterprise computing commonly concentrated application processing and data on a mainframe, while users worked through terminals (Figure 1-2). This does not mean every mainframe was a literal single point of failure, many supported redundancy, workload management, and high availability. For this historical comparison, the important characteristic is centralization, application logic and data were managed within one controlled environment. The example below models that arrangement in simplified form. One process owns a small set of user records and performs the work locally. No separate database or service call appears in the execution path. If the process is available, the state and logic are available with it. If it stops, the application stops as a whole.

Run this sample and each user is processed from memory. The example is deliberately small, but it shows why a centralized application can be straightforward to reason about. State remains local, so the program does not need to handle a network timeout or a remote service becoming unavailable midway through an operation.

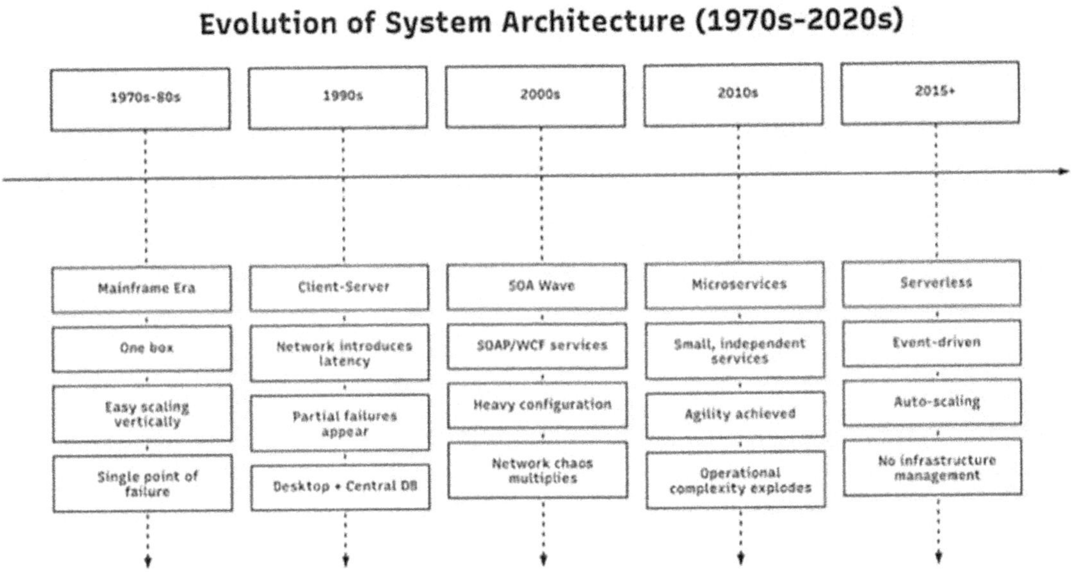

Figure 1-2. *Evolution*

This is a conceptual example, not an attempt to emulate a real mainframe. Mainframes were sophisticated systems with networking, concurrent workloads, and extensive reliability features. `MainframeSim` represents only the architectural idea needed here, application logic and data remain within one operational boundary. The client-server example that follows splits that boundary and introduces the possibility of partial failure.

```
using System;

public static class MainframeSim
{
    private static readonly string[] Users =
       { "Paddy", "Bob", "Carol" };

    public static void Main()
    {
        foreach (var user in Users)
        {
            Console.WriteLine($"Processing user: {user}");
        }
```

```
        Console.WriteLine($"Users in system: {Users.Length}");
    }
}
```

The code is direct because storage and processing remain local to one process. This reduces the number of independently failing components in an operation. The trade-off is concentration, capacity and availability depend on the central system, and adding resources usually means scaling that system vertically. Client-server architecture moved parts of the application onto different machines, making network latency and partial failure part of the normal execution path.

Client-Server: The Network Arrives

By the 1990s, PCs became widespread. Applications moved to a client-server model, a desktop app talking to a central database. Now the network entered the picture. Latency and partial failures appeared for the first time.

```
using System.Data.SqlClient;
public class ClientServerSim
{
    public static void Main()
    {
        using var conn = new SqlConnection("Server=.;Database=Demo;Trust
        ed_Connection=True;"
        );
        conn.Open();
        var cmd = new SqlCommand("SELECT COUNT(*) FROM Users",
        conn);
        int count = (int)cmd.ExecuteScalar();
        Console.WriteLine($"Users in DB: {count}");
    }
}
```

Run this with the database turned off, and the call throws. That's partial failure in its earliest form.

Service-Oriented Architecture (SOA): The First Wave of Distribution

In the 2000s, enterprises pushed further into distributed computing. The goal was modularity, reuse, and organizational scale. Rather than building one large application, teams exposed business capabilities as services, often over SOAP. In the Microsoft ecosystem, that usually meant Windows Communication Foundation, or WCF. The important change was not the syntax of a service contract. It was the fact that business operations now crossed process and machine boundaries routinely. A call that looked like a local method call in code was often a network hop underneath. That made systems more modular, but it also made latency, versioning, timeout handling, and partial failure part of everyday development.

The example below is important because it shows that shift directly. The client code appears straightforward, but the operation now depends on a remote endpoint, a transport protocol, a binding configuration, and a service being available at the other end. The code is simple, but the runtime behavior is no longer local.

```
using System;
using System.ServiceModel;

[ServiceContract]
public interface IOrderService
{
    [OperationContract]
    void PlaceOrder(int orderId);
}

public static class SoaClientSim
{
    public static void Main()
    {
        var binding = new BasicHttpBinding();
        var address = new EndpointAddress("http://localhost:8080/
        OrderService");

        var factory = new ChannelFactory<IOrderService>(binding, address);
        var client = factory.CreateChannel();
```

```
        client.PlaceOrder(42);

        Console.WriteLine("Order submitted.");
    }
}
```

This sample has been written to show how distribution became normalized during the SOA era. The method call looks small and tidy, but it now relies on a remote service and the network between them. That abstraction was powerful, but it also made failures harder to reason about. A call that looked like an ordinary method invocation could fail because of timeouts, unavailable endpoints, mismatched contracts, or transport-level issues. SOA improved organizational scaling, but it also brought the realities of distributed systems into mainstream enterprise development.

Microservices: Small, Fast-Moving Teams

By the 2010s, the pendulum swung again. Instead of heavyweight SOA, we embraced microservices. Each service was small, independently deployable, and often run in a container. With ASP.NET Core, you might expose a microservice like this in the middleware:

Program.cs

```
var builder = WebApplication.CreateBuilder(args);
var app = builder.Build();

app.MapPost("/orders", (Order order) =>
{
    Console.WriteLine($"Order {order.Id} placed.");
    return Results.Accepted();
});
app.Run();
```

This worked well for agility; teams could release features quickly. But distribution exploded, with dozens of services, dozens of databases, and endless inter-service calls.

This model worked well for team autonomy. Services could be built, deployed, and evolved independently. Teams moved faster, releases became smaller, and ownership was clearer. But the cost of distribution grew quickly. Dozens of services meant dozens of databases, many more network calls, and a sharp increase in partial failure scenarios. Observability became harder as a single user request now crossed multiple services and teams.

Microservices traded local complexity for system-wide complexity. The architecture scaled organizationally, but it also made latency, consistency trade-offs, and operational overhead unavoidable. The rest of this book explores what happens when you keep the benefits of independent units of work but move coordination, scaling, and reliability concerns into the platform itself.

Serverless architectures keep the idea of small, independently deployable units but shift much of the operational burden away from the application and into the runtime.

The Serverless Shift: Back to Focus

Serverless emerged in the mid-2010s as a reaction to growing system complexity. As applications became more distributed, developers increasingly spent time managing infrastructure, scaling rules, and operational plumbing rather than business logic. Cloud providers responded with Functions-as-a-Service, pushing more responsibility into the platform.

In Azure, this model appears through Azure Functions. A function is a small entry point that runs in response to an event such as an HTTP request, a message, or a timer. The example below is intentionally simple. It does not yet represent the full OrderProcessor system. Instead, it shows the core serverless idea in its smallest form: you provide the code that should run when an event occurs, while the platform handles hosting, scaling, and availability.

Serverless is not a radical departure from earlier architectures. It is the continuation of a long pendulum swing: from centralized systems to distributed systems to architectures burdened by operational complexity and back toward simplicity, this time built on cloud foundations rather than a single machine.

The example below is deliberately minimal. Its purpose is not to model a full order-processing workflow yet but to show how the serverless programming model shifts the developer's focus. Instead of creating and hosting a web application, defining routes, and managing the surrounding application structure, you write a small entry point that reacts to an event. The platform takes responsibility for hosting, scaling, and much of the execution infrastructure.

```
using System.Net;
using Microsoft.Azure.Functions.Worker;
using Microsoft.Azure.Functions.Worker.Http;
using Microsoft.Extensions.Logging;

namespace OrderProcessor;

public sealed class HelloFunction(ILogger<HelloFunction> logger)
{
    [Function("Hello")]
    public async Task<HttpResponseData> Run(
        [HttpTrigger(AuthorizationLevel.Function, "get")]
        HttpRequestData req,
        CancellationToken stopToken)
    {
        logger.LogInformation("Function executed.");

        var response = req.CreateResponse(HttpStatusCode.OK);
        await response.WriteStringAsync("Hello, Serverless World!",
        stopToken);
        return response;
    }
}
```

This is a trivial function by design. The business logic is almost nonexistent, because the point here is architectural, not functional. The example shows how serverless reduces the amount of visible infrastructure in application code and encourages developers to think in terms of event-driven units of work. Later chapters will build this into a more realistic system.

Lessons from History

Each stage in the evolution of software architecture solved a real problem, but never without introducing a new set of challenges. Mainframes delivered strong consistency and centralized control, but they were limited in how far they could scale horizontally. Client server architectures improved usability and distribution, yet they introduced network latency and tighter coupling between clients and servers. Service-oriented architecture pushed systems toward modularity and reuse, but often at the cost of heavy governance, complex standards, and significant operational overhead.

Microservices emerged as a reaction to that rigidity, offering faster iteration and team autonomy, but they also dramatically increased system complexity, especially in areas like deployment, observability, and failure handling. Serverless takes another step along this path by reducing much of the operational burden, but it reintroduces its own trade-offs, such as cold starts, vendor lock-in, and new debugging and monitoring patterns. The problems never truly disappear; they evolve. Understanding that history makes it easier to see serverless not as a radical break but as the latest point in a long and continuous architectural journey.

Enter Serverless

The story so far has been one of trade-offs. Each stage in the history of distributed computing gave us something new, scalability, modularity, and agility, at the expense of something else, simplicity, reliability, or manageability. By the time microservices became mainstream, many teams found themselves drowning in infrastructure concerns. They had escaped the monolith, but now spent more time configuring clusters, patching runtimes, wiring monitoring systems, and babysitting message queues than writing the code that mattered.

This set the stage for serverless computing, which emerged in the mid-2010s. The idea was radical in its simplicity: what if developers wrote nothing but business logic, and the cloud provider took care of everything else? No servers to provision. No clusters to patch. No capacity planning spreadsheets. Just code, triggered by events.

What "Serverless" Really Means

The term is misleading. There are still servers, CPUs, memory, and disks under the hood. The difference is you don't manage them. A serverless platform, like Azure Functions, abstracts all the infrastructure away.

Serverless is defined less by where your code runs and more by how it behaves at runtime. Execution is entirely event-driven; code does not sit around waiting for work; it is activated only in response to something happening, an HTTP request arriving, a message appearing on a queue, a timer firing, or a file being uploaded. When those events occur, the platform automatically handles scale for you, fanning out to hundreds or thousands of concurrent executions during traffic spikes and shrinking back down to zero when there is nothing to do. All of the underlying infrastructure is managed on your behalf. The cloud provider is responsible for patching operating systems, maintaining runtimes, and handling load balancing, which means your attention stays on business logic rather than servers. That execution model feeds directly into the pricing model. You pay only for the compute time your code actually consumes while handling events, with no cost for idle capacity sitting unused.

Deploy Your First Azure Function

Let's ground this with the simplest possible example. The function below responds to an HTTP request and returns a plain text response. There is no server to configure, no routing table to manage, and no infrastructure code in sight.

When you deploy this function, Azure provisions a Function App and exposes an HTTP endpoint for you. If a hundred users call it at once, the platform can scale out instances automatically. If no one calls it for hours, the app can scale down, and you pay nothing for idle time. What's missing is just as important as what's present: no IIS configuration, no load balancer setup, and no manual scaling rules. The code focuses entirely on what should happen when the event arrives.

```
using System.Net;
using Microsoft.Azure.Functions.Worker;
using Microsoft.Azure.Functions.Worker.Http;
using Microsoft.Extensions.Logging;

namespace OrderProcessor;

public sealed class HelloFunction(ILogger<HelloFunction> logger)
{
    [Function("Hello")]
    public async Task<HttpResponseData> Run(
        [HttpTrigger(AuthorizationLevel.Function, "get", "post")]
        HttpRequestData req,
        CancellationToken stopToken)
```

```
    {
        logger.LogInformation("Function executed at {Time}", DateTime.
        UtcNow);

        var response = req.CreateResponse(HttpStatusCode.OK);
        await response.WriteStringAsync("Hello, Serverless World!",
        stopToken);

        return response;
    }
}
```

This simplicity is powerful, but it doesn't remove the need to think about latency, failure, and consistency once functions start talking to each other.

When you deploy an HTTP-triggered Azure Function, Azure hosts it inside a function app and exposes it through a managed HTTP endpoint. The function runtime recognizes the HTTP trigger and wires that trigger into the platform's request pipeline. Under serverless hosting plans, Azure monitors incoming demand and scales out by adding more function instances when required, subject to the rules and limits of the selected plan. On Flex Consumption, this scaling is dynamic and the plan can scale to zero, although optional always-ready instances change the billing model. That is why no IIS configuration, custom load balancer setup, or manual server provisioning appears in the sample. Those concerns have not disappeared, but they are handled by the managed platform rather than by application code.

Beyond HTTP: Events Everywhere

The real power of serverless is not about replacing APIs. It is about treating events as the universal glue that holds systems together. In Azure, Functions can react to many different event sources: HTTP requests for APIs and webhooks, timers that behave like cron jobs, messages from queues and topics, file uploads in Blob Storage, and publish-subscribe notifications via Event Grid.

This breadth of triggers allows you to model systems around what happens, rather than around who calls whom. Instead of building chains of synchronous calls, you react to events and let the platform handle delivery and scale. The result is systems that are easier to evolve, more resilient to partial failure, and simpler to scale.

The example below reacts to a file being uploaded to Blob Storage. When a blob appears in the uploads container, the function runs and processes the file. There is no polling loop and no scheduled job. The function exists purely to respond to an event.

```
using Microsoft.Azure.Functions.Worker;
using Microsoft.Extensions.Logging;

namespace OrderProcessor;

public sealed class BlobProcessor(ILogger<BlobProcessor> logger)
{
    [Function("ProcessUpload")]
    public void Run(
        [BlobTrigger("uploads/{name}", Connection = "OrderStorage
        Connection")] Stream file,
        string name)
    {
        logger.LogInformation(
            "Processing file {Name}, size {Length} bytes",
            name,
            file.Length);
    }
}
```

In production, Blob Storage events are often delivered via Event Grid for lower latency and stronger delivery guarantees. Blob triggers remain a convenient abstraction, especially for simple scenarios.

Event-driven systems replace direct coupling with temporal decoupling, allowing components to evolve independently.

Orchestrating with Durable Functions

Many real systems involve multi-step workflows. Payment must succeed before inventory updates. Inventory must succeed before email is sent. Traditionally, we would write this as a chain of service calls, with all the latency and failure risks we saw earlier.

Durable Functions provide an orchestration framework that handles state, retries, and checkpoints for you.

Here's an example orchestration:

```
using Microsoft.Azure.Functions.Worker;
using Microsoft.Azure.Functions.Worker.Extensions.DurableTask;
using Microsoft.Extensions.Logging;

public static class OrchestratorExample
{

    [Function("OrderOrchestrator")]
    public static async Task RunOrchestrator([OrchestrationTrigger]
    TaskOrchestrationContext context)
    {
        var orderId = context.GetInput<int>();
        await context.CallActivityAsync("ProcessPayment", orderId);
        await context.CallActivityAsync("ReserveInventory", orderId);
        await context.CallActivityAsync("SendEmail", orderId);
    }

    [Function("ProcessPayment")]
    public static void ProcessPayment([ActivityTrigger] int orderId,
    FunctionContext ctx)
    {
        ctx.GetLogger("Payment").LogInformation($"Processing payment for
        order {orderId}");
    }

    [Function("ReserveInventory")]
    public static void ReserveInventory([ActivityTrigger] int orderId,
    FunctionContext ctx)
    {
        ctx.GetLogger("Inventory").LogInformation($"Reserving stock for
        order {orderId} ");
    }

    [Function("SendEmail")]
    public static void SendEmail([ActivityTrigger] int orderId,
    FunctionContext ctx)
```

```
    {
        ctx.GetLogger("Email").LogInformation($"Sending confirmation for
        order {orderId} ");
    }
}
[Function("ProcessPayment")]
public static void ProcessPayment([ActivityTrigger] int
orderId, FunctionContext ctx)
{
    ctx.GetLogger("Payment").LogInformation($"Processing
    payment for order {orderId}");
}

[Function("ReserveInventory")]
public static void ReserveInventory([ActivityTrigger] int
orderId, FunctionContext ctx)
{
    ctx.GetLogger("Inventory").LogInformation($"Reserving stock
    for order {orderId}");
}

[Function("SendEmail")]
public static void SendEmail([ActivityTrigger] int orderId,
FunctionContext ctx)
{
    ctx.GetLogger("Email").LogInformation($"Sending
    confirmation for order {orderId}");
}
```

If the payment step fails, Durable Functions will retry automatically. If the host crashes, the orchestration resumes from the last checkpoint. The complexity of reliability is handled by the platform.

Why .NET Developers Like This

For .NET developers, Azure's serverless offering feels immediately familiar because it builds on the same fundamentals you already use. Functions are just ordinary .NET projects, dependency injection is configured through IServiceCollection, NuGet provides access to the libraries you need, and async and await fit naturally into the programming model. You can test your code with xUnit or NUnit using the same patterns you would apply in any other application. The real difference shows up in deployment and execution rather than in how you write code. Instead of provisioning and managing servers, you publish Functions. Instead of manually wiring up queues and consumers, you bind directly to Service Bus. Instead of hand-rolling retry and orchestration logic, you let Durable Functions take care of it. What you end up with is not a new skill set but a natural extension of your existing .NET experience into the distributed, event-driven world.

The Limitations of Serverless

Of course, serverless isn't magic. It introduces new challenges:

- **Cold Starts**: Functions may take seconds to "wake up" if idle for long periods.
- **Vendor Lock-In**: Azure Functions use Azure-specific triggers and bindings.
- **Debugging Complexity**: Tracing across ephemeral instances requires new tools.
- **State Management**: Beyond Durable Functions, keeping long-lived state can be tricky.

The point is not that serverless removes all pain; it shifts the balance. Instead of spending 80% of your time on infrastructure and 20% on business logic, you spend 80% on business logic and only 20% on platform quirks.

Hello, Serverless World

By now we've looked at serverless as a concept. But nothing makes it real like writing and running your first Function. In this section, we'll go from zero to a deployed Azure Function, starting with the simplest possible example. Along the way, we'll contrast it with how you'd approach the same thing in a traditional server-hosted application.

The Simplest Function

Here's the canonical "hello world" in Azure Functions.

```
public static class HelloFunction
{
    [Function("HelloHttp")]
    public static HttpResponseData Run(
    [HttpTrigger(AuthorizationLevel.Anonymous, "get",
    "post")] HttpRequestData req,
    FunctionContext context)
    {
        var logger = context.GetLogger("HelloHttp");
        logger.LogInformation("Processing request at {Time}",
        DateTime.UtcNow);
        var response = req.CreateResponse(HttpStatusCode.OK);
        response.WriteString("Hello, Serverless World!");
        return response;
    }
}
```

A few things to notice:

- The [Function] attribute names this Function "HelloHttp". This is how Azure identifies it.
- The [HttpTrigger] binding means this Function runs when it receives an HTTP request.

- The logger is pulled from the FunctionContext, letting you log structured messages.
- The Function creates an HTTP response with a plain-text body. That's it. Deploy this, and Azure gives you a live endpoint like

  `https://<your-app>.azurewebsites.net/api/HelloHttp`

Hit it in your browser, and you'll see

```
Hello, Serverless World!
```

Comparing with ASP.NET Core

If you built the same thing as an ASP.NET Core API, it would look like this:

```
var builder = WebApplication.CreateBuilder(args);
var app = builder.Build();
app.MapGet("/hello", () => "Hello, ASP.NET Core World!");
app.Run();
```

The code may be small and elegant, but the operational burden does not disappear. You still have to deploy it somewhere, whether that is IIS, Kestrel, or a container. You must think about load balancing, decide how instances scale, and wire that scaling up manually or through something like Kubernetes. All of that capacity exists whether or not the endpoint is ever called, which means you continue to pay for idle resources even when /hello receives no traffic at all. A Function behaves very differently. When it is not being used, it scales all the way down to zero. When traffic arrives, it expands automatically to meet demand. The infrastructure is still there, but it is pushed entirely out of your way.

Triggered by More Than HTTP

While HTTP is a natural first demo, Functions shine when reacting to other kinds of events. Let's add a timer trigger:

```
public static class TimerFunction
{
    [Function("Heartbeat")]
```

```
    public static void Run([TimerTrigger("0 */5 * * * *")]
    TimerInfo timer, FunctionContext ctx)
    {
        var logger = ctx.GetLogger("Heartbeat");
        logger.LogInformation("Heartbeat at {Time}",
        DateTime.UtcNow);
    }
}
```

Package Note Timer triggers in isolated workers require the Microsoft.Azure.Functions.Worker.Extensions.Timers package. This runs every five minutes (the CRON expression 0 */5 * * **). It logs a heartbeat message, proving your Function app is alive.

In a monolith, you might write a Windows service or scheduled job for this. In serverless, it's just another Function: no daemon, no scheduler, and no ops overhead.

Testing Locally

Azure provides the Functions Core Tools so you can run these Functions on your machine before deploying. After installing them, run: func start.

You'll see logs like

```
[2025-09-16T14:00:00] Host started (PID 12345)
[2025-09-16T14:00:01] Function "HelloHttp" listening on: http://
localhost:7071/api/HelloHttp
```

You can now hit `http://localhost:7071/api/HelloHttp` and see your Function in action, no cloud deployment required.

Remember! Before you deploy to Production: 1. Change all HTTP triggers from AuthorizationLevel. Anonymous to AuthorizationLevel.Function. 2. Redeploy and call the endpoint with a function key, or proceed to the Security chapter to place endpoints behind API Management. AuthorizationLevel.Anonymous should only be used locally for development purposes.

Deployment in Seconds

When you're ready, deploy with a single command:

```
func azure functionapp publish my-first-func
```

Within a minute, you'll have a live endpoint on Azure. Scaling, logging, retries, all built in.

What About State?

You might wonder, where's the database? Where's the configuration? Functions are intentionally **stateless;** they execute in isolation and shouldn't depend on in-memory state. If you need persistence, you bind to external resources: Blob Storage, Service Bus, Cosmos DB, and SQL Database.

For example, to save greetings to Blob Storage:

```
using Microsoft.Azure.Functions.Worker;
using Microsoft.Azure.Functions.Worker.Http;
using Microsoft.Extensions.Logging;
using static System.Net.Mime.MediaTypeNames;

public static class BlobWriter
{
    [Function("SaveGreeting")]
    [BlobOutput("greetings/{rand-guid}.txt", Connection =
    "AzureWebJobsStorage")]
    public static async Task<string> Run(
    [HttpTrigger(AuthorizationLevel.Function, "post")]
    HttpRequestData req,
    FunctionContext ctx)
    {
        var text = await new
        StreamReader(req.Body).ReadToEndAsync();
        ctx.GetLogger("BlobWriter").LogInformation("Saved
        greeting: {Text}", text);
        return text;
    }
}
```

Package Note Isolated worker blob bindings require Microsoft.Azure.Functions.Worker.Extensions.Storage.Blobs. Here, the `[Blob]` binding automatically writes to a container called `greetings` with a random GUID as the filename. No SDK code. No connection boilerplate. The platform handles it.

Why Start Simple?

It might feel underwhelming to print "Hello, Serverless World!" or log a heartbeat. But these simple Functions illustrate the execution model:

- Functions are small, focused units of code.
- They're triggered by events.
- They're stateless.
- They scale automatically.

Everything else builds on these foundations.

Beyond HTTP: Event-Driven Flows

HTTP is often the gateway drug to Azure Functions. It's simple, familiar, and makes demos easy. But the real power of serverless comes when you stop thinking of Functions as "mini-APIs" and start treating them as reactions to events. An event is anything that happens in your system, such as a file upload, a message arriving on a queue, a new row in a database, or even a timer tick. Serverless thrives in these situations because Functions can be wired directly to the event sources without any glue code or background services.

The Event-Driven Mindset

The event-driven mindset flips the way most traditional systems are built. Instead of reacting to change, they tend to watch for it. You end up with background jobs that constantly poll, a Windows service checking a folder for new files, a cron job querying a table to see if rows have appeared, or a worker sitting in a tight loop waiting for messages. That approach is both wasteful and brittle. It consumes CPU even when nothing is happening and introduces an artificial delay between an event occurring and your system responding to it. In a serverless model, those events are pushed directly into your Functions. There is no polling and no idle work being done. The Function exists purely to handle the event, runs only when there is something to process, and then disappears again.

Blob Trigger: Reacting to File Uploads

One of the most common event types is a file arriving in blob storage.

With Functions, you can process it immediately:

```
using Microsoft.Azure.Functions.Worker;
using Microsoft.Extensions.Logging;
public static class ImageProcessor
{
    [Function("ProcessImage")]
    public static void Run(
    [BlobTrigger("uploads/{name}", Connection =
    "AzureWebJobsStorage")] Stream blob,
    string name,
    FunctionContext ctx)
    {
        var logger = ctx.GetLogger("ImageProcessor");
        logger.LogInformation("Processing blob {Name} ({Length}
        bytes)", name, blob.Length);
        // Imagine image resizing or virus scanning here
    }
}
```

Here the `[BlobTrigger]` binding wires the Function to the uploads container. As soon as a new file lands, Azure invokes your Function with the file stream. You don't write any file system watchers or loops; the platform handles it.

This pattern commonly appears in workflows where uploaded or incoming data must be processed before it can be used. Typical examples include resizing images for profile photos to ensure consistent dimensions and performance, scanning user uploads for viruses to protect the system and its users, and parsing CSV files into a structured format so the data can be validated, transformed, and stored reliably.

Queue Trigger: Decoupling Work

Queues are another natural fit for Functions. Suppose you want to send confirmation emails after orders are placed. Instead of calling the email service synchronously, push a message to a queue and let a Function handle it:

```
using Microsoft.Azure.Functions.Worker;
using Microsoft.Extensions.Logging;
public static class EmailSender
{
    [Function("SendEmail")]
    public static void Run(
    [QueueTrigger("emails", Connection =
    "AzureWebJobsStorage")] string message,
    FunctionContext ctx)
    {
        var logger = ctx.GetLogger("EmailSender");
        logger.LogInformation("Sending email: {Message}",
        message);
        // Pretend to send via SMTP or an API
    }
}
```

The advantage is decoupling; the API that enqueues the message returns instantly. Email sending happens asynchronously, and if the SMTP provider is slow, the queue provides natural buffering.

Event Grid: Pub/Sub at Scale

Azure Event Grid generalizes this idea with **publish/subscribe routing**. Services emit events (`"BlobCreated"`, `“ResourceUpdated"`), and subscribers react. This lets you build loosely coupled systems where producers don't need to know about consumers. A Function can subscribe like this:

```
using Microsoft.Azure.EventGrid.Models;
using Microsoft.Azure.Functions.Worker;
using Microsoft.Extensions.Logging;
```

```
public static class EventGridLogger
{
    [Function("LogEventGridEvent")]
    public static void Run(
    [EventGridTrigger] EventGridEvent eventGridEvent,
    FunctionContext ctx)
    {
        var logger = ctx.GetLogger("EventGridLogger");
        logger.LogInformation("Event received: {Id} - {Type}",
        eventGridEvent.Id, eventGridEvent.EventType);
    }
}
```

Now, any Event Grid publisher, Blob Storage, Service Bus, or custom apps, can trigger your Function. This creates rich pipelines without tight coupling.

Composing Flows

The real power shows up when you compose these triggers into a single flow. A user uploads a file, which immediately fires a Blob trigger. The first Function validates the file and, once it passes, pushes a message onto a queue. A second Function then consumes that queue message and persists the relevant metadata into Cosmos DB, after which Event Grid broadcasts a "FileProcessed" event to any downstream services that care about it. With well under a hundred lines of code, you end up with a distributed processing pipeline that scales automatically, moving cleanly from Blob Storage through validation and persistence and finally out to notification or integration handlers.

This is where serverless really pulls ahead of both monoliths and traditional microservices. There are no idle polling loops burning resources, no manual thread management to reason about, and no custom glue code needed just to wire services together. Producers and consumers are naturally decoupled, which removes tight runtime dependencies. Instead of centering the design on synchronous request and response flows, the system is built around events, and that shift alone makes the architecture more resilient and more scalable by default.

Why .NET Developers Should Care

By now, you've seen what Functions look like, how they scale, and how they connect to events. But you might still be asking, why does this matter to me as a .NET developer? After all, serverless platforms exist for JavaScript, Python, and even languages like PowerShell. Isn't this just another cloud fad?

The short answer is no. For .NET developers, serverless isn't a detour; it's a natural extension of the environment you already know. Functions run on .NET, use dependency injection, consume NuGet packages, support async/await, and can be tested with the same frameworks you already use. In other words, serverless lets you stay inside your comfort zone while expanding into distributed, event-driven systems.

Familiar Patterns in a New Runtime

When you create a Function app, you're really just creating a .NET project. You can add `Program.cs`, configure services with `IServiceCollection`, and use the same libraries you'd use in ASP.NET Core or a console app.

Here's an example with dependency injection:

```
// Program.cs
using Microsoft.Extensions.DependencyInjection;
using Microsoft.Extensions.Hosting;
var host = new HostBuilder()
.ConfigureFunctionsWorkerDefaults()
.ConfigureServices(services =>
    {
        services.AddSingleton<IGreetingService,
        GreetingService>();
    })
    .Build();
    host.Run();
    public interface IGreetingService
    {
        string Greet(string name);
    }
```

```
    public class GreetingService : IGreetingService
    {
        public string Greet(string name) => $"Hello, {name}!";
    }
```

And the Function consuming it:

```
using Microsoft.Azure.Functions.Worker;
using Microsoft.Azure.Functions.Worker.Http;
using System.Net;
public class GreetingFunction
{
    private readonly IGreetingService _greetingService;
    public GreetingFunction(IGreetingService greetingService)
    {
        _greetingService = greetingService;
    }
    [Function("Greet")]
    public HttpResponseData Run(
    [HttpTrigger(AuthorizationLevel.Anonymous, "get",
    "post")] HttpRequestData req,
    FunctionContext ctx)
    {
        var logger = ctx.GetLogger("GreetingFunction");
        var response = req.CreateResponse(HttpStatusCode.OK);
        response.WriteString(_greetingService.Greet("Serverless
        .NET Developer"));
        return response;
    }
}
```

If you've built ASP.NET Core APIs, this should feel second nature. The only difference is the trigger and context.

Async/Await and Scalability

One of .NET's strongest features is its async/await model. Serverless systems thrive on concurrency, so writing non-blocking code is essential. Functions make this seamless. For example, suppose you need to fetch two pieces of data from

different APIs:

For local use only

This Function uses `AuthorizationLevel.Anonymous` for demo simplicity. Do not deploy this endpoint publicly. We'll secure endpoints in the Security chapter; before publishing, switch triggers to `AuthorizationLevel.Function` or protect them behind API Management/Front Door.

API Management/Front Door.

```
using Microsoft.Azure.Functions.Worker;
using Microsoft.Azure.Functions.Worker.Http;
using System.Net;

public static class Example
{
    [Function("FetchData")]
    public static async Task<HttpResponseData> Run([HttpTrigger(Authorizati
    onLevel.Anonymous, "get")]
        HttpRequestData req,
        FunctionContext ctx)
        {
            var http = new HttpClient();
            var task1 = http.GetStringAsync("https://httpbin.org/
            delay/2");
            var task2 = http.GetStringAsync("https://httpbin.org/
            delay/3");

            await Task.WhenAll(task1, task2);
            var response = req.CreateResponse(HttpStatusCode.OK);
```

```
            response.WriteString($"Results: {task1.Result.Length},{
            task2.Result.Length} ");
          return response;
    }
}
```

Instead of waiting sequentially, the Function fires both requests and awaits them concurrently. This keeps the Function instance free to process other work. Serverless platforms reward this style of coding. Blocking calls waste CPU cycles and increases billing costs. Async/await turns efficient code into efficient billing.

NuGet and the .NET Environment

Functions can reference any NuGet package. Need to parse JSON with `System.Text.Json`? Validate data with `FluentValidation`? Connect to Cosmos DB with the official SDK? It all works out of the box. This is one of the biggest reasons .NET developers should care: you're not learning a new environment from scratch. You're leveraging the decades of libraries and tooling you already know.

Unit Testing Functions

Just like any .NET class, Functions can be tested. Because Functions are often small and stateless, they're easier to test than large controllers in a monolith.

Here's an example using xUnit:

```
public class GreetingFunctionTests
{
    [Fact]
    public async Task ReturnsGreeting()
    {
         var service = new GreetingService();
         var function = new GreetingFunction(service);var context =
         new DefaultFunctionContext();
         var request = new MockHttpRequestData(context);
         var result = function.Run(request, context);
         var response = await result.ReadAsStringAsync();
```

```
        Assert.Contains("Hello", response);
    }
}
```

By isolating your logic in services (`GreetingService`), Functions become thin wrappers. This makes them straightforward to test.

Tooling You Already Know

Azure Functions fit naturally into the tooling. You already use it day to day. You can press F5 in Visual Studio or VS Code and debug Functions locally with breakpoints, watches, and full step-through debugging, just as you would with any other .NET application. The Azure Functions Core Tools CLI lets you run, test, and manage Functions from the command line, which works well for scripting, CI pipelines, and local experimentation. When you are ready to deploy, you can publish directly to Azure from Visual Studio without learning a new deployment model or build system. Because the development experience feels familiar, and you are already invested in .NET tooling, you can adopt serverless incrementally, without a steep learning curve or a disruptive shift in how you build and debug software.

Why This Is More Than a Fad

Serverless is more than a passing trend or a shiny new abstraction. It aligns closely with the core strengths of the .NET environment. Strong typing and async and await encourage reliable, predictable code even under heavy concurrency, while built-in dependency injection makes it easy to keep Functions modular and testable. The NuGet ecosystem provides access to mature libraries without reinventing common solutions, and established testing frameworks allow you to validate behavior with the same confidence you expect from any production codebase. You are still writing the same C#, but it runs in an execution model that scales elastically, reacts to events in real time, and removes much of the operational burden that used to come with building distributed systems.

Case Study: E-Commerce Checkout

Abstract examples are useful, but nothing drives home the value of serverless like a concrete scenario. Let's imagine building a simplified e-commerce checkout process. At first glance, it seems straightforward: validate an order, process payment, update inventory, and send a confirmation email. In a monolithic application, you might put all of this inside one controller method. But in distributed systems, those steps quickly become fragile. Serverless gives us a way to handle each step as an event-driven component, resilient by design.

The Monolith Approach

Here's how it might look in an ASP.NET Core monolith:

```
[HttpPost("/checkout")]
public async Task<IActionResult> Checkout(Order order)
{
    if (!ModelState.IsValid) return BadRequest();
    var paymentResult = await _paymentService.Process(order);
    if (!paymentResult.Success) return StatusCode(502, "Payment
    failed");
    var inventoryResult = await
     _inventoryService.Reserve(order.Items);
    if (!inventoryResult.Success) return StatusCode(500,
    "Inventory failed");
    await _emailService.Send(order.CustomerEmail, "Order
    confirmed!");
    return Ok(new { order.Id, Status = "Confirmed" });
}
```

It's compact and easy to follow. But notice the risks:

- Each step is synchronous. If any one call stalls, the whole checkout hangs.
- A crash halfway through leaves the system in an inconsistent state (e.g., payment taken, inventory not reserved).
- Scaling means scaling everything together.

The Serverless Approach

Now let's rethink checkout with Functions. Each step becomes an event-driven Function, and Durable Functions orchestrates them.

Step 1: The Orchestrator

```
using Microsoft.Azure.Functions.Worker;
using Microsoft.DurableTask;

public static class OrchestratorExample
{
    [Function("CheckoutOrchestrator")]
    public static async Task RunOrchestrator([OrchestrationTrigger]
    TaskOrchestrationContext context)
    {
        var order = context.GetInput<Order>();
        await context.CallActivityAsync("ValidateOrder", order);

        await context.CallActivityAsync("ProcessPayment", order);
        await context.CallActivityAsync("ReserveInventory", order);
        await context.CallActivityAsync("SendConfirmationEmail", order);
     }
}
```

This is the workflow definition. Each call is a checkpoint; if the Function host crashes, Durable Functions resumes from the last completed activity.

Step 2: Validation Activity

```
using Microsoft.Azure.Functions.Worker;
using Microsoft.Extensions.Logging;
public static class ValidateExample
{
    [Function("ValidateOrder")]
    public static void Validate([ActivityTrigger] Order order,
    FunctionContext ctx)
```

```
    {
        var logger = ctx.GetLogger("ValidateOrder");
        if (order.Items.Count == 0) throw new InvalidOperationException("Em
        pty order");
        logger.LogInformation("Order {Id} validated with {Count} items",
        order.Id, order.Items.Count);
    }
}
```

Step 3: Payment Activity

```
using Microsoft.Azure.Functions.Worker;
using Microsoft.Extensions.Logging;
public static class PaymentExample
{
    [Function("ProcessPayment")]
    public static async Task ProcessPayment([ActivityTrigger] Order order,
FunctionContext ctx)
    {
        var logger = ctx.GetLogger("ProcessPayment");
        logger.LogInformation("Processing payment for order { Id} ",
        order.Id);
        // Simulate payment API call
        await Task.Delay(1000);
        if (new Random().Next(0, 10) < 2)
            throw new Exception("Random payment failure");
    }
}
```

This example includes a 20% chance of failure. Durable Functions automatically retries, saving you from writing manual retry loops.

Step 4: Inventory Reservation

```
using Microsoft.Azure.Functions.Worker;
using Microsoft.Extensions.Logging;
public static class ReserveExample
{
    [Function("ReserveInventory")]
    public static void Reserve([ActivityTrigger] Order order,
    FunctionContext ctx)
    {
        var logger = ctx.GetLogger("ReserveInventory");
        foreach (var item in order.Items)
        {
            logger.LogInformation("Reserving {Quantity} of { Product} ",
            item.Quantity, item.ProductId);
        }
    }
}
```

Step 5: Email Confirmation

```
using Microsoft.Azure.Functions.Worker;
using Microsoft.Extensions.Logging;
public static class ConfirmationExample
{
    [Function("SendConfirmationEmail")]
    public static void SendEmail([ActivityTrigger] Order order,
    FunctionContext ctx)
    {
        var logger = ctx.GetLogger("SendEmail");
        logger.LogInformation("Sending email to {Email} for order { Id} ",
        order.CustomerEmail, order.Id);
    }
}
```

Putting It Together

Now, when a client submits an order via an HTTP Function:

```
using Microsoft.Azure.Functions.Worker;
using Microsoft.Azure.Functions.Worker.Http;
using Microsoft.DurableTask.Client;
using System.Net;
public static class SubmitOrderExample
{
    [Function("SubmitOrder")]
    public static async Task<HttpResponseData> Run([HttpTrigger(Authorizati
    onLevel.Anonymous, "post")] HttpRequestData req,
    [DurableClient] DurableTaskClient client, FunctionContext ctx)
    {
        var order = await req.ReadFromJsonAsync<Order>();

        var instanceId = await client.ScheduleNewOrchestrationInstanceAsync
        ("CheckoutOrchestrator", order);
        var response =  req.CreateResponse(HttpStatusCode.Accepted);
        response.WriteString($"Order orchestration started. Instance ID: {
        instanceId} ");
        return response;
    }
}
```

The client doesn't wait for the whole workflow. Instead, they get an instance ID to query later. The orchestration runs independently, resiliently, and with retries (see Figure 1-3).

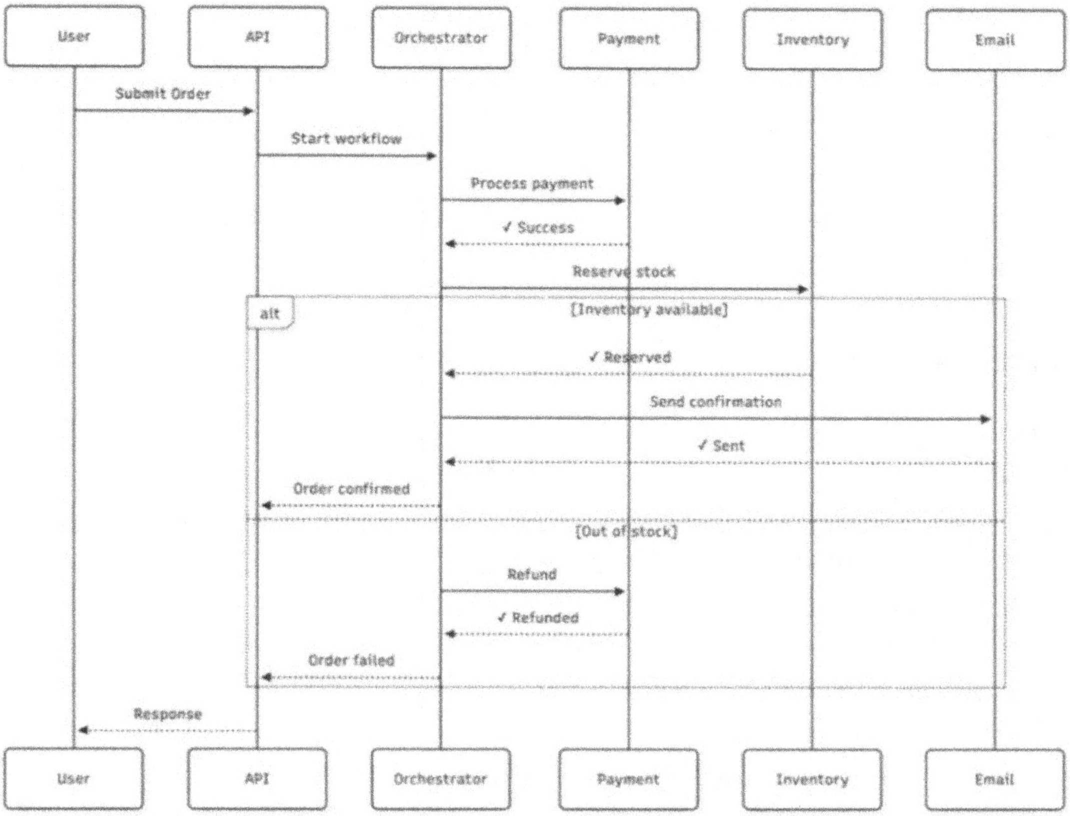

Figure 1-3. *Sequence Diagram*

Why This Is Better

- **Resilience**: If the host restarts during payment, Durable Functions resumes from the last checkpoint.
- **Scalability**: Payment processing can scale independently of email sending.
- **Transparency**: Durable Functions exposes state; you can query orchestration status at any time.
- **Cost Efficiency**: You only pay while Functions execute, not while waiting for an API to respond.

In short, checkout becomes a pipeline of events instead of one fragile synchronous block.

Anecdotes and Real-World Outages

Distributed systems theory can feel abstract until you see it play out in the real world. History is full of incidents where hidden assumptions about latency, partial failure, or consistency caused massive outages. In this section, we'll walk through a few real stories, some public, some anonymized, and reflect on what they teach us as .NET developers moving into serverless.

The S3 Outage That Broke the Internet (2017)

In February 2017, a simple typo at Amazon Web Services triggered one of the most infamous outages in cloud history. While debugging a billing subsystem, an engineer accidentally entered a command that removed more servers than intended. Unfortunately, those servers were part of the S3 (Simple Storage Service) metadata subsystem in the us-east-1 region.

The results were catastrophic; S3 became unavailable, which meant thousands of downstream systems, from image hosting to analytics dashboards, also went dark. Popular websites and apps around the world displayed broken images or crashed outright. **The lesson:** even "indestructible" cloud platforms are vulnerable.

Distributed systems rely on many layers of coordination, and partial failure in a single subsystem can ripple outward. For us as .NET developers, it's a reminder that even if you use serverless, you must plan for dependencies to fail. Circuit breakers, retries, and fallbacks aren't optional.

Azure AD Outage (2020)

Microsoft Azure Active Directory is a global identity service, and for many enterprises, it's the single point of authentication. In September 2020, an update to a backend service introduced a bug that caused token issuance to fail worldwide. For several hours, users couldn't log in to Office 365, Azure Portal, or any app integrated with Azure AD. The problem wasn't capacity or latency but consistency. The bug created a divergence in state across regions, and the system failed to reconcile.

The lesson: authentication is a distributed system too, and consistency matters. For serverless apps that rely on Azure AD or B2C, you should design graceful degradation paths, perhaps allowing cached tokens to continue for a short period or queuing requests until identity recovers.

Netflix and Chaos Monkey

Not all stories are about outages. Netflix famously pioneered the idea of deliberately breaking your own systems with a tool called Chaos Monkey. The tool randomly shuts down servers in production to test resilience.

At first, this seemed reckless. Why kill healthy services? But the practice forced Netflix engineers to design for partial failure. Services had to survive missing dependencies, reroute traffic, or retry intelligently.

The lesson: failures are not "if" but "when." By simulating them, you build confidence. In the serverless world, you can adopt the same mindset by running load tests, forcing Functions to throw exceptions, or experimenting with Azure's fault injection tooling.

The Retailer That Couldn't Checkout

At a global retailer I consulted with, Black Friday became a nightmare. Their checkout pipeline was built on microservices, payment, inventory, shipping, and loyalty points. Each had its own database, its own logs, its own dashboards. When an error appeared in checkout, no one knew which service was failing. Teams jumped from one log system to another, chasing timeouts. The outage lasted hours longer than it should have because operational complexity defeated the humans running the system.

The lesson: observability is as important as code. Serverless offers built-in application insights and distributed tracing, but you must adopt it early. Don't wait for Black Friday to wire correlation IDs.

A Smaller Story: The Startup with the Runaway Bill

A small startup built an event pipeline on serverless Functions. Everything worked beautifully until their Azure bill arrived. A bug in the client app was hammering the API with thousands of requests per second. Because Functions scale elastically, Azure kept up and charged accordingly. The startup hadn't put quotas or throttles in place. The incident nearly bankrupted them.

The lesson: elasticity is a double-edged sword. Serverless prevents outages by scaling with load, but it doesn't judge whether that load is real or accidental. Always combine serverless with governance, budgets, alerts, and throttles.

Pulling It Together

Pulling these stories together, they all surface the same underlying problems that show up again and again in distributed systems. Latency and failure are unavoidable once you cross network boundaries, something Netflix made painfully visible with Chaos Monkey. Consistency breaks down at global scale, as Azure AD's outage demonstrated. Partial failure is the norm rather than the exception, illustrated by a checkout pipeline where some steps succeed and others quietly fail. On top of that, operational complexity grows quickly, with teams spending hours chasing logs across services, and elastic scaling introducing its own risks when it translates directly into unexpected costs. Serverless does not make these problems disappear. What it does offer is a platform where handling retries, building resilience, wiring in monitoring, and enforcing governance are simpler and more consistent by default, rather than being responsibilities every team must reinvent from scratch.

Thought Experiments

So far we've looked at challenges, history, first Functions, and even a checkout pipeline. But distributed systems are not just about writing code; they're about designing with trade-offs. In this section, you'll explore a few thought experiments. These are not "right or wrong" questions; they're prompts to stretch your architectural thinking. Try sketching answers in a notebook, or even writing small Functions to simulate them.

Thought Experiment 1: File Ingestion Three Ways

Imagine your system must ingest user-uploaded files, validate them, and store metadata in a database. How would you implement it in three different models?

- **Monolith**: One controller action accepts the file, validates it, writes metadata, and returns success.
- **Microservices**: An upload service stores the file and publishes an event. A validator service consumes it, then calls a metadata service.
- **Serverless**: A Blob trigger fires on upload. A Function validates it. An Event Grid event routes metadata to Cosmos DB.

Ask yourself:

- Where does latency appear in each approach?
- What happens if validation fails?
- How would you debug an inconsistent state?

Try coding the serverless version with a Blob trigger and Cosmos DB output binding. Then imagine scaling each version to millions of files per day. Which feels most natural?

Thought Experiment 2: Availability Math

You have three services in series: A (99.9% uptime), B (99.9%), and C (99.9%). What's the combined uptime if all three must succeed? Mathematically: $0.999 \times 0.999 \times 0.999 = 0.997$ That's 99.7%, or nearly 8 hours of downtime per year. Now imagine adding retries, redundancy, or event-driven decoupling. How does that change the math?

In serverless, Functions and queues often decouple services. If B is down, the message waits instead of failing instantly. Does that increase availability for the user? Sketch a Function pipeline with retries and a dead-letter queue.

Thought Experiment 3: Consistency in a Social App

Imagine you're building a "likes" counter for posts in a social network. Strong consistency means users always see the exact count. But global replication latency slows writes. Eventual consistency means users may see stale counts, but writes are fast and scalable. Which do you choose?

Write two Functions to simulate it, one that increments a counter in a single in-memory dictionary (strong) and one that increments across two dictionaries with eventual reconciliation (eventual). How does the user experience change? Do you tolerate stale likes for scalability?

Thought Experiment 4: User Checkout Under Pressure

In the e-commerce case study, what happens if inventory is slow but payments are fast? In a monolith, the whole request blocks. In a microservice, the API gateway waits or times out. In serverless with Durable Functions, the orchestration waits, but retries can happen. Would you rather risk double-charging or overselling inventory? How do you design for idempotency?

Try modifying the `ProcessPayment` Function to generate a transaction ID and make it idempotent. Then imagine replaying the orchestration. Does it double-charge?

Thought Experiment 5: Operational Complexity Drill

Picture a bug report: "Some users see 500 errors when uploading files." In a monolith, you check one log file. In a microservice, you trace across upload, validator, and metadata services. In serverless, you search Application Insights for correlation IDs.

Which system gives you the fastest time to root cause? As a coding challenge, add correlation logging to your Functions. Trigger a workflow and trace it end-to-end. Could you hand those logs to a colleague and have them reconstruct the path?

Why Thought Experiments Are Important

Distributed systems are defined by trade-offs. Each of these scenarios forces you to confront them:

- Latency vs. responsiveness
- Consistency vs. availability
- Throughput vs. cost
- Resilience vs. complexity

Serverless doesn't remove trade-offs, but it changes the calculus. By externalizing state, wiring in retries, and scaling automatically, it pushes you toward designs that embrace distribution rather than fighting it.

EXERCISES

1. **Modify the Response**: Add a query parameter `?name=Alice` and greet the user personally.
2. **Compare with ASP.NET Core**: Write the same logic as a minimal API in ASP.NET Core. Which setup feels heavier?
3. **Cost Estimation**: Look up Azure Functions pricing. Estimate the cost of 1 million calls per month. Compare to a dedicated VM.

4. **Latency Measurement:** Modify the `LatencyDemo` to call three different endpoints in sequence. Measure total time. Then refactor to fire them in parallel with `Task.WhenAll`. How does this change user experience?

5. **Partial Failure Handling:** Adapt the `RandomFailure` function to be triggered by Service Bus. Configure retry policies in `host.json`. What happens when failures persist?

6. **Mainframe Simulation:** Modify `MainframeSim` to handle 100,000 users in memory. What happens as memory pressure increases?

7. **Client-Server Failure:** Run `ClientServerSim` with the database offline. How does the exception manifest? How might retries help?

8. **SOA Nostalgia:** Sketch a WCF service contract. How much boilerplate is required compared to a Function?

9. **Microservices Scaling:** Run two instances of the microservice. Send requests concurrently. How would you handle shared state between them?

10. **Serverless Reflection:** Compare the code size between the Function and the microservice. How does the developer experience differ?

11. **Hello, Function:** Create the `HelloFunction` example locally. Run it with the Azure Functions Core Tools. Call it with curl. Observe the logs.

12. **Blob Trigger:** Deploy the `BlobProcessor` Function. Drop a text file into the container. What happens if you upload 100 files at once?

13. **Durable Orchestration:** Deploy the `OrderOrchestrator`. Call it with an order ID. Kill the host midway. Restart. Does the orchestration resume where it left off?

14. **Reflection:** Sketch your current system. Which parts could be rewritten as event-driven Functions? Which would benefit least?

15. **Timer Demo:** Create the Heartbeat Function. Deploy it. Watch Application Insights logs to confirm it runs every five minutes, even without user input.

16. **Compare:** Build the equivalent ASP.NET Core API (/hello). Deploy both side by side. Compare scaling behavior and cost when idle.

17. **Queue Trigger:** Build the `SendEmail` Function. Push messages into the `emails` queue with Azure Storage Explorer. Confirm Functions pick them up automatically.

18. **Event Grid:** Configure a Blob Storage account to emit `BlobCreated` events into Event Grid. Subscribe to the `LogEventGridEvent` Function. Upload a blob and trace the event through Event Grid to the Function.

19. **DI Setup:** Implement the `GreetingService` example. Inject a second service (e.g., `ITimeService`) and include the current time in the response.

20. **Build the Pipeline:** Implement the `CheckoutOrchestrator` with all four activities. Submit an order. Query orchestration status with the Durable Functions API (`/runtime/webhooks/durabletask/instances/{id}`).

21. **Timeout Handling:** Add a timer to fail the orchestration if payment takes more than 30 seconds.

22. **Fan-Out/Fan-In:** Modify the orchestrator so inventory reservations run in parallel (`Task.WhenAll`). How much faster does checkout complete?

23. **Reflection:** Compare this pipeline with the monolith controller. Which version would be easier to debug after a partial failure?

24. **Consistency Demo:** Extend the "likes" counter simulation. Add reconciliation after a delay. Log when counts drift.

25. **Idempotency Test:** Modify `ProcessPayment` to accept a transaction ID. Replay the orchestration. Confirm no double charge.

26. **Correlation Audit:** Add correlation IDs across three Functions. Trace an error. How long does it take you to find the root cause compared to your current system?

Summary

Distributed systems form the backdrop of modern software development, introducing challenges that do not exist in single-process applications. Latency becomes unavoidable, failures are partial and unpredictable, and consistency shifts from certainty to compromise. As systems grow to support more users, features, and teams, they naturally evolve from monoliths into distributed architectures, each step bringing both benefits and new complexities. Serverless represents the latest stage in this evolution, not by eliminating these challenges, but by providing abstractions that make them manageable. By focusing on events, elastic scaling, and managed infrastructure, platforms like Azure Functions allow developers to build resilient systems without becoming overwhelmed by operational concerns. For .NET developers, this shift is both familiar and transformative: the same language, patterns, and tools remain, but they operate within a new execution model that prioritizes statelessness, reactivity, and cloud-native scalability.

Your first Function illustrates the essence of serverless, small units of business logic triggered by events and scaled automatically by the platform. Moving beyond HTTP reveals the true power of this model, where Functions respond directly to queues, blobs, and events to form end-to-end workflows without manual infrastructure glue. By composing triggers and integrating services such as Durable Functions, Event Grid, Service Bus, and Cosmos DB, serverless enables complex distributed pipelines that remain easier to reason about and operate than traditional synchronous systems. The e-commerce checkout example demonstrates how fragile monolithic workflows can be transformed into resilient event-driven processes, a pattern applicable to many real-world scenarios. Yet the lessons of past outages remind us that distributed systems remain inherently messy, requiring deliberate attention to resilience, observability, cost control, and design trade-offs. Developing intuition through thought experiments and practical examples prepares you to navigate these realities, ensuring that as you extend your .NET skills into the cloud-native era, you do so with a clear understanding of both the power and the responsibility that serverless systems bring.

Looking Ahead

In this chapter, we explored the messy reality of distributed systems and how serverless reshapes the landscape for .NET developers. We began with the challenges, latency, partial failures, consistency, and operational complexity. We then took a historical tour from mainframes through microservices before arriving at the promise of serverless. We wrote our first Functions, reacted to events beyond HTTP, and even walked through a case study in e-commerce checkout. Along the way, we saw real-world outages and ran thought experiments to stretch our architectural instincts.

But this is only the beginning. The code snippets so far have been intentionally simple, printing greetings, logging uploads, and simulating failures. The point was not to build production-ready software but to internalize the new mental model. Serverless requires you to think in terms of events, stateless execution, and orchestration, a different mindset from monoliths or microservices.

What's Next: Azure Functions in Depth

Chapter 2 will take us deeper into Azure Functions, the cornerstone of serverless on Azure. We'll explore

- **Triggers and Bindings in Detail**: HTTP, timers, blobs, queues, Event Grid, Service Bus
- **Function App Hosting Models**: Consumption, Premium, Dedicated
- **Execution Model**: Scaling behavior, cold starts, and concurrency
- **Configuration and Settings**: Connection strings, secrets, environment variables
- **Dependency Injection**: Structuring Functions with services and clean boundaries
- **Local Development and Testing**: Functions core tools, mocking bindings, unit tests

This is where we'll establish the working project that will carry through the rest of the book. Whereas Chapter 1 gave you the "why," Chapter 2 begins the "how."

How to Approach the Next Chapters

Approach them as a deliberate progression, rather than a collection of isolated topics. The book starts with the core building blocks, getting comfortable with Functions, Durable Functions, Event Grid, Service Bus, and Cosmos DB, and understanding what each one is responsible for. From there, it moves up a level to the patterns that emerge once those primitives are combined: fan-out and fan-in workflows, sagas, CQRS, event sourcing, and long-running or human-driven processes. With those patterns in place, the focus shifts to operations, covering how to observe what your system is doing, secure it properly, deploy it safely, and keep costs under control as it scales. Finally, the case studies pull everything together, applying the same ideas to real scenarios like streaming pipelines, orchestration-heavy systems, and multi-tenant architectures. Each chapter builds on the last by extending a single working project, so by the end you are not just familiar with the concepts but in possession of a complete reference architecture you can adapt to your own systems.

As we move forward, remember the lessons from this chapter:

- **Latency Is Real:** Design with async and queues.
- **Failures Are Partial:** Retries, poison queues, and orchestration are your friends.
- **Consistency Is a Trade-off**: Embrace eventual consistency where possible.
- **Observability Is Essential**: Correlation IDs and telemetry should be first-class citizens.
- **History Is Important:** Every "new" paradigm is built on old lessons.

Serverless is powerful, but it doesn't repeal the laws of distribution. It gives you a toolkit to work with them instead of against them.

Looking Ahead: Your Role As a .NET Developer

As a .NET developer, you're already equipped with the skills to thrive in serverless, strong typing, async/await, dependency injection, NuGet, and rich tooling. What changes is your focus, from building endpoints to orchestrating events, from managing infrastructure to designing workflows.

In Chapter 2, you'll see this shift in action. You'll create a Function App with multiple triggers, wire in DI, configure settings securely, and test Functions locally. You'll move from "hello world" to a real working project that forms the backbone of the book.

Distributed systems are hard; they always have been. But serverless changes the balance. Instead of spending your energy on servers, queues, and clusters, you spend it on business logic. That's the promise of serverless: complexity doesn't vanish, but it moves to the platform, leaving you free to deliver value. This chapter has given you the motivation and the mindset. The next will give you the tools.

CHAPTER 2

Azure Functions Deep Dive

Chapter 2 moves from architectural concepts to working code. In the previous chapter, we looked at how distributed systems evolved and why serverless emerged as a practical response to growing operational complexity. Now we make that shift concrete by building a real Azure Functions application in .NET and using it as the foundation for the rest of the book. This chapter introduces the `OrderProcessor` project and develops it step by step. We will scaffold a Function App, run it locally, explore triggers and bindings, examine hosting and scaling behavior, and put the supporting pieces in place for real-world development, configuration, dependency injection, and testing. The code begins simply, but that is deliberate. By the end of the chapter, you will have a working serverless foundation that is ready to grow into the distributed system we will expand throughout the chapters ahead.

From Concept to Code

Distributed systems sound intimidating in the abstract. It's one thing to talk about queues, triggers, and orchestration; it's another to see them in a real project. That's why this chapter begins not with more theory, but with code. We're going to scaffold a new Azure Function App in .NET, run it locally, and lay the foundation for a project we'll evolve throughout the rest of the book.

By the end of this section, you'll have a working Function App called `OrderProcessor`. At first, it will do almost nothing, just accept an HTTP request and log some data. But don't be fooled by its simplicity. This small Function App will grow chapter by chapter into a distributed system, events, queues, Durable orchestrations, Cosmos DB storage, observability, and secure endpoints.

© Patrick Kearns 2026
P. Kearns, *Serverless Distributed Systems in Modern .NET and Azure*,
https://doi.org/10.1007/979-8-8688-2839-3_2

In-Process vs. Isolated Worker

Before we write a line of code, let's clear up some terminology. Historically, Azure Functions ran in in-process mode; your Functions shared a process with the Functions runtime. This was convenient but limiting, especially as .NET evolved with its own hosting model and dependency injection system.

With .NET 5 and later, Microsoft introduced the isolated worker model. In this model, your Functions run in a separate process, hosting is managed through a `HostBuilder`, and you get the same flexibility as ASP.NET Core. For .NET 8 and beyond, this is the recommended model, and it's what we'll use in this book. The key takeaway: isolated worker = modern .NET development experience. You configure services in `Program.cs`, inject dependencies, and test with the same patterns you'd use anywhere else in the environment.

Scaffolding the Project

Let's set up the project. You'll need the Azure Functions Core Tools installed (which you can get via npm or Chocolatey) and the .NET 8 + SDK. In your terminal

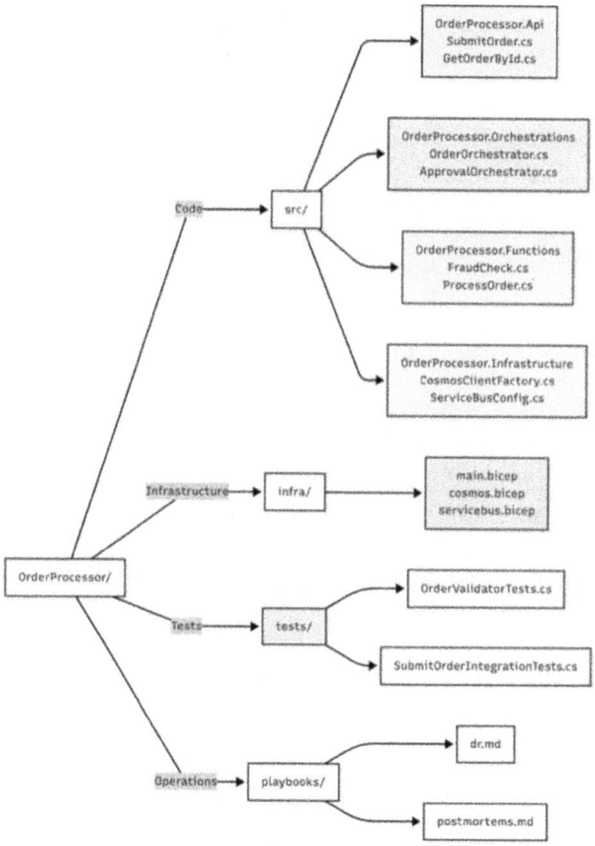

Figure 2-1. *Project Scaffolding*

```
func init OrderProcessor --worker-runtime dotnet-isolated --target-
framework net8.0

cd OrderProcessor

func new --name SubmitOrder --template "HttpTrigger"
```

This creates a new directory called `OrderProcessor` with the following layout (see Figure 2-1):

```
OrderProcessor/
├── Program.cs
├── SubmitOrder.cs
├── local.settings.json
├── host.json
└── .csproj
```

Let's look at each file:

- Program.cs: the entry point. Configures hosting, DI, and middleware.
- SubmitOrder.cs: our first Function, generated from the HTTP trigger template.
- local.settings.json: stores local configuration like connection strings.
- host.json: global runtime settings (e.g., retries, logging).
- .csproj: project file, which references Microsoft.Azure.Functions.Worker and related packages.

The Generated Function

Open `SubmitOrder.cs`. The template looks like this:

```
public class SubmitOrder
{
    private readonly ILogger _logger;
    public SubmitOrder(ILoggerFactory loggerFactory)
    {
        _logger = loggerFactory.CreateLogger<SubmitOrder>();
    }
    [Function("SubmitOrder")]
    public HttpResponseData Run(
    [HttpTrigger(AuthorizationLevel.Anonymous, "post")]
    HttpRequestData req,
    FunctionContext ctx)
    {
        _logger.LogInformation("SubmitOrder function processed
```

```
        a request.");
        var response = req.CreateResponse(HttpStatusCode.OK);
        response.WriteString("Order received!");
        return response;
    }
}
```

If you've written ASP.NET Core controllers, this feels familiar: dependency injection in the constructor, logging, a request object, and a response object. The difference is the [Function] attribute and the [HttpTrigger] binding, the glue that connects this method to the Azure Functions runtime.

Running the Function

Let's try it out. In the terminal

```
func start
```

You'll see output like

Functions:

```
SubmitOrder: [POST] http://localhost:7071/api/SubmitOrder
```

Send a request with `curl`:

```
curl -X POST http://localhost:7071/api/SubmitOrder
```

You'll get

Order received!

And in the console, a log line

`SubmitOrder` function processed a request.

That's it, your first Function. Simple, but significant, you didn't configure IIS, Nginx, or Kestrel; you didn't write boilerplate for routing or DI; you just wrote a method; and the platform took care of the rest.

Toward a Real Order Processor

Of course, "Order received!" isn't enough. Let's accept a JSON payload and echo it back. Add a simple `Order` model:

```
public record Order(string Id, string CustomerEmail, List<string> Items);
```

Now update the Function:

```
[Function("SubmitOrder")]
public async Task<HttpResponseData> Run(
[HttpTrigger(AuthorizationLevel.Anonymous, "post")]
HttpRequestData req,
FunctionContext ctx)
{
    var order = await req.ReadFromJsonAsync<Order>();
    if (order == null || order.Items.Count == 0)
    {
        var badResponse =
        req.CreateResponse(HttpStatusCode.BadRequest);
        badResponse.WriteString("Invalid order");
        return badResponse;
    }
    _logger.LogInformation("Received order {Id} for {Email}",
    order.Id, order.CustomerEmail);
    var response = req.CreateResponse(HttpStatusCode.Accepted);
    await response.WriteAsJsonAsync(new { order.Id, Status =
    "Pending" });
    return response;
}
```

Now test with

```
curl -X POST http://localhost:7071/api/SubmitOrder \
-H "Content-Type: application/json" \
-d '{"Id":"123","CustomerEmail":"alice@example.com","Items":
["Widget","Gadget"]}'
```

Response:

```
{ "id": "123", "status": "Pending" }
```

We now have the beginning of an order-processing pipeline. In Chapter 2, we'll keep extending this app with more triggers and bindings. In later chapters, we'll connect it to messaging, storage, orchestration, and identity.

Why This Is Important

At this point, you might think, I could have done this in ASP.NET Core *with a controller*. True.

But here's the difference:

1. In ASP.NET Core, you'd need to deploy a web server, scale it, manage its lifecycle, and pay for uptime.
2. In Functions, you wrote a single method. Azure will scale it on demand, retry it if it fails, and bill you only for the time it runs.

That's the serverless mindset. You stop thinking about servers and start thinking about events.

Triggers and Bindings

In the Functions world, everything begins with a trigger. A trigger tells Azure when to invoke your code. It might be an HTTP request, a queue message, a new blob, a scheduled timer, or an event published to Event Grid. Triggers are what make Functions reactive; instead of running all the time, they sit idle until something happens.

Paired with triggers are **bindings**. Bindings connect Functions to external resources, inputs to read from, or outputs to write to. The beauty of bindings is that they let you declare integrations in attributes rather than writing boilerplate code. You can focus on logic, not on wiring up SDKs.

This section introduces the most common triggers and bindings, with concrete .NET examples. We'll build several Functions into our OrderProcessor app so that by the end, it can handle HTTP submissions, queue processing, blob storage, timers, and events.

HTTP Triggers: The Entry Point

The most familiar trigger is HTTP. You've already seen it in `SubmitOrder`. Let's extend it with an output binding to place the order on a queue.

```
public class SubmitOrder
{
    private readonly ILogger _logger;
    public SubmitOrder(ILoggerFactory loggerFactory)
    {
        _logger = loggerFactory.CreateLogger<SubmitOrder>();
    }
    [Function("SubmitOrder")]
    [QueueOutput("orders", Connection =     "AzureWebJobsStorage")]
    public async Task<string> Run(
    [HttpTrigger(AuthorizationLevel.Anonymous, "post")]
    HttpRequestData req,
    FunctionContext ctx)
    {
        var order = await req.ReadFromJsonAsync<Order>();
        if (order == null || order.Items.Count == 0)
        throw new InvalidOperationException("Invalid
        order");_logger.LogInformation("Received order {Id}",
        order.Id);
        // Place on queue
        return JsonSerializer.Serialize(order);
    }
}
```

Now a single HTTP request not only validates the order but also enqueues it for downstream processing. The [QueueOutput] binding handles serialization and enqueuing behind the scenes.

Queue Triggers: Async Pipelines

Queues are ideal for decoupling. Instead of doing everything in the HTTP requests, you pass work to a queue and return immediately. A separate Function consumes the queue.

```
public class ProcessOrder
{
    private readonly ILogger _logger;
```

```
    public ProcessOrder(ILoggerFactory loggerFactory)
    {
        _logger = loggerFactory.CreateLogger<ProcessOrder>();
    }
    [Function("ProcessOrder")]
    public void Run(
    [QueueTrigger("orders", Connection =
    "AzureWebJobsStorage")] string message)
    {
        var order =
        JsonSerializer.Deserialize<Order>(message)!;
        _logger.LogInformation("Processing order {Id} with
        {Count} items", order.Id, order.Items.Count);
    }
}
```

Now we've split responsibilities: SubmitOrder enqueues and ProcessOrder consumes. If 100 orders arrive at once, Functions can scale out multiple processors in parallel.

Blob Triggers: File-Driven Flows

Suppose each order has an invoice PDF that must be processed. Blob triggers handle this. Whenever a file is uploaded, the Function runs.

```
public class ProcessInvoice
{
    private readonly ILogger _logger;
    public ProcessInvoice(ILoggerFactory loggerFactory)
    {
        _logger = loggerFactory.CreateLogger<ProcessInvoice>();
    }
    [Function("ProcessInvoice")]
    public void Run(
    [BlobTrigger("invoices/{name}", Connection =
```

```
    "AzureWebJobsStorage")] Stream invoice,
    string name)
    {
        _logger.LogInformation("Processing invoice {FileName},
        size {Bytes} bytes", name, invoice.Length);
    }
}
```

Just upload a blob to the `invoices` container, and the Function fires automatically. No polling, no SDK plumbing.

Timer Triggers: Scheduled Tasks

Some tasks need to run on a schedule: cleanup jobs, reminders, and nightly reports. Timer triggers work like CRON jobs.

```
public class CleanupOrders{
    private readonly ILogger _logger;
    public CleanupOrders(ILoggerFactory loggerFactory)
    {
        _logger = loggerFactory.CreateLogger<CleanupOrders>();
    }
    [Function("CleanupOrders")]
    public void Run([TimerTrigger("0 0 2 * * *")] TimerInfo
    timer)
    {
        _logger.LogInformation("Running cleanup at {Now}",
        DateTime.UtcNow);
    }
}
```

This runs every day at 2am UTC. The CRON expression format is flexible: `0 */5 * * * *` would mean every five minutes.

Event Grid Triggers: Pub/Sub Events

Event Grid enables pub/sub at scale. Instead of polling resources, you subscribe to events (like "blob created" or "resource deleted") and react to them. Here's a Function that reacts to new blob events:

```
public class InvoiceEventHandler
{
    private readonly ILogger _logger;
    public InvoiceEventHandler(ILoggerFactory loggerFactory)
    {
        _logger =
        loggerFactory.CreateLogger<InvoiceEventHandler>();
    }
    [Function("InvoiceEventHandler")]
    public void Run([EventGridTrigger] EventGridEvent ev)
    {
        _logger.LogInformation("Event received: {Type},
        Subject: {Subject}", ev.EventType, ev.Subject);
    }
}
```

Event Grid can route events from blob storage, resource groups, or custom sources. It's the backbone of many event-driven architectures.

Service Bus Triggers: Enterprise Messaging

For more advanced messaging, with topics, sessions, and guaranteed ordering, Azure Service Bus is the go-to. It's heavier than queues but more powerful.

```
public class ProcessPayment
{
    private readonly ILogger _logger;
    public ProcessPayment(ILoggerFactory loggerFactory)
    {
        _logger = loggerFactory.CreateLogger<ProcessPayment>();
    }
```

```
    [Function("ProcessPayment")]
    public void Run([ServiceBusTrigger("payments", Connection =
        "ServiceBusConnection")] string message)
    {
        _logger.LogInformation("Processing payment message:
        {Message}", message);
    }
}
```

Service Bus adds delivery guarantees, duplicate detection, and message sessions for ordered workflows. Later chapters will show how to combine Service Bus with Durable Functions for robust orchestration.

Why Bindings Are Important

In each of these examples, notice how little boilerplate there was. Without bindings, you'd need to instantiate SDK clients, authenticate, handle retries, and write error-handling code. Bindings abstract all that away. You declare intent, "this Function reads from queue X and writes *to blob Y,"* and the runtime wires it up. This simplicity encourages **event-driven design**. Instead of writing a massive controller method, you break workflows into small Functions, each triggered by its own event, each isolated and testable.

Hosting and Scaling Models

When you write a Function, it feels like magic; you focus on logic, and the platform takes care of the rest. But something still has to run your code. Serverless doesn't mean no servers; it means you don't manage them directly. Azure handles provisioning, scaling, and retiring instances, but you still choose the hosting plan. That choice affects cost, performance, and scale.

This section explores the three hosting models for Functions, Consumption, Premium, and Dedicated, and explains how Functions scale. But unlike abstract examples, we'll extend the `OrderProcessor` project to make these lessons tangible. You'll see how `SubmitOrder` reveals cold starts in real logs and how an `OrderBatchProcessor` demonstrates scale-out when faced with heavy load.

Consumption Plan: Elastic but Cold

The consumption plan is the default and the most serverless. You pay per execution, measured in GB-seconds. Azure automatically scales Functions up and down, even to zero when idle. This is perfect for spiky workloads. If your queue sits idle all day, you pay nothing. If a sudden surge of orders arrives, Azure spins up instances to drain it.

The trade-off is cold starts. When a Function App is idle for some time, Azure deallocates it. The next request requires spinning up a new container, loading assemblies, and initializing the runtime. That can add latency, usually under a second, but occasionally several. Let's expose this in our project.

SubmitOrder:

```
public class SubmitOrder
{
    private static readonly DateTime StartupTime =
    DateTime.UtcNow;
    private readonly ILogger _logger;
    public SubmitOrder(ILoggerFactory loggerFactory)
    {
        _logger = loggerFactory.CreateLogger<SubmitOrder>();
    }
    [Function("SubmitOrder")]
    [QueueOutput("orders", Connection = "AzureWebJobsStorage")]
    public async Task<string> Run(
    [HttpTrigger(AuthorizationLevel.Anonymous, "post")]
    HttpRequestData req,
    FunctionContext ctx)
    {
        _logger.LogInformation("App startup time: {Startup}",
        StartupTime);
        var order = await req.ReadFromJsonAs
        throw new InvalidOperationException("Invalid
        order");
```

```
        _logger.LogInformation("Received order {Id}",
        order.Id);
        return JsonSerializer.Serialize(order);
    }
}
```

Deploy this, leave it idle for 30 minutes, then submit an order. If the log shows a new StartupTime, you just witnessed a cold start.

Premium Plan: Pre-warmed Reliability

If your app is user-facing and latency matters, cold starts can be a dealbreaker. The Premium plan solves this by keeping instances pre-warmed. You pay for reserved capacity, but you also get

- **No cold starts** for most requests
- **VNET integration** (critical for enterprise networking)
- **Higher limits** (up to 60 minutes execution time, more concurrent connections)

Imagine `OrderProcessor` powering a checkout API. Customers expect instant confirmation. On consumption, 1 in 20 requests might feel sluggish due to a cold start. On Premium, every request hits a warm instance. The trade-off is cost; premium keeps at least one instance alive, whether it's used or not.

Dedicated Plan: The App Service Option

The Dedicated plan runs Functions on standard App Service plans. You pay for uptime, regardless of usage. This is rarely chosen for new serverless projects, but enterprises sometimes pick it to reuse existing App Service investments or to guarantee a fixed baseline of compute. For `OrderProcessor`, dedicated would make sense if it was one component of a larger App Service portfolio already paid for. But for a greenfield serverless pipeline, Consumption or Premium are better fits.

Scaling in Practice

Let's make scaling real in our project. So far, ProcessOrder simply logs each order. That's too quick to see scale-out. To force Azure to scale, we'll simulate heavy work in a new Function:

```
public class OrderBatchProcessor
{
    private readonly ILogger _logger;
    public OrderBatchProcessor(ILoggerFactory loggerFactory)
    {
        _logger =
        loggerFactory.CreateLogger<OrderBatchProcessor>();
    }
    [Function("OrderBatchProcessor")]
    public async Task Run([QueueTrigger("orders", Connection =
    "AzureWebJobsStorage")] string message,
    FunctionContext ctx)
    {
        var order = JsonSerializer.Deserialize<Order>(message)!;
        _logger.LogInformation("START order {Id} at {Time}",
        order.Id, DateTime.UtcNow);
        // Simulate 5s of heavy processing
        await Task.Delay(TimeSpan.FromSeconds(5));
        _logger.LogInformation("END order {Id} at {Time}",
        order.Id, DateTime.UtcNow);
    }
}
```

Now, if you submit 50 orders quickly through SubmitOrder, you'll notice overlapping logs, and multiple orders are processed at the same time. That's Functions scaling your app to handle the load.

Concurrency and Async

Scaling isn't just about creating more instances. Within a single Function host, multiple executions can run concurrently. Our `OrderBatchProcessor` uses await `Task.Delay`, which frees the thread to process other work. If we replaced it with `Thread.Sleep`, the thread would block, and throughput would drop.

Here's a quick experiment:

```
await Task.Delay(5000); // scalable
Thread.Sleep(5000); // unscalable
```

Run both versions with 20 queued orders. With `Task.Delay`, you'll see concurrent logs. With `Thread.Sleep`, orders will process sequentially. This highlights why async/await is essential in serverless .NET.

Cost Modeling

To make hosting choices concrete, let's estimate the cost for a million orders per month, each taking 1 second at 512MB memory:

- Consumption:
    1. 1M × 0.5 GB × 1s = 500k GB-s.
    2. At ~$0.000016/GB-s = ~$8, plus $0.20 for execution count.
    3. Total ≈ $8.20.
- Premium:
    1. One pre-warmed core ~ $130/month, regardless of usage.
- Dedicated:
    1. Smallest App Service plan ~ $70/month baseline. `OrderProcessor` is a perfect fit for consumption, cheap, elastic, and good enough unless latency SLAs require Premium.

Execution Model and Concurrency

When you submit a single order to the `OrderProcessor`, it feels simple; the Function runs, logs some data, enqueues a message, and finishes. But under the hood, the Functions runtime is juggling threads, scheduling tasks, and scaling instances. To design reliable serverless systems, you need to understand the execution model.

This section takes you behind the curtain. We'll look at what happens inside a Function App instance, how concurrency works, and why writing async .NET code is not just a best practice but a survival strategy. Along the way, we'll extend the `OrderProcessor` with an `OrderItemValidator` that demonstrates concurrency in action.

How the Functions Runtime Executes Code

A Function App runs as a process. Inside that process is a **host**, the Functions runtime, which manages triggers, bindings, logging, and dependency injection. When an event arrives (say, a new queue message), the runtime

1. Deserializes the message into the trigger parameter
2. Invokes your Function method
3. Manages its lifetime until completion

Multiple triggers can be active in one host. For example, if both `SubmitOrder` (HTTP) and `OrderBatchProcessor` (queue) are busy, the runtime interleaves their execution. The important thing is the runtime doesn't wait for one execution to finish before starting the next. It runs as many as the machine and runtime can handle, which means concurrency is the default.

Async Unlocks Concurrency

In .NET, async/await frees threads while waiting for I/O. That's perfect for serverless, where most work is I/O bound (reading messages, writing to storage, calling APIs).

Let's extend `OrderProcessor` with an `OrderItemValidator` that validates each item in an order by calling a (simulated) external API.

```
public class OrderItemValidator
{
    private readonly ILogger _logger;
```

```
    private static readonly HttpClient _http = new
        HttpClient();
    public OrderItemValidator(ILoggerFactory loggerFactory)
    {
        _logger =
        loggerFactory.CreateLogger<OrderItemValidator>();
    }
    [Function("OrderItemValidator")]
    public async Task Run(
        [QueueTrigger("orders", Connection =
        "AzureWebJobsStorage")] string message,
        FunctionContext ctx)
    {
        var order =
            JsonSerializer.Deserialize<Order>(message)!;
        _logger.LogInformation("Validating order {Id} with
        {Count} items", order.Id, order.Items.Count);
        var tasks = order.Items.Select(async item =>
    {
        var response = await _http.GetAsync($"https://
            httpbin.org/delay/2");
        _logger.LogInformation("Validated item {Item} with
            status {StatusCode}",
            item, response.StatusCode);
        });
        await Task.WhenAll(tasks);
        _logger.LogInformation("Completed validation for order
        {Id}", order.Id);
    }
}
```

Each item validation simulates a 2-second HTTP call. If you submit an order with five items, validation runs all calls concurrently, completing in ~2 seconds total (see Figure 2-2). If we had run them sequentially, it would take ~10 seconds.

Blocking Kills Throughput

Now, let's see what happens if we block threads. Replace the async API call with

```
Thread.Sleep(2000);
_logger.LogInformation("Validated item {Item}", item);
```

Run the same 5-item order. Validation now takes ~10 seconds. Worse, while the thread is blocked, the runtime can't schedule other work on it. This reduces concurrency across the whole Function App. If 50 orders arrive, throughput collapses. This is why async/await is not optional in serverless .NET. It's the difference between scaling elastically and grinding to a halt under load (see Figure 2-3).

Concurrency Across Instances

Concurrency happens inside an instance, but Azure also scales out by creating more instances. Suppose you enqueue 100 orders, each with 5 items. The runtime will

- Run multiple item validations concurrently in each host (thanks to async)
- Spin up additional instances of the Function App to handle load

You'll see interleaved logs with overlapping order IDs across different timestamps. This is normal and powerful.

Function Execution Model, Async vs. Blocking:

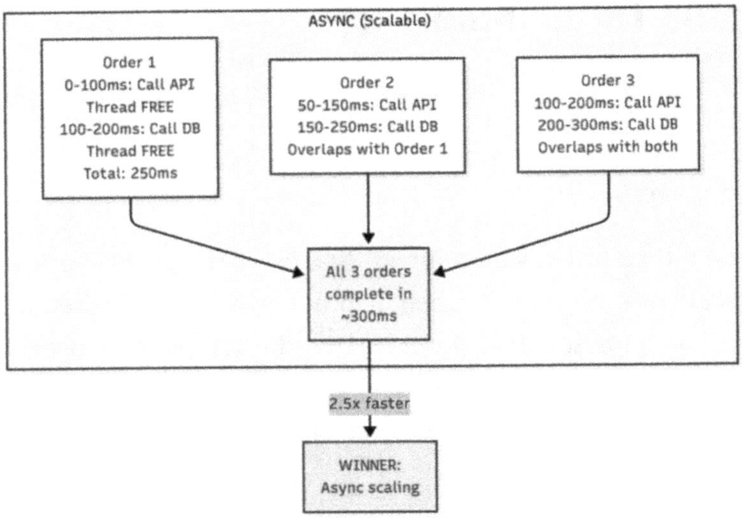

Figure 2-2. *Async*

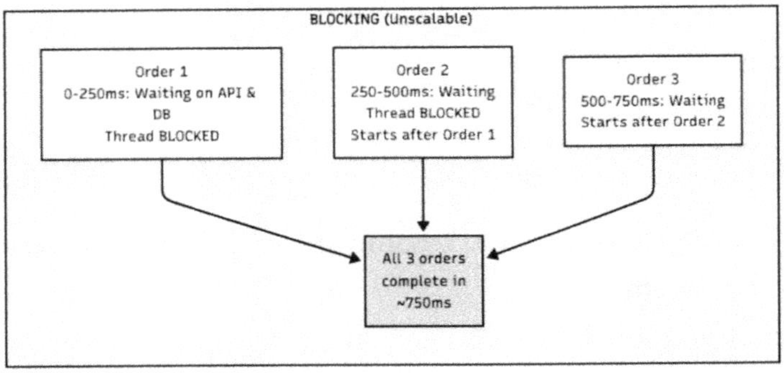

Figure 2-3. *Blocking*

Order of Execution is Not Guaranteed

The catch is that once you introduce concurrency, ordering is no longer guaranteed. As soon as work can run in parallel, the system no longer has a notion of "first" and "second." Order #1 may start first but finish last. Order #2 might complete straight away because it hit a warm instance or a faster network path. Validation logs might appear out of sequence compared to how items were submitted. Database writes can complete in a different order than requests were received. Even retries can overtake original executions if they land on a less busy worker. None of this indicates a bug. It's the natural result of concurrent execution. In distributed systems, time is not global and execution is not serial. Each worker processes messages independently, and progress depends on factors you don't control directly: CPU scheduling, IO latency, cold starts, garbage collection, network variance, and backpressure elsewhere in the system. When multiple instances are involved, there is no single clock or queue that defines a universal order of completion.

This is especially important to understand with serverless platforms and messaging-based architectures. Azure Functions, for example, will happily scale out and process multiple messages at once to maximize throughput. The runtime optimizes for efficiency, not determinism. If you assume "message A will finish before message B because it was enqueued first," that assumption will eventually fail under load.

If strict ordering is important to the business logic, it must be enforced explicitly at the design level. That might mean using Service Bus sessions so that related messages are processed sequentially by the same logical consumer. It could mean funneling work through a single-threaded Durable Function orchestrator, or introducing a sequence number and refusing to process item n + 1 until item n has been completed. All of these approaches deliberately trade throughput and scalability for determinism.

By default, though, Functions and similar systems choose throughput over order. They assume your handlers are idempotent, tolerant of reordering, and resilient to retries. Designing with that assumption in mind leads to systems that scale cleanly and behave predictably under load. Designing against it often results in subtle bugs that only appear in production.

The thing to remember is that if your system relies on execution order, that reliance must be made explicit. Otherwise, once concurrency is introduced, order is no longer guaranteed.

Observing Concurrency with Correlation IDs

Let's make it easier to trace what's happening. Add a correlation ID to each order, and flow it through logs.

Update SubmitOrder:

```
public record Order(string Id, string CustomerEmail,
List<string> Items, string CorrelationId);
public async Task<string> Run(
[HttpTrigger(AuthorizationLevel.Anonymous, "post")]
```

```
HttpRequestData req,
FunctionContext ctx)
{
    var order = await req.ReadFromJsonAsync<Order>();
    if (order == null) throw new
        InvalidOperationException("Invalid order");
    var correlationId = Guid.NewGuid().ToString();
    var enriched = order with { CorrelationId =
    correlationId };_logger.LogInformation("Order {Id} received,
    Correlation {CorrelationId}", order.Id, correlationId);
    return JsonSerializer.Serialize(enriched);
}
```

Update `OrderItemValidator` to log the correlation ID. Now when multiple orders overlap, you can trace items back to their parent order. This mirrors real-world observability practices.

Configuration and Settings

Every non-trivial system depends on external resources, storage accounts, databases, service buses, and APIs. Functions need to know how to connect to them. In a monolith, you might have hard-coded connection strings or config files checked into source control. In serverless, that approach is a recipe for trouble. Functions scale across instances and regions, and their configuration must be centralized, secure, and environment-aware. This section explores how Azure Functions manage configurations. We'll start with the local developer experience (`local.settings.json`), move to production app settings, and then show how to integrate Azure Key Vault for secrets. Along the way, we'll extend the `OrderProcessor` project by moving its queue storage connection into configuration, adding environment-specific settings, and preparing it for secure secret retrieval.

Local Settings: Fast Feedback

When you scaffolded **OrderProcessor**, a `local.settings.json` file was created:

```
{"IsEncrypted": false,
    "Values": {
        "AzureWebJobsStorage": "UseDevelopmentStorage=true",
        "FUNCTIONS_WORKER_RUNTIME": "dotnet-isolated"
    }
}
```

This is where local development secrets live. For now, it points AzureWebJobsStorage at Azurite (the local storage emulator). You can add custom settings here too. For example, let's add an API key setting that our order validator might use:

```
{
"IsEncrypted": false,
    "Values": {
        "AzureWebJobsStorage": "UseDevelopmentStorage=true",
        "FUNCTIONS_WORKER_RUNTIME": "dotnet-isolated",
        "ValidatorApiKey": "dev-secret-123"
    }
}
```

Inside a Function, you can read this value via

```
Environment.GetEnvironmentVariable:
var key =
Environment.GetEnvironmentVariable("ValidatorApiKey");
_logger.LogInformation("Using API key {Key}", key);
```

This is fine locally, but remember: `local.settings.json` should never be committed to source control. It's for dev only.

App Settings in Azure

When you deploy to Azure, configuration lives in Application Settings for the Function App. These are environment variables at runtime. The nice part is the same code you wrote locally (`Environment.GetEnvironmentVariable`) works unchanged in Azure. To add settings in the portal

1. Navigate to your Function App.
2. Under Configuration, click new application setting.
3. Add ValidatorApiKey with a production value.
4. Save and restart.

Now the deployed Function will see the production key instead of the dev key.

Strongly Typed Configuration with Options

Reading environment variables manually gets messy. Instead, we can bind them into strongly typed classes using .NET's `IOptions<T>` pattern.

Let's add a settings class:

```
public class ValidatorOptions
{
    public string ApiKey { get; set; } = string.Empty;
}
```

In Program.cs:

```
var host = new HostBuilder()
.ConfigureFunctionsWorkerDefaults()
.ConfigureServices(services =>
    {
        services.AddOptions<ValidatorOptions>()
        .Configure<IConfiguration>((settings,
        configuration) =>
    {
        configuration.GetSection("Validator").Bind(settings);
    });
})
.Build();
host.Run();
```

Now update `local.settings.json`:

```
"Validator": {
                "ApiKey": "dev-secret-123"
            }
```

And inject it into a Function:

```
public class ConfigDemo
{
    private readonly ValidatorOptions _options;
    private readonly ILogger _logger;
    public ConfigDemo(IOptions<ValidatorOptions> options,
    ILoggerFactory loggerFactory)
    {
        _options = options.Value;
        _logger = loggerFactory.CreateLogger<ConfigDemo>();
    }
    [Function("ConfigDemo")]
    public HttpResponseData Run(
    [HttpTrigger(AuthorizationLevel.Anonymous, "get")]
    HttpRequestData req)
    {
        var response = req.CreateResponse(HttpStatusCode.OK);
        response.WriteString($"Validator key:
        {_options.ApiKey}");
        return response;
    }
}
```

This keeps config clean, testable, and strongly typed.

Secrets and Key Vault

Storing secrets directly in App Settings works, but it's not ideal for high-security environments. Azure Key Vault is the best practice: a managed service for storing secrets, keys, and certificates. With Key Vault integration, you don't change your code. Instead, you

1. Store the secret in Key Vault.
2. Link the Key Vault to your Function App's managed identity.
3. Reference the secret in App Settings using the syntax:

```
@Microsoft.KeyVault(SecretUri=https://myvault.vault.azure.net/secrets/
ValidatorApiKey/...)
```

At runtime, the Functions host automatically resolves the secrets. Your code just sees it as an environment variable. This means our `ValidatorOptions` setup continues to work, but the secret value is securely stored in Key Vault, rotated automatically, and never exposed in plain text in the portal.

Environment-Specific Settings

Most real projects run in multiple environments: dev, test, staging, and production. Functions don't have `web.config` transforms like older ASP.NET apps. Instead, you manage environments by deploying to separate Function Apps, each with its own configuration. For `OrderProcessor`, that means

- **Dev**: Local Azurite storage, fake Validator API
- Test shared Azure Storage and test Key Vault secrets
- **Prod**: Production storage account, live Validator API, secure Key Vault integration

The Functions runtime doesn't know or care; it just reads whatever environment variables you give it. This encourages 12-factor app practices; config belongs to the environment, not the code.

`OrderProcessor` update

Let's make `OrderProcessor` more realistic by moving its storage connection string into settings. Update `local.settings.json`:

```
"Values": {
    "FUNCTIONS_WORKER_RUNTIME": "dotnet-isolated",
    "AzureWebJobsStorage": "UseDevelopmentStorage=true",
    "OrderStorageConnection": "UseDevelopmentStorage=true"
}
```

Now update `SubmitOrder` and `OrderBatchProcessor` to reference `OrderStorageConnection` instead of hardcoding `AzureWebJobsStorage`:

```
[QueueOutput("orders", Connection = "OrderStorageConnection")]
```

and

```
[QueueTrigger("orders", Connection = "OrderStorageConnection")]
```

This small change makes the project more portable. When you deploy to Azure, you can point `OrderStorageConnection` at a real storage account without touching the code. Later, we'll secure it with Key Vault.

Dependency Injection and Services

Serverless Functions are meant to be **small**. Each Function should do one thing: validate input, enqueue a message, or process a file. But "small" doesn't mean "stuff everything into one method." If you jam validation, logging, and business logic into your Function body, it quickly becomes untestable spaghetti.

The key is to keep Functions as thin entry points and move actual logic into services. Dependency Injection (DI) makes this possible. With DI, your Functions don't construct their own dependencies; they declare what they need, and the Functions host provides them. This mirrors ASP.NET Core's approach, so it feels natural to .NET developers.

In this section, we'll refactor the `OrderProcessor` project so that Functions call into injected services. We'll implement an `IOrderValidator` to check incoming orders and later add an `IDiscountService` to simulate business rules. Along the way, we'll unit test the services to prove that DI makes Functions more maintainable.

Why DI Is Important in Functions

Without DI, your Function might look like this:

```
[Function("SubmitOrderBad")]
public async Task<HttpResponseData> Run(
[HttpTrigger(AuthorizationLevel.Anonymous, "post")]
HttpRequestData req,
FunctionContext ctx)
```

```
{
    var body = await req.ReadAsStringAsync();
    var order = JsonSerializer.Deserialize<Order>(body);
    if (order == null ||
        string.IsNullOrWhiteSpace(order.CustomerEmail))
        throw new InvalidOperationException("Invalid order");
    var logger = ctx.GetLogger("SubmitOrderBad");
    logger.LogInformation("Processing order {Id}", order.Id);
    // Pretend to save to DB
    return req.CreateResponse(HttpStatusCode.Accepted);
}
```

This Function works, but

- Validation is hardcoded.
- No way to swap validators for testing.
- Business logic mixed with input/output code.

Refactoring with DI solves these issues.

Configuring DI in Program.cs

In the isolated worker model, DI is configured in `Program.cs` using `HostBuilder`.

```
var host = new HostBuilder()
.ConfigureFunctionsWorkerDefaults()
.ConfigureServices(services =>
{
    services.AddSingleton<IOrderValidator,
    OrderValidator>();
    services.AddScoped<IDiscountService,
    DiscountService>();})
    .Build();
    host.Run();
```

Here, `IOrderValidator` is registered as a singleton (one instance reused), while `IDiscountService` is scoped (new instance per Function execution).

Implementing Services

Let's start with an order validator.

```
public interface IOrderValidator
{
    bool IsValid(Order order, out string reason);
}
public class OrderValidator : IOrderValidator
{
    public bool IsValid(Order order, out string reason)
    {
        if (order == null)
        {
            reason = "Order was null";
            return false;
        }
        if (string.IsNullOrWhiteSpace(order.CustomerEmail) || !
            order.CustomerEmail.Contains("@")){
            reason = "Invalid customer email";
            return false;
        }
        if (order.Items == null || order.Items.Count == 0)
        {
            reason = "Order must contain at least one item";
            return false;
        }
        reason = string.Empty;
        return true;
    }
}
```

Now we can update SubmitOrder to depend on

```
IOrderValidator:
public class SubmitOrder
{
    private readonly ILogger _logger;
    private readonly IOrderValidator _validator;
    public SubmitOrder(ILoggerFactory loggerFactory,
    IOrderValidator validator)
    {
        _logger = loggerFactory.CreateLogger<SubmitOrder>();
        _validator = validator;
    }
    [Function("SubmitOrder")]
    [QueueOutput("orders", Connection =
    "OrderStorageConnection")]
    public async Task<string> Run(
    [HttpTrigger(AuthorizationLevel.Anonymous, "post")]
    HttpRequestData req)
    {
        var order = await req.ReadFromJsonAsync<Order>();
        if (!_validator.IsValid(order!, out var reason))
        {
            _logger.LogWarning("Invalid order: {Reason}",
                reason);
            throw new InvalidOperationException(reason);
        }
        _logger.LogInformation("Validated order {Id}",
            order!.Id);
        return JsonSerializer.Serialize(order);
    }
}
```

Now the Function is slim: it parses input, calls the validator, logs, and enqueues. The rules are isolated in a testable service.

Adding Business Rules: DiscountService

Next, let's simulate applying discounts with a service.

```
public interface IDiscountService
{
    decimal ApplyDiscount(Order order);
}
public class DiscountService : IDiscountService
{
    public decimal ApplyDiscount(Order order)
{
    if (order.Items.Count >= 5)
        return 0.10m; // 10% discount
        return 0m;
    }
}
```

We can inject this into a new Function, `CalculateDiscount`:

```
public class CalculateDiscount
{
    private readonly IDiscountService _discountService;
    private readonly ILogger _logger;
    public CalculateDiscount(IDiscountService discountService,
    ILoggerFactory loggerFactory)
    {
        _discountService = discountService;
        _logger =
        loggerFactory.CreateLogger<CalculateDiscount>();
    }
    [Function("CalculateDiscount")]
    public async Task<HttpResponseData> Run(
    [HttpTrigger(AuthorizationLevel.Anonymous, "post")]
    HttpRequestData req){
        var order = await req.ReadFromJsonAsync<Order>();
        var discount = _discountService.ApplyDiscount(order!);
        _logger.LogInformation("Applied discount {Discount:P}
```

```
        to order {Id}", discount, order!.Id);
        var response = req.CreateResponse(HttpStatusCode.OK);
                await response.WriteAsJsonAsync(new { order.Id,
        Discount = discount });
        return response;
    }
}
```

This separates business rules from Function logic, keeping things clean.

Unit Testing Services

Because services don't depend on the Functions runtime, they're easy to test.

Example with xUnit:

```
public class OrderValidatorTests
{
    [Fact]
    public void EmptyEmail_FailsValidation()
    {
        var validator = new OrderValidator();
        var order = new Order("123", "", new List<string>
        { "Widget" });
        Assert.False(validator.IsValid(order, out var reason));
        Assert.Equal("Invalid customer email", reason);
    }
    [Fact]
    public void ValidOrder_Passes()
    {
        var validator = new OrderValidator();
        var order = new Order("123", "alice@example.com", new
        List<string> { "Widget" });
        Assert.True(validator.IsValid(order, out var _));
    }}
```

These tests run fast, don't need the Functions host, and prove that business logic works independently.

Why DI Is Important for Scaling Projects

With clear layering and dependency injection, scaling becomes additive rather than destructive. New triggers plug into existing services. New rules extend existing behavior. New execution paths reuse the same core. The system grows by composition instead of modification, which is what allows it to scale in both throughput and complexity without collapsing under its own weight.

Local Development and Testing

Building Functions in the cloud is exciting, but constantly deploying to Azure just to see if your code works would be painful. Fortunately, the Functions runtime and tooling make it possible to develop, debug, and test locally, long before you hit the cloud. In this section, we'll explore how to run the `OrderProcessor` project on your machine, set breakpoints in Visual Studio and VS Code, write unit tests for services, and even run integration tests that simulate queues and HTTP requests. By the end, you'll have a full feedback loop: `write > run > test > debug`, without leaving your dev environment.

Running Functions Locally

The Functions runtime can run on your machine with Core Tools.

From the `OrderProcessor` directory:

```
func start
```

This launches the Functions host, reads your `local.settings.json`, and starts listening for triggers. You'll see output like

Functions:

```
SubmitOrder: [POST] http://localhost:7071/api/SubmitOrder
OrderBatchProcessor: queueTrigger
OrderItemValidator: queueTrigger
CalculateDiscount: [POST] http://localhost:7071/api/CalculateDiscount
```

This is your app running locally, with all triggers active.

Send a request to `SubmitOrder`:

```
curl -X POST http://localhost:7071/api/SubmitOrder \-H "Content-Type:
application/json" \
-d '{"Id":"123","CustomerEmail":"alice@example.com","Items":
["Widget","Gadget"]}'
```

You'll see the response immediately, and logs in the console show the queue output and validation activity.

Debugging in Visual Studio/VS Code

If you open the project in Visual Studio, you can press F5 to run Functions with full debugging. Breakpoints in `SubmitOrder`, `OrderValidator`, or `DiscountService` will hit just like an ASP.NET Core app. In VS Code, install the Azure Functions extension, which adds debug configurations. Press F5 and select the Function App. The runtime starts, and breakpoints light up. This parity between local and cloud development is powerful. You can iterate quickly, catch errors before deployment, and debug tricky concurrency issues.

Unit Testing Services

We've already seen that services like `OrderValidator` are easy to test because they don't depend on the Functions runtime. Let's add a few more.

Example for DiscountService:

```
public class DiscountServiceTests{
    [Fact]
    public void NoDiscount_WhenLessThanFiveItems()
    {
        var service = new DiscountService();
        var order = new Order("123", "alice@example.com", new
        List<string> { "Widget" });
        var discount = service.ApplyDiscount(order);
        Assert.Equal(0m, discount);
    }

    [Fact]
    public void Discount_WhenFiveOrMoreItems()
```

```
    {
        var service = new DiscountService();
        var order = new Order("123", "bob@example.com",
        new List<string> { "A","B","C","D","E" });
        var discount = service.ApplyDiscount(order);
        Assert.Equal(0.10m, discount);
    }
}
```

Run these with `dotnet test`. They execute instantly and catch regressions early.

Integration Testing Functions

Unit tests are great, but eventually you want to see the Functions in action. You can run integration tests against the Functions host. Here's a minimal xUnit test using `HttpClient`:

```
public class SubmitOrderIntegrationTests
{
    private readonly HttpClient _client;
    public SubmitOrderIntegrationTests()
    {
        // Point to local Functions runtime
        _client = new HttpClient { BaseAddress = new
        Uri("http://localhost:7071") };
    }
    [Fact]
    public async Task SubmitOrder_ReturnsAccepted()
    {var payload = new
    {
        Id = "999",
        CustomerEmail = "test@example.com",
        Items = new[] { "Widget" }
    };
    var response = await _client.PostAsJsonAsync("/api/
    SubmitOrder", payload);
```

```
    Assert.Equal(HttpStatusCode.Accepted,
    response.StatusCode);
    }
}
```

Run the Functions host with `func start`, then run this test. It hits your running Function just like a real client would.

Testing Queues Locally

Queues are trickier because they're event-driven. You can still simulate them using Azurite (the local storage emulator). Add a message:

```
az storage message put --queue-name orders --content '{"Id":"555","Customer
Email":"queue@test.com","Items":
["One","Two"]}' --connection-string “UseDevelopmentStorage=true"
```

The `OrderBatchProcessor` Function will fire automatically, logging start/end for the order. This lets you test queue-triggered Functions locally without touching Azure.

End-to-End Testing Strategy

In practice, you want a layered approach:

- **Unit Tests**: For services (`OrderValidator, DiscountService`). Fast, isolated.
- **Integration Tests**: For Functions, using HTTP/queues locally.
- **Cloud Tests**: A smaller set of tests against a deployed Function App, to confirm config and networking.

This balance keeps feedback fast while still giving confidence in production readiness.

CI/CD Testing

When you push code, you want the same tests to run in CI/CD. Azure DevOps, GitHub Actions, and others can

1. Run dotnet test for unit tests.
2. Start the Functions runtime in a build step (func start--verbose).
3. Run integration tests against it. This ensures your Functions don't just compile; they actually respond to requests.

OrderProcessor Update

To make testing concrete, let's add a dedicated **TestSupport** folder in the project:

```
OrderProcessor/
├── Functions/
├── Services/
├── Tests/
├── OrderValidatorTests.cs
├── DiscountServiceTests.cs
└── SubmitOrderIntegrationTests.cs
```

Here we keep both unit and integration tests. This mirrors how larger systems are structured, with a clear boundary between runtime code and test code.

EXERCISES

1. **Cold Start Detection:** Deploy the modified `SubmitOrder`. Submit once and note `StartupTime`. Leave idle for 30 minutes, and submit again. Did the time reset?
2. **Batch Scaling:** Deploy `OrderBatchProcessor`. Submit 50 orders quickly. Observe logs: did processing overlap? How many concurrent instances spun up?
3. **Async vs. Blocking:** Replace `Task.Delay` with `Thread.Sleep`. Re-run the batch. What happened to throughput?
4. **Cost Estimate:** Calculate monthly cost for 10M orders at 256MB and 0.5s each on consumption. Compare to Premium. Which would you choose?

5. **Scenario Reflection:** Would you run `OrderProcessor` on Consumption, Premium, or Dedicated? Why?
6. **Async Advantage:** Submit an order with five items. Compare validation time with async vs. `Thread.Sleep`.
7. **Batch Load:** Enqueue 20 orders with 5 items each. Watch logs: How many run concurrently? How many instances does Azure create?
8. **Correlation Tracing:** Add correlation IDs. Can you follow one order through interleaved logs?
9. **Sequential Enforcement**: Modify `OrderItemValidator` to process items sequentially (using foreach). Compare throughput. When might sequential processing be required?
10. **Throughput Reflection**: Imagine 1,000 orders with 10 items each. How long would it take sequentially vs. concurrently? Which hosting plan would best handle it?
11. **Custom Config:** Add a `DiscountRate` setting in `local.settings.json`. Create a Function that applies the discount to an order. Inject it via `IOptions<T>`.
12. **Environment Test:** Deploy `OrderProcessor` to Azure. Override the ValidatorApiKey app setting and confirm that the deployed Function uses the new value.
13. **Secret Hygiene:** Try committing `local.settings.json` to Git. Does Git ignore it? If not, update .gitignore. Why is this important?
14. **Key Vault Integration:** Create a Key Vault, add a secret, and reference it from App Settings. Confirm your Function resolves it automatically.
15. **Reflection:** How would you design configuration for an app that has five environments (dev, test, UAT, staging, prod)? What naming conventions would keep settings manageable?
16. **Refactor:** Move order validation into `OrderValidator`. Inject it into `SubmitOrder`. Confirm that invalid orders are rejected.
17. **Discount Rule:** Create a `DiscountService` that gives 20% off if the customer orders 10+ items. Inject and test it.

18. **Unit Tests:** Write tests for both `OrderValidator` and `DiscountService`. Run them with dotnet test.

19. **Mocking:** In a test, mock `IOrderValidator` to always return false. Confirm `SubmitOrder` throws.

20. **Reflection:** How does DI in Functions compare to ASP.NET Core? What benefits does it bring in a serverless context?

21. **Unit Test Coverage:** Write tests for invalid orders (empty items, bad emails). Confirm validator rejects them.

22. **Discount Testing:** Add a discount rule (20% for VIP customers). Write unit tests.

23. **Integration Tests:** Write a test that posts an order and then polls the orders queue to confirm it was enqueued.

24. **Queue Injection:** Manually push five messages into the orders queue via Azurite. Did `OrderBatchProcessor` handle them all?

25. **CI/CD:** Add a build step in GitHub Actions or Azure DevOps to run dotnet test. Then think: would you run integration tests in CI too, or only in a staging environment?

Summary

This section marked the real beginning of the `OrderProcessor` journey, starting with scaffolding a new .NET 8 + isolated worker Function App and running it locally. From that modest starting point, the project quickly evolved as we explored triggers and bindings, the core building blocks of Azure Functions. You saw how triggers determine when code runs, while bindings define how Functions interact with external systems, allowing you to compose reactive, focused pipelines. We layered multiple triggers together, HTTP endpoints feeding queues, queue processors writing to storage, blob triggers reacting to uploads, timer jobs performing background work, and event-driven integrations using Event Grid and Service Bus. As these pieces accumulated, `OrderProcessor` began to resemble a true distributed workflow rather than a simple sample, demonstrating how serverless systems naturally grow through loosely coupled, event-driven components.

We then zoomed out to the platform concerns that shape how these Functions behave in production. Hosting models revealed the trade-offs between Consumption, Premium, and Dedicated plans, balancing cost, cold starts, and enterprise capabilities, while scaling illustrated how Azure dynamically adds instances and executes workloads concurrently. You saw how asynchronous .NET code maximizes throughput and why blocking operations can cripple performance in highly concurrent environments. From there, we focused on the operational foundations that make serverless systems maintainable in the real world: configuration management through environment variables, strongly typed settings, and Key Vault integration; dependency injection to keep Functions thin and business logic testable; and local development and testing practices that create fast, reliable feedback loops. By the end of this section, `OrderProcessor` had transformed from a single HTTP Function into a multi-triggered, configurable, testable, and scalable event-driven foundation, ready to support the more advanced distributed system patterns explored in the rest of the book.

At the end of Chapter 2, `OrderProcessor` has

- Multiple triggers and bindings (HTTP, queue, blob, timer, Event Grid)
- Cold start logging and load simulation demonstrating scaling behavior
- Async concurrency and correlation IDs for traceability
- Environment-specific configuration via `IOptions<T>`
- Dependency injection with testable services
- Unit and integration tests running locally

What began as a single Function is now structured, testable, foundation-event-driven, configurable, and ready-to-grow into a distributed system.

In Chapter 3, we'll widen the lens from Functions to the messaging backbone of distributed systems: Event Grid and Service Bus. You'll see how to publish and subscribe to events, handle retries, and design flows where producers and consumers are decoupled. `OrderProcessor` will gain new capabilities: publishing order events to Event Grid, listening to Service Bus topics, and chaining Functions together into richer pipelines. This will take the project from a small demo to a distributed architecture with multiple event-driven pathways.

CHAPTER 3

Events, Messaging, and Decoupled Communication

Modern distributed systems rarely fail because a single component is badly built. More often, they fail because too many components depend on each other too tightly and too synchronously. A request enters one service, triggers calls to several others, and suddenly the health of the whole system depends on every downstream dependency responding quickly and correctly. That approach can work in simple systems, but as scale, traffic, and business complexity grow, it becomes fragile. Events and messages offer a more resilient alternative. Instead of forcing every component to participate in the same request at the same time, they allow systems to communicate through durable, asynchronous handoffs. Producers can publish facts or send work without needing to know who will react, when they will react, or whether they are currently available.

This chapter introduces the core communication patterns that make that style of architecture possible. Using the `OrderProcessor` project as a running example, we will explore why messaging is important, how events differ from commands, and where Azure Event Grid and Azure Service Bus each fit within a decoupled design. From there, we will examine how retries, dead-letter queues, and selective routing make distributed workflows more reliable under real production conditions. By the end of the chapter, you will have a practical understanding of how to move beyond brittle HTTP chains and design systems that are more scalable, more adaptable, and far more tolerant of failure.

© Patrick Kearns 2026
P. Kearns, *Serverless Distributed Systems in Modern .NET and Azure*,
https://doi.org/10.1007/979-8-8688-2839-3_3

Why Messaging Is Important

When you first build a distributed system, it's tempting to connect everything with HTTP calls. Service A receives a request, calls Service B over HTTP, which calls Service C, and so on. The chain looks neat on a diagram until you try it in production. Latency adds up. A hiccup in Service C drags the whole chain down. Spikes of traffic overwhelm the weakest link.

Messaging offers a different approach. Instead of synchronous request/response, components communicate asynchronously by publishing messages or events. Messages are durable, retried, and decoupled from immediate availability. The producer doesn't care whether the consumer is running right now; it just drops a message and moves on. In this section, we'll explore why messaging matters, how it changes the dynamics of distributed systems, and how the `OrderProcessor` project will use it.

The Problem with Synchronous Calls

Let's revisit `OrderProcessor`. Right now, `SubmitOrder` receives an order over HTTP, validates it, and enqueues it to a storage queue. That's already better than trying to do all the work inside the HTTP call, but imagine if we had chained it like this:

- `SubmitOrder` > HTTP call to Payment Service.
- `PaymentService` > HTTP call to Inventory Service.
- `InventoryService` > HTTP call to Email Service. If payment is slow, the whole request hangs. If inventory is down, the order fails entirely. Each HTTP call adds latency and fragility.

Here's a simple .NET sketch of the problem; this is just an example and NOT part of our project:

```
public class SynchronousOrderHandler
{
    private readonly HttpClient _http = new HttpClient();
    public async Task<bool> HandleOrderAsync(Order order)
    {
        var paymentResult = await
        _http.PostAsJsonAsync("https://payments/api/pay", order);
        if (!paymentResult.IsSuccessStatusCode) return false;
```

```
        var inventoryResult = await
        _http.PostAsJsonAsync("https://inventory/api/reserve", order);
        if (!inventoryResult.IsSuccessStatusCode) return false;
        var emailResult = await _http.PostAsJsonAsync("https://emails/api/
        send", order);
        return emailResult.IsSuccessStatusCode;
    }
}
```

This looks simple but is brittle. A single outage in any service breaks the whole chain.

The Messaging Alternative

Now take the messaging model. `SubmitOrder` publishes an `OrderCreated` event to a message broker. Payment, Inventory, and Email each subscribe to that event.

- If Payment is down, the message waits in the queue until it recovers.
- If Inventory is slow, it doesn't delay Payment or Email.
- Each service scales independently based on its own workload.

In .NET terms, the Function is simplified:

Functions/SubmitOrder.cs

```
[Function("SubmitOrder")]
[ServiceBusOutput("orders-topic", Connection =
"ServiceBusConnection")]
public async Task<string> Run(
[HttpTrigger(AuthorizationLevel.Anonymous, "post")]
HttpRequestData req,
FunctionContext ctx)
{
    var order = await req.ReadFromJsonAsync<Order>();
    return JsonSerializer.Serialize(order);
}
```

No HTTP chains, no waiting, just publish and forget.

Events vs. Messages

It's worth distinguishing events from messages:

- **Events** say *"something happened."* They're facts. For example, "OrderCreated," "InvoiceUploaded." They're lightweight and often fan out to many subscribers.
- **Messages** say *"do this work."* They're commands. For example, "ChargePayment," "ReserveInventory." They carry intent and usually have a single consumer.

Azure offers both: Event Grid for events and Service Bus for messages. In this chapter, we'll integrate both into `OrderProcessor`.

Real-World Analogy

Think about ordering a book online. Without messaging - You call the bookstore, the cashier calls the warehouse, the warehouse calls the courier, and the courier calls the email desk. If any person doesn't pick up, the whole order fails. With messaging - You place your order at the counter. Everyone else works from slips in their inbox: the cashier processes payment, the warehouse reserves stock, the courier schedules delivery, and email desk sends confirmation. If someone's inbox piles up, the work just waits until they catch up. The difference is resilience. Messaging means no single step can block the others.

Benefits of Messaging

Using a queue introduces a clean separation between producers and consumers, because neither side needs to know about the other's availability or internal implementation. This decoupling improves resilience, since if a consumer goes down, messages are safely held in the queue until it recovers rather than being lost or causing failures upstream. It also enables independent scalability. When payment traffic spikes, payment-related functions can scale out on their own without putting pressure on inventory processing. The model stays flexible over time. New consumers can be added simply by subscribing to the same events. An analytics service can start listening for `OrderCreated` events tomorrow without requiring any changes to the original `SubmitOrder` flow.

OrderProcessor: Preparing for Messaging

Up to now, OrderProcessor has used a storage queue (orders) as a simple way to decouple HTTP from batch processing. That was a good first step. In this chapter, we'll evolve it further:

- SubmitOrder will publish an OrderCreatedEvent to Event Grid.
- Other Functions (like OrderEventLogger) will subscribe to those events.
- For workflows needing durability and filtering, we'll add a Service Bus Topic.
- Functions will subscribe with filters, e.g., HighValueOrderHandler for large orders. By the end of the chapter, OrderProcessor will use both Event Grid and Service Bus, the backbone of Azure's messaging capabilities.

A First Taste: Logging Events

To prepare, let's add a simple subscriber that will eventually receive order events:

Functions/OrderEventLogger.cs

```
public class OrderEventLogger
{
    private readonly ILogger _logger;
    public OrderEventLogger(ILoggerFactory loggerFactory)
    => _logger =
    loggerFactory.CreateLogger<OrderEventLogger>();
    [Function("OrderEventLogger")]

    public void Run([EventGridTrigger] EventGridEvent ev)
    {
        _logger.LogInformation("Order event received:
        {EventType} | Subject: {Subject} | Id: {Id}",
        ev.EventType, ev.Subject, ev.Id);
    }
}
```

This Function doesn't yet receive real events, but it primes our project for the next section. Soon, `SubmitOrder` will publish to `EventGrid`, and `OrderEventLogger` will log them.

Event Grid: Pub/Sub Simplicity

If you need to broadcast facts across a system, Event Grid is the natural choice in Azure. It's lightweight, highly scalable, and purpose-built for fan-out pub/sub scenarios where many consumers need to react to the same event. Where Service Bus prioritizes durable messaging and controlled processing, Event Grid is about fast, low-friction notification. It excels at telling the rest of the system that something happened, without caring who reacts or how long that reaction takes. In this section, we introduce Event Grid and position it within an event-driven architecture. We then publish a custom `OrderCreatedEvent` from the `OrderProcessor` project and extend the existing `OrderEventLogger` subscriber to consume it. By the end, a single order creation will trigger multiple independent reactions through a shared event stream, demonstrating how pub/sub enables systems to grow in capability without increasing coupling or complexity.

What Is Event Grid?

Event Grid is Azure's event routing service. Its job is to take events emitted by one part of the system and deliver them to all interested subscribers. An event in this context is a fact about something that has already happened, represented as a small JSON payload. Event Grid does not process events or apply business logic. It simply moves information from producers to consumers quickly and reliably.

Event sources can be almost anything that emits events. Azure services such as Storage Accounts, Resource Groups, and IoT devices publish built-in events, but your own applications can publish custom events just as easily. Subscribers are endpoints that react to those events, commonly Azure Functions, Logic Apps, Webhooks, or Event Hubs. You can attach multiple subscribers to the same event without the source knowing or caring who they are.

A useful way to think about Event Grid is as a postman. Publishers drop events into the system, and Event Grid ensures they are delivered to every registered subscriber. Delivery is at least once, with automatic retries and optional dead-lettering when a subscriber cannot be reached. This makes Event Grid well suited to broadcasting facts across a system while keeping producers and consumers loosely coupled.

Why Event Grid Suits Pub/Sub

Event Grid is particularly well suited to pub/sub scenarios because it is optimized for fan-out. A single event can be delivered to many subscribers at the same time, each reacting independently. An `OrderCreatedEvent`, for example, might be consumed by analytics, auditing, email notifications, and payment initiation in parallel, without any coordination between those components.

Latency is also a key factor. Event Grid is designed to push events to subscribers within milliseconds, making it ideal for reactive workflows where fast notification is important. Also, it enforces loose coupling. Publishers have no knowledge of who consumes their events, and consumers do not need to know where those events originated.

Queues such as Service Bus serve a different purpose. They focus on durable, point-to-point work distribution, where a message is processed by one consumer and then removed. Both models are valuable and often used together, but when the goal is to broadcast the fact that something happened across a system, Event Grid is the better fit.

Designing the OrderCreatedEvent

Our `OrderProcessor` currently enqueues orders to a storage queue. Let's expand it – every time an order is accepted, we'll also publish an `OrderCreatedEvent` to Event Grid.

The event schema follows Event Grid's structure:

Example Event Grid payload

```
{
    "id": "abc123",
    "eventType": "OrderCreated",
    "subject": "orders/123",
    "eventTime": "2025-09-16T12:34:56Z",
    "data": {
            "OrderId": "123",
            "CustomerEmail": "paddy@example.com",
            "TotalItems": 3
        },
    "dataVersion": "1.0"
}
```

The outer envelope is required; data holds our custom payload.

Updating SubmitOrder to Publish

Let's modify SubmitOrder to publish an OrderCreatedEvent using the Event Grid output binding.

Functions/SubmitOrder.cs

```
using Azure.Messaging.EventGrid;
using System.Text.Json;
public class SubmitOrder
{
    private readonly ILogger _logger;
    private readonly IOrderValidator _validator;
    public SubmitOrder(ILoggerFactory loggerFactory,
    IOrderValidator validator)
    {
        _logger = loggerFactory.CreateLogger<SubmitOrder>();
        _validator = validator;
    }
[Function("SubmitOrder")]
[QueueOutput("orders", Connection =
"OrderStorageConnection")]
[EventGridOutput(Connection = "EventGridConnection",
TopicEndpointUri = "EventGridTopicUri", TopicKeySetting =
"EventGridKey")]
public async Task<(string queueMessage, EventGridEvent ev)>
Run(
[HttpTrigger(AuthorizationLevel.Anonymous, "post")]
HttpRequestData req)
{
    var order = await req.ReadFromJsonAsync<Order>();
    if (!_validator.IsValid(order!, out var reason))
    {
        _logger.LogWarning("Invalid order: {Reason}",
        reason);
```

```
        throw new InvalidOperationException(reason);
        }_logger.LogInformation("Validated order {Id}",
        order!.Id);
        var eventPayload = new
        {
            OrderId = order.Id,
            CustomerEmail = order.CustomerEmail,
            TotalItems = order.Items.Count
        };
        var ev = new EventGridEvent(
        subject: $"orders/{order.Id}",
        eventType: "OrderCreated",
        dataVersion: "1.0",
        data: eventPayload);
        return (JsonSerializer.Serialize(order), ev);
    }
}
```

This Function now has two outputs:

- The order goes to the orders queue for batch processing.
- An OrderCreatedEvent is published to Event Grid.

Both happen automatically when the Function completes successfully.

Subscribing with OrderEventLogger

Now let's revisit our OrderEventLogger Function. With an Event Grid trigger, it can subscribe to the topic and log incoming events:

```
using Azure.Messaging.EventGrid;
public class OrderEventLogger
{
    private readonly ILogger _logger;
    public OrderEventLogger(ILoggerFactory loggerFactory)
    {
        _logger =
```

```
        loggerFactory.CreateLogger<OrderEventLogger>();
        }[Function("OrderEventLogger")]
        public void Run([EventGridTrigger] EventGridEvent ev)
        {
            var orderData =
            ev.Data.ToObjectFromJson<OrderCreatedData>();
            _logger.LogInformation("Received event {Type} for order
            {Id} (Email: {Email}, Items: {Count})",
            ev.EventType, orderData!.OrderId,
            orderData.CustomerEmail, orderData.TotalItems);
        }
}
```

Models/Events/OrderCreatedData.cs

```
public class OrderCreatedData
{
    public string OrderId { get; set; } = string.Empty;
    public string CustomerEmail { get; set; } = string.Empty;
    public int TotalItems { get; set; }
}
```

Every new order now emits a broadcast fact: "OrderCreated." Multiple subscribers can act independently. For now, we just log, but in the next sections we'll add real downstream actions.

Testing Locally

Event Grid doesn't run in Azurite, but you can simulate events with the Functions CLI.

Run:

```
func start
```

Then send a test event to OrderEventLogger:

```
curl -X POST http://localhost:7071/runtime/webhooks/EventGrid?
functionName=OrderEventLogger \
-H "Content-Type: application/json" \
```

```
-d '[{"id": "test123",
"eventType": "OrderCreated",
"subject": "orders/test",
"eventTime": "2025-09-16T12:00:00Z",
"data": {
"OrderId": "test",
"CustomerEmail": "test@example.com",
"TotalItems": 1
},
"dataVersion": "1.0"
}]'
```

The Function should log:

```
Received event OrderCreated for order test (Email: test@example.com,
Items: 1)
```

This confirms the subscriber is wired correctly.

Scaling with Multiple Subscribers

The beauty of Event Grid is that you don't change the publisher to add more consumers. If you want an `OrderAnalytics` Function tomorrow, you just subscribe it to the topic. `SubmitOrder` doesn't know or care. This is loose coupling in action.

Service Bus: Enterprise Messaging

Event Grid provides high-scale event routing with minimal overhead, but there are many scenarios where that is not enough. Some workflows require strict ordering guarantees, coordinated processing using sessions, transactional boundaries, or more control over how messages are routed and consumed. In these cases, you often need the ability to fan out messages selectively, with well-defined filtering rules and stronger delivery semantics. That is where Azure Service Bus fits. It is Azure's enterprise-grade message broker, built for reliability, predictability, and mission-critical workloads.

In this section, we will introduce the core concepts behind Service Bus and position it alongside Azure Storage Queues and Event Grid, highlighting where each tool fits best. We will then extend the `OrderProcessor` project to publish orders to a Service Bus Topic and create multiple subscribers with filters. One subscriber will handle high-value orders, while another will process normal orders, demonstrating how Service Bus enables fine-grained routing and controlled fan-out within a distributed system.

Why Service Bus?

Service Bus exists to address a class of problems that Event Grid and storage queues are not designed to handle. Its primary strength is durability. Messages are persisted until they are successfully consumed, and messages that cannot be processed are moved to dead-letter queues rather than being lost. This makes Service Bus suitable for workflows where reliability and traceability matter more than immediacy.

Beyond durability, Service Bus provides stronger delivery guarantees and richer messaging semantics. It supports FIFO ordering through sessions, duplicate detection to protect against retries and client errors, and transactional messaging that allows multiple operations to succeed or fail as a unit. Topics add a controlled form of pub/sub by allowing subscribers to receive only the messages that match specific rules, rather than broadcasting every message to every consumer.

Service Bus also fits naturally into enterprise integration scenarios, particularly when interacting with legacy systems or workflows that depend on transactional boundaries. If Event Grid is a broadcast public address system, Service Bus is a disciplined switchboard, complete with call routing, queues, and operators that ensure every message is delivered to the right place, exactly once or in the correct order, and at the right time.

Queues vs. Topics

Queues and Topics solve related but distinct problems. A queue implements a point-to-point messaging pattern, where a producer sends messages to a single logical consumer. Each message is processed once and then removed from the queue. This model works well for work distribution, where multiple competing consumers can scale out to process tasks, but each task should only be handled by one worker.

A topic, by contrast, implements a pub/sub model within Service Bus. A single producer publishes messages to the topic, and each subscription receives its own copy of every message that matches its rules. Subscriptions can apply filters so that consumers only see the messages relevant to them, rather than everything published to the topic. This allows fan-out with control, rather than simple broadcast.

For the `OrderProcessor` project, a topic is the better fit. All orders can be published to a single stream, while different subscribers handle them in different ways. One subscriber might process high-value orders, another might handle standard fulfillment, and a third could trigger auditing or reporting, all without coupling those concerns to the order submission logic.

Adding a Service Bus Topic

To begin, we'll define a new Service Bus Topic called orders-topic. This topic will act as the central channel through which all order messages are published, allowing multiple subscribers to react independently. In Azure, the topic can be created using the Azure CLI:

```
az servicebus topic create \
  --resource-group buy-ci-common-ResourceGroup \
  --namespace-name buy-orders-namespace \
  --name orders-topic
```

With the topic in place, we can now extend the `SubmitOrder` flow to publish messages to it. From this point on, every order submission will emit a message to the topic, making it available to any interested subscribers without introducing direct dependencies between the order processor and downstream consumers.

Updating SubmitOrder to Service Bus

```
public class SubmitOrder
{
    private readonly ILogger<SubmitOrder> _logger;
    private readonly IOrderValidator _validator;
    public SubmitOrder(ILoggerFactory loggerFactory,
    IOrderValidator validator)
    {
```

```
        _logger = loggerFactory.CreateLogger<SubmitOrder>();
        _validator = validator;
    }

    // POCO that carries BOTH outputs
    public class SubmitOutputs
    {
        [QueueOutput("orders", Connection =
        "OrderStorageConnection")]
        public string? QueueMessage { get; set; }
        [ServiceBusOutput("orders-topic", Connection =
        "ServiceBusConnection")]
    }
    [Function("SubmitOrder")]
    public async Task<SubmitOutputs> Run(
    [HttpTrigger(AuthorizationLevel.Anonymous, "post")]
    HttpRequestData req)
    {
        var order = await req.ReadFromJsonAsync<Order>();
        if (!_validator.IsValid(order!, out var reason))
        {
            _logger.LogWarning("Invalid order: {Reason}",
                reason);
            throw new InvalidOperationException(reason);
        }
        _logger.LogInformation("Validated order {Id}",
            order!.Id);
        var json = JsonSerializer.Serialize(order);
        return new SubmitOutputs
        {
            QueueMessage = json,
            TopicMessage = json
        };
    }
}
```

Now each new order goes to:

- The orders storage queue (for batch processing).
- The orders-topic Service Bus Topic (for enterprise-grade subscribers).

Creating Subscribers with Filters

We'll create two subscriptions on the Topic:

1. **HighValueOrders**: only receives orders where `TotalValue` > 1000.
2. **NormalOrders**: receives everything else.

Create subscriptions via CLI:

```
az servicebus topic subscription create \
--resource-group buy-ci-common-ResourceGroup \
--namespace-name buy-orders-namespace \
--topic-name orders-topic \
--name HighValueOrders \
--rule-name HighValueFilter \
--filter-sql-expression "TotalValue > 1000"

az servicebus topic subscription create \
--resource-group buy-ci-common-ResourceGroup \
--namespace-name buy-orders-namespace \
--topic-name orders-topic \
--name NormalOrders \
--rule-name Default
```

High-Value Order Handler

Now add a Function to process high-value orders:

Functions/HighValueOrderHandler.cs

```
using System.Text.Json;
using Microsoft.Azure.Functions.Worker;
using Microsoft.Extensions.Logging;
```

```
using Microsoft.Azure.Functions.Worker.Extensions.ServiceBus;

public class HighValueOrderHandler
{
    private readonly ILogger<HighValueOrderHandler> _logger;
    public HighValueOrderHandler(ILoggerFactory loggerFactory)
    {
        _logger =
        loggerFactory.CreateLogger<HighValueOrderHandler>();
    }
    [Function("HighValueOrderHandler")]
    public void Run(
    [ServiceBusTrigger("orders-topic", "HighValueOrders",
    Connection = "ServiceBusConnection")]
    string message)
    {
        var order = JsonSerializer.Deserialize<Order>(message);
        _logger.LogInformation("High-value order {Id} worth
        special handling!", order!.Id);
    }
}
```

Normal Order Handler

Functions/NormalOrderHandler.cs

```
public class NormalOrderHandler
{
    private readonly ILogger _logger;
    public NormalOrderHandler(ILoggerFactory loggerFactory)
    {
        _logger =
        loggerFactory.CreateLogger<NormalOrderHandler>();
    }
    [Function("NormalOrderHandler")]
    public void Run(
```

```
        [ServiceBusTrigger("orders-topic", "NormalOrders",
        Connection = "ServiceBusConnection")]
        string message)
        {
            var order = JsonSerializer.Deserialize<Order>(message);
            _logger.LogInformation("Processing normal order {Id}",
            order!.Id);
        }
}
```

Now orders are automatically routed by Service Bus: big ones go to `HighValueOrderHandler` and the rest to `NormalOrderHandler`.

Comparing Event Grid and Service Bus

Event Grid and Service Bus are not competing technologies; they are complementary. Each is optimized for a different style of communication, and mature systems often use both together. Event Grid excels at announcing that something happened. It is lightweight, fast, and well suited to broadcasting facts across a system so that any interested component can react.

Service Bus, by contrast, is designed to carry out the work that follows those announcements. It provides durable messaging, stronger delivery guarantees, ordering, and transactional support, making it a better fit for long-running or business-critical workflows. In practice, a common pattern is to use Event Grid to publish high-level domain events and then hand off specific tasks to Service Bus for reliable processing. This combination allows systems to remain loosely coupled while still meeting strict reliability and consistency requirements.

Reliable Delivery: Retries and Dead Letters

Distributed systems have a way of reminding you that failure is inevitable. A downstream service might be overloaded, a Function might throw an exception, or a transient network blip might strike at the worst possible time. The question isn't if this happens, but what then?

Both Event Grid and Service Bus are designed with reliability in mind. They don't just drop a message on the floor if something goes wrong. Instead, they retry delivery. If retries fail persistently, the message ends up in a dead letter destination for later inspection. In this section, we'll look at how retries work, how dead lettering saves data from being lost, and how the `OrderProcessor` project can handle these scenarios with deliberate failures and a new `DeadLetterHandler` Function.

Event Grid Retry Behavior

When an Event Grid subscriber, such as our `OrderEventLogger`, fails to process an event, Event Grid does not immediately give up. Instead, it automatically retries delivery using an exponential backoff strategy with random jitter. The first retry typically happens within seconds, and subsequent retries are spaced further apart, with intervals increasing up to roughly an hour. By default, Event Grid retains events for up to 24 hours, continuing delivery attempts throughout that window.

If the subscriber never succeeds within the retention period, Event Grid moves the event to a dead letter destination. This is typically a blob container or a storage queue in a storage account that you configure ahead of time. Rather than silently losing events, failures are captured for later inspection and recovery.

For example, if the `OrderEventLogger` crashes repeatedly due to a bug or misconfiguration, the event is not discarded. It is written to the dead letter container, where it can be analyzed, replayed, or used to diagnose the underlying issue.

Service Bus Retry and DLQs

Service Bus offers reliability guarantees similar to Event Grid, but it layers on a set of controls that are designed for enterprise workloads where failure handling must be explicit and auditable. When a Function triggered by a Service Bus queue or topic subscription throws an exception, Service Bus does not immediately abandon the message. Instead, it retries delivery according to the configuration of the queue or subscription, treating failures as part of the normal lifecycle of message processing rather than as exceptional edge cases.

Each time a message is delivered to a consumer, it is locked for a fixed period. If processing fails or the consumer crashes before completing the message, the lock eventually expires and the message becomes visible again for redelivery. This cycle continues until the message is successfully processed or the maximum delivery count is reached. By default, Service Bus allows ten delivery attempts, but this limit can be tuned to match the tolerance and behavior of a given workflow.

When the maximum delivery count is exceeded, the message is moved to the dead-letter queue associated with that queue or subscription. Importantly, every queue and every topic subscription has its own dedicated dead letter queue. This ensures that problematic messages do not block healthy ones and that failures are isolated to the specific workflow that encountered them. No message is silently lost. Every failure is preserved, along with metadata about why it failed and how many times it was retried.

This model gives operators clear visibility into system health. Dead letter queues act as a safety net and a diagnostic tool, allowing teams to inspect failed messages, identify patterns, and decide whether to fix the underlying issue, replay the messages, or discard them intentionally. In production systems, this explicit failure handling is often the difference between a system that degrades gracefully and one that fails unpredictably under load or during partial outages.

Simulating Failure in OrderProcessor

To see this in action, let's add a deliberately unreliable Function:

Functions/FlakyOrderHandler.cs

```
public class FlakyOrderHandler
{
    private readonly ILogger _logger;
    private static readonly Random _rng = new();
    public FlakyOrderHandler(ILoggerFactory loggerFactory)
    {
        _logger =
        loggerFactory.CreateLogger<FlakyOrderHandler>();
    }
    [Function("FlakyOrderHandler")]
    public void Run(
    [ServiceBusTrigger("orders-topic", "NormalOrders",
    Connection = "ServiceBusConnection")]
    string message)
    {
```

```
        var order =
        JsonSerializer.Deserialize<Order>(message)!;
        // Simulate random failure
        if (_rng.NextDouble() < 0.5)
        {
            _logger.LogError("Failed to process order {Id}",
            order.Id);
            throw new InvalidOperationException("Random
            failure!");
        }
        _logger.LogInformation("Successfully processed order
        {Id}", order.Id);
    }
}
```

Roughly half the time, this Function will throw. Service Bus will retry the message a few times. If it keeps failing, the message ends up in the NormalOrders/DeadLetterQueue.

Handling Dead Letters

A dead letter queue is just another queue. You can attach a Function to it like any other:

Functions/DeadLetterHandler.cs

```
using Azure.Messaging.ServiceBus;
using Microsoft.Azure.Functions.Worker;
using Microsoft.Extensions.Logging;

namespace OrderProcessor.Functions;

public sealed class DeadLetterHandler( ILogger< DeadLetterHandler> logger,
ServiceBusClient serviceBusClient) { [Function("DeadLetterHandler")]

public async Task Run( [TimerTrigger("0 */1 * * * *")] TimerInfo timer,
CancellationToken stopToken) {
await using ServiceBusReceiver receiver = serviceBusClient.CreateReceiver(
topicName: "orders-topic", subscriptionName: "NormalOrders", options: new
ServiceBusReceiverOptions { SubQueue = SubQueue.DeadLetter });
```

```
    IReadOnlyList<ServiceBusReceivedMessage> messages =
        await receiver.ReceiveMessagesAsync(
            maxMessages: 25,
            maxWaitTime: TimeSpan.FromSeconds(5),
            cancellationToken: stopToken);

    foreach (ServiceBusReceivedMessage message in messages)
    {
        logger.LogWarning(
            "Dead-lettered message. MessageId: {MessageId}, Body:
            {Message}",
            message.MessageId,
            message.Body.ToString());

        await receiver.CompleteMessageAsync(message, stopToken);
    }
}

}
```

This Function doesn't fix the order, but it makes sure no failed message goes unnoticed. In a real system, you might

- Alert operations when DLQs grow
- Write DLQ messages to storage for forensic analysis
- Attempt repair/replay of failed messages

Event Grid Dead Letter Demo

For Event Grid, we can also simulate failure. Change `OrderEventLogger` to throw every time:

```
public void Run([EventGridTrigger] EventGridEvent ev)
{
    throw new InvalidOperationException("Always failing!");
}
```

If you configure a storage account as the dead letter destination for the Event Grid subscription, you'll see the events written there after retries are exhausted. This proves Event Grid won't drop them silently.

Operational Considerations

Dead letter queues should be treated as a first-class signal of system health. They are often the earliest indication that something is wrong, whether that is a breaking schema change, a downstream dependency outage, or an unexpected edge case in business logic. Monitoring DLQs is therefore essential. A growing dead letter count is the messaging equivalent of a canary in the coal mine, warning you about failures long before users start reporting visible issues.

It's also important to distinguish between transient failures and poison messages. Transient failures, such as brief network interruptions or temporary database outages, are usually resolved through retries and eventually succeed. Poison messages, on the other hand, will never succeed. They might be malformed, violate validation rules, or reference data that no longer exists. Retrying these messages repeatedly only wastes resources and delays the processing of healthy messages, which is why they ultimately end up in a dead-letter queue (see Figure 3-1).

Every system needs a clear replay strategy. You should decide in advance how dead-lettered messages are handled once the underlying issue is resolved. In some cases, messages can be replayed automatically after a fix is deployed. In others, manual inspection and intervention are required to correct the data before reprocessing. Without a deliberate approach to dead letter handling, failures remain invisible and unresolved. With it, you gain visibility, control, and the ability to respond when things inevitably go wrong.

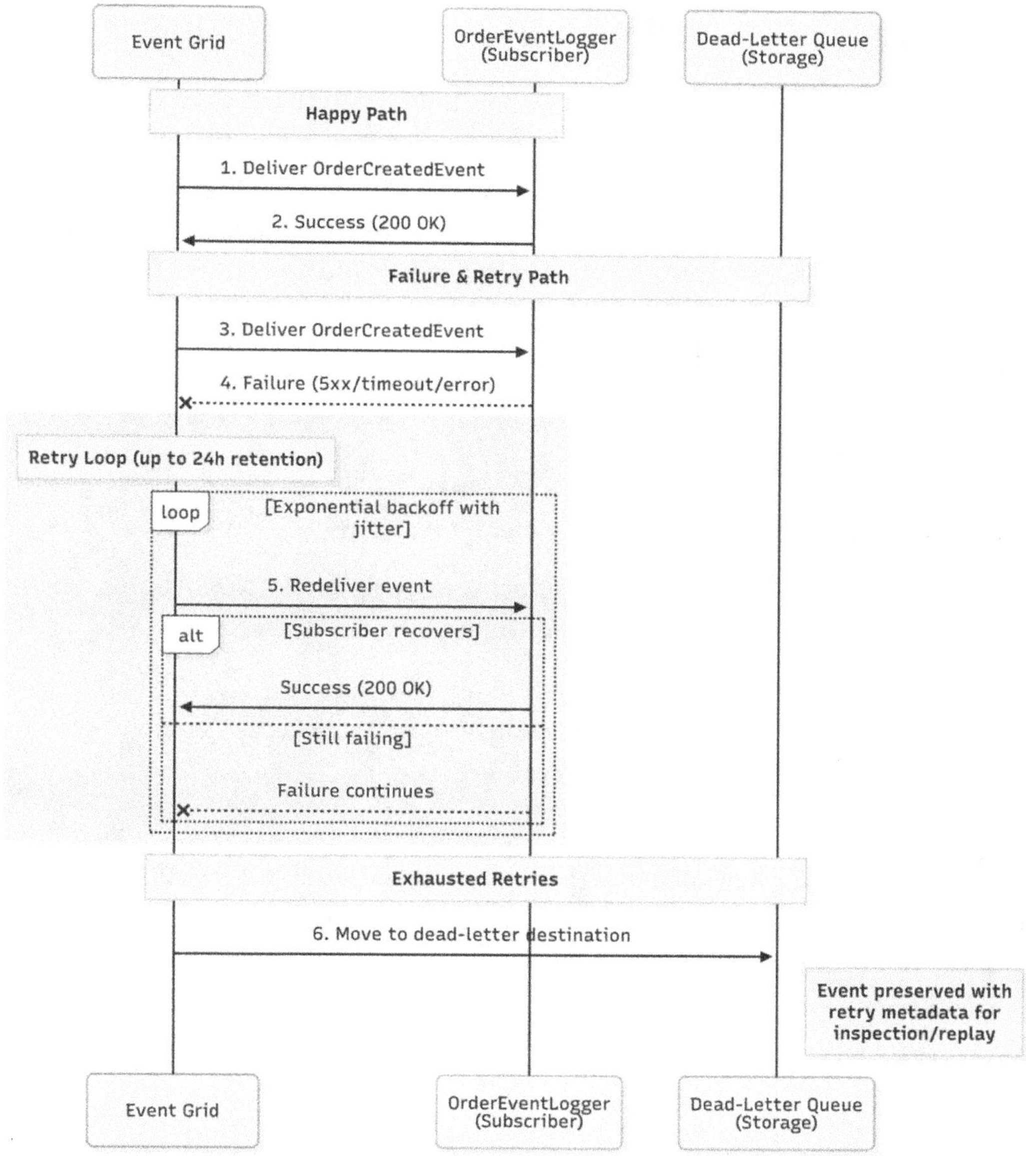

Figure 3-1. *Retry Behavior*

Designing Flows with Events and Messages

By now, you've seen Event Grid and Service Bus individually. Each has strengths: Event Grid excels at lightweight broadcasts and Service Bus at durable workflows. But in practice, the most effective systems don't pick one; they combine them. In this section, we'll explore how to design flows that blend events and messages. We'll use the `OrderProcessor` project as a case study, chaining Event Grid and Service Bus to model a realistic order lifecycle: order received > event broadcast > downstream workflows (payment, inventory, notifications).

Why Combine Both?

Imagine a new order comes in. You want different reactions:

- **Notifications**: Broadcast to multiple systems (analytics, dashboards, CRM). Event Grid is perfect here: low latency, fan-out, and subscribers can come and go.
- **Critical Workflows**: Payment and inventory must succeed reliably. You need ordered, durable, retryable messaging. That's Service Bus territory.

If you rely only on Event Grid, you risk losing critical workflows if a subscriber fails. If you rely only on Service Bus, you lose the easy broadcast and low coupling. Combining them gives you the best of both, agility plus durability.

The Order Lifecycle

- Let's sketch a flow for OrderProcessor:
- Order submitted > SubmitOrder publishes OrderCreatedEvent to Event Grid.
- Broadcast fan-out > Multiple subscribers react:

    1. `OrderEventLogger` logs.
    2. `OrderAnalytics` updates dashboards.
    3. `OrderNotifier` sends an email.

- Workflow initiation > An Event Grid subscription routes the same event into a Service Bus Topic.
- Durable processing > Subscribers on the Service Bus Topic:
    1. `PaymentHandler` processes payment.
    2. `InventoryHandler` reserves stock.
    3. `HighValueOrderHandler` flags big orders for review.

This hybrid flow separates "inform everyone" from "do critical work."

Routing Event Grid to Service Bus

Azure makes it easy to link Event Grid to Service Bus. You can create an Event Grid subscription with a Service Bus Topic as its endpoint:

```
az eventgrid event-subscription create \
--source-resource-id /subscriptions/<sub>/resourceGroups/<rg>/providers/
Microsoft.EventGrid/topics/orders-topic \--name OrdersToServiceBus \
--endpoint-type servicebusqueue \
--endpoint /subscriptions/<sub>/resourceGroups/<rg>/providers/

Microsoft.ServiceBus/namespaces/buy-orders-namespace/topics/orders-topic
```

With this setup:

- `SubmitOrder` publishes an Event Grid event.
- Event Grid automatically forwards it into a Service Bus Topic.
- Durable subscribers pick it up reliably.

Implementing PaymentHandler

Here's a new Function that consumes from Service Bus:

Functions/PaymentHandler.cs

```
public class PaymentHandler
```

```
{
    private readonly ILogger<PaymentHandler> _logger;
    public PaymentHandler(ILoggerFactory loggerFactory)
    {
        _logger = loggerFactory.CreateLogger<PaymentHandler>();
    }
    [Function("PaymentHandler")]
    public void Run(
    [ServiceBusTrigger("orders-topic", "Payments",
    Connection = "ServiceBusConnection")]
    string message)
    {
        var order =
        JsonSerializer.Deserialize<Order>(message)!;
        _logger.LogInformation("Processing payment for order
        {Id} (Email: {Email})",
        order.Id, order.CustomerEmail);
        // Simulate payment processing
        if (order.Items.Count == 0)
            throw new InvalidOperationException("Cannot process
        empty order");_logger.LogInformation("Payment for order {Id}
        succeeded", order.Id);
    }
}
```

This subscriber runs independently of analytics or notifications. If it fails, Service Bus retries. If retries fail, the message ends up in the DLQ for Payment.

Implementing InventoryHandler

Functions/InventoryHandler.cs

```
public class InventoryHandler
{
    private readonly ILogger _logger;
    public InventoryHandler(ILoggerFactory loggerFactory)
```

```
{
    _logger =
    loggerFactory.CreateLogger<InventoryHandler>();
}
[Function("InventoryHandler")]
public void Run(
[ServiceBusTrigger("orders-topic", "Inventory",
Connection = "ServiceBusConnection")]
string message)
{
    var order =
    JsonSerializer.Deserialize<Order>(message)!;
    _logger.LogInformation("Reserving inventory for order
    {Id}", order.Id);
    // Pretend inventory update
    foreach (var item in order.Items)
    _logger.LogInformation("Reserved {Item}", item);
    _logger.LogInformation("Inventory reserved for order
    {Id}", order.Id);
}}
```

Now orders trigger both payment and inventory workflows, decoupled but coordinated (see Figure 3-2).

Visualizing the Flow

This architecture demonstrates separation of concerns - Event Grid handles notifications and broad fan-out; Service Bus handles durable, ordered, critical workflows (see Figure 3-3).

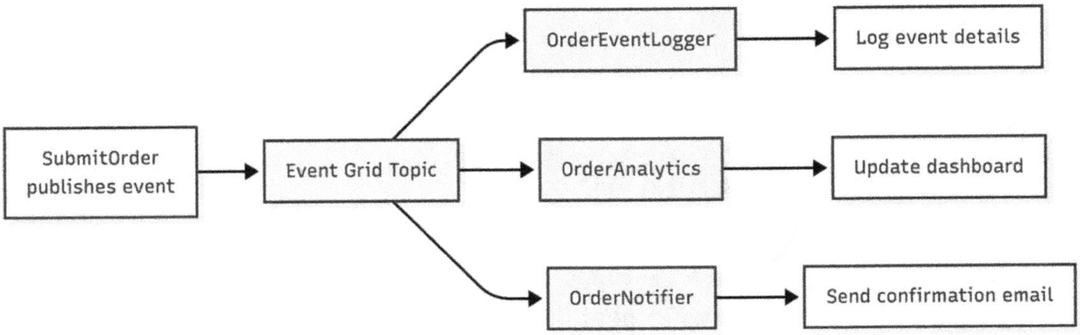

***Figure 3-2.** Broadcast Fan-Out*

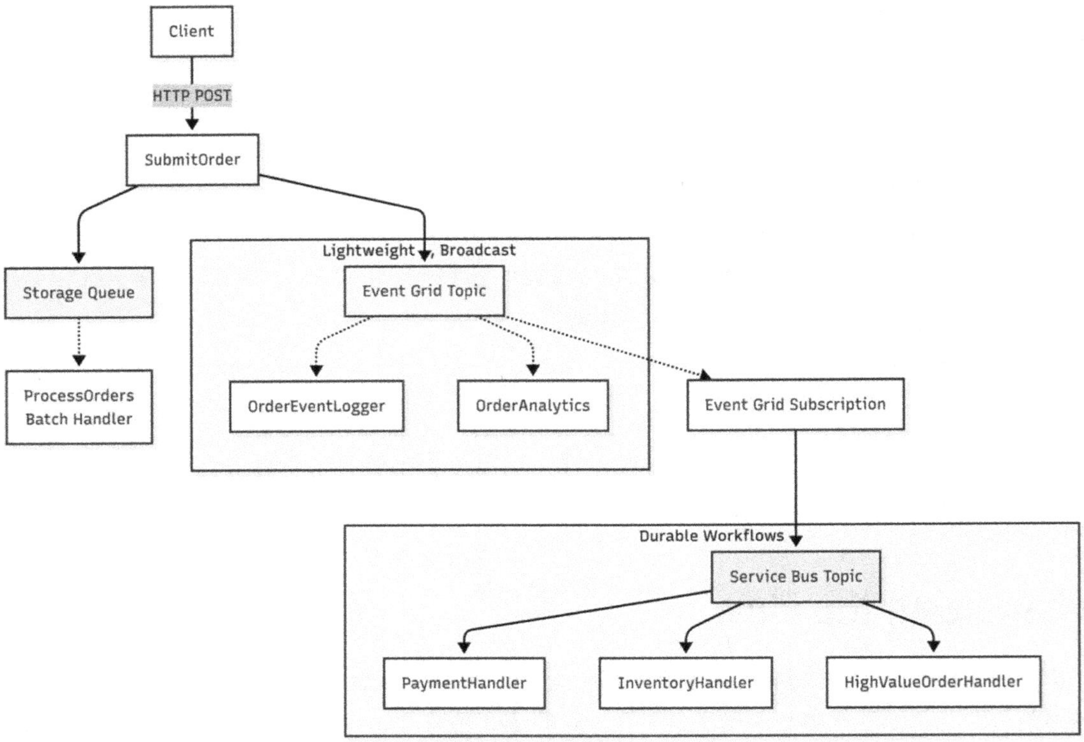

***Figure 3-3.** Higher-Level Architecture*

Benefits of the Hybrid Approach

- **Scalability**: Analytics subscribers don't slow down payments. Each scales independently.
- **Flexibility**: New Event Grid subscribers can join with zero impact.

- **Durability**: Payment and inventory can fail/retry without losing orders.
- **Clarity**: Events declare *what happened*; messages drive *what to* do.

This is the essence of event-driven design: different tools for different jobs, working together.

EXERCISES

1. **Synchronous Fragility**: Write a Function that calls three HTTP endpoints in sequence (use httpbin.org). Simulate one being slow. How does latency compound?
2. **Queue Alternative**: Replace the synchronous calls with queue messages (one per step). Compare resilience.
3. **Events vs. Messages:** Create a list of actions in `OrderProcessor`. Which are events (facts)? Which are messages (commands)?
4. **Reflection:** Think about your own systems. Where are you chaining HTTP calls today? Could they be replaced with messaging?
5. **Custom Payload:** Add `OrderValue` to the `OrderCreatedEvent`. Update `OrderEventLogger` to log it.
6. **Multiple Subscribers**: Create another Function `OrderEmailNotifier` subscribed to Event Grid. For now, just log "send email."
7. **Manual Event**: Post a test event to `OrderEventLogger`. What happens if you omit `dataVersion`?
8. **Replay Thought Experiment:** Unlike queues, Event Grid doesn't store events long term. What happens if a subscriber is offline? How would you design for replay if needed?
9. **Reflection**: Where in your own systems would Event Grid's broadcast model fit better than direct API calls?
10. **Topic Publishing:** Add `TotalValue` to orders. Publish it with the message. Confirm that only high-value orders reach `HighValueOrderHandler`.

11. **Multiple Subscribers:** Add a third subscriber `AnalyticsHandler` that logs every order for reporting.

12. **Manual Test:** Use `az servicebus topic` send to publish a fake message. Confirm the right handler processes it.

13. **Failure Simulation:** Throw an exception in `NormalOrderHandler`. What happens to the message? Where does it end up?

14. **Reflection:** When would you choose Service Bus over Event Grid? When might you use both?

15. **Random Failure:** Run `FlakyOrderHandler` by publishing 10 messages. How many succeed? How many land in DLQ?

16. **Dead Letter Trigger:** Hook up `DeadLetterHandler` and confirm it logs failed messages.

17. **Event Grid DLQ:** Configure a blob container as Event Grid's dead-letter destination. Force failures and inspect the blob content.

18. **Poison Message:** Publish an invalid order JSON. What happens? Does it end up in DLQ?

19. **Reflection:** In your own systems, who would be responsible for DLQ monitoring and replay? Developers? Ops? Both?

20. **New Subscriber:** Add an `OrderNotifier` subscriber to Event Grid that logs "Email sent to customer."

21. **Hybrid Test:** Post an order. Confirm Event Grid subscribers fire instantly, while Service Bus handlers pick up reliably.

22. **Failure Injection:** Make `PaymentHandler` throw for orders with ID ending in 9. Watch retries and DLQ.

23. **Analytics Expansion:** Write `OrderAnalytics` that logs total order count. How would you persist state across events?

24. **Reflection:** In your own systems, can you separate concerns into "broadcast facts" and "durable workflows"?

Summary

Synchronous chains are simple but fragile, which is why modern distributed systems rely on messaging patterns built on events and commands. Messaging introduces decoupling, resilience, scalability, and flexibility, allowing systems to evolve without tight dependencies between components. In the `OrderProcessor` system, this shift begins when a single `SubmitOrder` call produces multiple asynchronous side effects. Orders are queued for processing while an `OrderCreatedEvent` is broadcast through Event Grid, enabling immediate consumption by subscribers such as the `OrderEventLogger` and any future listeners that can be added without changing the publisher. Event Grid excels at lightweight pub/sub by efficiently broadcasting that "something happened," while Azure Service Bus complements it by providing durable, ordered, enterprise-level messaging designed for workflows that must reliably complete. Within `OrderProcessor`, this means orders flow through both systems; Event Grid distributes notifications broadly, while Service Bus Topics route filtered, persistent messages to specialized subscribers that process high-value and normal orders differently. Together, they form a hybrid messaging backbone that balances agility with reliability, ensuring that events can trigger reactions quickly while critical work is handled with guaranteed delivery.

Reliable delivery is the center of this architecture because distributed systems inevitably experience failures. Both Event Grid and Service Bus provide built-in retries and dead-letter handling, ensuring that undeliverable messages are never silently lost. In `OrderProcessor`, this is demonstrated through simulated subscriber failures and a `DeadLetterHandler` that surfaces and manages problematic messages so they can be analyzed and recovered. As the system evolves, it transitions from a simple HTTP-triggered function into a small, distributed environment. Orders are submitted via HTTP, queued for batch processing, broadcast through Event Grid for analytics and monitoring, forwarded into Service Bus for durable workflows, and consumed by downstream services such as payment and inventory processors. Failures trigger automated retries, and unrecoverable messages are isolated safely in dead letter queues. The result is a hybrid event-driven design in which Event Grid communicates that something occurred and Service Bus ensures required work is completed, and together they provide a resilient, scalable messaging foundation for real-world serverless systems.

So far, our project passes data around, but where does it live? How do we query orders, update them, and ensure consistency across services? In Chapter 4, we'll turn to Data in a Distributed World. We'll explore Cosmos DB and SQL in serverless contexts, dive into consistency models, and introduce patterns like event sourcing and CQRS. With messaging as our backbone, we're ready to tackle the heart of distributed systems: managing state.

CHAPTER 4

State, Data, and Consistency in Serverless Systems

State is where distributed systems become difficult. Messaging and serverless triggers can decouple work, but correctness depends on data. Once a state is spread across Functions, queues, databases, and external services, the simple assumptions of a monolith begin to fail. Reads can be stale, writes can conflict, and operations that appear to succeed independently can still leave the system in an inconsistent state.

This chapter examines that reality through the `OrderProcessor` project. It introduces the core problems of distributed data, including concurrency, partitioning, and consistency, then shows how Azure data services such as Cosmos DB change the way state must be modeled and protected. From there, it explores optimistic concurrency, event sourcing, and CQRS as practical patterns for building serverless systems that remain correct under scale, parallelism, and partial failure.

Why Data Is Hard in Distributed Systems

If messaging is the backbone of distributed systems, data is the beating heart. And hearts are fragile. You can get away with rough edges in messaging; retries and dead letters patch over a lot. But when it comes to the state, correctness matters. Did the order get paid? Was the inventory reduced? Did two customers just buy the same last item?

In single-process apps, data feels easy. One SQL database, one transaction, strong consistency. But spread that across Functions, regions, or databases, and the assumptions fall apart. Suddenly you're living with stale reads, conflicting writes, and strange edge cases that don't show up in your unit tests.

© Patrick Kearns 2026
P. Kearns, *Serverless Distributed Systems in Modern .NET and Azure*,
https://doi.org/10.1007/979-8-8688-2839-3_4

This section introduces the core challenge: data is hard in distributed systems because consistency is relative, not absolute. We'll revisit the CAP theorem, explore scenarios where assumptions break, and extend the `OrderProcessor` project with a race-condition demo that shows how even a simple counter can betray you once concurrency enters the picture.

The Comforting World of Monoliths

In a monolith backed by a relational database, you lean on `transactions`.

For example:

```
BEGIN TRANSACTION;
UPDATE Inventory
SET Quantity = Quantity - 1
WHERE ProductId = 42;
COMMIT;
```

This guarantees atomicity, consistency, isolation, and durability (ACID). Either the entire operation succeeds or nothing happens at all. If two requests attempt to purchase the same product at the same time, the database engine coordinates access through locks and isolation levels. One transaction waits while the other completes, preventing overselling or a corrupted state.

Most importantly, failure is predictable. If something goes wrong halfway through execution, the database rolls everything back automatically. The application developer rarely needs to reason about partial completion, retries, or conflicting updates. Concurrency exists, but it is contained inside the database boundary.

The monolith feels safe because there is a single source of truth, a single transactional boundary, and a single moment in time where data becomes valid.

The Messy World of Distributed Systems

Distributed systems remove that safety net. Once functionality is split across services or Functions, there is no longer one database or one transactional boundary coordinating everything. A single business operation might now involve multiple independently executing components, each running on different machines and persisting state in different storage technologies.

One Function might update Cosmos DB, another writes metadata to blob storage, while a third publishes an event to a queue for downstream processing. All of these steps can execute in parallel, succeed independently, or fail at different times.

There is no practical way to wrap these operations in a single ACID transaction. Even if it were technically possible, the latency and coupling would defeat the purpose of distribution. Instead of immediate consistency, systems move toward eventual consistency, where correctness emerges over time rather than instantly.

This shift forces developers to confront trade-offs that were previously hidden. The CAP theorem describes these constraints. In a distributed environment you must balance consistency, availability, and partition tolerance. Network partitions are not theoretical events but normal operating conditions. Machines restart, networks glitch, and regions temporarily lose connectivity.

Because partitions cannot be avoided, systems must choose whether to reject requests to preserve strict consistency or continue operating while accepting temporarily stale data. Platforms such as Azure expose configuration choices, and services like Cosmos DB provide multiple consistency levels, but these are tuning controls rather than escape routes. The trade-off never disappears.

In distributed systems, correctness is no longer enforced by a transaction manager. It becomes an architectural concern that must be designed, observed, and recovered from explicitly. The difference between transactional monolith consistency and distributed coordination is illustrated in Figure 4-1.

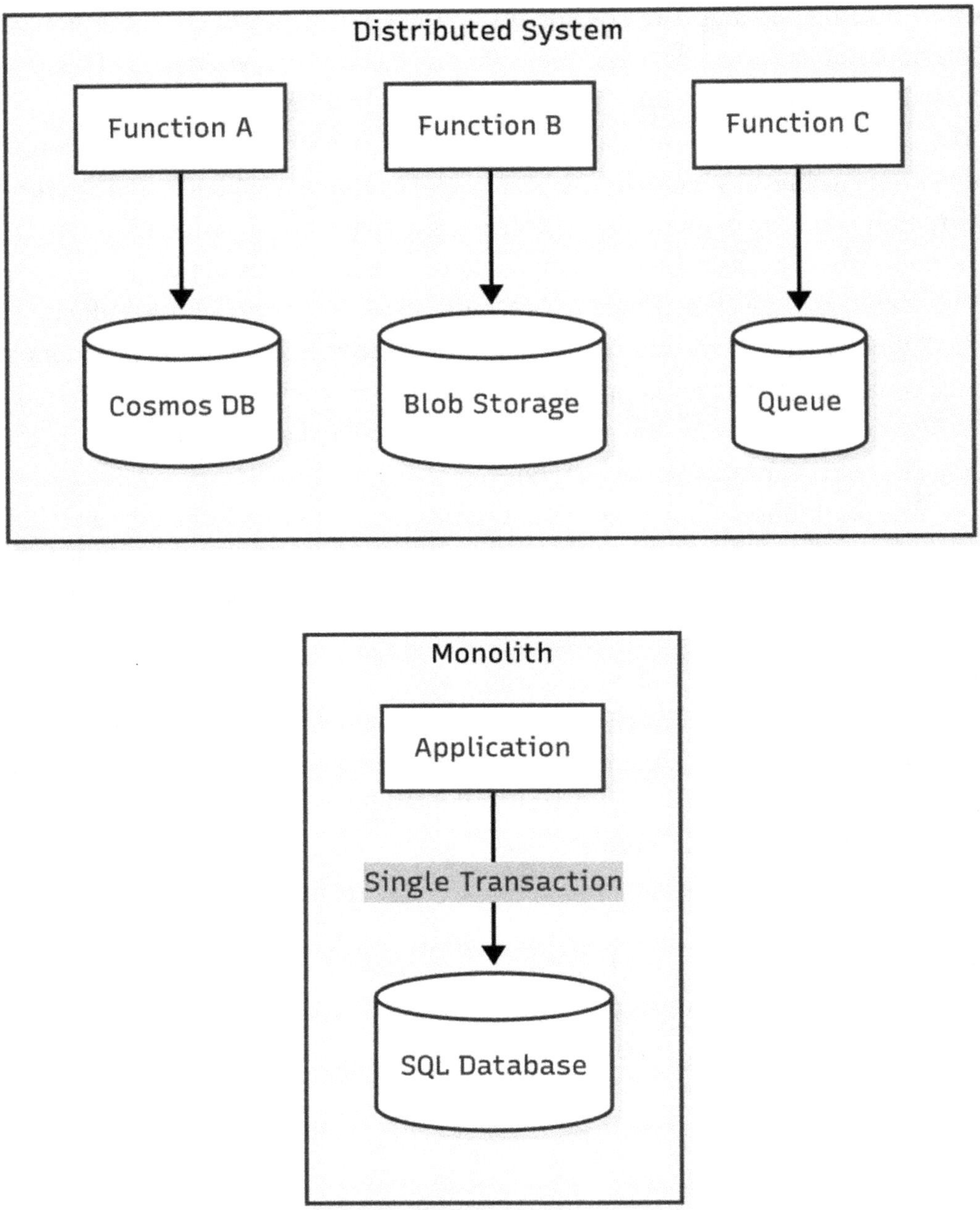

Figure 4-1. *Monolith vs. Distributed*

Scenarios That Bite

Distributed system failures rarely look dramatic. Systems usually appear to work correctly until subtle timing or network conditions expose hidden assumptions. The most dangerous problems are not crashes but silent correctness failures.

Concurrent updates happen when two Functions process purchase requests at nearly the same time. Both read the current inventory value before either write is complete. Each independently decrements the quantity and writes the result back successfully. No exception is thrown. No retry occurs. From the perspective of each Function, everything worked exactly as expected. Yet inventory has now been oversold because both operations were based on the same original state. In a monolith, database locking would serialize access automatically. In a distributed system, concurrency control becomes your responsibility.

Stale reads happen when a Function reads from a replica just before an update arrives. The read succeeds, but it returns outdated information. Decisions are now made using data that is technically valid, yet already obsolete. Users experience this as confusing behavior rather than failure. Changes appear to take time to show up or appear to revert temporarily.

Lost updates happen when a Function reads a record, modifies one field, and writes the entire object back. Meanwhile, another process updates a different field. Because the first Function writes an older snapshot, the second change disappears without warning. No conflict is detected. No error is raised. These bugs often survive testing because they require precise timing windows that rarely occur in development environments.

Partitioned writes happen during a transient network partition where different parts of your system talk to different replicas or regions. Both sides continue accepting writes to remain available. When connectivity is restored, the system must reconcile diverging histories. Conflicts emerge, ordering becomes ambiguous, and determining which version represents truth becomes a business decision rather than a technical one. At this point, consistency is no longer enforced automatically. It must be reconstructed.

Each of these scenarios is subtle, intermittent, and difficult to reproduce locally. They rarely appear under light load or single-user testing. Instead, they emerge in production when scale, latency, and failure combine in ways that traditional transactional thinking never anticipated. Distributed systems do not fail loudly. They fail slowly, quietly, and convincingly enough to look correct.

OrderProcessor: A Race-Condition Demo

Let's simulate this pain in our project with a deliberately naive in-memory store. We'll create a ConcurrentOrderStore that tracks how many times an order has been updated. Then we'll write a Function endpoint and hit it with parallel requests. The point is not to build a good counter. The point is to create a tiny, reproducible window where "read then write" becomes unsafe under concurrency.

Important The code in this section is intentionally broken for demonstration purposes. It exists to reproduce a race condition in a small, controlled example so the failure mode is easy to see. It is not a production pattern and is not intended to be carried forward into the final OrderProcessor implementation.

In-Memory Store (Intentionally Broken)

Stores/ConcurrentOrderStore.cs

```
using System.Collections.Concurrent;
using System.Threading;

namespace OrderProcessor;

public static class ConcurrentOrderStore
{
   private static readonly ConcurrentDictionary<string, int> Updates
   = new();

   public static void Increment(string orderId)
   {
       Updates.TryAdd(orderId, 0);

       var current = Updates[orderId];

       // Deliberately widen the race window so the lost-update bug
       // reproduces under concurrent load.
       Thread.SpinWait(50_000);

       Updates[orderId] = current + 1;
   }
```

```
    public static int GetCount(string orderId) =>
        Updates.TryGetValue(orderId, out var count) ? count : 0;
}
```

Updater Function

Functions/RaceConditionUpdater.cs

```
using System.Net;
using Microsoft.Azure.Functions.Worker;
using Microsoft.Azure.Functions.Worker.Http;
using Microsoft.Extensions.Logging;

namespace OrderProcessor;

public sealed class RaceConditionUpdater
{
    private readonly ILogger<RaceConditionUpdater> _logger;

    public RaceConditionUpdater(ILogger<RaceConditionUpdater> logger)
    {
        _logger = logger;
    }

    [Function("RaceConditionUpdater")]
    public async Task<HttpResponseData> Run(
        [HttpTrigger(AuthorizationLevel.Anonymous, "post")]
        HttpRequestData req,
        CancellationToken stopToken)
    {
        var query = System.Web.HttpUtility.ParseQueryString(req.Url.Query);
        var orderId = query["orderId"];

        if (string.IsNullOrWhiteSpace(orderId))
        {
            var bad = req.CreateResponse(HttpStatusCode.BadRequest);
            await bad.WriteStringAsync(
                "Missing required query parameter 'orderId'.",
```

```
                stopToken);

            return bad;
        }

        ConcurrentOrderStore.Increment(orderId);

        var currentCount = ConcurrentOrderStore.GetCount(orderId);

        _logger.LogInformation(
            "Updated order {OrderId}, count is now {Count}",
            orderId,
            currentCount);

        var response = req.CreateResponse(HttpStatusCode.OK);
        await response.WriteStringAsync(
            $"Order {orderId} update count: {currentCount}",
            stopToken);

        return response;
    }
}
```

Simulating the Race

Fire 50 parallel requests.

```
seq 1 50 | xargs -n1 -P10 curl -s "http://localhost:7071/api/RaceCondition
Updater?orderId=123"
```

You would expect the count to end at 50. In practice, you'll usually see something lower. Updates got lost because two concurrent executions read the old value and overwrote each other. This tiny demo mirrors the bug class that appears in real distributed systems, but it does so inside a single process so you can reproduce it easily. Figure 4-2 shows how concurrent executions overwrite state even though both operations succeed.

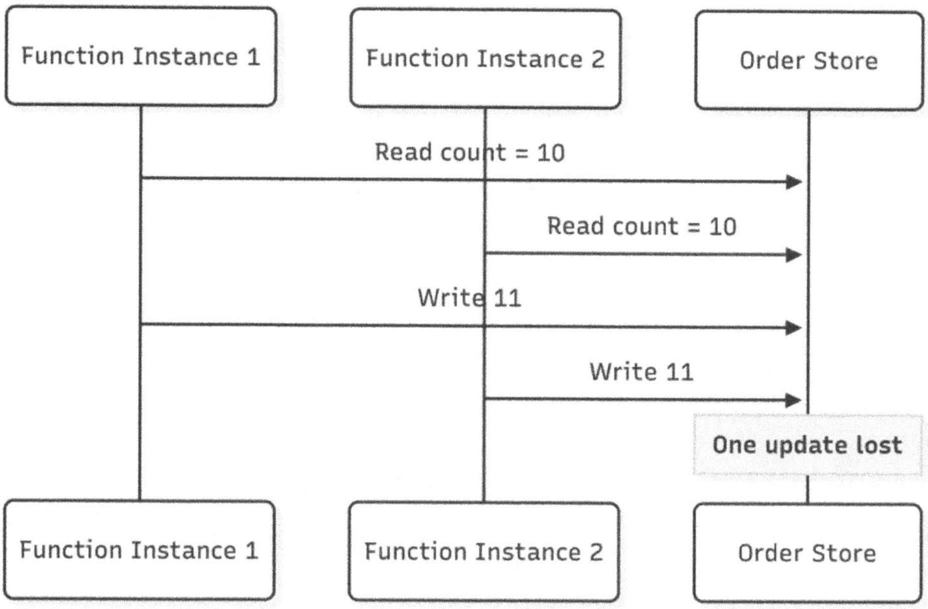

Figure 4-2. *Race Condition Timeline*

Lessons from the Demo

Concurrency is invisible until you load test. Your Function works fine with one request, and all your happy-path tests pass, but then the cracks show when multiple requests hit it simultaneously. Local locks do not scale across hosts either. Even if you add a lock in Increment, Azure Functions scale by adding instances, so your in-memory protection only applies inside one process. Idempotency matters because retries can make correctness worse. If you retry blindly, you might double-count. If you avoid retries, you might lose updates. Data stores make or break you because the store defines what forms of concurrency and consistency are available. SQL transactions and Cosmos optimistic concurrency are designed to detect and prevent lost updates, while an in-memory dictionary is not.

Azure Storage vs. Cosmos DB vs. SQL Database

Now that we've seen why data is tricky in distributed systems, the next question is where the data should live. Azure gives you multiple options, each with different trade-offs. Picking the wrong one can mean poor performance, high costs, or broken correctness guarantees. Picking the right one makes scaling and reliability far easier.

Azure Storage is the foundation: cheap, scalable, and versatile. Blob Storage is ideal for large unstructured data like files, images, and invoices. Queue Storage is great for simple messaging. Table Storage is the relevant option for persistence. It is fast and inexpensive, but limited. Queries are narrow, joins do not exist, and complex filtering becomes awkward. It can hold business records, but it shines more as a low-cost store for metadata, logs, and archival records than as the beating heart of business state.

Cosmos DB is Azure's distributed document database built for globally distributed systems. It stores JSON natively, partitions automatically for scale, provides a SQL-like query language and LINQ support, and offers five consistency levels that let you trade off freshness against availability and latency. It also gives you optimistic concurrency through ETags so you can detect lost updates instead of silently overwriting data. Cosmos is more expensive than Table Storage and requires careful partition key design, but it is far more capable when your domain model is naturally document-shaped.

Azure SQL Database is the relational heavyweight. If you need joins, multi-row transactions, relational constraints, stored procedures, and strong consistency across a normalized model, SQL is the best fit. It feels familiar to .NET developers using EF Core. The trade-off is that horizontal scaling is harder, schema evolution can be slower, and if you choose a serverless tier, it can introduce its own scaling and resume characteristics that you must account for.

For `OrderProcessor`, Cosmos DB is the best fit. Orders arrive as JSON, the model evolves, the workload is distributed, and we want to query orders by customer and by criteria without imposing a rigid relational schema.

Preparing the Project

We will partition orders by `CustomerEmail`. This keeps queries like "all orders for Alice" efficient and predictable.

At this point, OrderProcessor has grown quite a bit. To keep the project tidy as we introduce models, we'll add them in a "Models" folder.

Models/Order.cs

```
public sealed class Order
{
    public string Id { get; set; } = Guid.NewGuid().ToString();
    public string CustomerEmail { get; set; } = string.Empty;
    public List<string> Items { get; set; } = new();
```

```
    public decimal TotalValue { get; set; }

    public string Status { get; set; } = "Created";

    // Partition key for Cosmos DB (container partitioned on /
    CustomerEmail)
    public string PartitionKey => CustomerEmail;

    public bool HighValue => TotalValue > 1000;
}
```

Working with Cosmos DB in Functions

So far, the `OrderProcessor` project has been passing orders around through queues and topics. That's useful for workflow, but not enough for a real business system. At some point you need to persist state. Customers want to query orders later. Operators need to see what's been processed. Analytics needs historical data.

Cosmos DB is a natural fit because it stores JSON documents directly and scales across partitions and regions. Azure Functions integrates with Cosmos DB in two main ways. Bindings work well for point reads and simple writes. The Cosmos SDK is better for queries and any scenario where you want explicit control over partition targeting, RU cost, or consistency options.

A common mistake is trying to stack multiple output binding attributes on a single method and hoping the runtime "figures it out." The stable pattern is to return a single output object where each property is bound.

Program.cs Update: Register CosmosClient

Program.cs

```
using Microsoft.Azure.Cosmos;
using Microsoft.Azure.Functions.Worker;
using Microsoft.Extensions.DependencyInjection;
using Microsoft.Extensions.Hosting;

namespace OrderProcessor;

var builder = FunctionsApplication.CreateBuilder(args);
```

```
builder.ConfigureFunctionsWebApplication();

builder.Services
    .AddApplicationInsightsTelemetryWorkerService()
    .ConfigureFunctionsApplicationInsights();

builder.Services.AddSingleton(sp =>
{
    var configuration = sp.GetRequiredService<IConfiguration>();
    var connectionString = configuration["CosmosDbConnection"]
        ?? throw new InvalidOperationException("CosmosDbConnection setting
        is missing.");

    return new CosmosClient(connectionString, new CosmosClientOptions
    {
        SerializerOptions = new CosmosSerializationOptions
        {
            PropertyNamingPolicy = CosmosPropertyNamingPolicy.CamelCase
        }
    });
});

// Existing service registrations from earlier chapters
builder.Services.AddSingleton<IOrderValidator, OrderValidator>();

builder.Build().Run();
```

Extending SubmitOrder with Queue, Topic, and Cosmos Outputs

In this example, expected request and validation failures should be handled explicitly, while unexpected failures should be allowed to fail the Function invocation. Because output bindings do not expose remote write failures to function code, this pattern is useful for demonstration but is not sufficient when a workflow requires precise control over partial success and recovery.

Functions/SubmitOrder.cs

```
using System.Text.Json;
using Microsoft.Azure.Functions.Worker;
using Microsoft.Azure.Functions.Worker.Http;
using Microsoft.Extensions.Logging;

public sealed record SubmitOrderOutputs(
    [property: QueueOutput("orders", Connection =
    "OrderStorageConnection")]
    string QueueMessage,

    [property: ServiceBusOutput("orders-topic", Connection = "Service
    BusConnection")]
    string TopicMessage,

    [property: CosmosDBOutput(
        databaseName: "OrderDb",
        containerName: "Orders",
        Connection = "CosmosDbConnection",
        CreateIfNotExists = true,
        PartitionKey = "/CustomerEmail")]
    Order CosmosDocument
);

public sealed class SubmitOrder
{
    private readonly ILogger _logger;
    private readonly IOrderValidator _validator;

    public SubmitOrder(ILoggerFactory loggerFactory, IOrderValidator
    validator)
    {
        _logger = loggerFactory.CreateLogger<SubmitOrder>();
        _validator = validator;
    }

    [Function("SubmitOrder")]
    public async Task<SubmitOrderOutputs> Run(
```

```
        [HttpTrigger(AuthorizationLevel.Anonymous, "post")]
        HttpRequestData req,
        CancellationToken stopToken)
    {
        var order = await req.ReadFromJsonAsync<Order>(cancellationToken:
        stopToken);

        if (order is null)
            throw new InvalidOperationException("Request body could not be
            parsed as an Order.");

        if (!_validator.IsValid(order, out var reason))
        {
            _logger.LogWarning("Invalid order: {Reason}", reason);
            throw new InvalidOperationException(reason);
        }

        _logger.LogInformation("Validated order {Id}", order.Id);

        var json = JsonSerializer.Serialize(order);

        return new SubmitOrderOutputs(
            QueueMessage: json,
            TopicMessage: json,
            CosmosDocument: order
        );
    }
}
```

This chains three side effects in a single Function. It is still a trade-off. When you tie three outputs to one trigger, you must accept that partial failure becomes possible. In practice, you might use patterns like outbox, retries, or compensations to manage that risk. For the purposes of this chapter, it keeps the flow concrete and lets you see how state becomes durable.

Reading Orders with a Cosmos DB Input Binding

Cosmos DB point reads require both the document id and the partition key. That is why the route includes {email}.

Functions/GetOrderById.cs

```
using System.Net;
using Microsoft.Azure.Functions.Worker;
using Microsoft.Azure.Functions.Worker.Http;
using Microsoft.Extensions.Logging;

public sealed class GetOrderById
{
    private readonly ILogger _logger;

    public GetOrderById(ILoggerFactory loggerFactory)
    {
        _logger = loggerFactory.CreateLogger<GetOrderById>();
    }

    [Function("GetOrderById")]
    public async Task<HttpResponseData> Run(
        [HttpTrigger(AuthorizationLevel.Anonymous, "get", Route = "orders/
        {id}/{email}")]
        HttpRequestData req,
        [CosmosDBInput(
            databaseName: "OrderDb",
            containerName: "Orders",
            Connection = "CosmosDbConnection",
            Id = "{id}",
            PartitionKey = "{email}")]
        Order? order,
        CancellationToken stopToken)
    {
        if (order is null)
        {
            var notFound = req.CreateResponse(HttpStatusCode.NotFound);
            await notFound.WriteStringAsync("Order not found", stopToken);
```

```
            return notFound;
        }

        var ok = req.CreateResponse(HttpStatusCode.OK);
        await ok.WriteAsJsonAsync(order, cancellationToken: stopToken);
        return ok;
    }
}
```

Example call:

```
curl "http://localhost:7071/api/orders/123/alice@example.com"
```

Querying and Reading Data

Persisting data is only half the story. The other half is getting data back out. This is where distributed systems reveal their quirks. A relational database promises that after commit, reads see the latest state. Cosmos DB gives you choices. You can tune consistency, but you must accept the trade-offs between latency, availability, and freshness.

For queries beyond point reads, the Cosmos SDK is the cleanest approach. It avoids subtle quoting errors, makes partition targeting explicit, and gives you a clear path to talk about RU cost and cross-partition fan-out.

GetOrdersByCustomer

This query is efficient because it targets a single partition by using the partition key value.

Functions/GetOrderByCustomer.cs

```
using System.Net;
using Microsoft.Azure.Cosmos;
using Microsoft.Azure.Functions.Worker;
using Microsoft.Azure.Functions.Worker.Http;
using Microsoft.Extensions.Logging;

public sealed class GetOrdersByCustomer
{
```

```
private readonly CosmosClient _client;
private readonly ILogger _logger;

public GetOrdersByCustomer(CosmosClient client, ILoggerFactory
loggerFactory)
{
    _client = client;
    _logger = loggerFactory.CreateLogger<GetOrdersByCustomer>();
}

[Function("GetOrdersByCustomer")]
public async Task<HttpResponseData> Run(
    [HttpTrigger(AuthorizationLevel.Anonymous, "get", Route =
    "customers/{email}/orders")]
    HttpRequestData req,
    string email,
    CancellationToken stopToken)
{
    var container = _client.GetContainer("OrderDb", "Orders");

    var query = new QueryDefinition("SELECT * FROM c WHERE
    c.CustomerEmail = @email")
        .WithParameter("@email", email);

    var iterator = container.GetItemQueryIterator<Order>(
        query,
        requestOptions: new QueryRequestOptions { PartitionKey = new
        PartitionKey(email) });

    var results = new List<Order>();


    while (iterator.HasMoreResults)
    {
        var page = await iterator.ReadNextAsync(stopToken);
        results.AddRange(page);
    }

    var response = req.CreateResponse(HttpStatusCode.OK);
```

```
        await response.WriteAsJsonAsync(results, cancellationToken:
        stopToken);
        return response;
    }
}
```

Call it with:

```
curl "http://localhost:7071/api/customers/alice@example.com/orders"
```

Filtering by Value

A query like “orders above €500” is intentionally expensive if you do not filter by partition key. Cosmos must fan out across partitions, and that costs more RUs. This is not a Cosmos problem; it’s the reality of distributed partitioned storage. The point of including this endpoint is to make the trade-off visible.

Functions/GetHighValueOrders.cs

```
using System.Net;
using Microsoft.Azure.Cosmos;
using Microsoft.Azure.Functions.Worker;
using Microsoft.Azure.Functions.Worker.Http;
using Microsoft.Extensions.Logging;

public sealed class GetHighValueOrders
{
    private readonly CosmosClient _client;
    private readonly ILogger _logger;

    public GetHighValueOrders(CosmosClient client, ILoggerFactory
    loggerFactory)
    {
        _client = client;
        _logger = loggerFactory.CreateLogger<GetHighValueOrders>();
    }

    [Function("GetHighValueOrders")]
    public async Task<HttpResponseData> Run(
```

```
        [HttpTrigger(AuthorizationLevel.Anonymous, "get", Route = "orders/
        highvalue")]
        HttpRequestData req,
        CancellationToken stopToken)
    {
        var container = _client.GetContainer("OrderDb", "Orders");

        var query = new QueryDefinition("SELECT * FROM c WHERE c.Total
        Value > 500");

        var iterator = container.GetItemQueryIterator<Order>(
            query,
            requestOptions: new QueryRequestOptions { MaxConcurrency
            = -1 });

        var results = new List<Order>();

        while (iterator.HasMoreResults)
        {
            var page = await iterator.ReadNextAsync(stopToken);
            results.AddRange(page);
        }

        var response = req.CreateResponse(HttpStatusCode.OK);
        await response.WriteAsJsonAsync(results, cancellationToken:
        stopToken);
        return response;
    }
}
```

Call it with:

```
curl "http://localhost:7071/api/orders/highvalue"
```

Eventual Consistency in Action

Cosmos DB offers five consistency levels. Strong consistency gives you the closest thing to a single logical copy of the data, but at a cost in latency and throughput. Eventual consistency gives the fastest reads and highest availability, but reads may lag behind writes under replication and distributed conditions. Session sits in the middle and is often the best default for user-facing systems because it guarantees that a client sees its own writes.

The important point is that consistency is a design decision. If you query immediately after writing, a strong-consistent read will see the write once it commits, while weaker levels may return older data depending on replication timing and where the read is served from. In single-region development setups you may not always observe staleness, which is exactly why these problems show up later in production.

Handling Consistency and Partitioning

When you move beyond simple inserts and queries, Cosmos DB forces you to face two unavoidable realities of distributed data. Consistency is not absolute, and partitioning shapes everything. These are not abstract concerns. They directly affect how your Functions behave, how your queries perform, and how your users experience the system.

The Five Consistency Models

Strong consistency means every read sees the latest committed write, closest to the mental model of a single database, but it reduces availability and throughput. Bounded staleness guarantees reads lag behind writes by at most a configured version or time window, which can work well when you want predictability without paying the full cost of strong reads. Session consistency guarantees that within a session a client sees its own writes, while other clients may see lag. A consistent prefix guarantees that reads never observe out-of-order writes but may miss the latest. Eventual consistency provides the weakest guarantees and the highest availability, useful for scenarios where freshness is not critical.

Testing Consistency with Per-Request Override

The Cosmos SDK lets you override consistency for a specific request. Whether you observe staleness depends on the account configuration and replication conditions, but the point of this Function is to make the knob real and let you test it under conditions that matter.

Functions/ConsistencyExperiment.cs

```
using System.Net;
using System.Linq;
using Microsoft.Azure.Cosmos;
using Microsoft.Azure.Functions.Worker;
using Microsoft.Azure.Functions.Worker.Http;
using Microsoft.Extensions.Logging;

namespace OrderProcessor;

public sealed class ConsistencyExperiment
{
    private readonly CosmosClient _client;
    private readonly ILogger<ConsistencyExperiment> _logger;

    public ConsistencyExperiment(
        CosmosClient client,
        ILogger<ConsistencyExperiment> logger)
    {
        _client = client;
        _logger = logger;
    }

    [Function("ConsistencyExperiment")]
    public async Task<HttpResponseData> Run(
        [HttpTrigger(AuthorizationLevel.Anonymous, "get", Route =
        "consistency/{email}/{level}")]
        HttpRequestData req,
        string email,
        string level,
        CancellationToken stopToken)
```

```
{
    if (!Enum.TryParse<ConsistencyLevel>(level, ignoreCase: true, out
    var consistencyLevel))
    {
        var bad = req.CreateResponse(HttpStatusCode.BadRequest);
        await bad.WriteStringAsync(
            "Invalid consistency level. Use Strong, BoundedStaleness,
            Session, ConsistentPrefix, or Eventual.",
            stopToken);

        return bad;
    }

    var container = _client.GetContainer("OrderDb", "Orders");


    var query = new QueryDefinition(
            "SELECT TOP 1 * FROM c WHERE c.CustomerEmail = @email ORDER
            BY c._ts DESC")
        .WithParameter("@email", email);

    var options = new QueryRequestOptions
    {
        PartitionKey = new PartitionKey(email),
        ConsistencyLevel = consistencyLevel
    };

    var iterator = container.GetItemQueryIterator<Order>(
        query,
        requestOptions: options);

    Order? latest = null;


    if (iterator.HasMoreResults)
    {
        var page = await iterator.ReadNextAsync(stopToken);
        latest = page.Resource.FirstOrDefault();
    }
```

```
        _logger.LogInformation(
            "Consistency experiment for {Email} using {ConsistencyLevel}",
            email,
            consistencyLevel);

        var response = req.CreateResponse(HttpStatusCode.OK);

        if (latest is null)
        {
            await response.WriteStringAsync(
                "No recent orders found (possible stale read under weaker
                consistency).",
                stopToken);

            return response;
        }

        await response.WriteAsJsonAsync(latest, cancellationToken:
        stopToken);
        return response;
    }
}
```

Example calls:

```
curl "http://localhost:7071/api/consistency/alice@example.com/Strong"
curl "http://localhost:7071/api/consistency/alice@example.com/Eventual"
```

Partitioning Revisited

Partitioning is how Cosmos DB scales horizontally. A partition key determines where a document lives, and all documents with the same key value live in the same logical partition. Queries restricted to one partition are efficient. Queries spanning many partitions are slower and cost more RUs. Write throughput is also distributed. Hot partitions, where one key receives disproportionate traffic, throttle performance.

In `OrderProcessor` we chose `CustomerEmail` as the partition key because customer-centric queries are common and intuitive. In real systems you sometimes need synthetic keys or composite strategies if one tenant dominates traffic. There is no universal right answer. There is only "right for your workload."

Optimistic Concurrency with ETags

So far, we've inserted and read orders without worrying about updates. But if two Functions update the same order at once, one update can overwrite the other. Cosmos DB offers optimistic concurrency via ETags. Every document has an `_etag`. When you read a document, you receive its ETag. When you write back, you can specify that the write should only succeed if the ETag has not changed. If another writer changed it, Cosmos rejects the write with `412 Precondition Failed`.

Functions/UpdateOrderStatus.cs

```
using System.Net;
using Microsoft.Azure.Cosmos;
using Microsoft.Azure.Functions.Worker;
using Microsoft.Azure.Functions.Worker.Http;
using Microsoft.Extensions.Logging;

public sealed class UpdateOrderStatus
{
    private readonly CosmosClient _client;
    private readonly ILogger _logger;

    public UpdateOrderStatus(CosmosClient client, ILoggerFactory
    loggerFactory)
    {
        _client = client;
        _logger = loggerFactory.CreateLogger<UpdateOrderStatus>();
    }

    [Function("UpdateOrderStatus")]
    public async Task<HttpResponseData> Run(
        [HttpTrigger(AuthorizationLevel.Anonymous, "post", Route = "orders/
        {id}/{email}/status/{status}")]
        HttpRequestData req,
        string id,
        string email,
        string status,
        CancellationToken stopToken)
    {
```

```
var container = _client.GetContainer("OrderDb", "Orders");

try
{
    var read = await container.ReadItemAsync<Order>(
        id,
        new PartitionKey(email),
        cancellationToken: stopToken);

    var doc = read.Resource;
    var etag = read.ETag;

    doc.Status = status;

    var replace = await container.ReplaceItemAsync(
        doc,
        id,
        new PartitionKey(email),
        new ItemRequestOptions { IfMatchEtag = etag },
        cancellationToken: stopToken);

    var ok = req.CreateResponse(HttpStatusCode.OK);
    await ok.WriteAsJsonAsync(replace.Resource, cancellationToken:
    stopToken);
    return ok;
}
catch (CosmosException ex) when (ex.StatusCode == HttpStatusCode.
PreconditionFailed)
{
    var failed = req.CreateResponse(HttpStatusCode.
    PreconditionFailed);
    await failed.WriteStringAsync("Precondition failed: order was
    updated by someone else.", stopToken);
    return failed;
}
catch (CosmosException ex) when (ex.StatusCode == HttpStatusCode.
NotFound)
{
```

```
            var notFound = req.CreateResponse(HttpStatusCode.NotFound);
            await notFound.WriteStringAsync("Order not found.", stopToken);
            return notFound;
        }
    }
}
```

Without ETags, last write wins silently. With ETags, you detect conflicts and can choose how to handle them, retry, merge, reject, or escalate. Combined with consistency levels, you decide how fresh your reads must be before applying updates. This is the essence of distributed data design. You cannot avoid conflicts, but you can detect and handle them.

Event Sourcing Basics

So far, we've treated orders like documents that get overwritten as the status changes. That works, but it hides history. Did the order go from Created to Paid to Shipped, or was it Created then Cancelled? All you know is the current snapshot.

Event sourcing flips the model. Instead of overwriting state, you append events to an immutable log and derive state by replaying those events. In distributed systems this has two important benefits. First, append-only writes reduce a whole class of lost-update problems because multiple writers can append without overwriting each other. Second, the event log becomes an audit trail you can replay to rebuild derived models.

One practical detail matters immediately. If you want to replay an order, your partition key should make that replay efficient. That means events should be partitioned by `OrderId`, not by `CustomerEmail`. You can still index or project by customer later, but the core read pattern for event sourcing is "load the aggregate's events."

Modeling Events

Models/OrderEvent.cs

```
public abstract class OrderEvent
{
    public string Id { get; set; } = Guid.NewGuid().ToString();

    // Partition key for the event store
```

```
    public string OrderId { get; set; } = string.Empty;

    public string EventType { get; set; } = string.Empty;
    public DateTime Timestamp { get; set; } = DateTime.UtcNow;
}

public sealed class OrderCreated : OrderEvent
{
    public string CustomerEmail { get; set; } = string.Empty;
    public List<string> Items { get; set; } = new();
    public decimal TotalValue { get; set; }
}

public sealed class OrderPaid : OrderEvent
{
    public decimal Amount { get; set; }
    public string PaymentReference { get; set; } = string.Empty;
}

public sealed class OrderShipped : OrderEvent
{
    public string TrackingNumber { get; set; } = string.Empty;
}
```

Writing Events to Cosmos DB

Instead of replacing an order document, we append events to a container named `OrderEvents`. Each event is partitioned by `OrderId` so that replay remains a single-partition query.

Functions/RecordOrderCreated.cs

```
using System.Net;
using Microsoft.Azure.Cosmos;
using Microsoft.Azure.Functions.Worker;
using Microsoft.Azure.Functions.Worker.Http;

public sealed class RecordOrderCreated
{
    private readonly CosmosClient _client;
```

```
    public RecordOrderCreated(CosmosClient client)
    {
        _client = client;
    }

    [Function("RecordOrderCreated")]
    public async Task<HttpResponseData> Run(
        [HttpTrigger(AuthorizationLevel.Anonymous, "post", Route = "orders/
        create")]
        HttpRequestData req,
        CancellationToken stopToken)
    {
        var order = await req.ReadFromJsonAsync<Order>(cancellationToken:
        stopToken);
        if (order is null)
            throw new InvalidOperationException("Request body could not be
            parsed as an Order.");

        var container = _client.GetContainer("OrderDb", "OrderEvents");

        var evt = new OrderCreated
        {
            OrderId = order.Id,
            CustomerEmail = order.CustomerEmail,
            Items = order.Items,
            TotalValue = order.TotalValue,
            EventType = nameof(OrderCreated)
        };

        await container.CreateItemAsync(evt, new PartitionKey(evt.OrderId),
        cancellationToken: stopToken);

        var response = req.CreateResponse(HttpStatusCode.OK);
        await response.WriteAsJsonAsync(evt, cancellationToken: stopToken);
        return response;
    }
}
```

Reconstructing State

In a production event-sourced system, you would configure polymorphic serialization and build projections. For a book example, the simplest robust approach is to replay as a `JsonDocument` and branch on `EventType`. This avoids "serializer magic" and makes the idea explicit.

Functions/GetOrderState.cs

```
using System.Net;
using System.Text.Json;
using Microsoft.Azure.Cosmos;
using Microsoft.Azure.Functions.Worker;
using Microsoft.Azure.Functions.Worker.Http;

public sealed class GetOrderState
{
    private readonly CosmosClient _client;

    public GetOrderState(CosmosClient client)
    {
        _client = client;
    }

    [Function("GetOrderState")]
    public async Task<HttpResponseData> Run(
        [HttpTrigger(AuthorizationLevel.Anonymous, "get", Route = "orders/
        {id}/state")]
        HttpRequestData req,
        string id,
        CancellationToken stopToken)
    {
        var container = _client.GetContainer("OrderDb", "OrderEvents");

        var query = new QueryDefinition(
                "SELECT * FROM c WHERE c.OrderId = @id ORDER BY
                c.Timestamp")
            .WithParameter("@id", id);

        var iterator = container.GetItemQueryIterator<JsonDocument>(
```

```
        query,
        requestOptions: new QueryRequestOptions { PartitionKey = new
        PartitionKey(id) });

    var events = new List<JsonDocument>();

    while (iterator.HasMoreResults)
    {
        var batch = await iterator.ReadNextAsync(stopToken);
        events.AddRange(batch);
    }

    var status = "Unknown";
    decimal total = 0;

    foreach (var doc in events)
    {
        var root = doc.RootElement;
        var eventType = root.GetProperty("EventType").GetString();

        if (eventType == nameof(OrderCreated))
        {
            status = "Created";
            if (root.TryGetProperty("TotalValue", out var tv))
                total = tv.GetDecimal();
        }
        else if (eventType == nameof(OrderPaid))
        {
            status = "Paid";
        }
        else if (eventType == nameof(OrderShipped))
        {
            status = "Shipped";
        }
    }

    var response = req.CreateResponse(HttpStatusCode.OK);
```

```
        await response.WriteAsJsonAsync(new { OrderId = id, Status =
        status, Total = total }, cancellationToken: stopToken);
        return response;
    }
}
```

Event sourcing isn't free. Reads can be slower if you replay on demand, and data volume grows over time. In practice you maintain snapshots or read models, which leads naturally into CQRS.

CQRS in Practice

Event sourcing gives us a durable log of everything that happened. That's great for correctness and auditability, but it introduces a new challenge. Queries become expensive if you replay events every time. For one order that might be a handful of events. For a customer or tenant with thousands of orders, replay becomes a tax.

Command query responsibility segregation (CQRS) separates the write path from the read path. Commands change state by appending events. Queries are read from a separate optimized model. Instead of replaying the event log for every read, you maintain read models, also called projections, that store derived state in a shape that answers queries efficiently.

For `OrderProcessor` we'll build a `CustomerOrderSummary` read model that stores, per customer, the total number of orders, total value of orders, and date of last order. This lets us answer, "What is this customer's total spend?" instantly without replaying everything.

Projection Function Using the Change Feed

Once the `OrderEvents` container holds multiple event types, the trigger must bind to something that can represent them all. A clean approach is to bind to `JsonDocument` and filter by `EventType`. This also keeps the example robust without requiring polymorphic serializer configuration.

Because projections update shared state, they also create a new concurrency problem. Two change feed batches can race and overwrite the summary. We solve that with ETags in the projection updater, applying the same concurrency control in a new context.

Models/CustomerOrderSummary.cs

```
using System.Net;
using System.Text.Json;
using Microsoft.Azure.Cosmos;
using Microsoft.Azure.Functions.Worker;
using Microsoft.Extensions.Logging;

public sealed class CustomerOrderSummary
{
    public string Id { get; set; } = string.Empty; // same as CustomerEmail
    public string CustomerEmail { get; set; } = string.Empty;
    public int TotalOrders { get; set; }
    public decimal TotalValue { get; set; }
    public DateTime LastOrder { get; set; }
}
```

Functions/CustomerOrderSummaryUpdater.cs

```
using System.Net;
using System.Text.Json;
using Microsoft.Azure.Cosmos;
using Microsoft.Azure.Functions.Worker;weqQQW saz\
using Microsoft.Extensions.Logging;

namespace OrderProcessor;

public sealed class CustomerOrderSummaryUpdater
{
   private readonly CosmosClient _client;
   private readonly ILogger<CustomerOrderSummaryUpdater> _logger;

   public CustomerOrderSummaryUpdater(
       CosmosClient client,
       ILogger<CustomerOrderSummaryUpdater> logger)
   {
       _client = client;
       _logger = logger;
   }
```

```
[Function("CustomerOrderSummaryUpdater")]
public async Task Run(
    [CosmosDBTrigger(
        databaseName: "OrderDb",
        containerName: "OrderEvents",
        Connection = "CosmosDbConnection",
        LeaseContainerName = "leases",
        CreateLeaseContainerIfNotExists = true)]
    IReadOnlyList<JsonDocument> input,
    CancellationToken stopToken)
{
    if (input is null || input.Count == 0)
    {
        return;
    }

    var container = _client.GetContainer("OrderDb", "Customer
    Summaries");

    foreach (var doc in input)
    {
        var root = doc.RootElement;

        if (!root.TryGetProperty("EventType", out var eventTypeProp))
        {
            continue;
        }

        var eventType = eventTypeProp.GetString();
        if (!string.Equals(eventType, nameof(OrderCreated), String
        Comparison.Ordinal))
        {
            continue;
        }

        var email = root.GetProperty("CustomerEmail").GetString();
        if (string.IsNullOrWhiteSpace(email))
        {
```

```
        continue;
    }

    var totalValue = root.TryGetProperty("TotalValue", out var tv)
        ? tv.GetDecimal()
        : 0m;

    var timestamp = root.TryGetProperty("Timestamp", out var ts)
        ? ts.GetDateTime()
        : DateTime.UtcNow;

    var id = email;
    var pk = new PartitionKey(email);

    for (var attempt = 1; attempt <= 10; attempt++)
    {
        stopToken.ThrowIfCancellationRequested();

        try
        {
            var read = await container.ReadItemAsync<CustomerOrde
            rSummary>(
                id,
                pk,
                cancellationToken: stopToken);

            var summary = read.Resource;
            var etag = read.ETag;

            summary.TotalOrders += 1;
            summary.TotalValue += totalValue;
            summary.LastOrder = timestamp;

            await container.ReplaceItemAsync(
                summary,
                id,
                pk,
                new ItemRequestOptions { IfMatchEtag = etag },
                cancellationToken: stopToken);
```

```
        _logger.LogInformation(
            "Updated customer summary for {Email} on attempt
            {Attempt}",
            email,
            attempt);

        break;
    }
    catch (CosmosException ex) when (ex.StatusCode ==
    HttpStatusCode.NotFound)
    {
        try
        {
            var summary = new CustomerOrderSummary
            {
                Id = email,
                CustomerEmail = email,
                TotalOrders = 1,
                TotalValue = totalValue,
                LastOrder = timestamp
            };

            await container.CreateItemAsync(summary, pk,
            cancellationToken: stopToken);

            _logger.LogInformation(
                "Created customer summary for {Email} on attempt
                {Attempt}",
                email,
                attempt);

            break;
        }
        catch (CosmosException createEx) when (createEx.
        StatusCode == HttpStatusCode.Conflict)
        {
```

```
                    // Another updater created it first. Retry and
                    update instead.
                    continue;
                }
            }
            catch (CosmosException ex) when (ex.StatusCode ==
            HttpStatusCode.PreconditionFailed)
            {
                // Another updater changed it first. Retry with a
                fresh read.
                continue;
            }

            if (attempt == 10)
            {
                _logger.LogWarning(
                    "Failed to update customer summary for {Email} after
                    {Attempts} attempts",
                    email,
                    attempt);
            }
        }
    }
  }
}
```

Querying the Summary

Functions/GetCustomerSummary.cs

```
using System.Net;
using Microsoft.Azure.Cosmos;
using Microsoft.Azure.Functions.Worker;
using Microsoft.Azure.Functions.Worker.Http;

public sealed class GetCustomerSummary
{
```

```
private readonly CosmosClient _client;

public GetCustomerSummary(CosmosClient client)
{
    _client = client;
}

[Function("GetCustomerSummary")]
public async Task<HttpResponseData> Run(
    [HttpTrigger(AuthorizationLevel.Anonymous, "get", Route =
    "customers/{email}/summary")]
    HttpRequestData req,
    string email,
    CancellationToken stopToken)
{
    var container = _client.GetContainer("OrderDb",
    "CustomerSummaries");

    try
    {
        var read = await container.ReadItemAsync<CustomerOrderSummary>(
            email,
            new PartitionKey(email),
            cancellationToken: stopToken);

        var ok = req.CreateResponse(HttpStatusCode.OK);
        await ok.WriteAsJsonAsync(read.Resource, cancellationToken:
        stopToken);
        return ok;
    }
    catch (CosmosException ex) when (ex.StatusCode == HttpStatusCode.
    NotFound)
    {
        var notFound = req.CreateResponse(HttpStatusCode.NotFound);
        await notFound.WriteStringAsync("No summary found for this
        customer.", stopToken);
```

```
                return notFound;
            }
        }
    }
```

At this point, OrderProcessor has a clear split. Commands append events and write orders. Projections consume changes and update derived read models. Queries read from the models designed for fast reads. That separation introduces eventual consistency by design. Summaries may lag behind the event log, but they are fast, cheap to query, and easy to shape for specific read needs (see Figure 4-3).

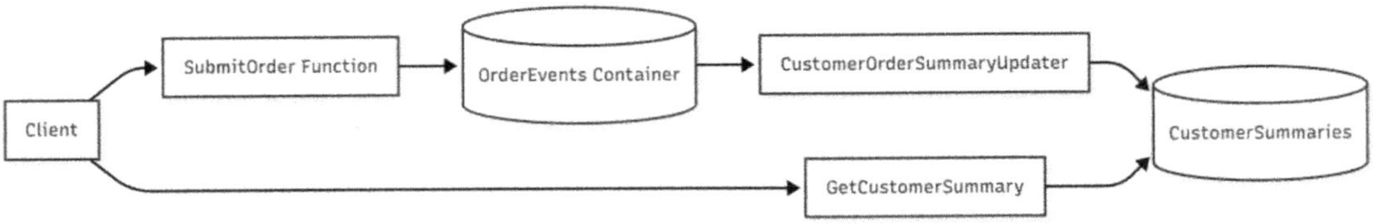

Figure 4-3. *CQRS and Event Flow*

EXERCISES

1. Run the race demo by firing 50 parallel requests at `RaceConditionUpdater`. Record the final count and repeat the test three times. Notice how the result varies even though the code never changes.
2. Increase the race demo to 200 requests with higher concurrency. Observe how increasing load increases the frequency and severity of lost updates.
3. Add a lock to `ConcurrentOrderStore.Increment` and rerun the test. Confirm that it fixes the race inside a single process. Then explain why this does not solve correctness in a scaled-out Function App.
4. Modify the race demo so the Function returns the update count plus the current `Environment.MachineName`. Repeat the test. Use the output to reason about what would happen if multiple machines were involved.
5. Post three valid orders using `SubmitOrder` and confirm that each order is written to Cosmos DB and also emitted to the queue and the topic. Then explain

what "partial success" would mean in this specific Function if one output destination becomes unavailable.

6. Call `GetOrderById` with a correct id but the wrong email partition key. Confirm it returns not found. Use that behavior to explain why Cosmos DB requires partition key values for point reads.
7. Post multiple orders for two different customers and then call `GetOrdersByCustomer` for each. Confirm the results are partition targeted and discuss why this query stays efficient at scale.
8. Populate orders across many customers and run `GetHighValueOrders` repeatedly. Compare the latency and RU charge to `GetOrdersByCustomer`. Explain why cross-partition fan-out is the trade-off you pay for horizontal scale.
9. Change the partition key choice in your own notes by imagining orders partitioned by Id instead of `CustomerEmail`. Explain which queries become cheaper and which become more expensive, and whether that trade-off fits the `OrderProcessor` workload.
10. Run `ConsistencyExperiment` using Strong and Eventual while rapidly writing and reading. If you do not observe staleness locally, describe what environmental conditions would make it observable and why production is where this typically appears.
11. Add a deliberate artificial delay between writing an order and reading it back inside your own test harness. Use it to reason about why "I tested it locally and it looked fine" is not evidence of correctness under replication.
12. Call `UpdateOrderStatus` twice in parallel for the same order and same email. Confirm that one of the requests can fail with 412 Precondition Failed under true concurrency. Then implement a basic retry loop with bounded attempts and log how many retries were needed.
13. Modify `UpdateOrderStatus` so that if it receives 412, it re-reads the order and only applies the status update if the current status is still compatible with the requested transition. Explain how this starts moving you toward a real domain model.

14. Add an `OrderPaid` event writer endpoint and an `OrderShipped` event writer endpoint that append to the `OrderEvents` container. Confirm that appends do not overwrite each other even under concurrent calls.

15. Extend `GetOrderState` so it also folds a Cancelled state if you append an `OrderCancelled` event. Decide whether Cancelled should override Shipped, and write down the business rule that your fold function implements.

16. Create a second projection container that tracks high-value orders per customer, for example, count and total value for orders above €1,000. Use the change feed to update it and compare the results with an on-demand query.

17. Create a projection that stores a denormalized `OrderSnapshot` per order id, updated from events, so that queries do not need to replay the entire event stream. Describe how this changes the read performance and what it costs in complexity.

18. Intentionally introduce a race in `CustomerOrderSummaryUpdater` by removing the ETag-based conditional replace and rerun your event writes under concurrency. Observe how counts can drift and explain why projections need concurrency protection too.

19. Measure or estimate how many writes per second a single "hot customer" could generate in your current partitioning scheme. Explain what a hot partition is, why it happens, and what partition key strategies might reduce the risk.

20. Reflection exercise. Pick one real system you know: payments, seat reservations, inventory, or underwriting. Identify where stale reads and lost updates could occur. Then decide whether you would rather reject requests to preserve strict consistency or accept availability and design a conflict-resolution strategy.

Summary

Data is the hardest part of distributed systems because it is where correctness lives. In a monolith, the database gives you a clear boundary for truth. Transactions serialize concurrent operations, rollbacks repair partial failures, and reads after commit match the mental model developers build early in their careers. In distributed serverless systems that boundary dissolves. Functions scale out, writes happen in multiple stores, reads can come from replicas, and partitions become normal. That changes the nature of bugs. The most dangerous failures are not the ones that throw exceptions but the ones that succeed while quietly producing incorrect states. Concurrency, stale reads, lost updates, and partitions are not "edge cases" in distributed systems; they are the steady-state reality you must design for.

In `OrderProcessor`, we made those ideas concrete. We started with an intentionally broken in-memory counter to show how trivial logic fails under concurrency. We then moved state into Cosmos DB and explored the two forces that shape every distributed data design: consistency and partitioning. We used partition keys to make customer queries efficient, and we used ETags to detect and prevent lost updates when multiple writers compete. We then shifted from mutable documents to immutable event streams, which aligns better with distributed flows and creates a built-in audit log. Finally, we introduced CQRS with projections so reads become fast without giving up the event log. `OrderProcessor` now behaves like a real distributed system; it persists state durably, it makes partition decisions explicit, it detects write conflicts rather than hiding them, and it separates write concerns from read concerns in a way that scales.

So far, we've built reactive flows. Functions trigger from queues, topics, and change feeds, and state evolves through writes, events, and projections. That model scales well, but it is still fundamentally reactive. Each step runs independently, and coordination is implicit. When the path is simple, that's fine. When the path spans multiple steps, includes retries, or must wait on external systems, the complexity leaks back into your code.

This is where Durable Functions come in. Durable Functions give you a way to orchestrate long-running workflows while keeping the reliability properties you need in a distributed system. Instead of stitching together state transitions with ad hoc queues and timers, you model the workflow explicitly using an orchestrator and activity functions. In Chapter 5, we'll use Durable Functions to extend `OrderProcessor` into a workflow-driven system and cover the core patterns you'll use in real serverless systems: fan-out and fan-in, retries, stateful orchestration, and saga-style coordination.

PART II

Patterns

CHAPTER 5

Orchestration with Durable Functions

`OrderProcessor` can now persist orders, publish events, and query state efficiently, but it still lacks one critical capability: coordination. Real workflows do not end at data storage or event publication. They span multiple dependent steps, include failures and retries, and often pause for time-based rules or human decisions. In a distributed system, that kind of process needs more than independent event handlers. It needs orchestration.

This chapter introduces Durable Functions as the mechanism for modeling that coordination explicitly. We will use it to turn `OrderProcessor` into a workflow-driven system and then extend that workflow with fan-out and fan-in, approvals, retries, compensation, sub-orchestrations, and Durable Entities. The result is a serverless design that is easier to follow, easier to debug, and more reliable under real-world failure and scale.

Why Orchestration Is Important

In the last chapter, we built out persistence with Cosmos DB and learned how events and CQRS help us query distributed state efficiently. With that in place, our `OrderProcessor` system can ingest orders, broadcast them to interested services, and store them durably. But something's missing, coordination. When you think about the lifecycle of an order in the real world, it isn't just a single insert and forget. It's a multi-step process that spans services, people, and time:

© Patrick Kearns 2026
P. Kearns, *Serverless Distributed Systems in Modern .NET and Azure*,
https://doi.org/10.1007/979-8-8688-2839-3_5

- Validate the order.
- Reserve inventory.
- Process payment.
- Ship the items.
- Notify the customer.

Some steps can happen in parallel. Some must wait for others. Some may fail and need retrying. Some may require human approval. Pure event-driven flows (like we've built so far) handle independence well. Each service reacts to an event and does its piece. But once you need coordination, ensuring that payment happens before shipping or that an order is cancelled if payment fails, events alone aren't enough.

This is where orchestration comes in.

Choreography vs. Orchestration

When designing distributed systems, two coordination styles come up again and again: choreography and orchestration. Both are used to manage how services work together across a wider workflow, but they do so in very different ways. Understanding the difference is important because it affects how your system behaves, how easy it is to change, and how difficult it is to debug when something goes wrong.

Choreography

In a distributed serverless system, each service responds independently to events rather than relying on a single central coordinator. That means there is no single "brain" controlling the full workflow. Instead, when an `OrderCreated` event is published, the Payment service may attempt to take payment, the Inventory service may reserve stock, and the Shipping service may wait for an `OrderPaid` event before beginning fulfillment. This style gives you flexibility and loose coupling, but it also introduces complexity. Event contracts must be designed very carefully so each service knows exactly how to react, and troubleshooting can become difficult when a workflow stalls and an order appears to be stuck somewhere in the chain.

Orchestration

With orchestration, a central workflow is responsible for defining the sequence of steps and coordinating how services are called, whether in order or in parallel. The orchestrator maintains state, handles retries, and keeps the overall process moving. For example, it might receive an order, call one activity to take payment, then, if that succeeds, call another activity to reserve inventory, and finally trigger shipping. This approach makes the process much easier to follow because the workflow is expressed explicitly in code rather than being spread across loosely connected event handlers. In Azure, Durable Functions provides this orchestration model directly within Azure Functions, making it a strong fit for long-running and stateful serverless workflows.

The Limits of Choreography in OrderProcessor

The current `OrderProcessor` relies entirely on choreography. When an `OrderCreated` event is published, payment processing begins, inventory attempts to reserve stock, and notifications may fire, all as independent reactions. That works for simple flows, but the cracks start to show as soon as the process becomes more complex. There is nothing enforcing dependency order, so one part of the system could move ahead before another critical step has completed. Failure handling becomes awkward too, because if payment fails after inventory has already reserved stock, something needs to decide how to compensate. Human approval introduces another problem, since an expensive order might need to pause and wait for a decision, which is difficult to model cleanly with pure event chaining. Time-based rules create the same issue, such as cancelling an order if payment has not been completed within ten minutes, because some part of the system must track that waiting period. On top of all that, visibility suffers. You can inspect logs and piece events together, but there is no single, reliable view showing exactly where an order is in the workflow. Those are all signs that you are dealing with orchestration problems rather than simple event-driven coordination.

Durable Functions to the Rescue

This is where Durable Functions become useful. Durable Functions extends Azure Functions with a built-in orchestration model, giving you a structured way to manage long-running and stateful workflows. At the center of that model are Orchestrator Functions, which define the workflow in C# code, call activity functions, wait for results, and preserve state as the process moves forward. The Durable runtime keeps that orchestration deterministic and resilient. Activity Functions handle the actual work such as charging a card, reserving stock, or sending an email, and they can fail, retry, and scale independently. Durable Client Functions act as the entry point, typically receiving an HTTP request, starting the orchestration, and returning an orchestration ID that can be used to track progress. Together, these pieces let you write business workflows in a clear, code-driven way that feels almost synchronous, while still running reliably across a distributed system with retries, checkpoints, and built-in resilience.

Example: Orchestrating an Order

Package Note This chapter needs the following NuGet packages. Microsoft.Azure.Functions.Worker.Extensions.DurableTask Microsoft.Azure.Cosmos

Here's a first sketch of an orchestrator for our OrderProcessor:

Orchestrators/OrderOrchestrator.cs

```
using Microsoft.Azure.Functions.Worker;
using Microsoft.DurableTask;

namespace OrderProcessor;

public static class OrderOrchestrator
{
    [Function("OrderOrchestrator")]
    public static async Task Run(
        [OrchestrationTrigger] TaskOrchestrationContext context)
    {
        var order = context.GetInput<Order>()
            ?? throw new InvalidOperationException("Order input is
            required.");

        var paymentOk = await context.CallActivityAsync<bool>(
            "ProcessPaymentActivity",
            order);
```

```
        if (!paymentOk)
        {
            await context.CallActivityAsync(
                "NotifyFailureActivity",
                new FailureNotice(order, "Payment failed"));

            return;
        }

        var warehouseIds = new[] { "W1", "W2", "W3" };

        var inventoryTasks = warehouseIds.Select(warehouseId =>
            context.CallActivityAsync<bool>(
                "CheckWarehouseActivity",
                new WarehouseRequest(order, warehouseId)));

        var inventoryResults = await Task.WhenAll(inventoryTasks);

        if (!inventoryResults.Any(result => result))
        {
            await context.CallActivityAsync("RefundPaymentActivity",
            order);

            await context.CallActivityAsync(
                "NotifyFailureActivity",
                new FailureNotice(order, "Out of stock"));

            return;
        }

        await context.CallActivityAsync("ShipOrderActivity", order);
        await context.CallActivityAsync("NotifySuccessActivity", order);
    }
}
```

At first glance, this looks like synchronous code. But behind the scenes, Durable Functions

- Saves checkpoints between calls
- Retries failed activities
- Allows the workflow to pause for minutes or days
- Lets you query orchestration status via APIs

Updating the OrderProcessor Lifecycle

With Durable Functions in place, the order lifecycle becomes far more structured. An incoming `SubmitOrder` HTTP request starts the orchestration, which then hands control to an `OrderOrchestrator`. From there, the workflow executes each step in a defined sequence, processing payment first, then checking inventory, and finally moving on to shipping and success notification when the required conditions are met. If payment, inventory, or a later stage fails, the orchestrator can switch into the appropriate compensation path, such as issuing a refund and sending a failure notification. Instead of relying on loosely connected services to react independently and hope the overall flow stays consistent, you now have a central coordinator that enforces ordering, manages failures, and keeps the workflow under control.

Instead of loosely coupled services reacting independently, we now have a coordinator ensuring steps happen in order and failures are handled.

When to Use Orchestration

Use choreography when each step can react independently, execution order is not especially important, and you want the system to stay flexible and loosely coupled. Use orchestration when the workflow has clear dependencies between steps, failures need coordinated handling, timeouts or approvals must be tracked, or the business process needs a single source of control. In practice, most production systems use a mix of both. Events are useful for decoupled notifications and side effects, while orchestrations are better suited to critical workflows where consistency, visibility, and control matter. That is the direction `OrderProcessor` should now take.

Anatomy of Durable Functions

In the previous section, we argued for orchestration: sometimes events alone aren't enough, and you need a conductor to coordinate the dance. Now let's open up the box and see how Durable Functions actually work. Understanding the anatomy of Durable Functions is essential before we scaffold our first orchestrator in `OrderProcessor`.

The Three Building Blocks

Durable Functions is built around three core function types that work together to model reliable workflows. Orchestrator Functions define the workflow itself, deciding what happens next, waiting for results, handling timers, and pausing for external events when needed. Because the runtime may replay them to rebuild state, they must remain deterministic. Activity Functions perform the real work, such as calling APIs, writing to a database, or sending emails. They can fail, retry, and scale independently, and they should always be designed to be idempotent so repeated execution does not create unwanted side effects. Durable Client Functions act as the entry point into the workflow, usually triggered by HTTP, Service Bus, or Event Grid, and they start orchestrations while returning an orchestration ID that can be used to check progress later. Together, these three building blocks let you write workflows that read clearly in code while executing asynchronously and reliably across a distributed system.

Deterministic Replay

One of the most unusual but also most important ideas in Durable Functions is deterministic replay. Each time an orchestration runs, the runtime records the decisions it makes. If that orchestrator crashes, restarts, or is resumed on another host, the runtime can replay that history to rebuild its state and continue safely. That only works if the orchestrator is deterministic, meaning the same input must always lead to the same result. Because of that, certain things should not be done directly inside an orchestrator. You should not call `DateTime.UtcNow` directly and should use the orchestration context time instead; you should not generate random values yourself and should rely on the context for that too, and you should not make direct HTTP calls from the orchestrator but push that work into activity functions. This replay model is what gives Durable Functions much of its resilience, allowing workflows to pause for minutes, days, or even months without losing their place.

Scaffolding OrderOrchestrator

Let's scaffold our first orchestrator in **OrderProcessor**. It won't do real work yet, just stub activity calls, but it lays the foundation.

Durable Client (Starter)

We'll start orchestrations via HTTP:

Functions/StartOrderOrchestration.cs

```
using System.Net;
using Microsoft.Azure.Functions.Worker;
using Microsoft.Azure.Functions.Worker.Http;
using Microsoft.DurableTask.Client;
using Microsoft.Extensions.Logging;

namespace OrderProcessor;

public sealed class StartOrderOrchestration
{
   private readonly ILogger<StartOrderOrchestration> _logger;

   public StartOrderOrchestration(ILogger<StartOrderOrchestration> logger)
   {
       _logger = logger;
   }

   [Function("StartOrderOrchestration")]
   public async Task<HttpResponseData> Run(
       [HttpTrigger(AuthorizationLevel.Function, "post", Route = "orders/
       orchestrate")]
       HttpRequestData req,
       [DurableClient] DurableTaskClient client,
       CancellationToken stopToken)
   {
       var order = await req.ReadFromJsonAsync<Order>(cancellationToken:
       stopToken);

       if (order is null || string.IsNullOrWhiteSpace(order.Id) || string.
```

```
IsNullOrWhiteSpace(order.CustomerEmail))
        {
            var bad = req.CreateResponse(HttpStatusCode.BadRequest);
            await bad.WriteStringAsync("Invalid order payload.", stopToken);
            return bad;
        }

        var instanceId = await client.ScheduleNewOrchestrationInstanceAsync(
            "OrderOrchestrator",
            order,
            cancellation: stopToken);

        _logger.LogInformation("Started orchestration with ID {InstanceId}
        for order {OrderId}", instanceId, order.Id);

        var response = req.CreateResponse(HttpStatusCode.Accepted);
        await response.WriteAsJsonAsync(new
        {
            instanceId,
            orderId = order.Id,
            statusQuery = $"/api/orchestrations/{instanceId}"
        }, cancellationToken: stopToken);

        return response;
    }
}
```

This Function receives an Order via HTTP and starts an orchestration instance.

Orchestrator

Now the heart of the workflow:

Orchestrators/OrderOrchestrator.cs

```
using Microsoft.Azure.Functions.Worker;
using Microsoft.DurableTask;

namespace OrderProcessor;
```

```
public static class OrderOrchestrator
{
   [Function("OrderOrchestrator")]
   public static async Task Run(
       [OrchestrationTrigger] TaskOrchestrationContext context)
   {
       var order = context.GetInput<Order>()
           ?? throw new InvalidOperationException("Order input is
           required.");

       if (order.TotalValue > 10_000m)
       {
           using var approvalTimeoutCts = new CancellationTokenSource();

           var timeoutTask = context.CreateTimer(
               context.CurrentDateTimeUtc.AddHours(24),
               approvalTimeoutCts.Token);

           var approvalTask = context.WaitForExternalEvent<string>("Manager
           Approval");

           var winner = await Task.WhenAny(approvalTask, timeoutTask);

           if (winner == timeoutTask)
           {
               await context.CallActivityAsync(
                   "NotifyFailureActivity",
                   new FailureNotice(order, "Approval timed out"));

               return;
           }

           var decision =  await approvalTask;

           if (!string.Equals(decision, "Approved", StringComparison.
           OrdinalIgnoreCase))
           {
               await context.CallActivityAsync(
                   "NotifyFailureActivity",
```

```
                new FailureNotice(order, $"Approval rejected:
                {decision}"));

            return;
        }

        approvalTimeoutCts.Cancel();
    }

    var paymentOk = await context.CallActivityAsync<bool>("ProcessPaymen
    tActivity", order);

    if (!paymentOk)
    {
        await context.CallActivityAsync(
            "NotifyFailureActivity",
            new FailureNotice(order, "Payment failed"));

        return;
    }

    var warehouseIds = new[] { "W1", "W2", "W3" };
    var tasks = warehouseIds.Select(warehouseId =>
        context.CallActivityAsync<bool>(
            "CheckWarehouseActivity",
            new WarehouseRequest(order, warehouseId)));

    var results = await Task.WhenAll(tasks);

    if (!results.Any(r => r))
    {
        await context.CallActivityAsync("RefundPaymentActivity", order);
        await context.CallActivityAsync(
            "NotifyFailureActivity",
            new FailureNotice(order, "Out of stock"));

        return;
    }
```

```
        await context.CallActivityAsync("ShipOrderActivity", order);
        await context.CallActivityAsync("NotifySuccessActivity", order);
    }
}
```

Notice how linear it looks, but behind the scenes, Durable Functions manages state and retries.

Stub Activities

Note These activities are intentionally minimal stubs used to establish the orchestration shape. In later sections, they are expanded with real integration logic, retry handling, error classification, idempotency, and compensation.

Finally, let's add stubs for each activity:

Activities/PaymentActivities.cs

```
using Microsoft.Azure.Functions.Worker;
using Microsoft.Extensions.Logging;

namespace OrderProcessor;

public sealed class PaymentActivities
{
    private readonly ILogger<PaymentActivities> _logger;

    public PaymentActivities(ILogger<PaymentActivities> logger)
    {
        _logger = logger;
    }

    [Function("ProcessPaymentActivity")]
    public Task<bool> ProcessPayment([ActivityTrigger] Order order)
    {
        _logger.LogInformation("Processing payment for order {OrderId}",
        order.Id);
        return Task.FromResult(true);
```

```
    }

    [Function("RefundPaymentActivity")]
    public Task RefundPayment([ActivityTrigger] Order order)
    {
        _logger.LogInformation("Refunding payment for order {OrderId}",
        order.Id);
        return Task.CompletedTask;
    }
}
```

Activities/WarehouseActivities.cs

```
using Microsoft.Azure.Functions.Worker;
using Microsoft.Extensions.Logging;

namespace OrderProcessor;

public sealed class WarehouseActivities
{
    private readonly ILogger<WarehouseActivities> _logger;

    public WarehouseActivities(ILogger<WarehouseActivities> logger)
    {
        _logger = logger;
    }

    [Function("CheckWarehouseActivity")]
    public Task<bool> CheckWarehouse([ActivityTrigger] WarehouseRequest
    request)
    {
        _logger.LogInformation(
            "Checking warehouse {WarehouseId} for order {OrderId}",
            request.WarehouseId,
            request.Order.Id);

        return Task.FromResult(request.WarehouseId == "W2");
    }
}
```

Activities/ShippingActivities.cs

```
using Microsoft.Azure.Functions.Worker;
using Microsoft.Extensions.Logging;

namespace OrderProcessor;

public sealed class ShippingActivities
{
    private readonly ILogger<ShippingActivities> _logger;

    public ShippingActivities(ILogger<ShippingActivities> logger)
    {
        _logger = logger;
    }

    [Function("ShipOrderActivity")]
    public Task ShipOrder([ActivityTrigger] Order order)
    {
        _logger.LogInformation("Shipping order {OrderId}", order.Id);
        return Task.CompletedTask;
    }
}
```

Activities/NotificationActivities.cs

```
using Microsoft.Azure.Functions.Worker;
using Microsoft.Extensions.Logging;

namespace OrderProcessor;

public sealed class NotificationActivities
{
    private readonly ILogger<NotificationActivities> _logger;

    public NotificationActivities(ILogger<NotificationActivities> logger)
    {
        _logger = logger;
    }

    [Function("NotifyFailureActivity")]
```

```
    public Task NotifyFailure([ActivityTrigger] FailureNotice notice)
    {
        _logger.LogWarning(
            "Order {OrderId} failed: {Reason}",
            notice.Order.Id,
            notice.Reason);

        return Task.CompletedTask;
    }

    [Function("NotifySuccessActivity")]
    public Task NotifySuccess([ActivityTrigger] Order order)
    {
        _logger.LogInformation(
            "Order {OrderId} succeeded for {CustomerEmail}",
            order.Id,
            order.CustomerEmail);

        return Task.CompletedTask;
    }
}
```

Each activity is stubbed; it just logs. Later, we'll replace these stubs with real integrations: charging payments, updating Cosmos DB, and sending emails.

Lifecycle of an Orchestrated Order

The flow is now much more explicit. A `POST /orders/orchestrate` request starts the process by calling `StartOrderOrchestration`, which acts as the client function and kicks off the workflow. Control then moves to `OrderOrchestrator`, where the lifecycle is managed step by step through activities such as `ProcessPaymentActivity`, `CheckWarehouseActivity`, `ShipOrderActivity`, and `NotifySuccessActivity`. In the fan-out case, the orchestrator can start multiple `CheckWarehouseActivity` calls in parallel and then wait for the combined result before deciding whether fulfillment can continue. If payment or inventory fails at any point, the orchestrator can immediately switch to the appropriate compensating path, such as issuing a refund or sending a failure notification. Instead of relying on separate services to react correctly on their own, the workflow now has a clear coordinator that controls both the happy path and the failure path (see Figure 5-1).

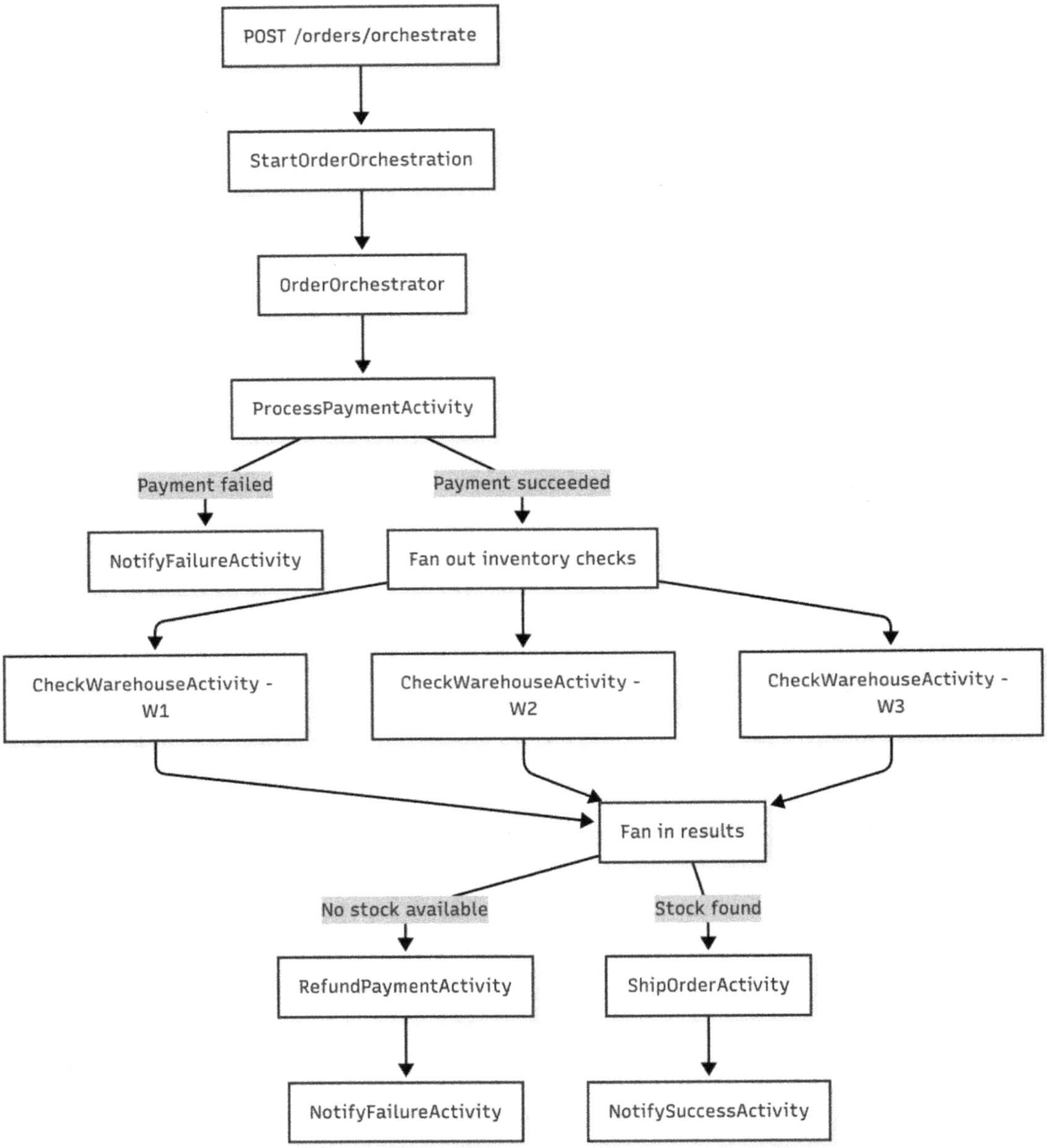

Figure 5-1. *Durable order orchestration with parallel inventory checks and compensation paths*

Fan-Out/Fan-In

So far, our orchestrator has executed activities sequentially: payment first, then inventory, then shipping. This works when each step depends strictly on the previous one. But many workflows contain steps that could run in parallel. A classic example is inventory checks. If your products are stocked in multiple warehouses, you don't want to check them one by one. You want to fan out requests to all warehouses at once, then fan in their results to decide if the order can proceed. Durable Functions makes this pattern first-class: fan-out is just launching multiple activity calls, and fan-in is waiting for them to complete with `Task.WhenAll`.

Why Fan-Out Is Important

Fan-out is important because it turns a slow, fragile workflow into one that is fast, scalable, and far more resilient under real load. If an orchestration needs to contact five independent inventory sources and it does so one after another, the total latency becomes the sum of every call, so five one-second checks quickly become a five-second delay before the workflow can move on. In contrast, a fan-out approach starts those checks in parallel, allowing the overall step to complete in roughly the time of the slowest single call rather than the sum of all of them. That reduction in end-to-end latency is often the difference between a responsive system and one that feels sluggish under pressure. Fan-out also improves scalability because each downstream activity can run independently and scale according to its own workload characteristics rather than being forced through a single sequential bottleneck. Just as importantly, it improves resilience. If one warehouse, provider, or dependency is slow or temporarily unavailable, that failure can be isolated and handled without preventing the rest of the checks from completing. For an `OrderProcessor` workflow, this is especially valuable during inventory validation, where availability may need to be checked across multiple stock locations or supplier systems at the same time. Instead of waiting on each source in turn, the orchestrator can fan out requests to all relevant inventory providers, gather the results through a fan-in step, and then make a single coordinated decision based on the combined outcome. The result is a workflow that is quicker, more fault-tolerant, and much better suited to real-world distributed processing.

Updating the Orchestrator

Let's extend OrderOrchestrator to fan out inventory checks across multiple warehouses.

Orchestrator Code

Orchestrators/OrderOrchestrator.cs

```
using Microsoft.Azure.Functions.Worker;
using Microsoft.DurableTask;
using System.Linq;

namespace OrderProcessor;

public static class OrderOrchestrator
{
    [Function("OrderOrchestrator")]
    public static async Task Run(
        [OrchestrationTrigger] TaskOrchestrationContext context)
    {
        var order = context.GetInput<Order>()
            ?? throw new InvalidOperationException("Order input is
            required.");

        var paymentOk = await context.CallActivityAsync<bool>(
            "ProcessPaymentActivity",
            order);

        if (!paymentOk)
        {
            await context.CallActivityAsync(
                "NotifyFailureActivity",
                new FailureNotice(order, "Payment failed"));

            return;
        }

        var warehouseIds = new[] { "W1", "W2", "W3" };

        var inventoryTasks = warehouseIds.Select(warehouseId =>
```

```
            context.CallActivityAsync<bool>(
                "CheckWarehouseActivity",
                new WarehouseRequest(order, warehouseId)));

        var inventoryResults = await Task.WhenAll(inventoryTasks);

        if (!inventoryResults.Any(result => result))
        {
            await context.CallActivityAsync("RefundPaymentActivi
            ty", order);

            await context.CallActivityAsync(
                "NotifyFailureActivity",
                new FailureNotice(order, "Out of stock"));

            return;
        }

        await context.CallActivityAsync("ShipOrderActivity", order);
        await context.CallActivityAsync("NotifySuccessActivity", order);
    }
}
```

Here It first fans out by starting `CheckWarehouseActivity` for every relevant warehouse rather than checking them one at a time. That means all availability checks run concurrently, which keeps the workflow fast even when several downstream systems are involved. It then fans in by awaiting all of those operations together with `Task.WhenAll`, allowing the orchestrator to gather the complete set of results before making a decision. Once all responses have been received, the workflow can evaluate the overall outcome in one place. If none of the warehouse checks succeed, the order cannot be fulfilled, so the orchestration moves into its compensation path by issuing a refund and notifying the customer that fulfillment failed. If at least one warehouse succeeds, the process can continue to the next stage with confidence that inventory has been found. This pattern is powerful because it combines speed with clear decision-making, letting the workflow act on the combined result of several independent activities without turning the orchestration into a slow sequential chain.

Supporting Types

```
public record WarehouseRequest(Order Order, string WarehouseId);
```

Activity Function

Activities/WarehouseActivities.cs

```
using Microsoft.Azure.Functions.Worker;
using Microsoft.Extensions.Logging;

namespace OrderProcessor;

public sealed class WarehouseActivities
{
    private readonly ILogger<WarehouseActivities> _logger;

    public WarehouseActivities(ILogger<WarehouseActivities> logger)
    {
        _logger = logger;
    }

    [Function("CheckWarehouseActivity")]
    public Task<bool> CheckWarehouse([ActivityTrigger] WarehouseRequest
    request)
    {
        _logger.LogInformation(
            "Checking warehouse {WarehouseId} for order {OrderId}",
            request.WarehouseId,
            request.Order.Id);

        return Task.FromResult(request.WarehouseId == "W2");
    }
}
```

Visualizing the Flow

Instead of waiting on one warehouse at a time, all checks run in parallel (see Figure 5-2).

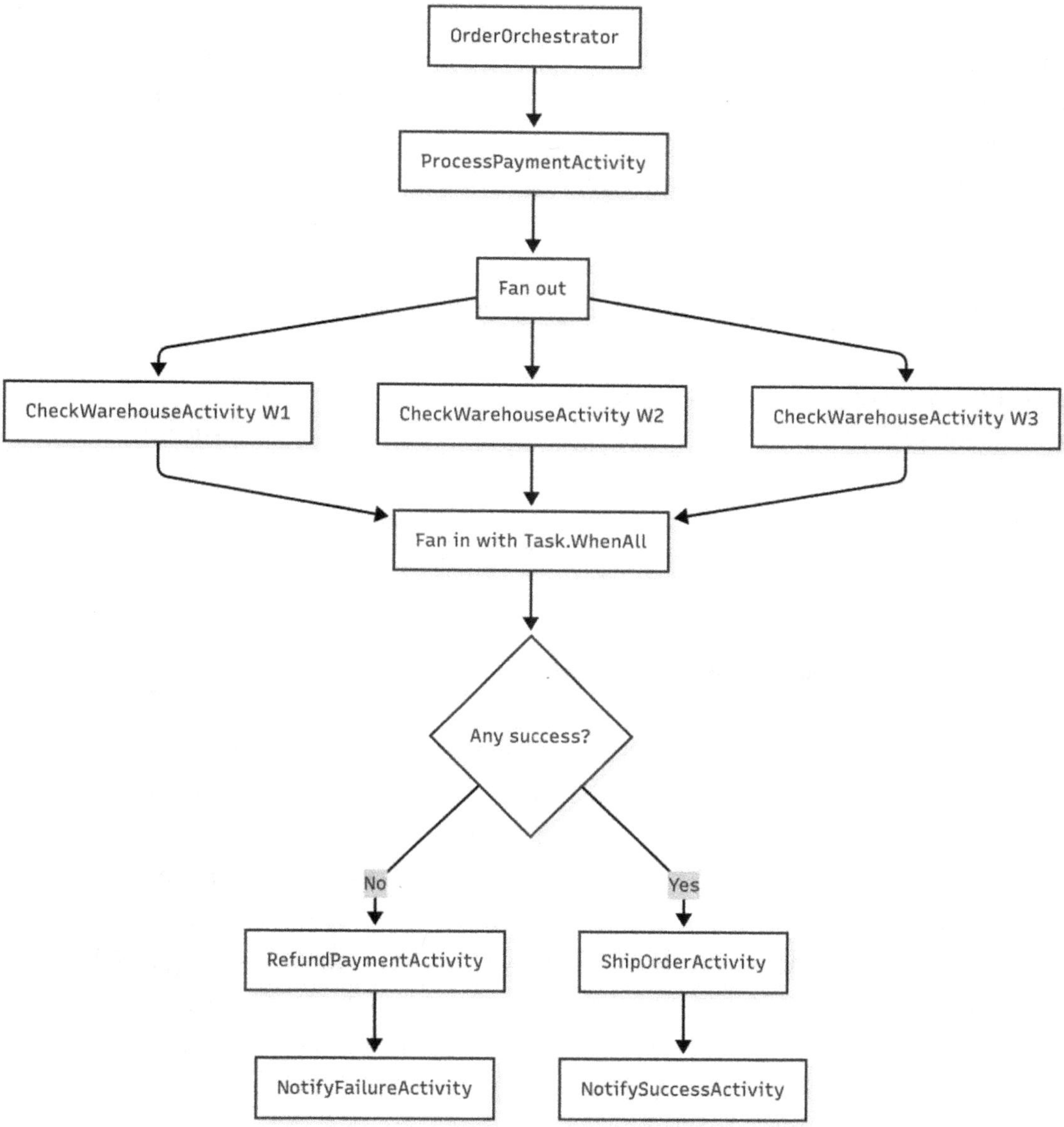

***Figure 5-2.** Fan-out/fan-in inventory checks within the order orchestration*

Deterministic Replay Considerations

Fan-out in Durable Functions is safe because it fits the orchestration model that Durable Functions was designed around. Each activity call is treated as an external operation, so the orchestrator can schedule it without executing the underlying work directly during replay, which keeps the workflow replay-safe and deterministic. When those activity tasks are later combined with `Task.WhenAll`, the pattern remains deterministic as long as the set of inputs is stable and the orchestration is not relying on non-deterministic values such as random numbers, current timestamps, or mutable in-memory state. That makes parallel execution both reliable and predictable, even when the orchestrator is replayed many times as part of Durable Functions' normal execution model. Another major advantage is scale. This pattern allows you to fan out to hundreds or even thousands of parallel activity calls, making it ideal for workloads such as checking many warehouses, processing large document sets, or coordinating many independent external operations at once. That said, fan-out is not infinite. If you try to launch millions of parallel tasks in a single orchestration, the execution history can grow so large that it puts pressure on the orchestrator's history storage and slows the workflow significantly. At that point, the issue is no longer correctness but operational scale. For very large workloads, the better approach is to combine fan-out with batching so the orchestration schedules manageable groups of work at a time rather than flooding the history table with an excessive number of entries.

Long-Running Workflows and Human Interaction

So far, our orchestrations have been short-lived, with payment, inventory checks, and shipping all completing within seconds. Real-world workflows are rarely that simple. Many business processes stretch across hours, days, or even weeks because they depend on people, documents, or decisions outside the system. A loan application may need manager approval, an insurance claim may pause until a customer uploads missing documents, and a purchase order may require several levels of sign-off before it can continue. In our `OrderProcessor`, we are about to introduce the same kind of complexity with a new rule: any order above €10,000 must be approved by a manager before payment can be processed. That changes the workflow from a short-running transaction into a long-running process. Instead of moving straight to the next activity, the orchestrator must pause, preserve its state, and wait for external input. Durable Functions supports this directly through durable timers and external events.

External Events

External events allow an orchestration to pause and wait for a signal from outside the workflow. Inside the orchestrator, you define an event name and wait for it explicitly. A separate Function, HTTP endpoint, or other external caller can then raise that event when the required action has happened. This makes external events a natural fit for human approval scenarios. Instead of polling or building custom state tracking, the orchestrator can simply pause and remain durable until a manager sends an Approved or Rejected signal.

Extending OrderOrchestrator

Let's update the orchestrator to handle approvals:

Orchestrators/OrderOrchestrator.cs

```
using Microsoft.Azure.Functions.Worker;
using Microsoft.DurableTask;

namespace OrderProcessor;

public static class OrderOrchestrator
{
    [Function("OrderOrchestrator")]
    public static async Task Run(
        [OrchestrationTrigger] TaskOrchestrationContext context)
    {
        var order = context.GetInput<Order>()
            ?? throw new InvalidOperationException("Order input is
            required.");

        if (order.TotalValue > 10_000m)
        {
            using var approvalTimeoutCts = new CancellationTokenSource();

            var timeoutTask = context.CreateTimer(
                context.CurrentDateTimeUtc.AddHours(24),
                approvalTimeoutCts.Token);

            var approvalTask = context.WaitForExternalEvent<string>("Manage
            rApproval");

            var winner = await Task.WhenAny(approvalTask, timeoutTask);

            if (winner == timeoutTask)
```

```
        {
            await context.CallActivityAsync(
                "NotifyFailureActivity",
                new FailureNotice(order, "Approval timed out"));

            return;
        }

        var decision = approvalTask.Result;

        if (!string.Equals(decision, "Approved", StringComparison.
        OrdinalIgnoreCase))
        {
            await context.CallActivityAsync(
                "NotifyFailureActivity",
                new FailureNotice(order, $"Approval rejected:
                {decision}"));

            return;
        }

        approvalTimeoutCts.Cancel();
    }

    var paymentOk = await context.CallActivityAsync<bool>(
        "ProcessPaymentActivity",
        order);

    if (!paymentOk)
    {
        await context.CallActivityAsync(
            "NotifyFailureActivity",
            new FailureNotice(order, "Payment failed"));

        return;
    }

    var warehouseIds = new[] { "W1", "W2", "W3" };

    var inventoryTasks = warehouseIds.Select(warehouseId =>
```

```
            context.CallActivityAsync<bool>(
                "CheckWarehouseActivity",
                new WarehouseRequest(order, warehouseId)));

        var inventoryResults = await Task.WhenAll(inventoryTasks);

        if (!inventoryResults.Any(result => result))
        {
            await context.CallActivityAsync("RefundPaymentActivi
            ty", order);

            await context.CallActivityAsync(
                "NotifyFailureActivity",
                new FailureNotice(order, "Out of stock"));

            return;
        }

        await context.CallActivityAsync("ShipOrderActivity", order);
        await context.CallActivityAsync("NotifySuccessActivity", order);
    }
}
```

Key additions:

- Orders > €10,000 trigger an approval step.
- The orchestrator waits for either an approval signal or a 24-hour timer.
- If no approval arrives in time, the order fails.

Raising the Approval Event

We need a Function to raise the external event when a manager decides:

Functions/ApprovalFunctions.cs

```
using System.Net;
using Microsoft.Azure.Functions.Worker;
using Microsoft.Azure.Functions.Worker.Http;
```

```
using Microsoft.DurableTask.Client;
using Microsoft.Extensions.Logging;

namespace OrderProcessor;

public sealed class ApprovalFunctions
{
    private readonly ILogger<ApprovalFunctions> _logger;

    public ApprovalFunctions(ILogger<ApprovalFunctions> logger)
    {
        _logger = logger;
    }

    [Function("RaiseApproval")]
    public async Task<HttpResponseData> Run(
        [HttpTrigger(AuthorizationLevel.Function, "post", Route = "orders/
        {instanceId}/approval/{decision}")]
        HttpRequestData req,
        string instanceId,
        string decision,
        [DurableClient] DurableTaskClient client,
        CancellationToken stopToken)
    {
        if (!string.Equals(decision, "Approved", StringComparison.
        OrdinalIgnoreCase) &&
            !string.Equals(decision, "Rejected", StringComparison.
            OrdinalIgnoreCase))
        {
            var bad = req.CreateResponse(HttpStatusCode.BadRequest);
            await bad.WriteStringAsync("Decision must be Approved or
            Rejected.", stopToken);
            return bad;
        }

        _logger.LogInformation("Raising manager approval event for
        {InstanceId} with decision {Decision}", instanceId, decision);
```

```
        await client.RaiseEventAsync(instanceId, "ManagerApproval",
        decision, cancellation: stopToken);

        var response = req.CreateResponse(HttpStatusCode.OK);
        await response.WriteStringAsync($"Approval decision '{decision}'
        sent to orchestration {instanceId}.", stopToken);
        return response;
    }
}
```

Managers can now POST to /orders/{instanceId}/approval/Approved or / Rejected.

To see this in action, start by submitting a high-value order to /orders/orchestrate. The response will return an instanceId, which identifies the running orchestration. If you do nothing after that and no approval event is raised within the allowed window, the orchestration will eventually time out, automatically follow its failure path, and call NotifyFailureActivity. For testing, you will probably want to shorten the timeout rather than wait a full 24 hours. If approval is raised before the timeout expires, for example by sending a POST request to /orders/{instanceId}/approval/Approved, the orchestrator will receive the external event, cancel the timer, and continue with the rest of the workflow.

Why This Is Important

This pattern solves a large class of real-world workflow problems. It works well when a process must wait for human approval, escalate if nobody responds, cancel stale orders after a timeout, or pause until a customer provides more information. Without Durable Functions, you usually end up polling a database, building your own scheduling logic, or stitching several moving parts together just to hold state and resume later. Durable Functions gives you those capabilities out of the box, which makes long-running workflows much easier to build, reason about, and maintain.

Error Handling and Retries in Orchestrations

In a perfect world, payment gateways would never time out, and inventory systems would always respond on the first attempt. Real systems do not behave that way. Networks drop packets, downstream services throttle requests, and transient faults are part of everyday distributed computing. The real challenge is knowing when a failure is worth retrying because it is temporary and when the workflow should stop because the problem is permanent. Durable Functions treats retries as a first-class capability, letting you apply retry policies around activity calls with exponential backoff, limits on the number of attempts, and call-level timeout control. In this section, we will separate transient failures from permanent ones and apply retry policies through TaskOptions.FromRetryPolicy(...), signal non-retryable conditions through domain exceptions, introduce compensation paths such as refunds that run only after final failure, add correlation-friendly logging for diagnosis, and keep activities idempotent so retries remain safe.

Transient vs. Permanent: Decide Before You Code

Before you add retries, you need to decide what kind of failure you are dealing with. Transient failures are temporary and may succeed on a later attempt, such as HTTP 429 throttling responses, 502, 503, or 504 gateway errors, TCP timeouts, payment gateway hiccups, or Cosmos DB rate limiting. Permanent failures are different because waiting will not change the outcome. A declined card, insufficient funds, an invalid SKU, a rejected approval, or a malformed request will still fail no matter how many times you retry. Your activities should make that distinction explicit. A common pattern is to throw a custom `TransientException` when a retry has a realistic chance of succeeding, and a custom `PermanentException` when retrying would be pointless. The orchestrator can then apply retry policies for temporary problems while using catch blocks to stop cleanly and handle permanent failures in the right way.

Retry Options in Durable Functions

Durable orchestrators can call activities with a retry policy:

Services/RetryPolicies.cs

```
using Microsoft.DurableTask;
```

```
namespace OrderProcessor;

public static class RetryPolicies
{
    public static RetryPolicy ShortBackoff(int attempts = 5) => new(
        maxNumberOfAttempts: attempts,
        firstRetryInterval: TimeSpan.FromSeconds(2),
        backoffCoefficient: 2.0,
        maxRetryInterval: TimeSpan.FromSeconds(30),
        retryTimeout: TimeSpan.FromMinutes(2));

    public static RetryPolicy ShippingBackoff(int attempts = 6) => new(
        maxNumberOfAttempts: attempts,
        firstRetryInterval: TimeSpan.FromSeconds(3),
        backoffCoefficient: 2.0,
        maxRetryInterval: TimeSpan.FromSeconds(60),
        retryTimeout: TimeSpan.FromMinutes(5));
}
```

Then:

```
var retryOptions = TaskOptions.FromRetryPolicy(RetryPolicies.
ShortBackoff());

var paymentOk = await context.CallActivityAsync<bool>(
    "ProcessPaymentActivity",
    order,
    options: retryOptions);
```

If the activity throws, Durable waits, backs off, and tries again without losing orchestration state.

Tip Use shorter retry windows for user-facing steps (perceived latency) and longer ones for background steps (batch).

Updating OrderProcessor: Exceptions and Utilities

First, define exception types shared by activities:

```
public class TransientException : Exception{
    public TransientException(string message) : base(message){}

    public TransientException(string message, Exception
inner) : base(message, inner) { }
}

public class PermanentException : Exception
{
    public PermanentException(string message) : base(message) {}
}
```

Depending on the Durable Functions version you're on, you may or may not be able to pass a Handle predicate directly. If not, simply let all errors retry and throw `PermanentException` after the final attempt (i.e., perform the classification inside the activity).

Making Activities Classify Failures

Payment: Transient vs. Permanent

Activities/PaymentActivities.cs

```
using Microsoft.Azure.Functions.Worker;
using Microsoft.Extensions.Logging;

namespace OrderProcessor;

public sealed class PaymentActivities
{
   private readonly ILogger<PaymentActivities> _logger;

   public PaymentActivities(ILogger<PaymentActivities> logger)
   {
       _logger = logger;
   }
```

```
    [Function("ProcessPaymentActivity")]
    public bool ProcessPayment([ActivityTrigger] Order order)
    {
        _logger.LogInformation("Processing payment for order {OrderId},
        value {TotalValue}", order.Id, order.TotalValue);

        var rnd = Random.Shared.Next(0, 10);

        if (rnd <= 2)
        {
            _logger.LogWarning("Transient payment failure for order
            {OrderId}, rnd={Rnd}", order.Id, rnd);
            throw new TransientException("Payment gateway timeout or
            throttling.");
        }

        if (rnd == 3)
        {
            _logger.LogWarning("Permanent payment failure for order
            {OrderId}", order.Id);
            throw new PermanentException("Card declined.");
        }

        _logger.LogInformation("Payment succeeded for order {OrderId}",
        order.Id);
        return true;
    }

    [Function("RefundPaymentActivity")]
    public Task RefundPayment([ActivityTrigger] Order order)
    {
        _logger.LogInformation("Refunding payment for order {OrderId}",
        order.Id);
        return Task.CompletedTask;
    }
}
```

A couple of details are worth calling out here. We are deliberately modeling both transient and permanent outcomes so the workflow can respond differently depending on the type of failure. When a permanent exception is thrown during a retried call, the current attempt should fail immediately and bubble back to the orchestrator rather than continuing through further retries. That matters because retrying a genuinely permanent failure just wastes time and adds noise. If your runtime does not support a Handle filter for retry control, a practical alternative is to catch `PermanentException` inside the activity and only rethrow after retry handling is complete or return a typed result that makes the failure explicit without relying entirely on exceptions.

Inventory: Mostly Transient

Activities/WarehouseActivities.cs

```
using Microsoft.Azure.Functions.Worker;
using Microsoft.Extensions.Logging;

namespace OrderProcessor;

public sealed class WarehouseActivities
{
    private readonly ILogger<WarehouseActivities> _logger;

    public WarehouseActivities(ILogger<WarehouseActivities> logger)
    {
        _logger = logger;
    }

    [Function("CheckWarehouseActivity")]
    public Task<bool> CheckWarehouse([ActivityTrigger] WarehouseRequest
    request)
    {
        _logger.LogInformation(
            "Checking warehouse {WarehouseId} for order {OrderId}",
            request.WarehouseId,
            request.Order.Id);

        if (Random.Shared.Next(0, 5) == 0)
        {
```

```
            _logger.LogWarning(
                "Transient inventory failure for warehouse {WarehouseId},
                order {OrderId}",
                request.WarehouseId,
                request.Order.Id);

            throw new TransientException("Inventory service unavailable.");
        }

        if (request.Order.Items.Count > 100)
        {
            _logger.LogWarning(
                "Permanent inventory failure for warehouse {WarehouseId},
                order {OrderId}",
                request.WarehouseId,
                request.Order.Id);

            throw new PermanentException("Out of stock.");
        }

        return Task.FromResult(request.WarehouseId == "W2");
    }
}
```

Orchestrator: Wrap with Retry and Handle Outcomes

Update `OrderOrchestrator` to use retry for both payment and inventory and compensate on final failure:

Orchestrators/OrderOrchestrator.cs

```
using Microsoft.Azure.Functions.Worker;
using Microsoft.DurableTask;

namespace OrderProcessor;

public static class OrderOrchestrator
{
   [Function("OrderOrchestrator")]
   public static async Task Run(
```

```
        [OrchestrationTrigger] TaskOrchestrationContext context)
    {
        var order = context.GetInput<Order>()
            ?? throw new InvalidOperationException("Order input is
            required.");

        var retryOptions = TaskOptions.FromRetryPolicy(RetryPolicies.
        ShortBackoff());

        bool paymentOk;

        try
        {
            paymentOk = await context.CallActivityAsync<bool>(
                "ProcessPaymentActivity",
                order,
                options: retryOptions);
        }
        catch (TaskFailedException ex) when (ex.FailureDetails?.IsCausedBy
        <PermanentException>() == true)
        {
            await context.CallActivityAsync(
                "NotifyFailureActivity",
                new FailureNotice(order, "Payment permanent failure"));

            return;
        }
        catch (TaskFailedException)
        {
            await context.CallActivityAsync(
                "NotifyFailureActivity",
                new FailureNotice(order, "Payment failed after retries"));

            return;
        }

        if (!paymentOk)
        {
```

```
    await context.CallActivityAsync(
        "NotifyFailureActivity",
        new FailureNotice(order, "Payment returned false"));

    return;
}

var warehouses = new[] { "W1", "W2", "W3" };

var inventoryTasks = warehouses.Select(warehouseId =>
    context.CallActivityAsync<bool>(
        "CheckWarehouseActivity",
        new WarehouseRequest(order, warehouseId),
        options: retryOptions));

bool anyAvailable;

try
{
    var inventoryResults = await Task.WhenAll(inventoryTasks);
    anyAvailable = inventoryResults.Any(r => r);
}
catch (TaskFailedException)
{
    await context.CallActivityAsync("RefundPaymentActivity", order);
    await context.CallActivityAsync(
        "NotifyFailureActivity",
        new FailureNotice(order, "Inventory check failed after
        retries"));

    return;
}

if (!anyAvailable)
{
    await context.CallActivityAsync("RefundPaymentActivity", order);
    await context.CallActivityAsync(
        "NotifyFailureActivity",
        new FailureNotice(order, "Out of stock"));
```

```
            return;
        }

        try
        {
            await context.CallActivityAsync(
                "ShipOrderActivity",
                order,
                options: retryOptions);
        }
        catch (TaskFailedException)
        {
            await context.CallActivityAsync("RefundPaymentActivity", order);
            await context.CallActivityAsync(
                "NotifyFailureActivity",
                new FailureNotice(order, "Shipping failed after retries"));

            return;
        }

        await context.CallActivityAsync("NotifySuccessActivity", order);
    }
}
```

There are a few important things happening here now. Each activity call is wrapped with a retry policy, so resilience is handled consistently by the Durable Functions runtime rather than by handwritten retry loops inside the orchestrator. We also make a clear distinction between a `PermanentException`, which should fail fast immediately, and a failure caused by exhausting all retry attempts, which means the system gave the operation multiple chances before giving up. Compensation only runs after that final failure point, so something like `RefundPaymentActivity` is triggered only when inventory has definitively failed after payment already succeeded. That keeps the workflow explicit and prevents compensation from running too early. For longer-running background work, such as overnight fulfillment or slower back office processing, it often makes sense to use a more patient retry policy with a `firstRetryInterval` of around ten seconds, `maxAttempts` somewhere in the 10 to 15 range, and a `MaxRetryInterval` of up to five minutes.

Idempotency: Make Retries Safe

Retries are only safe when your activities are idempotent. In practice, that means the same activity can be called more than once without causing duplicate side effects. `ProcessPaymentActivity` should use an idempotency key, such as the order ID, when calling the payment gateway so a replay does not charge the customer twice. If the gateway does not support that directly, you can store a payment status record in Cosmos DB keyed by something like `{OrderId, Operation}` and return success when the operation has already completed. `RefundPaymentActivity` should behave as a no-op when the payment has already been refunded, either by checking Cosmos DB or querying the payment provider. `ShipOrderActivity` should follow the same principle by using a shipment record keyed by order ID, so if a shipment already exists, the activity simply returns the existing tracking number instead of creating another one. This is what makes retries safe. Without idempotency, a retry can make the situation worse. With it, a retry becomes a recovery mechanism rather than a source of damage.

Surfacing Failures Clearly (Logging + Correlation)

When failures happen, logs need to help you understand the story quickly rather than force you to reconstruct it from scattered messages. That means every log entry should carry the order ID and a correlation ID, while orchestrator logs should also include the Durable Functions instance ID so the full execution can be traced end to end. It is also useful to capture retry attempt numbers, either from retry metadata or by passing an explicit counter in the activity payload when you need more control. Before the orchestrator exits on a final failure, it should emit one clear summary message describing what failed and why. A simple way to standardize that is to use a small payload such as `FailureNotice(Order Order, string Reason)` and pass it into `NotifyFailureActivity`, where the failure reason can be logged consistently and then forwarded to email, SMS, or Teams hooks if needed.

A tiny payload to standardize failure notifications:

```
public record FailureNotice(Order Order, string Reason);
```

And in

Activities/NotificationActivities.cs

```
using Microsoft.Azure.Functions.Worker;
using Microsoft.Extensions.Logging;

namespace OrderProcessor;

public sealed class NotificationActivities
{
    private readonly ILogger<NotificationActivities> _logger;

    public NotificationActivities(ILogger<NotificationActivities> logger)
    {
        _logger = logger;
    }

    [Function("NotifyFailureActivity")]
    public Task NotifyFailure([ActivityTrigger] FailureNotice notice)
    {
        _logger.LogWarning("Order {OrderId} failed: {Reason}", notice.
        Order.Id, notice.Reason);
        return Task.CompletedTask;
    }

    [Function("NotifySuccessActivity")]
    public Task NotifySuccess([ActivityTrigger] Order order)
    {
        _logger.LogInformation("Order {OrderId} succeeded for
        {CustomerEmail}", order.Id, order.CustomerEmail);
        return Task.CompletedTask;
    }
}
```

Circuit Breakers (Optional Advanced Pattern)

Retries are useful for short-lived transient faults, but they are the wrong tool when a dependency is genuinely down. In that situation, repeated retries only add pressure to an already failing system. A circuit breaker helps by stopping that retry storm at the activity boundary. The basic idea is to keep a small piece of state, for example, in Cosmos

DB or a Durable Entity, that tracks recent failures. If those failures cross a defined threshold, the circuit opens for a short period such as 60 seconds. While it is open, the activity fails fast instead of continuing to hammer the downstream service, typically by throwing a `TransientException` that works with a longer backoff policy. This gives the dependency time to recover, reduces unnecessary load, and helps protect both your own workflow and the systems it depends on.

Timeouts and Per-Try Limits

Do not let activities hang indefinitely. At the activity boundary, set explicit HTTP client timeouts, usually somewhere around five to ten seconds for downstream calls. When a timeout occurs, treat it as a `TransientException` so Durable Functions can retry according to the policy you have defined. In most cases, short timeouts combined with controlled retries are a better strategy than a single long-running request, because they recover from temporary blips more smoothly and avoid tying up threads while a dependency remains unresponsive.

Putting It All Together: The Happy, the Flaky, the Fail-Fast

When you put these pieces together, the workflow becomes resilient by default. If the payment gateway times out, the orchestrator does not fail immediately but retries the payment activity with backoff because the problem may be temporary. If the payment is declined, that is treated as a permanent failure, so the workflow stops at once and sends a failure notification rather than wasting time on pointless retries. If a warehouse endpoint flickers or becomes briefly unavailable, the orchestrator can retry the inventory check against that dependency without collapsing the whole process. If no warehouse has stock at all, the workflow follows its compensation path by refunding the payment and notifying the customer of the failure. If shipping fails because of a temporary issue, the orchestrator retries that step as well, and only after those retries are exhausted does it move to final failure handling, which may include a notification and, depending on the business rules, a refund. That is what resilient by default looks like in practice: temporary faults are absorbed, permanent failures are handled cleanly, and compensating actions run only when they are truly needed.

Sub-orchestrations and Modular Workflows

As workflows grow, a single all-knowing orchestrator quickly becomes difficult to manage. Payment rules become more involved, inventory checks fan out across multiple warehouses, and shipping starts to include carrier selection, label generation, customs declarations, and fraud checks. Before long, one orchestration file has swollen into hundreds of lines of fragile logic that is hard to read, test, and evolve. Sub-orchestrations solve that by letting you split a large workflow into smaller, composable modules. Each module is its own Durable orchestrator with dedicated activities, retry behavior, and state management. The parent orchestrator can then call these child workflows through the `CallSubOrchestrator` APIs, await their results like normal tasks, and handle success or failure with much clearer boundaries. In this section, we will look at when it makes sense to extract parts of a workflow into sub-orchestrations, build a dedicated `ShippingOrchestrator` with its own activities, call it from `OrderOrchestrator` with retries and compensation, propagate custom status and parent-child correlation IDs, and explore practical patterns for versioning, fan-out, testing, and surfacing nested progress through a simple status API.

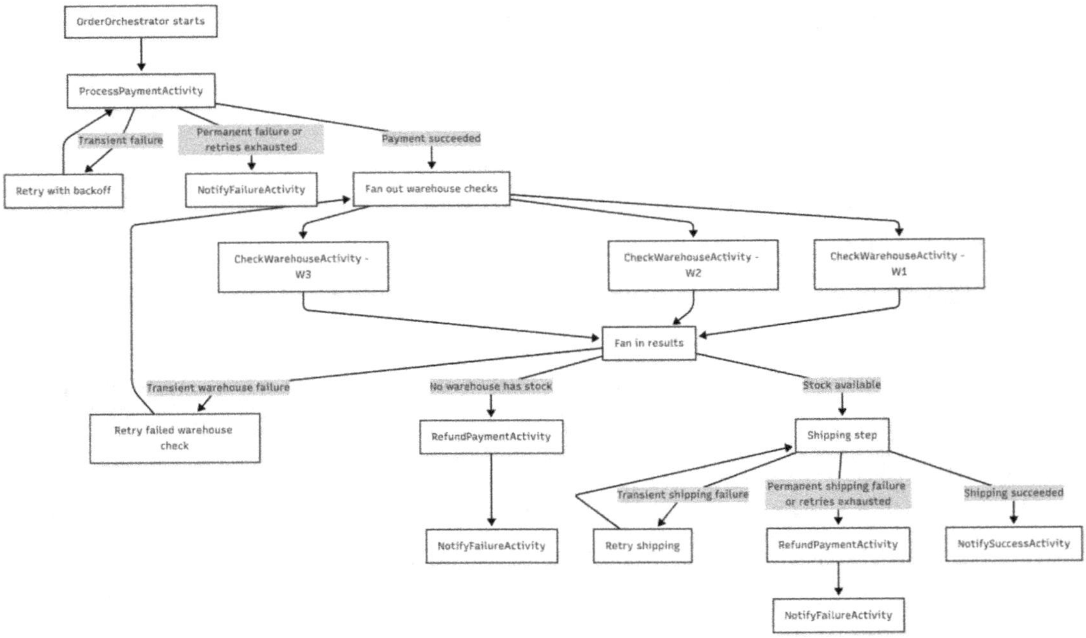

***Figure 5-3.** Order orchestration with retries, failure handling, and compensation paths*

Figure 5-3 shows retry and compensation flow in the order orchestration. Transient faults are retried with backoff, permanent failures fail fast, and compensating actions such as refunds run only after the workflow can no longer continue.

Why Sub-orchestrations?

Sub-orchestrations are useful because they let each part of the workflow evolve on its own without turning the parent process into a monolith. Payment, inventory, and shipping all have different rules, failure modes, and rates of change, so keeping each one in its own orchestrator helps preserve clear boundaries and cohesive logic. That also improves reuse, since something like `ShippingOrchestrator` can be called not only from the main order flow but also from other scenarios, such as a reshipment process. Another advantage is that each sub-orchestrator can apply retry behavior that matches its own needs, so shipping can use slower or more patient retry policies without complicating the parent workflow. Observability improves as well, because every orchestrator has its own instance ID, execution history, and custom status, which makes failures easier to trace and diagnose. On top of that, sub-orchestrations make versioning much more practical, allowing you to deploy something like `ShippingOrchestratorV2` alongside `V1`, route new work to the newer version, and let existing in-flight instances complete on the original one (see Figure 5-4).

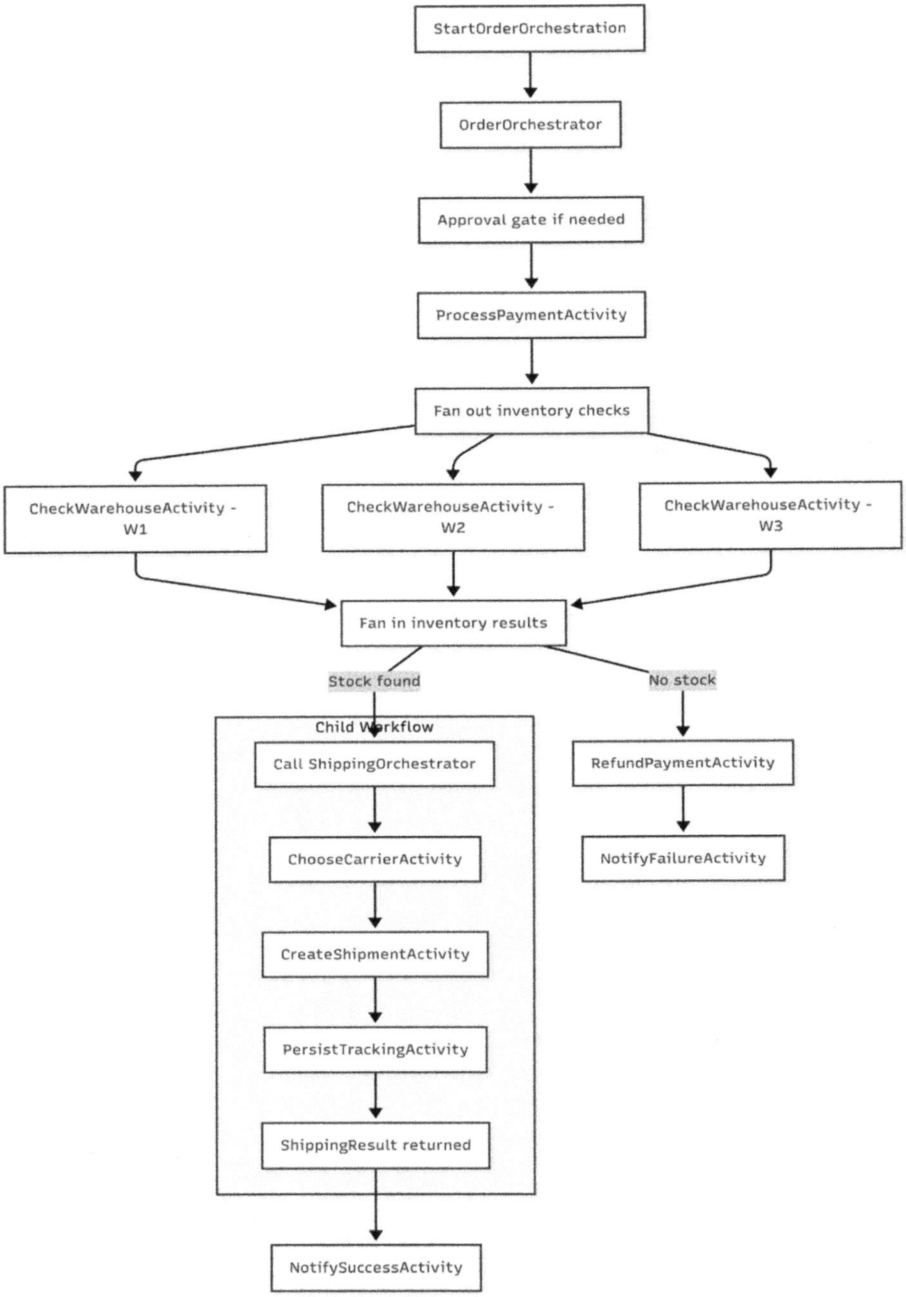

Figure 5-4. *Order Orchestration with Payment Validation, Parallel Warehouse Checks, and Compensation on Inventory Failure*

Shipping As a Sub-orchestrator

We will model shipping as its own sub-orchestrated workflow. The process begins by choosing a carrier based on rules such as order value, destination region, and required delivery speed. From there, the workflow creates the shipment by calling the carrier API, generates the shipping label, updates the order with the tracking number, and finally notifies the warehouse. Each of these steps is implemented as a separate activity, while `ShippingOrchestrator` coordinates the full sequence and handles the flow as a single shipping process.

Data Contracts

Models/ShippingRequest.cs

```
public record ShippingRequest(
Order Order,
string ServiceLevel = "Standard"); // "Express",
"Overnight", etc.
public record ShippingResult(
bool Succeeded,
string? Carrier = null,
string? TrackingNumber = null,
string? LabelUrl = null,
string? FailureReason = null);
```

Models/ShippingItem.cs

```
namespace OrderProcessor;

public sealed record ShipmentWorkItem(ShippingRequest Request,
    string Carrier);
```

Implementing ShippingOrchestrator

Orchestrators/ShippingOrchestrator.cs

```
using Microsoft.Azure.Functions.Worker;
using Microsoft.DurableTask;
```

```
namespace OrderProcessor;

public static class ShippingOrchestrator
{
    [Function("ShippingOrchestrator")]
    public static async Task<ShippingResult> Run(
        [OrchestrationTrigger] TaskOrchestrationContext context)
    {
        var request = context.GetInput<ShippingRequest>()
            ?? throw new InvalidOperationException("Shipping request is
            required.");

        context.SetCustomStatus(new
        {
            Stage = "Start",
            OrderId = request.Order.Id,
            ServiceLevel = request.ServiceLevel
        });

        var carrier = await context.CallActivityAsync<string>("ChooseCarrie
        rActivity", request);

        context.SetCustomStatus(new
        {
            Stage = "CarrierChosen",
            Carrier = carrier
        });

        var workItem = new ShipmentWorkItem(request, carrier);
        var retryOptions = TaskOptions.FromRetryPolicy(RetryPolicies.
        ShippingBackoff());

        bool created;

        try
        {
            created = await context.CallActivityAsync<bool>(
                "CreateShipmentActivity",
                workItem,
```

```
        options: retryOptions);
}
catch (TaskFailedException ex) when (ex.FailureDetails?.IsCausedBy<
PermanentException>() == true)
{
    return new ShippingResult(false, FailureReason: "Carrier
    rejected shipment.");
}
catch (TaskFailedException)
{
    return new ShippingResult(false, FailureReason: "Shipment
    creation failed after retries.");
}

if (!created)
{
    return new ShippingResult(false, FailureReason: "Carrier
    rejected shipment.");
}

context.SetCustomStatus(new
{
    Stage = "ShipmentCreated",
    Carrier = carrier
});

var labelUrl = await context.CallActivityAsync<string>("GenerateLab
elActivity", workItem);

context.SetCustomStatus(new
{
    Stage = "LabelGenerated",
    LabelUrl = labelUrl
});

var trackingNumber = await context.CallActivityAsync<string>("Assig
nTrackingActivity", workItem);
```

```
        context.SetCustomStatus(new
        {
            Stage = "TrackingAssigned",
            TrackingNumber = trackingNumber
        });

        await context.CallActivityAsync(
            "NotifyWarehouseActivity",
            new WarehouseNotification(request.Order.Id, carrier, labelUrl,
            trackingNumber));

        context.SetCustomStatus(new
        {
            Stage = "Completed",
            TrackingNumber = trackingNumber
        });

        return new ShippingResult(
            Succeeded: true,
            Carrier: carrier,
            TrackingNumber: trackingNumber,
            LabelUrl: labelUrl);
    }
}
```

We use SetCustomStatus at key milestones so progress becomes visible through the status API, giving you a clearer view of how the workflow is moving. Shipment creation also runs with its own retry policy, independent of the parent orchestrator, which allows shipping specific failures to be handled with the right level of resilience without complicating the broader order flow.

Shipping Activities (Stubs with Real Shape)

Models/WarehouseNotification.cs

```
namespace OrderProcessor;

public sealed record WarehouseNotification(
```

```
    string OrderId,
    string Carrier,
    string LabelUrl,
    string TrackingNumber);
```

Activities/ShippingActivities.cs

```
using Microsoft.Azure.Functions.Worker;
using Microsoft.Extensions.Logging;

namespace OrderProcessor;

public sealed class ShippingActivities
{
    private readonly ILogger<ShippingActivities> _logger;

    public ShippingActivities(ILogger<ShippingActivities> logger)
    {
        _logger = logger;
    }

    [Function("ChooseCarrierActivity")]
    public string ChooseCarrier([ActivityTrigger] ShippingRequest request)
    {
        var carrier = request.Order.TotalValue > 1000m ? "FastExpress" :
        "EconomyShip";

        _logger.LogInformation("Chosen carrier {Carrier} for order
        {OrderId}", carrier, request.Order.Id);
        return carrier;
    }

    [Function("CreateShipmentActivity")]
    public async Task<bool> CreateShipment([ActivityTrigger]
    ShipmentWorkItem workItem)
    {
        _logger.LogInformation(
            "Creating shipment with {Carrier} for order {OrderId}",
            workItem.Carrier,
```

```
            workItem.Request.Order.Id);

        if (Random.Shared.Next(0, 6) == 0)
        {
            throw new TransientException("Carrier API timeout.");
        }

        if (workItem.Request.Order.Items.Contains("HAZMAT", StringComparer.
        OrdinalIgnoreCase))
        {
            throw new PermanentException("Carrier rejected hazardous
            materials.");
        }

        await Task.Delay(10);
        return true;
    }

    [Function("GenerateLabelActivity")]
    public Task<string> GenerateLabel([ActivityTrigger] ShipmentWorkItem
    workItem)
    {
        var url = $"https://labels.example/{workItem.Request.Order.Id}.pdf";

        _logger.LogInformation("Generated label {LabelUrl} for order
        {OrderId}", url, workItem.Request.Order.Id);
        return Task.FromResult(url);
    }

    [Function("AssignTrackingActivity")]
    public Task<string> AssignTracking([ActivityTrigger] ShipmentWorkItem
    workItem)
    {
        var prefix = workItem.Request.Order.Id.Length >= 8
            ? workItem.Request.Order.Id[..8]
            : workItem.Request.Order.Id;

        var tracking = $"TRK-{prefix}-{Random.Shared.Next(1000, 9999)}";
```

```
        _logger.LogInformation("Assigned tracking {TrackingNumber} for order
        {OrderId}", tracking, workItem.Request.Order.Id);
        return Task.FromResult(tracking);
    }

    [Function("NotifyWarehouseActivity")]
    public Task NotifyWarehouse([ActivityTrigger] WarehouseNotification
    notification)
    {
        _logger.LogInformation(
            "Notified warehouse for order {OrderId}, carrier {Carrier},
            tracking {TrackingNumber}",
            notification.OrderId,
            notification.Carrier,
            notification.TrackingNumber);

        return Task.CompletedTask;
    }

    [Function("ShipOrderActivity")]
    public Task ShipOrder([ActivityTrigger] Order order)
    {
        _logger.LogInformation("Shipping order {OrderId}", order.Id);
        return Task.CompletedTask;
    }
}
```

Activities are idempotent-friendly: if replayed, the effects won't cause double shipments (in a real system, you'd persist "shipment created " & "tracking number " keyed by {OrderId} to guard against duplicates).

Calling the Sub-orchestrator from the Parent

Update `OrderOrchestrator` to delegate shipping:

Orchestrators/OrderOrchestrator.cs

```
using Microsoft.Azure.Functions.Worker;
using Microsoft.DurableTask;
```

```
namespace OrderProcessor;

public static class OrderOrchestrator
{
    [Function("OrderOrchestrator")]
    public static async Task Run(
        [OrchestrationTrigger] TaskOrchestrationContext context)
    {
        var order = context.GetInput<Order>()
            ?? throw new InvalidOperationException("Order input is
            required.");

        var retryOptions = TaskOptions.FromRetryPolicy(RetryPolicies.
        ShortBackoff());

        if (order.TotalValue > 10_000m)
        {
            using var approvalTimeoutCts = new CancellationTokenSource();

            var timeoutTask = context.CreateTimer(
                context.CurrentDateTimeUtc.AddHours(24),
                approvalTimeoutCts.Token);

            var approvalTask = context.WaitForExternalEvent<string>
            ("ManagerApproval");

            var winner = await Task.WhenAny(approvalTask, timeoutTask);

            if (winner == timeoutTask)
            {
                await context.CallActivityAsync(
                    "NotifyFailureActivity",
                    new FailureNotice(order, "Approval timed out"));

                return;
            }

            var decision = approvalTask.Result;

            if (!string.Equals(decision, "Approved", StringComparison.
            OrdinalIgnoreCase))
```

```
    {
        await context.CallActivityAsync(
            "NotifyFailureActivity",
            new FailureNotice(order, $"Approval rejected:
            {decision}"));

        return;
    }

    approvalTimeoutCts.Cancel();
}

bool paymentOk;

try
{
    paymentOk = await context.CallActivityAsync<bool>(
        "ProcessPaymentActivity",
        order,
        options: retryOptions);
}
catch (TaskFailedException ex) when (ex.FailureDetails?.IsCausedBy<
PermanentException>() == true)
{
    await context.CallActivityAsync(
        "NotifyFailureActivity",
        new FailureNotice(order, "Payment permanent failure"));

    return;
}
catch (TaskFailedException)
{
    await context.CallActivityAsync(
        "NotifyFailureActivity",
        new FailureNotice(order, "Payment failed after retries"));

    return;
```

```
}

if (!paymentOk)
{
    await context.CallActivityAsync(
        "NotifyFailureActivity",
        new FailureNotice(order, "Payment returned false"));

    return;
}

var warehouses = new[] { "W1", "W2", "W3" };

var inventoryTasks = warehouses.Select(warehouseId =>
    context.CallActivityAsync<bool>(
        "CheckWarehouseActivity",
        new WarehouseRequest(order, warehouseId),
        options: retryOptions));

bool anyAvailable;

try
{
    var inventoryResults = await Task.WhenAll(inventoryTasks);
    anyAvailable = inventoryResults.Any(result => result);
}
catch (TaskFailedException)
{
    await context.CallActivityAsync("RefundPaymentActivi
    ty", order);

    await context.CallActivityAsync(
        "NotifyFailureActivity",
        new FailureNotice(order, "Inventory check failed after
        retries"));

    return;
}
```

```
if (!anyAvailable)
{
    await context.CallActivityAsync("RefundPaymentActivi
    ty", order);

    await context.CallActivityAsync(
        "NotifyFailureActivity",
        new FailureNotice(order, "Out of stock"));

    return;
}

var shippingRequest = new ShippingRequest(order, "Standard");

ShippingResult shipping;

try
{
    shipping = await context.CallSubOrchestratorAsync<Shippi
    ngResult>(
        "ShippingOrchestrator",
        shippingRequest);
}
catch (TaskFailedException ex)
{
    var reason = ex.FailureDetails?.ErrorMessage ?? "Unknown
    shipping failure";

    await context.CallActivityAsync("RefundPaymentActivi
    ty", order);

    await context.CallActivityAsync(
        "NotifyFailureActivity",
        new FailureNotice(order, $"Shipping failed: {reason}"));

    return;
}

if (!shipping.Succeeded)
```

```
        {
            await context.CallActivityAsync("RefundPaymentActivi
            ty", order);

            await context.CallActivityAsync(
                "NotifyFailureActivity",
                new FailureNotice(order, $"Shipping failed: {shipping.
                FailureReason}"));

            return;
        }

        await context.CallActivityAsync(
            "PersistTrackingActivity",
            new PersistTrackingRequest(
                order.Id,
                order.CustomerEmail,
                shipping.TrackingNumber!,
                shipping.Carrier!,
                shipping.LabelUrl!));

        await context.CallActivityAsync("NotifySuccessActivity", order);
    }
}
```

Persisting Tracking (Activity)

Models/PersistTrackingRequest.cs

```
namespace OrderProcessor;

public sealed record PersistTrackingRequest(
   string Id,
   string CustomerEmail,
   string TrackingNumber,
   string Carrier,
   string LabelUrl);
```

Activities/OrderPersistenceActivities.cs

```
using Microsoft.Azure.Cosmos;
using Microsoft.Azure.Functions.Worker;
using Microsoft.Extensions.Logging;

namespace OrderProcessor;

public sealed class OrderPersistenceActivities
{
    private readonly CosmosClient _client;
    private readonly ILogger<OrderPersistenceActivities> _logger;

    public OrderPersistenceActivities(
        CosmosClient client,
        ILogger<OrderPersistenceActivities> logger)
    {
        _client = client;
        _logger = logger;
    }

    [Function("PersistTrackingActivity")]
    public async Task PersistTracking([ActivityTrigger]
    PersistTrackingRequest request)
    {
        var container = _client.GetContainer("OrderDb", "Orders");

        var response = await container.ReadItemAsync<Order>(
            request.Id,
            new PartitionKey(request.CustomerEmail));

        var document = response.Resource;
        document.TrackingNumber = request.TrackingNumber;
        document.Carrier = request.Carrier;
        document.LabelUrl = request.LabelUrl;

        await container.UpsertItemAsync(
            document,
            new PartitionKey(request.CustomerEmail));

        _logger.LogInformation(
```

```
            "Persisted tracking {TrackingNumber} for order {OrderId}",
            request.TrackingNumber,
            request.Id);
    }
}
```

Observability: Parent/Child IDs and Custom Status

Observability becomes much stronger once you start breaking workflows into parent and child orchestrations. Every orchestration instance has its own instance ID, and when a parent starts a sub-orchestrator, Durable Functions creates a child instance with its own ID as well. By default that child ID is derived from the parent relationship, although you can supply a custom ID when you need more control. This gives you two useful levels of visibility. You can inspect the parent orchestration to understand the overall order lifecycle, and you can inspect the child orchestration separately to see the progress of a specific part of the workflow, such as shipping. When combined with `SetCustomStatus`, this makes it much easier to expose meaningful progress information instead of treating the whole workflow as a black box.

Status API (HTTP) for Any Instance

Functions/OrchestrationStatusApi.cs

```
using System.Net;
using Microsoft.Azure.Functions.Worker;
using Microsoft.Azure.Functions.Worker.Http;
using Microsoft.DurableTask.Client;

namespace OrderProcessor;

public sealed class OrchestrationStatusApi
{
    [Function("GetOrchestrationStatus")]
    public async Task<HttpResponseData> Run(
        [HttpTrigger(AuthorizationLevel.Function, "get", Route =
        "orchestrations/{instanceId}")]
```

```
        HttpRequestData req, string instanceId,
        [DurableClient] DurableTaskClient client)
    {
        var status = await client.GetInstanceAsync(instanceId,
        getInputsAndOutputs: true);

        if (status is null)
        {
            var notFound = req.CreateResponse(HttpStatusCode.NotFound);
            await notFound.WriteStringAsync($"No orchestration found for
            instance ID '{instanceId}'.");
            return notFound;
        }

        var response = req.CreateResponse(HttpStatusCode.OK);

        await response.WriteAsJsonAsync(new
        {
            status.RuntimeStatus,
            status.CreatedTime,
            status.LastUpdatedTime,
            status.CustomStatus,
            status.Input,
            status.Output
        });

        return response;
    }
}
```

If you log the child instance ID from `ShippingOrchestrator` (e.g., via an activity or by generating it yourself and using `CallSubOrchestratorAsync<T>(name, instanceId, input)`), you can fetch its status separately to see fine-grained shipping stages.

Versioning and Evolution

Sub-orchestrations are especially useful when workflows need to evolve over time. Because each one has a narrower responsibility, you can version and replace them more safely than a single large orchestration. For example, you might deploy a new ShippingOrchestratorV2 with an improved carrier selection algorithm, then route only new orders to that version behind a feature flag or configuration switch. Existing V1 instances can continue running to completion without disruption because Durable Functions preserves their execution history and determinism. That gives you a practical way to roll forward workflow changes gradually, reduce migration risk, and evolve complex processes without breaking in flight orchestrations.

```
var shippingName = useV2 ? "ShippingOrchestratorV2" :
"ShippingOrchestrator";

shipping = await
context.CallSubOrchestratorAsync<ShippingResult>(shippingName,
shipRequest);
```

No big bang migrations, no breaking replay.

Fan-Out of Sub-orchestrations (Advanced)

Need to split a massive order into line-level shipments across regions? Launch multiple child orchestrators in parallel:

```
var childTasks = order.Items
.GroupBy(i => RegionFor(i))
.Select(group =>
{
    var childReq = new ShippingRequest(order with { Items =
    group.ToList()
}, "Standard");var childId = $"{context.InstanceId}:ship:{group.Key}";
return
context.CallSubOrchestratorAsync<ShippingResult>("ShippingOrchestrator",
childId, childReq);
});
var childResults = await Task.WhenAll(childTasks);
```

This composes naturally with Durable's fan-in, aggregates child results, then finalizes.

Testing Sub-orchestrations

Testing sub-orchestrations becomes much more manageable when you treat each layer separately. Activities can be unit tested directly without involving the Durable runtime at all, which keeps those tests fast and focused. Orchestrator tests can then concentrate on workflow behavior, either by using Durable Functions testing helpers or by writing thin behavioral tests with stubbed activities and asserting that the correct branches are taken. Integration tests should cover the full end-to-end path by starting an orchestration over HTTP, polling its status until it reaches Completed or Failed, and then verifying outputs and side effects such as Cosmos DB documents, emitted logs, or notifications. Because sub-orchestrators each handle a smaller and more focused part of the overall workflow, the tests around them are usually easier to write, easier to understand, and much faster to diagnose when something breaks.

Error Handling and Compensation Recap

A few rules keep error handling clean here. If `ShippingOrchestrator` throws a `PermanentException`, for example, because a HAZMAT shipment is rejected, the parent orchestrator should treat that as a final business failure and take responsibility for compensation, such as issuing a refund and notifying the customer. If the child workflow hits transient faults instead, its own activities should retry according to the retry policy defined within that shipping orchestration without forcing the parent to manage those temporary blips directly. As always, the shipping activities themselves must remain idempotent, especially around tracking assignment and label generation, so that retries do not create duplicate shipments or inconsistent downstream states.

Durable Entities for State

Not all states need to live in a database. Sometimes what you really need is a small, strongly consistent piece of state that many workflows can update safely without worrying about race conditions. Using Cosmos DB for every tiny increment adds latency and RU cost, and you still have to deal with optimistic concurrency on top. Durable

Entities give you a different option: an in-process, durable, single-threaded state tied to a logical key. You can think of an entity as a small durable object identified by an ID, with operations that can be called from orchestrations, activities, or HTTP endpoints. Because the Durable runtime guarantees serial access for each entity key, they work well for things like per customer spend totals, credit limits, rate limits, idempotency guards, loyalty points, and other lightweight aggregates. In this section, we will add a `CustomerEntity` to the `OrderProcessor` project to track total spend, a configurable credit limit, loyalty points, a sliding window of recent orders for rate limiting, and a set of processed order IDs for idempotency. We will then integrate that entity into the orchestration so each order can check policy before payment and update spend and points after success, all without double counting during retries or compensation flows.

What Durable Entities Are (and Aren't)

Durable Entities are durable, single-threaded state machines identified by an `EntityId`, typically a combination of a name and key, that expose operations you can call like methods. The Durable runtime rehydrates their state when needed, serializes access for that specific key, and persists changes automatically, which makes them very useful for small coordination heavy state. What they are not is a general-purpose cache or a replacement for a real database. Entities work best when the state is small, the decisions need to be fast, and multiple workflows need a safe coordination point. Large datasets, rich queries, reporting, and long-term storage still belong in Cosmos DB or SQL. They are a good fit when you need atomic increments or decisions, such as approving an order only if a limit has not been exceeded; when you need low latency coordination across concurrent orchestrations; or when you want to avoid building custom concurrency control in a database just to manage a small amount of shared state.

Designing CustomerEntity

We will key `CustomerEntity` by customer email, which aligns neatly with the Cosmos DB partition key already used elsewhere in the system. The entity will hold a small but important set of customer-level state: `TotalSpend`, `CreditLimit`, `LoyaltyPoints`, a `RecentOrders` queue for sliding window rate limiting, a `ProcessedOrderIds` set for idempotency, and an `UpdatedUtc` timestamp for auditing. On top of that state, the entity will expose a focused set of operations. `CanPlace(amount, orderId)` acts as an idempotent gate that checks both rate limits and credit limits before an order is allowed to proceed. `RecordSuccess(amount, orderId)` updates spend and loyalty totals and remembers that the order has already been applied. `Compensate(amount, orderId)` reverses those changes when a previously recorded order needs to be rolled back. `SetCreditLimit(limit)` gives operations or admin workflows a way to adjust customer limits, while `Get()` returns the current snapshot of the entity state.

Entity Implementation

Works with the Durable Task extension for .NET isolated. The signatures here match the isolated worker style you've used so far.

Entities/CustomerEntity.cs

```
using Microsoft.Azure.Functions.Worker;
using Microsoft.DurableTask.Entities;

namespace OrderProcessor;

public sealed record CustomerSnapshot(
    string CustomerEmail,
    decimal TotalSpend,
    decimal CreditLimit,
    int LoyaltyPoints,
    int OrdersLastHour,
    DateTime UpdatedUtc);

public sealed record CanPlaceOrderRequest(
    decimal Amount,
    string OrderId,
    DateTime NowUtc);

public sealed record RecordOrderRequest(
    decimal Amount,
    string OrderId,
    DateTime NowUtc);

public sealed class CustomerState
{
```

```
    public decimal TotalSpend { get; set; }
    public decimal CreditLimit { get; set; } = 20_000m;
    public int LoyaltyPoints { get; set; }
    public Queue<DateTime> RecentOrdersUtc { get; set; } = new();
    public HashSet<string> ProcessedOrderIds { get; set; } = new();
    public DateTime UpdatedUtc { get; set; } = DateTime.UtcNow;

    public void TrimOldOrders(DateTime nowUtc)
    {
        var threshold = nowUtc.AddHours(-1);

        while (RecentOrdersUtc.Count > 0 && RecentOrdersUtc.Peek() <
        threshold)
        {
            RecentOrdersUtc.Dequeue();
        }
    }
}

public sealed class CustomerEntity : TaskEntity<CustomerState>
{
    public CustomerSnapshot Get()
    {
        var nowUtc = DateTime.UtcNow;
        State.TrimOldOrders(nowUtc);

        return new CustomerSnapshot(
            CustomerEmail: Context.Id.Key,
            TotalSpend: State.TotalSpend,
            CreditLimit: State.CreditLimit,
            LoyaltyPoints: State.LoyaltyPoints,
            OrdersLastHour: State.RecentOrdersUtc.Count,
            UpdatedUtc: State.UpdatedUtc);
    }

    public void SetCreditLimit(decimal limit)
    {
        State.CreditLimit = limit;
```

```
    State.UpdatedUtc = DateTime.UtcNow;
}

public bool CanPlace(CanPlaceOrderRequest request)
{
    State.TrimOldOrders(request.NowUtc);

    if (State.ProcessedOrderIds.Contains(request.OrderId))
    {
        return true;
    }

    var projectedSpend = State.TotalSpend + request.Amount;
    var underRateLimit = State.RecentOrdersUtc.Count < 5;
    var underCreditLimit = projectedSpend <= State.CreditLimit;

    return underRateLimit && underCreditLimit;
}

public void RecordSuccess(RecordOrderRequest request)
{
    if (State.ProcessedOrderIds.Contains(request.OrderId))
    {
        return;
    }

    State.TotalSpend += request.Amount;
    State.LoyaltyPoints += CalculatePoints(request.Amount);
    State.ProcessedOrderIds.Add(request.OrderId);
    State.RecentOrdersUtc.Enqueue(request.NowUtc);
    State.TrimOldOrders(request.NowUtc);
    State.UpdatedUtc = request.NowUtc;
}

public void Compensate(RecordOrderRequest request)
{
    if (!State.ProcessedOrderIds.Contains(request.OrderId))
    {
        return;
```

```
        }

        State.TotalSpend = Math.Max(0, State.TotalSpend - request.Amount);
        State.LoyaltyPoints = Math.Max(0, State.LoyaltyPoints -
        CalculatePoints(request.Amount));
        State.ProcessedOrderIds.Remove(request.OrderId);
        State.UpdatedUtc = request.NowUtc;
    }

    [Function(nameof(CustomerEntity))]
    public Task Run([EntityTrigger] TaskEntityDispatcher dispatcher)
    {
        return dispatcher.DispatchAsync(this);
    }

private static int CalculatePoints(decimal amount)
        => (int)Math.Floor(amount / 10m);
}
```

Why this works well

- Each customer's entity is single-threaded: no races on spend/points.
- Idempotency is built in via `ProcessedOrderIds`.
- Rate limiting is a quick in-memory trim of last-hour timestamps.

Calling the Entity from the Orchestrator

Rather than replacing the final parent orchestration from the section "Sub-orchestrations and Modular Workflows," this snippet shows how that existing workflow can be extended with a policy gate backed by a Durable Entity. Before charging the customer, the orchestrator asks the entity whether the order can proceed. After a successful charge, it records the spend and awards points. If a later step such as inventory or shipping fails and the order is refunded, the workflow should also compensate the entity so the customer summary remains correct.

Orchestrators/OrderOrchestrator.cs

```
using Microsoft.Azure.Functions.Worker;
using Microsoft.DurableTask;
using Microsoft.DurableTask.Entities;

namespace OrderProcessor;

public static class OrderOrchestrator
{
    [Function("OrderOrchestrator")]
    public static async Task Run(
        [OrchestrationTrigger] TaskOrchestrationContext context)
    {
        var order = context.GetInput<Order>()
            ?? throw new InvalidOperationException("Order input is
            required.");

        var entityId = new EntityInstanceId(nameof(CustomerEntity), order.
        CustomerEmail);

        var allowed = await context.Entities.CallEntityAsync<bool>(
            entityId,
            "CanPlace",
            new CanPlaceOrderRequest(order.TotalValue, order.Id, context.
            CurrentDateTimeUtc));

        if (!allowed)
        {
            await context.CallActivityAsync(
                "NotifyFailureActivity",
                new FailureNotice(order, "Rejected by customer policy
                (limit or rate)"));

            return;
        }

        var retryOptions = TaskOptions.FromRetryPolicy(RetryPolicies.
        ShortBackoff());
```

```
        bool paymentOk;

        try
        {
            paymentOk = await context.CallActivityAsync<bool>(
                "ProcessPaymentActivity",
                order,
                options: retryOptions);
        }
        catch
        {
            await context.CallActivityAsync(
                "NotifyFailureActivity",
                new FailureNotice(order, "Payment failed after retries"));

            return;
        }

        if (!paymentOk)
        {
            await context.CallActivityAsync(
                "NotifyFailureActivity",
                new FailureNotice(order, "Payment declined"));

            return;
        }

        await context.Entities.SignalEntityAsync(entityId, "RecordSuccess",
        new RecordOrderRequest(order.TotalValue, order.Id, context.Current
        DateTimeUtc));

// Continue with inventory fan-out and shipping steps here.
// If a later step fails after payment succeeded, compensate the entity
   as well:
// await context.Entities.SignalEntityAsync(
// entityId,
// "Compensate",
```

```
// new RecordOrderRequest(order.TotalValue, order.Id, context.
   CurrentDateTimeUtc));
// await context.CallActivityAsync("RefundPaymentActivity", order);

            await context.CallActivityAsync("NotifySuccessActivity", order);
        }
}
```

A few design choices matter here. We use `CallEntityAsync` for `CanPlace` because that is a request-response decision, and the orchestrator needs the answer immediately before it can continue. For follow-up actions such as `RecordSuccess` and Compensate, we use `SignalEntityAsync` instead because those updates do not need to block the workflow and can be applied asynchronously while still being serialized and persisted by the entity runtime. This separation keeps the orchestration responsive without sacrificing correctness. It also matters for compensation: if shipping or inventory fails after payment has already succeeded, the workflow should both refund the payment and compensate the entity so that spend totals, loyalty points, and policy counters stay accurate.

Admin/Ops HTTP Endpoints (Optional)

Allow ops to adjust credit limit or check a customer summary:

Functions/CustomerEntityApi.cs

```
using System.Net;
using Microsoft.Azure.Functions.Worker;
using Microsoft.Azure.Functions.Worker.Http;
using Microsoft.DurableTask.Client;
using Microsoft.DurableTask.Entities;

namespace OrderProcessor;

public sealed class CustomerEntityApi
{
    [Function("GetCustomerPolicy")]
    public async Task<HttpResponseData> Get(
        [HttpTrigger(AuthorizationLevel.Anonymous, "get", Route =
        "customers/{email}/policy")]
```

```
        HttpRequestData req,
        string email,
        [DurableClient] DurableTaskClient client)
    {
        var entityId = new EntityInstanceId(nameof(CustomerEntity), email);
        var state = await client.Entities.ReadEntityStateAsync<CustomerSnap
        shot>(entityId);

        if (!state.EntityExists)
        {
            var notFound = req.CreateResponse(HttpStatusCode.NotFound);
            await notFound.WriteStringAsync($"No customer policy found for
            '{email}'.");
            return notFound;
        }

        var response = req.CreateResponse(HttpStatusCode.OK);
        await response.WriteAsJsonAsync(state.EntityState);
        return response;
    }

    [Function("SetCustomerCreditLimit")]
    public async Task<HttpResponseData> SetLimit(
        [HttpTrigger(AuthorizationLevel.Anonymous, "post", Route =
        "customers/{email}/limit/{amount:decimal}")]
        HttpRequestData req,
        string email,
        decimal amount,
        [DurableClient] DurableTaskClient client)
    {
        var entityId = new EntityInstanceId(nameof(CustomerEntity), email);

        await client.Entities.SignalEntityAsync(entityId, "SetCreditLimit",
        amount);

        var response = req.CreateResponse(HttpStatusCode.Accepted);
```

```
        await response.WriteStringAsync($"Limit update signaled for
        {email}: {amount:N2}");
        return response;
    }
}
```

Entities vs. Cosmos DB: When to Choose What

Durable Entities and Cosmos DB solve different problems, and most real systems benefit from using both. Entities are best when you need to manage a very small amount of highly contended state with atomic updates and low latency. They give you a natural coordination point for a single key, such as a customer, tenant, or SKU, but they are limited to key-based access and are not designed for ad hoc querying. Cosmos DB is the better fit for persistent records, larger documents, reporting, analytics, and CQRS-style projections. It gives you flexible storage and query capabilities, but concurrency is handled through optimistic techniques such as ETags rather than the single-threaded execution model that entities provide. A practical pattern is to keep orders, events, and read models in Cosmos DB while using entities for hot path decisions such as limits, counters, throttling, and idempotency checks.

Idempotency and Retries (Crucial with Orchestrations)

Idempotency matters even more once orchestrations begin retrying automatically, because the same logical step may be executed more than once. To prevent spend, points, or policy counters from being applied twice, we introduced `ProcessedOrderIds` as a simple but effective guard. `RecordSuccess` first checks whether the order has already been recorded and only applies its updates once, while Compensate only reverses state when that order was previously applied in the first place. That makes the entity safe under retries and reliable during compensation, which is exactly what you need in a workflow that may pause, resume, and replay over time.

The full order workflow has now evolved well beyond a simple sequence of function calls. What began as a basic orchestrator now brings together policy checks, approval gates, retry handling, parallel inventory validation, compensation paths, shipping sub-orchestrations, and final persistence into a single coordinated flow. Figure 5-5 shows how these pieces fit together end-to-end in the finished `OrderProcessor` design.

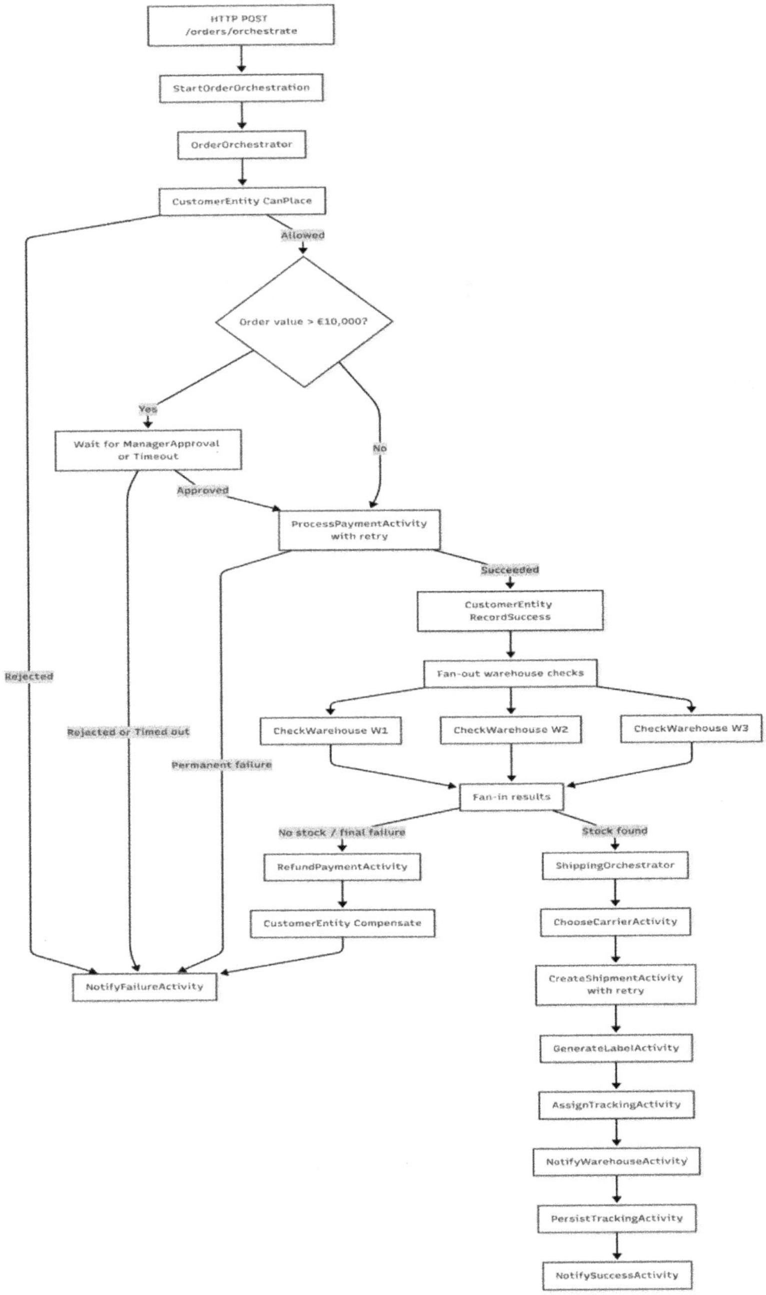

Figure 5-5. *End-to-End Durable Functions Workflow*

EXERCISES

1. **Sketch the Workflow**: Draw your own diagram of the order lifecycle. Which steps must happen sequentially? Which can run in parallel?
2. **Failure Analysis**: Suppose payment fails after inventory is reserved. How should the orchestrator handle it? Write pseudocode.
3. **Approval Scenario**: Add a step for manager approval if the order value is greater than €10,000. Where would it fit?
4. **Reflection**: What visibility benefits does orchestration bring to debugging distributed workflows?
5. **Run the Orchestrator**: Submit a new order via `/orders/orchestrate`. Check the logs. Do you see each activity fire in sequence?
6. **Simulate Failure**: Change `ProcessPaymentActivity` to return false. Does the orchestrator skip to `NotifyFailureActivity`?
7. **Determinism Test:** Try adding `DateTime.UtcNow` inside the orchestrator. What error do you get? Replace it with `context.CurrentUtcDateTime`.
8. **Parallel Logs**: Run `/orders/orchestrate` and check logs. Do you see warehouse checks for W1, W2, and W3 logged almost simultaneously?
9. **Scale Test**: Add 10 warehouses to the list. Does performance change compared to 3?
10. **Approval Timeout**: Reduce the timeout to 1 minute for testing. Submit a high-value order and do nothing. What happens?
11. **Rejection Path**: Submit an order and `POST /Rejected`. Does the orchestrator stop?
12. **Tune Payment Retries**: Change the payment retry policy to `first=1s`, `attempts=6`, `MaxRetryInterval=20s`. Force a few runs until you see at least one retry. How long did the end-to-end flow take?
13. **Permanent vs. Transient**: Make `ProcessPaymentActivity` throw `PermanentException` for orders ending with "9". Verify the orchestrator does not retry and immediately notifies failure.

14. **Idempotent Refund**: Call `RefundPaymentActivity` twice. Ensure it behaves as a no-op the second time.
15. **Wire It Up**: Call `/orders/orchestrate` and watch the logs. Identify the parent instance ID and the shipping child instance ID.
16. **Custom Status Drill-Down**: Hit `/api/orchestrations/{childInstanceId}` while shipping is in progress. Do you see stages such as `CarrierChosen` and `ShipmentCreated` over time?
17. **Version Switch**: Duplicate the shipping orchestrator as `ShippingOrchestratorV2`, add a feature flag, and route to V2. Prove both versions can run in parallel.
18. **Rate-Limit Test**: Submit 6 orders within a minute for the same customer through `/orders/orchestrate`. Confirm the sixth is rejected by `CanPlace`.
19. **Compensation Path**: Make inventory fail after payment. Ensure the parent orchestrator signals compensate and calls `RefundPaymentActivity`. Verify the entity's `TotalSpend` returns to the pre-order value.
20. **Idempotency Under Retries**: Force `ProcessPaymentActivity` to throw a transient error twice, then succeed. Confirm `RecordSuccess` is applied once and `ProcessedOrderIds` contains the order ID.

Summary

This chapter shows the move from loosely coordinated, event-driven behavior to explicit, stateful orchestration with Durable Functions. It starts by establishing why choreography alone breaks down once workflows need sequencing, compensation, timeouts, human approval, and clear visibility. From there, it introduces the core Durable Functions model, orchestrators, activities, and durable clients and uses `OrderProcessor` to show how an order lifecycle can be expressed as a central workflow rather than a scattered set of reactions.

The chapter then expands that foundation into real distributed systems patterns. It introduces fan-out and fan-in to parallelize warehouse checks, durable timers and external events to support long-running approvals, and retry policies to distinguish between transient faults and permanent business failures. It also stresses the importance of idempotency, compensation, and correlation-friendly logging so that retries remain safe and failures stay diagnosable. The result is an orchestration model that is not only more reliable but also much easier to reason about under load and failure.

Finally, the chapter shows how to keep workflows maintainable as they grow. Shipping is extracted into a sub-orchestrator with its own retries, custom status, and versioning path, while Durable Entities are added to manage customer policy state such as credit limits, rate limits, spend totals, loyalty points, and idempotency guards. Together, these patterns turn `OrderProcessor` into a much more production-ready system, one that can coordinate complex workflows, evolve safely over time, and combine Cosmos DB, messaging, orchestration, and entities into a coherent serverless architecture.

So far, `OrderProcessor` has focused on orchestration inside a controlled environment. We introduced durable workflows, compensation, retries, human approval, sub-orchestrations, and entity-backed policy checks, all within boundaries we largely control. That gave us a clear view of how Durable Functions coordinate state, time, and failure without the added complexity of external dependencies.

In the next chapter, that changes. We will begin integrating with systems outside the workflow itself, including external APIs, partner services, and long-running external processes. Those integrations introduce new concerns such as latency, rate limits, authentication, and partial failure, and they require us to apply the orchestration patterns from this chapter in less predictable environments.

Chapter 6 takes `OrderProcessor` into that next stage. We will look at how orchestrations interact safely with external systems while remaining deterministic, resilient, and observable. This is where the workflow begins to move from a structured internal process toward a more realistic distributed application.

CHAPTER 6

Integrating with External Systems

OrderProcessor has so far operated within boundaries we largely control. Orders are accepted, state is persisted, workflows are orchestrated, and failures are handled inside a predictable serverless environment. Real systems are rarely that contained. They depend on external APIs, partner platforms, human approvals, legacy applications, and specialist services that introduce new forms of latency, failure, cost, and uncertainty.

This chapter explores how to integrate with those external systems without losing the reliability benefits of orchestration. We will use Durable Functions to model outbound API calls, long-running callbacks, human interaction, and hybrid workflows that span serverless components, microservices, and monoliths. Along the way, we will focus on the patterns that matter most in production, including retries, idempotency, compensation, observability, and resilience at scale.

Integrating with External APIs

Until now, the OrderProcessor system has behaved as a closed loop. It processes orders, validates inventory, charges payments through a stubbed implementation, ships goods, and sends notifications. That model is useful for learning the mechanics of orchestration, but real systems do not live in isolation. In production, distributed applications almost always depend on external services such as payment providers, fraud detection platforms, tax calculation APIs, ERP systems, and email or SMS gateways.

The moment an orchestration crosses a boundary into an external API, the reliability model changes. You no longer control the uptime of the dependency, its latency profile, or the rate limits it may enforce. External contracts can also evolve over time, with new

© Patrick Kearns 2026
P. Kearns, *Serverless Distributed Systems in Modern .NET and Azure*,
https://doi.org/10.1007/979-8-8688-2839-3_6

API versions, changed response fields, and different authentication requirements. Security becomes more important as well, because access tokens expire, TLS must be enforced, and sensitive customer or financial data must be handled carefully.

There is also a financial and operational cost to consider. Some external services charge per request, which means retries are not always free. A badly designed retry policy can increase both spend and risk. Idempotency becomes critical too, because the system must be able to retry safely without double-charging a payment card, submitting the same order twice, or registering a shipment more than once. These are not edge cases. They are normal concerns in any serious distributed workflow.

In this section, we will look at how Durable Functions orchestrations can interact with external APIs in a safe and controlled way. To make this concrete, we will extend `OrderProcessor` with a `FraudCheck` step that calls an external REST API before payment is attempted. This reflects a common business rule in domains such as e-commerce and insurance: do not accept or progress an order until an external fraud service has approved it.

Why Orchestrations Help with APIs

In Chapter 5, we saw how orchestrations handle retries and compensations for internal activities. Those same principles still apply when working with external APIs, but the need for discipline is even greater because these dependencies sit outside your control. External services can be slow, unavailable, rate-limited, or inconsistent, so the orchestration layer needs to protect the wider workflow from those failures.

One of the most important rules is determinism. An orchestrator must never call an external API directly, because replaying the orchestration would repeat the call and could produce unintended side effects. Instead, all API communication should be pushed into activity functions. That keeps the orchestrator deterministic while still allowing the workflow to interact with the outside world safely.

Retries also become far more important with external dependencies. Transient failures are common, so applying `TaskOptions.FromRetryPolicy(...)` to activity calls is usually the right default for API-facing work. Timeouts should also remain short. It is generally better to fail fast after five to ten seconds and retry according to policy than to let a workflow sit blocked behind a long-running HTTP call.

Idempotency is another core requirement. Every outbound request that could create, update, or charge something should include an idempotency key such as the order ID. That gives the external service a way to recognize repeated attempts as the same operation rather than treating them as duplicates. Without this safeguard, a retry can quickly become a business incident.

Finally, a resilient design needs to know when to stop pushing. If an external API is failing repeatedly, continuing to hammer it just increases pressure on both systems. This is where circuit breaker thinking becomes useful. Backing off for longer periods, pausing requests, or switching to a fallback path can prevent a temporary outage from turning into a larger cascade of failures.

Adding a FraudCheck Step

Next, we will introduce a fraud check before payment is processed. This changes the workflow so that an order is first submitted, then evaluated by an external fraud service, and only proceeds to payment if that service returns an approval. If the fraud check does not approve the order, the workflow stops and the order is rejected. This is a common real-world pattern because it prevents the system from committing financial or fulfillment actions before a risk decision has been made.

Conceptually, the flow now becomes very simple. An order is submitted, the orchestration calls the external `FraudCheck` step, and the result determines the next branch. An approved result allows the workflow to continue into payment processing. A rejected result ends the process early, often with a status that can be surfaced back to customer support, downstream systems, or the customer-facing application.

To support this step, we can model the request and response as small contract records. The request contains the order identifier, the customer email, and the total order value, which together provide enough context for a basic fraud decision. The response returns a boolean approval flag and a reason string, allowing the orchestration to decide whether to continue and to capture why a transaction was rejected when needed (see Figure 6-1).

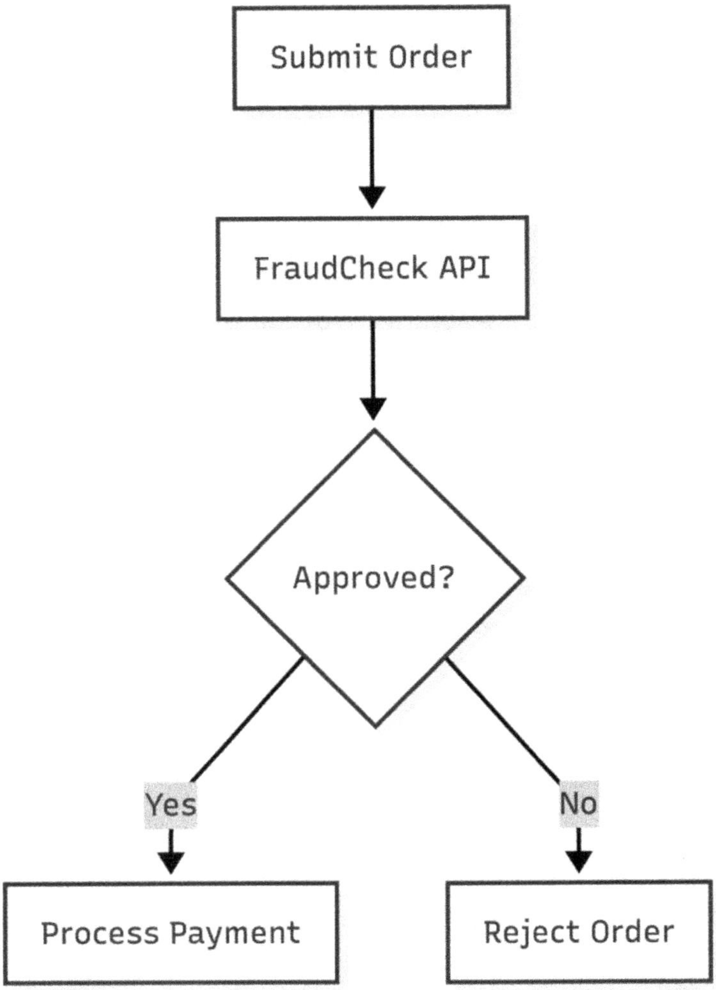

Figure 6-1. *Adding Fraud Check*

Package Note This chapter needs the following NuGet Package.Microsoft.
Extensions.Http

FraudCheck Activity

This is where we actually call the external service. For the demo, we'll call a fake endpoint at `https://fraud-checker.example/api/check.`

Activities/FraudActivities.cs

```
using System.Net.Http.Json;
using Microsoft.Azure.Functions.Worker;
using Microsoft.Extensions.Logging;

namespace OrderProcessor;

public sealed record FraudCheckRequest(
    string OrderId,
    string CustomerEmail,
    decimal TotalValue);

public sealed record FraudCheckResponse(
    bool Approved,
    string Reason);

public sealed class FraudActivities
{
    private readonly HttpClient _http;
    private readonly ILogger<FraudActivities> _logger;

    public FraudActivities(
        IHttpClientFactory httpFactory,
        ILogger<FraudActivities> logger)
    {
        _http = httpFactory.CreateClient("FraudCheck");
        _logger = logger;
    }

    [Function("FraudCheckActivity")]
    public async Task<FraudCheckResponse> FraudCheck([ActivityTrigger]
    FraudCheckRequest request)
    {
        using var httpRequest = new HttpRequestMessage(HttpMethod.Post, "/
        api/check")
        {
            Content = JsonContent.Create(request)
        };

        httpRequest.Headers.Add("Idempotency-Key", request.OrderId);
```

```
        _logger.LogInformation(
            "Calling fraud check for order {OrderId}",
            request.OrderId);

        using var response = await _http.SendAsync(
            httpRequest,
            HttpCompletionOption.ResponseHeadersRead);

        if (!response.IsSuccessStatusCode)
        {
            var body = await response.Content.ReadAsStringAsync();

            _logger.LogWarning(
                "Fraud check failed for order {OrderId}. Status
                {StatusCode}. Body: {Body}",
                request.OrderId,
                response.StatusCode,
                body);

            throw new TransientException($"Fraud API returned {response.
            StatusCode}");
        }

        var result = await response.Content.ReadFromJsonAsync<FraudCheckRe
        sponse>();

        if (result is null)
        {
            _logger.LogError(
                "Fraud API returned null response for order {OrderId}",
                request.OrderId);

            throw new InvalidOperationException("Fraud API returned an
            invalid response.");
        }

        return result;
    }
}
```

A few details matter here. This logic runs inside an activity rather than an orchestrator, which is important because outbound HTTP calls should never be made directly from orchestration code. On non-success responses, it throws a `TransientException` so the Durable Functions retry policy can handle temporary failures automatically. The activity uses `IHttpClientFactory` to manage sockets, timeouts, and related policies cleanly, and it sends the order ID as an idempotency key in the request headers so retried calls do not accidentally create duplicate external side effects.

Orchestrator with FraudCheck

Update OrderOrchestrator:

Orchestrators/OrderOrchestrator.cs

```
using Microsoft.Azure.Functions.Worker;
using Microsoft.DurableTask;

namespace OrderProcessor;

public static class OrderOrchestrator
{
    [Function("OrderOrchestrator")]
    public static async Task Run(
        [OrchestrationTrigger] TaskOrchestrationContext context)
    {
        var order = context.GetInput<Order>()
            ?? throw new InvalidOperationException("Order input is
            required.");

        context.SetCustomStatus(new { Stage = "FraudCheckPending" });

        var fraudRetryOptions = TaskOptions.FromRetryPolicy(RetryPolicies.
        ShortBackoff());

        FraudCheckResponse fraudResult;
        try
        {
            fraudResult = await context.CallActivityAsync<FraudCheck
            Response>(
                "FraudCheckActivity",
```

```
                new FraudCheckRequest(order.Id, order.CustomerEmail, order.
                TotalValue),
                options: fraudRetryOptions);
        }
        catch (TaskFailedException ex)
        {
            var reason = ex.FailureDetails?.ErrorMessage ?? "Unknown fraud
            API failure";

            await context.CallActivityAsync(
                "NotifyFailureActivity",
                new FailureNotice(order, $"Fraud check failed after
                retries: {reason}"));

            return;
        }

        context.SetCustomStatus(new
        {
            Stage = "FraudCheckResult",
            Approved = fraudResult.Approved
        });

        if (!fraudResult.Approved)
        {
            await context.CallActivityAsync(
                "NotifyFailureActivity",
                new FailureNotice(order, $"Rejected by fraud service:
                {fraudResult.Reason}"));

            return;
        }

        // Continue with payment and later workflow steps.
    }
}
```

Now every order goes through fraud screening before payment is attempted.

Configuring HttpClient

In `Program.cs`:

```
builder.Services.AddHttpClient("FraudCheck", client =>
{
    client.BaseAddress = new Uri("https://fraud-
        checker.example/");
    client.Timeout = TimeSpan.FromSeconds(10); // short timeout
});
```

This ensures short-lived, connection-pooled clients with consistent policies.

Security: Handling API Keys

Never hardcode keys in the source. Store them in Azure Key Vault or App Config and inject them:

```
builder.Services.AddHttpClient("FraudCheck", (sp, client) =>
{
    var config = sp.GetRequiredService<IConfiguration>();
    client.BaseAddress = new Uri(config["FraudApi:BaseUrl"]);
    client.DefaultRequestHeaders.Authorization =
        new AuthenticationHeaderValue("Bearer",
    config["FraudApi:Token"]);
});
```

Keys rotate without redeploys. You can even combine this with Managed Identity if the API supports Microsoft Entra ID tokens.

Observability: Custom Status

For long calls, update custom status so ops can see where an order is stuck:

```
context.SetCustomStatus(new { Stage = "FraudCheckPending" });
// call FraudCheck
context.SetCustomStatus(new { Stage = "FraudCheckResult",
Approved = fraudResult.Approved });
```

Ops dashboards can poll the status API and know instantly if orders are blocked on fraud review.

Long-Running External Tasks

Some external integrations complete in seconds, like the fraud API we added in 6.1, but many real-world dependencies take far longer. A tax authority may calculate compliance asynchronously, a logistics provider may only confirm shipment after transport is booked, a payment clearing system may settle hours later, and a KYC or identity verification process may pause while waiting for human review. In each of these cases, the pattern is the same: your system sends a request, the external partner continues the work offline, and the result arrives later either through a callback such as a webhook or through repeated polling for completion.

This is exactly the kind of problem Durable Functions handles well. An orchestrator can pause without tying up compute resources, wait for an external event raised from a webhook, or resume itself on a timer to poll again until the work completes or a timeout is reached. Instead of building custom schedulers, background loops, and state tables just to remember where the workflow left off, you can express the waiting logic directly in the orchestration.

In this section, we will extend `OrderProcessor` to integrate with a Tax Calculation Service whose response may take hours to arrive. That gives us a practical example of how to model long-running external work in a way that stays durable, traceable, and easy to reason about.

Scenario: External Tax Service

Before an order can be shipped, it now needs to be validated by an external regional tax service. That service follows a common asynchronous integration pattern: we send a POST request to /tax/submit with the order details, it responds immediately with a `submissionId`, and the real outcome arrives later through a callback indicating either `TaxCalculated` or `TaxRejected`. In other words, the initial request only starts the work; it does not complete it.

This fits naturally into a Durable Functions workflow. The orchestrator can submit the order to the tax service through an activity, then pause and wait for the external result to arrive as an event raised by a webhook. That keeps the workflow durable and avoids wasting resources while the external system continues its processing. To keep the process safe, the orchestrator should also enforce a timeout. If no tax result arrives within twelve hours, the workflow can fail cleanly rather than waiting forever. That gives us a clear three step pattern for this scenario: submit to the tax service, wait for the callback event, and stop with a timeout if the partner never responds.

Tax Submission Activity

This activity calls the external API and returns a submission ID.

Activities/TaxActivities.cs

```
using System.Net.Http.Json;
using Microsoft.Azure.Functions.Worker;
using Microsoft.Extensions.Logging;

namespace OrderProcessor;

public sealed record TaxSubmissionRequest(
    string OrderId,
    decimal TotalValue,
    string CustomerEmail);

public sealed record TaxSubmissionResponse(string SubmissionId);

public sealed class TaxActivities
{
    private readonly HttpClient _http;
    private readonly ILogger<TaxActivities> _logger;

    public TaxActivities(
        IHttpClientFactory httpFactory,
        ILogger<TaxActivities> logger)
    {
        _http = httpFactory.CreateClient("TaxService");
        _logger = logger;
    }

    [Function("SubmitTaxActivity")]
```

```
public async Task<TaxSubmissionResponse> SubmitTax([ActivityTrigger]
TaxSubmissionRequest request)
{
    using var httpRequest = new HttpRequestMessage(HttpMethod.Post, "/
    tax/submit")
    {
        Content = JsonContent.Create(request)
    };

    httpRequest.Headers.Add("Idempotency-Key", request.OrderId);

    _logger.LogInformation(
        "Submitting tax validation for order {OrderId}",
        request.OrderId);

    using var response = await _http.SendAsync(
        httpRequest,
        HttpCompletionOption.ResponseHeadersRead);

    response.EnsureSuccessStatusCode();

    var result = await response.Content.ReadFromJsonAsync<TaxSubmission
    Response>();

    return result ?? throw new InvalidOperationException("Invalid tax
    response");
}}
```

Orchestrator Update

Add the tax submission step after payment but before shipping:

```
// Step X: Submit to tax authority
var taxRetryOptions = TaskOptions.FromRetryPolicy(RetryPolicies.
ShortBackoff());

var taxResponse = await context.CallActivityAsync<TaxSubmissionResponse>(
    "SubmitTaxActivity",
    new TaxSubmissionRequest(order.Id, order.TotalValue, order.CustomerEmail),
```

```
    options: taxRetryOptions);

context.SetCustomStatus(new
{
    Stage = "TaxSubmitted",
    SubmissionId = taxResponse.SubmissionId
});

// Wait for external webhook event
using var taxTimeoutCts = new CancellationTokenSource();

var timeoutTask = context.CreateTimer(
    context.CurrentDateTimeUtc.AddHours(12),
    taxTimeoutCts.Token);

var taxEventTask = context.WaitForExternalEvent<string>(
    $"TaxResult-{taxResponse.SubmissionId}");

var winner = await Task.WhenAny(taxEventTask, timeoutTask);

if (winner == timeoutTask)
{
    await context.CallActivityAsync(
        "NotifyFailureActivity",
        new FailureNotice(order, "Tax validation timed out"));

    return;
}

if (!string.Equals(taxEventTask.Result, "Approved", StringComparison.
OrdinalIgnoreCase))
{
    await context.CallActivityAsync(
        "NotifyFailureActivity",
        new FailureNotice(order, $"Tax validation rejected: {taxEventTask.
        Result}"));
```

```
    return;
}

taxTimeoutCts.Cancel();

context.SetCustomStatus(new { Stage = "TaxApproved" });
```

Here we uniquely name the external event with the `submissionId`. We wait up to 12 hours. The webhook (below) will raise the event when tax results are ready.

Webhook to Resume Orchestration

Functions/TaxWebhookFunctions.cs

```
using System.Net;
using Microsoft.Azure.Functions.Worker;
using Microsoft.Azure.Functions.Worker.Http;
using Microsoft.DurableTask.Client;
using Microsoft.Extensions.Logging;

namespace OrderProcessor;

public sealed record TaxResultMessage(string OrderId, string Status);

public sealed class TaxWebhookFunctions
{
    private readonly ILogger<TaxWebhookFunctions> _logger;

    public TaxWebhookFunctions(ILogger<TaxWebhookFunctions> logger)
    {
        _logger = logger;
    }

    [Function("TaxWebhook")]
    public async Task<HttpResponseData> Run(
        [HttpTrigger(AuthorizationLevel.Function, "post", Route = "tax/
        result/{submissionId}")]
        HttpRequestData req,
        string submissionId,
        [DurableClient] DurableTaskClient client)
```

```
    {
        var payload = await req.ReadFromJsonAsync<TaxResultMessage>();

        if (payload is null || string.IsNullOrWhiteSpace(payload.OrderId) ||
        string.IsNullOrWhiteSpace(payload.Status))
        {
            var bad = req.CreateResponse(HttpStatusCode.BadRequest);
            await bad.WriteStringAsync("Invalid payload.");
            return bad;
        }

        _logger.LogInformation(
            "Received tax result for submission {SubmissionId}: {Status}",
            submissionId,
            payload.Status);

        // Demo simplification:
        // assume OrderId is the orchestration instance ID.
        var instanceId = payload.OrderId;

        await client.RaiseEventAsync(
            instanceId,
            $"TaxResult-{submissionId}",
            payload.Status);

        var ok = req.CreateResponse(HttpStatusCode.Accepted);
        await ok.WriteStringAsync("Result accepted.");
        return ok;
    }
}
```

This webhook is called by the external tax authority. It raises the event back into the orchestrator, resuming the workflow (see Figure 6-2).

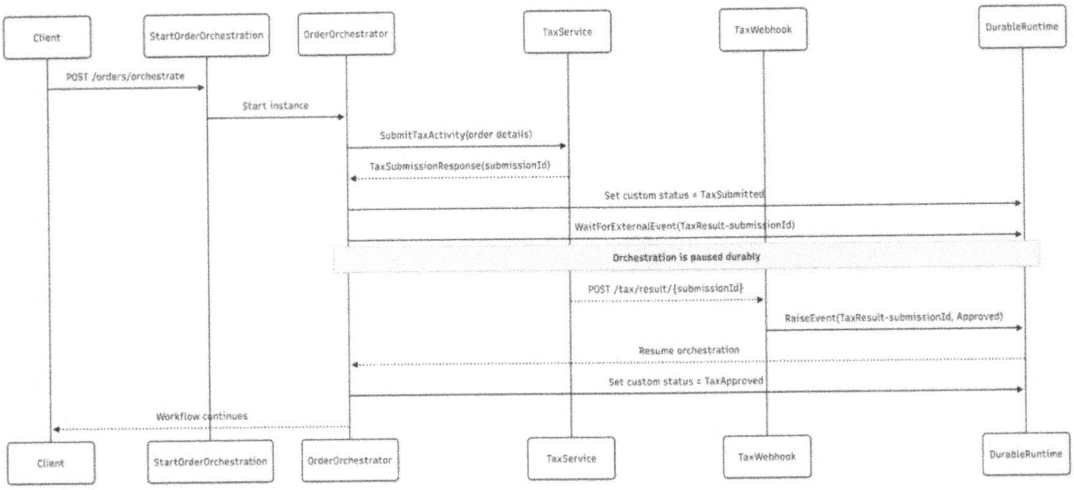

Figure 6-2. *Tax Authority Webhook Flow*

Observability

Observability matters here because long-running external work can otherwise look like the system has simply stalled. By updating custom status as the workflow progresses, operators can see exactly where the orchestration is waiting. Before the callback arrives, the order can show a stage such as `TaxSubmitted`, making it obvious that processing is paused while the external tax service completes its work. Once the callback is received, that status can move to something like `TaxApproved` or switch to a failure state if the tax service rejects the order. That small amount of visibility makes a big difference, because it tells operators whether an order is genuinely stuck or simply waiting for an external dependency to respond.

Durable Polling Alternative

Not every external provider supports callbacks. When that happens, the orchestration can still stay durable by switching to a polling pattern. The first step is to store the `submissionId` returned by the external service, because that identifier is needed for future status checks. From there, the orchestrator can enter a loop that waits on a durable timer for a few minutes, wakes up, calls a polling activity to check the external status, and then either completes, fails, or goes back to sleep and tries again. This gives you the same long-running reliability as a webhook-driven design but without relying on the provider to push results back to you.

```
while (true)
{
    var result = await context.CallActivityAsync<string>(
        "PollTaxStatusActivity",
        taxResponse.SubmissionId);

    if (string.Equals(result, "Approved", StringComparison.
    OrdinalIgnoreCase))
    {
        context.SetCustomStatus(new { Stage = "TaxApproved" });
        break;
    }

    if (string.Equals(result, "Rejected", StringComparison.
    OrdinalIgnoreCase))
    {
        await context.CallActivityAsync(
            "NotifyFailureActivity",
            new FailureNotice(order, "Tax validation rejected"));

        return;
    }

    context.SetCustomStatus(new
    {
        Stage = "TaxPolling",
        SubmissionId = taxResponse.SubmissionId,
        LastKnownStatus = result
    });

    await context.CreateTimer(
        context.CurrentDateTimeUtc.AddMinutes(10),
        CancellationToken.None);
}
```

This pattern works but costs more executions. Webhooks are preferred.

Human Interaction (Approvals via External Systems)

Distributed systems don't just integrate machines with machines. Sooner or later, you'll need to integrate humans into your workflows. An order might require customer confirmation, supplier acknowledgement, or compliance officer approval. These are tasks that no algorithm can shortcut. In our `OrderProcessor` project, we already saw manager approval for high-value orders (5.4). That worked via Durable Functions' `WaitForExternalEvent`. In this section, we'll generalize that pattern to support external users, customers, suppliers, or partners, who must approve or reject via their own portals or emails.

Why Humans Complicate Workflows

Human interaction makes workflows harder because people do not behave like predictable system dependencies. A user might approve something immediately, ignore it for hours, or never respond at all. They may act through different channels such as email links, SMS messages, web portals, or mobile apps, which means the workflow has to handle input arriving from more than one direction. On top of that, approvals and rejections cannot just be accepted blindly. They must be tied to authenticated identities, and every decision needs a proper audit trail showing who acted, when they acted, and how the action was taken.

That combination of uncertainty, multiple input channels, security requirements, and auditability is what makes human-driven workflow steps fundamentally different from normal service-to-service calls. You are no longer waiting on a fast, deterministic dependency; you are coordinating a business process that crosses technical and human boundaries.

Durable Functions fits this well because it allows an orchestration to pause safely, preserve its state, and wait for input without consuming resources while idle. When the user eventually acts, whether that is seconds later or days later, the workflow can resume from the same point with the context intact and the decision captured as part of the orchestration history.

Scenario: Supplier Confirmation

Consider an order that cannot move to shipping until a supplier confirms they can fulfill it. In that case, the orchestration pauses after inventory allocation and sends the supplier an email, for example through SendGrid, containing a unique approval link. When the supplier clicks either Approve or Reject, that action calls back into our API, which then raises an external event to the waiting orchestration. The workflow can then resume from the exact point where it paused and either continue toward shipping or fail cleanly based on the supplier's decision. This pattern is a good example of how Durable Functions can coordinate business processes that depend on human action without resorting to polling loops, custom schedulers, or manually stitched state tracking (see Figure 6-3).

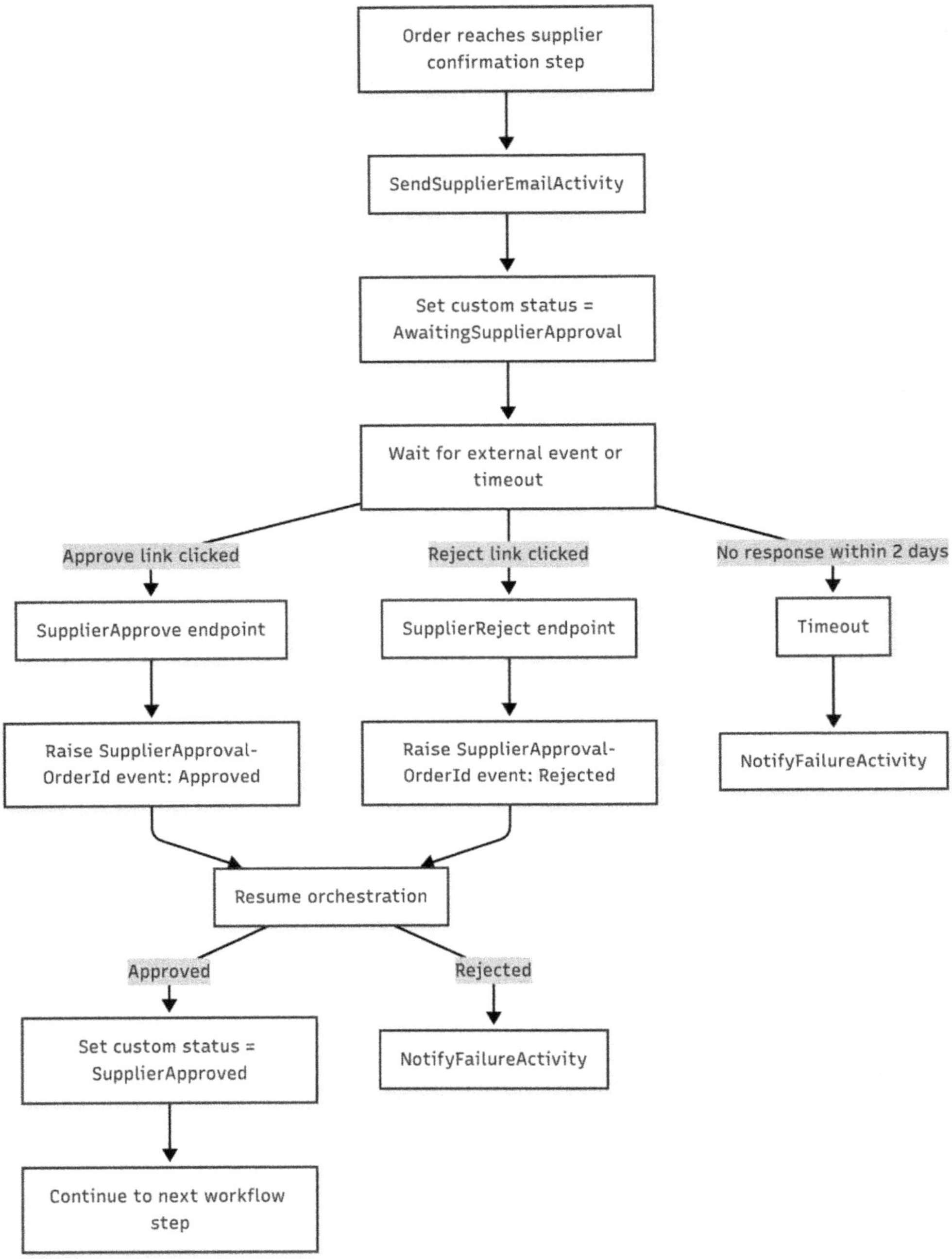

Figure 6-3. *Supplier Approval Flow Using External Events, Timeout Handling, and Orchestration Resume*

Orchestrators/OrderOrchestrator.cs

Replace the existing supplier confirmation block after the inventory check succeeds with:

```
// Step: Supplier confirmation required
var supplierEmail = "supplier@example.com";

await context.CallActivityAsync(
    "SendSupplierEmailActivity",
    new SupplierEmailRequest(order, supplierEmail));

context.SetCustomStatus(new
{
    Stage = "AwaitingSupplierApproval",
    OrderId = order.Id
});

using var supplierTimeoutCts = new CancellationTokenSource();

var timeoutTask = context.CreateTimer(
    context.CurrentDateTimeUtc.AddDays(2),
    supplierTimeoutCts.Token);

var decisionTask = context.WaitForExternalEvent<string>(
    $"SupplierApproval-{order.Id}");

var winner = await Task.WhenAny(decisionTask, timeoutTask);

if (winner == timeoutTask)
{
    await context.CallActivityAsync(
        "NotifyFailureActivity",
        new FailureNotice(order, "Supplier did not respond in time"));

    return;
}

if (!string.Equals(decisionTask.Result, "Approved", StringComparison.
OrdinalIgnoreCase))
{
    await context.CallActivityAsync(
```

```
        "NotifyFailureActivity",
        new FailureNotice(order, "Supplier rejected the order"));

    return;
}

supplierTimeoutCts.Cancel();

context.SetCustomStatus(new { Stage = "SupplierApproved" });
```

Sending the Approval Email

Activity to send supplier an email with approval/reject links
Activities/SupplierActivities.cs

```
using Microsoft.Azure.Functions.Worker;
using Microsoft.Extensions.Logging;

namespace OrderProcessor;

public sealed record SupplierEmailRequest(
    Order Order,
    string Email);

public sealed class SupplierActivities
{
    private readonly ILogger<SupplierActivities> _logger;

    public SupplierActivities(ILogger<SupplierActivities> logger)
    {
        _logger = logger;
    }

    [Function("SendSupplierEmailActivity")]
    public Task SendSupplierEmail([ActivityTrigger] SupplierEmailRequest
    request)
    {
        var approveUrl = $"https://myapi.example.com/api/orders/{request.
        Order.Id}/supplier/approve";
```

```
        var rejectUrl = $"https://myapi.example.com/api/orders/{request.
        Order.Id}/supplier/reject";

        var subject = $"Order {request.Order.Id} requires your
        confirmation";

        var body = $"""
            Please confirm the order:

            Value: {request.Order.TotalValue:C}
            Approve: {approveUrl}
            Reject: {rejectUrl}
            """;

        _logger.LogInformation(
            "Sending supplier email to {Email}. Subject: {Subject}. Body:
            {Body}",
            request.Email,
            subject,
            body);

        return Task.CompletedTask;
    }
}
```

Webhook Endpoints for Approval

Suppliers click links > Functions endpoints raise events:

Functions/SupplierApprovalFunctions.cs

```
using System.Net;
using Microsoft.Azure.Functions.Worker;
using Microsoft.Azure.Functions.Worker.Http;
using Microsoft.DurableTask.Client;
using Microsoft.Extensions.Logging;

namespace OrderProcessor;

public sealed class SupplierApprovalFunctions
```

```
{
    private readonly ILogger<SupplierApprovalFunctions> _logger;

    public SupplierApprovalFunctions(ILogger<SupplierApprovalFunctio
    ns> logger)
    {
        _logger = logger;
    }

    [Function("SupplierApprove")]
    public async Task<HttpResponseData> Approve(
        [HttpTrigger(AuthorizationLevel.Anonymous, "get", Route = "orders/
        {orderId}/supplier/approve")]
        HttpRequestData req,
        string orderId,
        [DurableClient] DurableTaskClient client)
    {
        _logger.LogInformation("Supplier approved order {OrderId}",
        orderId);

        await client.RaiseEventAsync(orderId, $"SupplierApproval-
        {orderId}", "Approved");

        var response = req.CreateResponse(HttpStatusCode.OK);
        await response.WriteStringAsync("Thank you. Order approved.");
        return response;
    }

    [Function("SupplierReject")]
    public async Task<HttpResponseData> Reject(
        [HttpTrigger(AuthorizationLevel.Anonymous, "get", Route = "orders/
        {orderId}/supplier/reject")]
        HttpRequestData req,
        string orderId,
        [DurableClient] DurableTaskClient client)
    {
        _logger.LogInformation("Supplier rejected order {OrderId}",
        orderId);
```

```
        await client.RaiseEventAsync(orderId, $"SupplierApproval-
        {orderId}", "Rejected");

        var response = req.CreateResponse(HttpStatusCode.OK);
        await response.WriteStringAsync("Order rejected.");
        return response;
    }
}
```

This is the human-facing surface: a supplier approves/rejects by clicking a secure link.

Security Considerations

A workflow like this also needs proper security around the human interaction points. Approval links should never expose a raw `orderId` on their own. A better approach is to include a signed token, such as a JWT or HMAC-based value, that encodes the order reference and an expiry time so the link cannot be tampered with or reused indefinitely. In higher trust scenarios, you may go further and require the supplier to authenticate through a portal before submitting their decision, with the portal then posting that decision into your API and raising the event from there. Whatever path you choose, every approval or rejection should be fully audited, including the timestamp, caller identity, and source details such as IP address, so the workflow remains traceable and compliant.

Combining Serverless with Microservices and Monoliths

So far, `OrderProcessor` has followed a largely serverless-first design, built around Functions, queues, topics, orchestrations, and entities. Real systems are rarely that clean. Most teams have to work with what already exists, which usually means a mix of containerized microservices, older monoliths, and newer serverless components living side by side. Microservices may already expose focused APIs for specific business capabilities, while monoliths often continue to own critical rules, transactions, or core data that cannot be replaced overnight. In that kind of environment, serverless is not a replacement for everything else. More often, it becomes the connective tissue. Azure Functions and Durable Functions can sit between these systems, coordinate calls, trigger workflows, and introduce new behavior without forcing a disruptive rewrite of the applications that are already in place.

The Integration Challenge

The challenge is that different architectural styles solve different problems well. Microservices can give you strong separation and independent deployment, monoliths often provide stability and mature business logic, and serverless works well for event-driven processing, orchestration, and elastic background workflows. Most organizations end up with some mix of all three. That is normal. The goal is not to force everything into one model, but to connect these parts in a way that is deliberate and understandable. In practice, success comes less from architectural uniformity and more from choosing clear integration patterns so each system can play to its strengths without turning the whole landscape into a mess.

Scenario: ERP Integration

Let's extend `OrderProcessor` to integrate with an existing ERP system that runs as a legacy monolith, exposes a REST API, and must receive each confirmed order so invoicing can proceed in the system of record. This is a very typical enterprise shape. The newer serverless workflow coordinates events, retries, approvals, and state transitions, while the older ERP still owns the authoritative business record for finance and downstream processing. That does mean the integration has to account for slow response times and higher latency, but that is exactly the kind of boundary Durable Functions can handle well.

This scenario also highlights why hybrid architectures are so common. A monolith often provides rich functionality and centralized data, but it can be hard to scale, slower to change, and full of hidden coupling. Microservices offer clearer boundaries and independent scaling, but they introduce cross-service latency, consistency challenges, and a need for stronger orchestration. Serverless fits best where you need event-driven coordination, rapid extension, and pay-per-use execution, although its stateless nature means you need patterns like Durable Functions when workflows become long-running or stateful. The point is not that one style wins. It is that each style brings tradeoffs, and a system like `OrderProcessor` often sits in the middle, connecting them deliberately.

ERP Activity Function

We wrap ERP calls in an activity:

Activities/ErpActivities.cs

```
using System.Net.Http.Json;
using Microsoft.Azure.Functions.Worker;
using Microsoft.Extensions.Logging;

namespace OrderProcessor;

public sealed record ErpOrderRequest(
    string OrderId,
    string CustomerEmail,
    decimal TotalValue);

public sealed record ErpOrderResponse(
    bool Success,
    string ErpId);

public sealed class ErpActivities
{
    private readonly HttpClient _http;
    private readonly ILogger<ErpActivities> _logger;

    public ErpActivities(
        IHttpClientFactory httpFactory,
        ILogger<ErpActivities> logger)
    {
        _http = httpFactory.CreateClient("ErpApi");
        _logger = logger;
    }

    [Function("RegisterErpOrderActivity")]
    public async Task<ErpOrderResponse> RegisterOrder([ActivityTrigger]
    ErpOrderRequest request)
    {
        _logger.LogInformation(
            "Registering order {OrderId} with ERP",
```

```
            request.OrderId);

        using var httpRequest = new HttpRequestMessage(HttpMethod.Post, "/
        orders")
        {
            Content = JsonContent.Create(request)
        };

        httpRequest.Headers.Add("x-correlation-id", request.OrderId);
        httpRequest.Headers.Add("Idempotency-Key", request.OrderId);

        using var response = await _http.SendAsync(
            httpRequest,
            HttpCompletionOption.ResponseHeadersRead);

        if (!response.IsSuccessStatusCode)
        {
            var body = await response.Content.ReadAsStringAsync();

            _logger.LogWarning(
                "ERP call failed for order {OrderId}. Status {StatusCode}.
                Body: {Body}",
                request.OrderId,
                response.StatusCode,
                body);

            throw new TransientException("ERP unavailable");
        }

        var result = await response.Content.ReadFromJsonAsync<ErpOrderRe
        sponse>();

        return result ?? new ErpOrderResponse(false, string.Empty);
    }
}
```

Orchestrator Integration

We add ERP registration after successful shipping:

Orchestrators/OrderOrchestrator.cs

Add or update the ERP registration step in `OrderOrchestrator` as follows:

```
// Step: Register order in ERP
var erpRetryOptions = TaskOptions.FromRetryPolicy(RetryPolicies.
LongBackoff());

ErpOrderResponse erpResponse;

try
{
    erpResponse = await context.CallActivityAsync<ErpOrderResponse>(
        "RegisterErpOrderActivity",
        new ErpOrderRequest(order.Id, order.CustomerEmail, order.
TotalValue),
        options: erpRetryOptions);
}
catch
{
    await context.CallActivityAsync(
        "NotifyFailureActivity",
        new FailureNotice(order, "ERP registration failed after retries"));

    return;
}

if (!erpResponse.Success)
{
    await context.CallActivityAsync(
        "NotifyFailureActivity",
        new FailureNotice(order, "ERP rejected order"));

    return;
}

context.SetCustomStatus(new
{
    Stage = "ErpRegistered",
    ErpId = erpResponse.ErpId
});
```

This ensures ERP gets every confirmed order, even if it takes multiple retries.

Observability Across Boundaries

Observability becomes even more important once a workflow crosses boundaries between Functions, microservices, and legacy systems. Correlation IDs should flow end to end, with the order ID propagated as a header into the ERP and any downstream services so a single business transaction can be traced across the whole path. Application Insights distributed tracing can then stitch those hops together, giving operators a clearer view of how a request moved through Azure Functions and into the ERP API. It also helps to store ERP response IDs back into Cosmos DB alongside the order document so that support teams have a clean reconciliation point between the serverless workflow and the external system of record.

A few integration patterns work especially well in these hybrid environments. One common approach is to place Azure API Management or Front Door in front of a monolith so legacy APIs can be exposed through a cleaner, more consistent surface that Functions can consume. Another is event-based bridging, where Functions publish events into Event Grid and microservices or monoliths subscribe and react, which reduces direct coupling between systems. When a legacy platform cannot push updates back, Functions can fall back to polling on a schedule, with Durable orchestrations managing the polling loop without losing workflow state. And for large-scale data movement, batch-oriented tools such as Data Factory or Logic Apps can extract and synchronize data from monolithic databases into modern storage that serverless components can use more effectively.

Combining Orchestrations and Microservices

Durable Functions orchestrations often work best as the control plane that sits above existing services and coordinates how they are used. Activities can wrap calls to microservices over REST, GraphQL, or gRPC, allowing the orchestrator to drive containerized services without embedding transport logic directly into workflow code. Those same workflows can pause and wait for events published by microservices through Event Grid, then resume when the right signal arrives. If a service fails, the orchestrator can apply fallback logic, trigger compensation, or switch to an alternative provider instead of letting the whole process collapse. That is what makes this model so practical in mixed environments: you can introduce new business workflows around services that already exist, adding coordination, resilience, and visibility without having to rewrite the services themselves.

Example: Payment as a Microservice

A good example is moving payment handling out of `OrderProcessor` and into a dedicated `PaymentService` running as a containerized microservice. In that setup, the orchestration does not implement payment rules itself. Instead, an activity calls the `PaymentService` API and waits for the result. The payment service owns the sensitive concerns such as PCI compliance, token handling, charge execution, and refunds, while the `OrderProcessor` workflow remains focused on coordination. That split is useful because it keeps high risk payment logic inside a service designed for that responsibility, while Durable Functions still provides the surrounding resilience, retry handling, compensation, and stateful workflow control.

Patterns for Resilience and Integration at Scale

By now, you've seen `OrderProcessor` evolve beyond a purely serverless sandbox. It talks to external APIs, waits for long-running external tasks, involves humans in the loop, and integrates with legacy ERP and microservices. Each integration brought its own quirks and risks. At a small scale, you might get by with ad hoc fixes. At enterprise scale, you need patterns. This section pulls together recurring solutions to the messy problems of integration, showing how Durable Functions and serverless glue can keep the system robust even as dependencies multiply.

The Integration Tax

Every integration introduces cost. Each extra dependency adds latency, increases the number of failure points, and brings its own behavioral quirks. Legacy systems, modern APIs, human approvals, and external services all fail differently and on different timelines. Left unmanaged, that integration tax turns workflows brittle and hard to support. The answer is not to avoid integration, but to apply a set of patterns that absorb the complexity in a controlled way.

Pattern 1 – The Circuit Breaker

When an external API is struggling, repeated retries often make the situation worse. A circuit breaker protects both your system and the dependency by tripping after repeated failures, and short-circuiting further calls for a cooldown period. In `OrderProcessor`, you might place `FraudCheckActivity` behind a circuit breaker entity so that after too many consecutive failures, new orders fail fast with a clear message instead of continuing to hammer the fraud service.

Pattern 2 – The Idempotency Key

Retries are unavoidable in distributed systems, which means repeated requests must be safe. That is where idempotency keys matter. Payment calls should send the order ID as an idempotency key, ERP integrations should reject duplicate submissions of the same order, and `CustomerEntity` should use `ProcessedOrderIds` so spend and loyalty points are not applied twice. Without idempotency, retries cause damage. With it, retries become a recovery tool.

Pattern 3 – Compensation

Not every failure can be prevented, and many workflows fail only after some earlier steps have already succeeded. Compensation is the mechanism that lets you undo those earlier changes. If payment succeeds but inventory allocation later fails, the workflow should issue a refund and signal Compensate on `CustomerEntity`. If an ERP rejects an order after shipping has started, the response may involve reversing the shipment and alerting operations. Compensation is what keeps distributed workflows consistent even when there is no global transaction.

Pattern 4 – Event-Driven Integration

Direct API calls create tight coupling between systems. Events loosen that dependency. Instead of calling the ERP directly, `OrderProcessor` could publish an `OrderConfirmed` event into Event Grid, allowing ERP integration Functions, analytics pipelines, and CRM systems to subscribe independently. That makes the workflow easier to extend, reduces direct backpressure on the orchestrator, and allows new consumers to be added without changing the core flow.

Pattern 5 – Custom Status and Observability

At scale, the hardest problem is often not failure itself, but understanding what the system is doing. Durable orchestrations expose custom status so workflows do not become black boxes. A fraud check might surface `FraudCheckPending`, a tax service might show `TaxSubmitted`, a supplier step might report `AwaitingSupplierApproval`, and an ERP handoff might display `ErpRegistered`. These status values give operators a clear view of why an order is paused and make dashboards and troubleshooting much more effective.

Pattern 6 – Hybrid Integration (Serverless + Legacy)

Pure serverless systems are uncommon in real organizations. More often, serverless succeeds by augmenting what is already there. Durable orchestrations coordinate the workflow, the ERP remains the source of truth, a payment microservice owns compliance-sensitive logic, and Cosmos DB stores projections for fast reads while another platform keeps canonical data. This hybrid approach avoids disruptive rewrites and allows value to be added incrementally.

Pattern 7 – Resilience by Design

Resilience is not something you bolt on at the end. It has to be designed in from the start. That means assuming partial failure, planning for eventual consistency, measuring latency and retry behavior, and exposing status and correlation IDs so humans can support the system when things go wrong. These are not just implementation techniques. They are architectural commitments that make distributed workflows survivable in the real world.

EXERCISES

1. **Fraud Retry Simulation:** Make `FraudCheckActivity` randomly throw `TransientException`. Start several orchestrations and confirm the fraud step retries instead of failing immediately.
2. **Fraud Rejection Path:** Return `Approved = false` from the fraud API for selected orders. Verify the workflow stops before payment is attempted and sends a failure notification.

3. **Fraud Timeout Drill:** Lower the fraud `HttpClient` timeout to one second and confirm the activity fails fast, retries according to policy, and does not leave the workflow hanging.

4. **Secure Fraud Configuration:** Move the fraud API token out of configuration files and into Azure Key Vault or App Configuration. Wire it into the `HttpClient` setup and verify the activity still works.

5. **Fraud Circuit Breaker:** Add a `FraudCircuit` Durable Entity that opens after repeated failures. Confirm new orders fail fast while the breaker is open rather than continuing to hammer the fraud service.

6. **Tax Webhook Happy Path:** Submit an order, then POST an approved tax result to the webhook endpoint. Verify the orchestration resumes from the waiting state and continues.

7. **Tax Rejection Path:** Send a rejected tax result through the webhook and confirm the order fails cleanly with the correct failure reason.

8. **Tax Timeout Path:** Start an order but do not send any tax result. Shorten the waiting window for testing and confirm the orchestration fails when the timer expires.

9. **Polling Variant:** Replace the webhook-driven tax result with a polling activity. Verify the orchestration wakes on each timer interval, checks status, and eventually succeeds or fails correctly.

10. **Webhook Plus Polling Fallback:** Implement a hybrid design where the orchestration prefers the webhook result but falls back to polling if no callback arrives after a defined period.

11. **Supplier Approval Happy Path:** Submit an order that requires supplier confirmation, click the approval link, and verify the orchestration resumes and continues.

12. **Supplier Rejection Path:** Trigger the reject link and confirm the workflow stops with a failure notice instead of progressing to shipping.

13. **Supplier Timeout Path:** Do not click either approval link. Shorten the timeout for testing and confirm the order fails after the supplier response window expires.

14. **Approval Audit Logging:** Extend the supplier approval endpoint so that each decision is written to Cosmos DB with a timestamp, identity, and outcome.
15. **Signed Approval Links:** Replace raw approval URLs with signed JWT or HMAC-based links and verify that tampered or expired links are rejected.
16. **ERP Retry and Latency Test:** Make the ERP API respond slowly or intermittently fail. Confirm the orchestrator uses its longer retry policy and eventually succeeds without losing state.
17. **ERP Outage Test:** Force the ERP integration to stay unavailable for an extended period. Verify the orchestration survives the outage and follows the failure path only after retries are exhausted.
18. **Payment As a Microservice:** Move payment handling behind a dedicated `PaymentService` and update the orchestration to call it through an activity rather than performing payment logic directly in `OrderProcessor`.
19. **Compensation After Downstream Failure:** Force payment to succeed, then make shipping or ERP registration fail. Confirm the workflow issues a refund and applies the appropriate compensation steps.
20. **Operations Dashboard:** Build a simple status endpoint or dashboard that groups orchestrations by custom status values such as `FraudCheckPending`, `TaxSubmitted`, `AwaitingSupplierApproval`, and `ErpRegistered`.

Summary

This chapter moved `OrderProcessor` out of the safe confines of an internal demo and into the messier reality of external integration. The workflow now talks to external APIs, waits on third-party systems that respond hours later, incorporates human approvals, and hands confirmed orders off to legacy ERP boundaries. Along the way, Durable Functions proved why orchestration is such a strong fit for these problems. It lets workflows remain deterministic by pushing external calls into activities, pause safely while waiting for callbacks or human action, and resume later without losing state or forcing teams to build their own schedulers and persistence logic.

The chapter also showed that integration is never just about making a call succeed once. The real work is in dealing with timeouts, retries, idempotency, compensation, authentication, observability, and the awkward realities of systems you do not control. Fraud screening introduced safe outbound API calls with retry and configuration discipline. Tax validation showed how to model long-running external work through webhooks, timers, and durable polling. Supplier approval demonstrated how humans can be brought into orchestrated workflows without sacrificing traceability or reliability. ERP registration then grounded the discussion in enterprise reality, where serverless systems often sit beside monoliths and microservices rather than replacing them.

By the end of the chapter, the main lesson is clear: resilient integration is a design problem, not a plumbing exercise. Circuit breakers, idempotency keys, compensation paths, event-driven boundaries, custom status, and hybrid integration are not optional extras once systems begin to scale; they are the patterns that keep workflows survivable. `OrderProcessor` now looks far more like a real production system, one that can coordinate external dependencies, absorb partial failure, remain observable under load, and evolve safely inside a mixed architecture of Functions, legacy platforms, and specialized services.

CHAPTER 7

Observability in Serverless Distributed Systems

As `OrderProcessor` grows from a simple serverless workflow into a distributed system, understanding what the platform is doing becomes just as important as making it work. A single order may now pass through HTTP endpoints, Durable Functions orchestrations, activity functions, queues, external APIs, and persistence layers before the workflow is complete. That kind of architecture brings flexibility and scale, but it also makes failures harder to see and performance harder to explain. When something slows down, retries unexpectedly, or disappears into a queue, traditional logging on its own is no longer enough. The system needs to become observable in a way that matches its distributed nature.

This chapter introduces the practical observability foundations that make that possible in `OrderProcessor`. It begins with distributed tracing so requests can be followed across services and workflow boundaries, then moves into structured logging so telemetry becomes queryable rather than just readable. From there, it looks at monitoring cost and scale in Azure Functions, turning dashboards and alerts into actionable operational tools, and finally pulling everything together into an observability playbook for running the system with confidence. The aim is not simply to generate more telemetry. It is to make `OrderProcessor` understandable, diagnosable, and operable when real workloads and real failures arrive.

© Patrick Kearns 2026
P. Kearns, *Serverless Distributed Systems in Modern .NET and Azure*,
https://doi.org/10.1007/979-8-8688-2839-3_7

Distributed Tracing Basics

When an application runs on a single server, debugging is usually straightforward. You inspect the logs, follow the execution path, and work out where the request began and where it failed. In a distributed system, those assumptions break down very quickly. A single business action may enter through an HTTP endpoint, move into a Function trigger, publish a queue message, resume an orchestration, call one or more downstream services, and write to storage before the user ever sees a result. By the time something goes wrong, the path that led to the failure may already span several runtimes and infrastructure boundaries. That is the problem distributed tracing is designed to solve. Instead of treating each request, dependency call, or log line as an isolated event, tracing follows one logical operation across all of the components that participate in it. For `OrderProcessor`, that matters because the system is no longer a simple request-response application. An order may begin at the API boundary, move through a Durable Functions orchestration, fan out into activities such as fraud and tax checks, call external APIs, and then continue later based on asynchronous events. If the workflow stalls or fails, the team needs a way to see the whole journey rather than trying to reconstruct it from disconnected fragments.

What Distributed Tracing Is

Distributed tracing works by attaching a shared correlation context to an operation as it moves through the system. In practice, that usually means a trace identifier for the overall transaction and span identifiers for the individual pieces of work inside it. Standards such as W3C Trace Context define how that information is propagated between components, most commonly through headers such as `traceparent` and `tracestate`. Tools such as Application Insights and OpenTelemetry can then record those spans and rebuild the full path of the request.

That gives you more than just a prettier request timeline. It tells you where time was spent, which dependency introduced latency, and which step actually broke the chain. In a serverless workflow, those answers matter because the business question is rarely “which instance handled this request?” It is usually “why is this order stuck?”, “which external dependency slowed everything down?”, or “where in the journey did the failure occur?”

Why It Matters in Serverless Systems

Tracing becomes even more important in serverless systems because the runtime is more fragmented than in a traditional hosted application. Azure Functions scale dynamically, so the same type of operation may run on different instances from one moment to the next. Queues and events break direct synchronous call chains. Durable Functions replay orchestrations to rebuild state, which means naïve logging can become noisy and hard to interpret. Retries can multiply the number of individual operations involved in one logical business flow.

For `OrderProcessor`, that means observability has to follow the business transaction rather than the infrastructure it happened to pass through. The important thing is not which worker instance handled the fraud check. The important thing is that the fraud check, tax call, approval step, and ERP registration all belong to the same order journey and can be understood together.

Tracing the Order Journey in `OrderProcessor`

The clearest way to introduce tracing in `OrderProcessor` is to anchor it to a real workflow. A good starting point is the order submission path from the HTTP boundary into the orchestration, then onwards into external dependencies such as `FraudCheck`, `TaxService`, and ERP. Once that path is visible, the same tracing model can be extended across the rest of the system. Figure 7-1 shows the core flow we want to make visible. The goal is simple. Every execution should carry a trace identifier, outbound dependency calls should preserve that context, and the orchestration should appear as part of the same overall transaction rather than as an isolated process. In practice, that means enabling telemetry collection in the Functions host, letting outbound HTTP calls flow trace context through the normal `HttpClient` pipeline, and adding a correlation layer so that each invocation has a usable trace identifier even when one is not supplied upstream (see Figure 7-1).

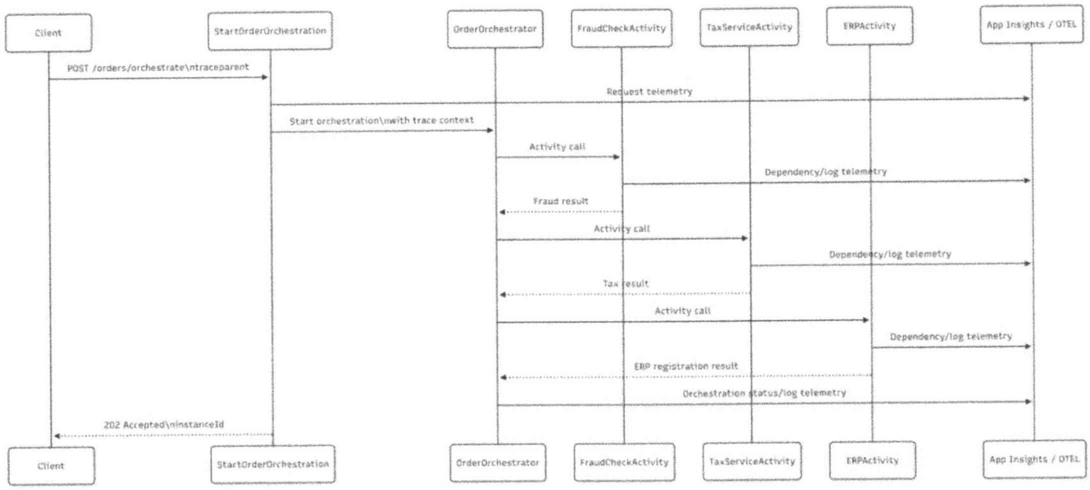

Figure 7-1. *Observability Across the OrderProcessor Orchestration and Activity Pipeline*

Enabling Application Insights in the Functions Host

At the host level, the first step is to enable telemetry collection for the isolated worker. In `Program.cs`, that begins with Application Insights:

Program.cs

```
builder.Services.AddApplicationInsightsTelemetryWorkerService();
builder.Services.ConfigureFunctionsApplicationInsights();
```

This gives the Functions host a telemetry pipeline capable of recording requests, dependencies, and traces. On its own, that does not yet guarantee that every order journey will be easy to follow, but it provides the foundation the rest of the tracing model depends on.

Letting Outbound Dependency Calls Carry Trace Context

Once tracing is enabled at the host level, outbound calls also need to preserve the same tracing context. That matters because `OrderProcessor` does not stop at the Function boundary. It talks to other services, and those dependency calls need to remain part of the same trace if the end-to-end picture is going to make sense.

In .NET, `HttpClient` integrates with `Activity.Current`, which means outgoing requests can automatically include `traceparent` when diagnostics are active. A named client registration is enough to make that dependency path explicit in the project:

Program.cs

```
builder.Services.AddHttpClient("FraudCheck")
    .AddHttpMessageHandler(() => new HttpClientHandler
    {
        AllowAutoRedirect = true
    });
```

The important point here is not the redirect setting. It is that outbound dependency calls now move through the standard `HttpClient` pipeline, where trace context can flow with them. That allows a call from `OrderProcessor` into `FraudCheck`, `TaxService`, or ERP to appear as part of the same transaction rather than as an unrelated external request.

Adding Correlation Middleware

Although upstream callers will often provide a trace context, that cannot always be assumed. For that reason, `OrderProcessor` should ensure that every execution has a correlation identifier even when one did not arrive from the caller. A middleware layer is a good place to do that because it sits close to the function boundary and can stamp the execution context consistently.

A simple correlation middleware could look like this:

Middleware/CorrelationMiddleware.cs

```
public class CorrelationMiddleware : IFunctionsWorkerMiddleware
{
    public async Task Invoke(FunctionContext context,
    FunctionExecutionDelegate next)
    {
        var traceId = context.TraceContext.TraceParent ?? Guid.NewGuid().
        ToString();

        context.Items["TraceId"] = traceId;

        var logger = context.GetLogger("Correlation");
        logger.LogInformation("Trace ID: {TraceId}", traceId);
```

```
        await next(context);
    }
}
```

This does two useful things. First, it ensures that the current execution always has a trace identifier attached to it. Second, it makes that identifier visible in logs from the start of execution, which helps bridge distributed tracing and structured logging later in the chapter.

Register the middleware in `Program.cs`:

Program.cs

```
builder.Services.AddSingleton<IFunctionsWorkerMiddleware,
CorrelationMiddleware>();
```

At this point, `OrderProcessor` has the beginnings of a consistent tracing model at the execution boundary rather than relying entirely on whatever the caller happened to send.

Orchestration Trace Flow

Durable Functions adds another layer of complexity because orchestrators replay. That means naïve logging inside an orchestrator can make telemetry noisy or misleading if replayed steps appear as repeated events. The answer is not to avoid tracing. It is to use the orchestrator carefully. For `OrderProcessor`, the better approach is to let tracing flow through the orchestration while using replay-safe practices for logs and progress reporting. `context.SetCustomStatus` can expose meaningful business progress such as `FraudCheck`, `Tax`, `SupplierApproval`, or ERP without flooding the logs with repeated control-flow messages. Business-level logs still matter, but they should be written with replay in mind so the trace remains useful rather than cluttered.

Once this is in place, Application Insights can show an order submission flowing across its major steps in one connected view. A submission request can be linked to outbound dependency calls such as `FraudCheck`, `TaxService`, and ERP, with timing and failure data preserved as part of the same transaction.

OpenTelemetry As an Alternative

Application Insights is a strong default for Azure-hosted systems, but OrderProcessor does not have to be tied to a single tracing backend forever. If greater portability or finer control is needed, OpenTelemetry provides a more vendor-neutral option. That can be useful if the system later needs to export traces to a different backend or if observability standards need to stay portable across teams and platforms.

A basic OpenTelemetry setup:

Program.cs

```
builder.Services.AddOpenTelemetry()
    .WithTracing(b =>
    {
        b.AddAspNetCoreInstrumentation();
        b.AddHttpClientInstrumentation();
        b.AddSource("OrderProcessor");
        b.AddAzureMonitorTraceExporter(o =>
        {
            o.ConnectionString =
                builder.Configuration["APPLICATIONINSIGHTS_CONNECTION_
                STRING"];
        });
    });
```

For this book, the important thing is not to force one tracing stack over another. It is to show that the tracing model in OrderProcessor is built on standard correlation concepts that can carry forward even if the tooling changes.

Project Addition: Distributed Tracing Foundation for OrderProcessor

This section introduces the first real distributed tracing foundation for OrderProcessor. The Functions host now enables telemetry collection; outbound HttpClient calls can participate in the same trace context, and a correlation middleware ensures that each execution has a usable trace identifier whether or not one was supplied upstream. From this point on, an order is no longer observed only as a sequence of disconnected log messages. It becomes a traceable transaction that can be followed from submission through orchestration, activity execution, and downstream integration boundaries.

Structured Logging in Serverless Systems

Logs are still one of the most useful tools in a developer's toolkit, but in a distributed system they stop being useful very quickly if they are treated as free text alone. A handful of plain-text messages may be enough when one application runs on one server and one request stays inside one process. In a serverless distributed system, that breaks down. `OrderProcessor` now spreads work across HTTP endpoints, orchestrations, activity functions, queues, and external dependencies. If each part logs in its own style, with its own wording and no shared structure, the result is noise rather than observability.

That is why structured logging matters. The goal is not simply to write more logs. It is to write logs in a consistent, machine-queryable shape so they can be filtered, grouped, correlated, and analyzed across the whole workflow. In the section "Distributed Tracing Basics," distributed tracing gave `OrderProcessor` a way to follow a request across boundaries. Structured logging now gives that traced request meaningful business context such as the order ID, the workflow stage, the outcome, and the reason for failure. Figure 7-2 shows how that structured context sits alongside tracing and application flow.

What Structured Logging Is

Structured logging means recording events as named fields rather than as one undifferentiated sentence. Instead of writing something like `"Order 123 failed because ERP timed out,"` the application writes a message together with separate properties such as `OrderId`, `Stage`, `Outcome`, `Reason`, and `TraceId`. The message is still useful to a human reading the log stream, but the surrounding properties are what make the entry valuable to the system. That structure matters because modern observability backends do more than store strings. Application Insights, Log Analytics, Elasticsearch, Splunk, and similar systems can index those fields and let the team ask much more useful questions. Instead of scanning log lines manually, you can ask for all ERP failures in the last hour, group failed orders by stage, or filter every record associated with one trace ID. In other words, the log stream stops being a diary and becomes a dataset.

Why It Matters in Serverless Systems

Serverless systems multiply log volume quickly. Each Function execution emits its own telemetry. Durable orchestrations replay, which can repeat control-flow logs if the code is careless. Queue-triggered retries add more executions. Fan-out patterns multiply the number of related activity logs for a single business operation. Without structure, the sheer number of entries makes diagnosis slow and frustrating.

For `OrderProcessor`, the most important question is rarely "what did this Function instance print?" It is usually "what happened to this order?" That means the logs need to preserve the business key the team cares about most, which is the order itself, while still linking back to the trace ID introduced in the section "Distributed Tracing Basics." Structured logging is the bridge between technical telemetry and business workflow state.

Logging Consistently in `OrderProcessor`

A useful pattern for `OrderProcessor` is to make sure every meaningful business log carries the same small set of fields. The most important ones are `TraceId`, so the log can be correlated with distributed tracing; `OrderId`, because that is the business identifier the team will search for most often; `Stage`, so the reader knows which part of the workflow produced the event; and `Outcome`, so the success or failure state is explicit rather than implied.

Once those fields exist consistently, the log stream becomes much easier to query. A trace can be followed from the HTTP boundary into the orchestration and then into individual activities. Failures can be grouped by stage. Queries can focus on a single order or on a failure trend across many orders. Figure 7-2 shows the relationship between those structured fields and the wider observability flow.

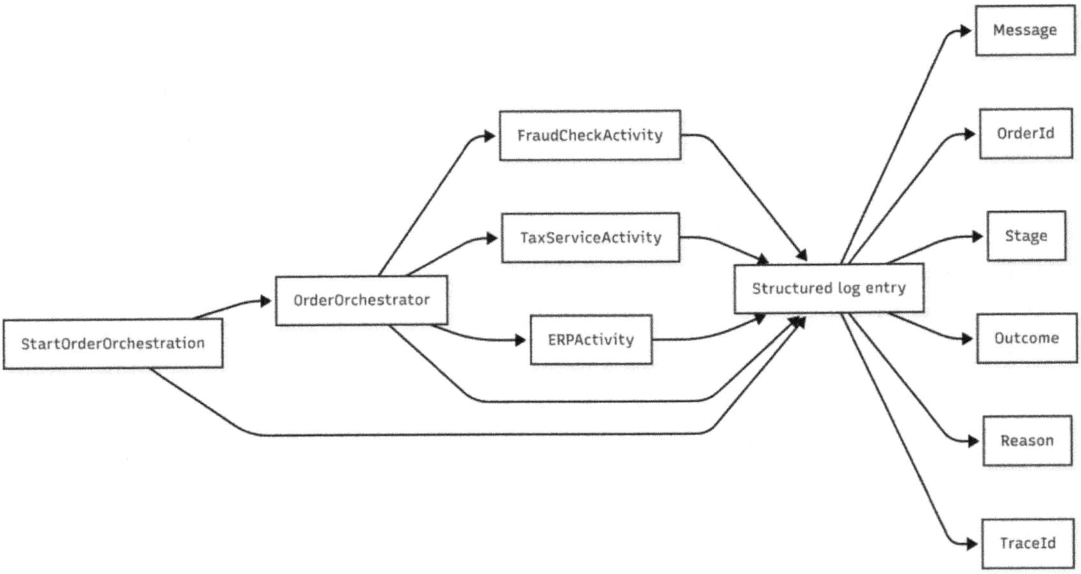

Figure 7-2. *Wider Observability Flow*

A Simple StructuredLogger Helper

One practical way to keep logs consistent is to use a small helper that standardizes the fields each log entry should contain. The point is not to create a universal logging framework. It is simply to reduce the chance that every activity logs in a different shape.

A simple helper for OrderProcessor might look like this:

Logging/StructuredLogger.cs

```
public class StructuredLogger
{
    private readonly ILogger _logger;

    public StructuredLogger(ILogger logger)
    {
        _logger = logger;
    }

    public void Info(
        string message,
        string orderId,
```

```
        string stage,
        string outcome,
        string traceId)
    {
        _logger.LogInformation(
            "{EventMessage} | Order={OrderId} Stage={Stage}
            Outcome={Outcome} Trace={TraceId}",
            message,
            orderId,
            stage,
            outcome,
            traceId);
    }

    public void Error(
        string message,
        string orderId,
        string stage,
        string outcome,
        string reason,
        string traceId,
        Exception? ex = null)
    {
        _logger.LogError(
            ex,
            "{EventMessage} | Order={OrderId} Stage={Stage}
            Outcome={Outcome} Reason={Reason} Trace={TraceId}",
            message,
            orderId,
            stage,
            outcome,
            reason,
            traceId);
    }
}
```

This pattern is intentionally simple because the chapter is teaching the shape of structured logging rather than trying to lock you into one reusable library. The important thing is that business logs now have a predictable schema rather than relying on ad hoc phrasing.

Using Structured Logging in an Activity

The benefit becomes more obvious when the helper is used inside one of the workflow activities. An ERP registration step is a good example because it is a business-critical dependency and one the operations team would care about immediately if it started failing.

This activity is shown as a representative example rather than as a complete production integration. It assumes the orchestrator has already created a valid ErpOrderRequest, that trace or correlation context has been established at the function boundary, and that StructuredLogger is the shared helper introduced earlier in the section. The important point is the shape of the telemetry; each business-relevant log entry carries the order ID, stage, outcome, and trace context in a consistent form.

Functions/RegisterErpOrderActivity.cs

```
[Function("RegisterErpOrderActivity")]
public async Task<ErpOrderResponse> Run(
    [ActivityTrigger] ErpOrderRequest req,
    FunctionContext ctx)
{
        ArgumentNullException.ThrowIfNull(req);

    var traceId = ctx.TraceContext.TraceParent ?? Guid.NewGuid().
    ToString();
    var logger = new StructuredLogger(ctx.GetLogger("ERP"));

    try
    {
        await Task.Delay(100);

        var erpId = Guid.NewGuid().ToString("N");

        logger.Info(
            "ERP registration succeeded",
```

```
            req.OrderId,
            "ERP",
            "Success",
            traceId);

        return new ErpOrderResponse(true, erpId);
    }
    catch (Exception ex)
    {
        logger.Error(
            "ERP registration failed",
            req.OrderId,
            "ERP",
            ex.Message,
            traceId,
            ex);
        throw;    }
}
```

Again, the point here is not that the `Task.Delay(100)` is realistic production code. The point is that the activity logs success and failure using the same core fields every time. That gives you a concrete `OrderProcessor` example while still keeping the section focused on the pattern.

JSON Logging and Machine Readability

Structured logging becomes even more useful when the host emits logs in a format that downstream systems can parse naturally. In practice, that usually means JSON output rather than plain-text console lines. Once the log entries are emitted in a structured format, observability tools can ingest the fields directly without relying on brittle parsing rules.

A host configuration for JSON-style output might look like this:

host.json

```
{
  "logging": {
    "applicationInsights": {
```

```
      "enableLiveMetrics": true,
      "samplingSettings": {
        "isEnabled": true
      }
    },
    "logLevel": {
      "default": "Information",
      "Host": "Warning",
      "Function": "Information"
    },
    "console": {
      "isEnabled": true,
      "formatterName": "json"
    }
  }
}
```

The exact mechanics may vary depending on the hosting path and logging sink, but the architectural idea is straightforward. If logs are already being written as structured events, the runtime and telemetry pipeline should preserve that structure rather than flattening everything back into text.

Orchestrator-Specific Considerations

Durable Functions needs a little more care because orchestrators replay. That means not every log statement belongs inside the orchestrator, and certainly not every log statement should be treated the same way as an activity log. Control-flow logging inside a replaying orchestrator can become repetitive and misleading very quickly.

For `OrderProcessor`, the cleaner approach is to log idempotent facts rather than noisy orchestration control flow. If a business event matters, such as an ERP registration succeeding with a specific identifier, that is worth recording. If the log simply says the orchestrator is entering a stage that may replay several times, that often belongs in `SetCustomStatus` instead or should be guarded by replay checks.

A simple replay-safe pattern might look like this:

```
if (!context.IsReplaying)
{
    logger.Info("Starting ERP registration", order.Id, "ERP", "Pending",
    traceId);
}
```

That keeps the trace and log stream useful without allowing orchestrator replay to flood the telemetry with repeated control-flow entries.

Querying Structured Logs

Once structured logs are flowing into Application Insights or Log Analytics, the real benefit appears in querying. A reader or operator is no longer forced to scan plain-text lines manually. They can search directly on the business fields the system already emits.

A query for one order might look like this:

```
traces
| where customDimensions.OrderId == "o-1001"
| project timestamp, customDimensions.Stage, message, severityLevel
```

A broader query grouping failures by stage and reason might look like this:

```
traces
| where customDimensions.Outcome == "Failure"
| summarize count() by customDimensions.Stage, customDimensions.Reason
```

These kinds of queries are what make structured logging genuinely operationally useful. The logs are no longer just there in case someone needs them. They can now support diagnosis, reporting, and trend analysis across the workflow.

Project Addition: Structured Logging Foundation for `OrderProcessor`

This section adds the first structured logging foundation for `OrderProcessor`. The workflow now has a consistent way to record business-relevant events using shared fields such as `OrderId`, `Stage`, `Outcome`, and `TraceId`, and those fields line up directly with the distributed tracing model introduced in the section "Distributed Tracing Basics." From this point on, the log stream is no longer just a collection of textual messages emitted by isolated Functions. It becomes a queryable record of how orders moved through the workflow and where they succeeded, stalled, or failed.

Monitoring Costs and Scale in Azure Functions

One of the selling points of serverless computing is that it scales automatically and charges only for what you use. That promise is broadly true, but it becomes meaningful only if the team can see what the platform is actually doing. In a workflow system such as `OrderProcessor`, cost and scale are not abstract platform concerns sitting outside the application. They are direct consequences of how the workflow is designed. Every orchestration replay, every activity invocation, every queue-triggered retry, and every fan-out branch affects both runtime behavior and cost. That is why observability in a serverless system cannot stop at traces and logs. `OrderProcessor` also needs visibility into how often Functions execute, how long they run, how queue backlogs behave, whether cold starts are affecting latency, and how retries or orchestration patterns are changing the shape of the workload. The point of this section is not to turn you into a billing specialist. It is to show that a serverless system becomes much easier to operate when the team understands not just whether it works, but how it scales and what that behavior is likely to cost.

The Economics of Azure Functions

Azure Functions changes the way application cost behaves because the bill is tied to runtime behavior rather than to one static server footprint. On the Consumption plan, execution count, execution duration, memory usage, storage interaction, and network behavior all contribute to cost. On the Premium plan, reserved capacity introduces a different pricing model, but the workload shape still matters because over-provisioning or unnecessary activity can waste that capacity just as easily. For `OrderProcessor`, that means a single business action can expand into many billable operations. An order enters through the API boundary, starts an orchestration, triggers multiple activities, fans out across inventory or validation work, calls external systems, and may retry when something goes wrong. Durable Function replays can add more executions. Queue-triggered processing can multiply load further. A system like that can still be cost-effective, but only if the team can observe how those patterns behave under real traffic.

What to Watch in OrderProcessor

The most useful cost and scale signals are not financial reports alone. They are workload metrics that explain why the platform is behaving the way it is. In OrderProcessor, the important questions include how many times each Function is running, which activities dominate execution volume, whether retries are multiplying work, how quickly queue-triggered Functions consume backlog, and whether cold starts are introducing latency that pushes the team toward a different hosting plan.

Azure Functions, Application Insights, and Azure Monitor already expose much of that information. The job of the application team is to decide which signals are actually meaningful for this workflow. Execution count matters because it reflects how often work is happening. Failures matter because they often drive retries and duplicate processing. Queue length matters because it reveals whether the system is keeping up with demand. Cold starts matter because they affect user-visible latency. Together, those signals tell the team whether the serverless platform is scaling as intended or whether the design of the workflow is causing unexpected pressure.

Enabling Richer Runtime Telemetry

To make Durable Functions and activity execution more visible, the host configuration can be tuned to emit a richer telemetry stream. A representative host.json configuration might look like this:

Host.json

```
{
  "logging": {
    "applicationInsights": {
      "samplingSettings": {
        "isEnabled": true,
        "maxTelemetryItemsPerSecond": 20
      }
    }
  },
  "extensions": {
    "durableTask": {
      "hubName": "OrderHub",
```

```
      "tracing": {
        "traceInputsAndOutputs": true,
        "traceReplayEvents": true
      }
    }
  }
}
```

This does not turn the platform into a complete cost model on its own, but it does make the runtime much easier to observe. Replay events, durable activity execution, and orchestration timing become visible in a way that supports both diagnosis and workload analysis. In a chapter about observability, that is the important point. The platform now emits enough signal for the team to reason about behavior instead of guessing.

Seeing Execution Patterns in Application Insights

Once telemetry is flowing, one of the first useful questions is simply which Functions are running most often. In a workflow such as `OrderProcessor`, that tells the team which parts of the design are driving the overall workload. Fan-out bursts, retries, and replay-heavy paths all become much easier to spot when they are viewed as time-based execution spikes rather than as isolated Function invocations.

A simple query showing request volume by Function might look like this:

```
requests
| summarize count() by name, bin(timestamp, 1m)
```

That kind of view is useful because it shows the operational shape of the workload. If one activity suddenly dominates execution volume, the cause may be legitimate demand, but it may also be a retry storm or an overly chatty workflow. Either way, the team now has an entry point for asking the right question.

Retry behavior can be explored in a similar way. Because retries multiply cost and execution count, they are worth watching explicitly rather than treating them as a hidden implementation detail. A dependency or queue-focused query can reveal whether the system is falling into repeated retry paths more often than expected:

```
dependencies
| where type == "Azure queue"
| summarize count() by operation_Name, success
```

Estimating Cost Per Order

One of the most useful ways to make cost visible is to tie it back to the business transaction the team already cares about. In `OrderProcessor`, that means cost should be made visible per order, or at least approximated per order, rather than only at the subscription or Function App level. The numbers will never be perfectly precise from inside the application, but even a rough application-level metric can make trade-offs much easier to understand.

A simple helper for recording an approximate order cost might look like this:

Services/MetricsLogger.cs

```
public class MetricsLogger
{
    private readonly TelemetryClient _telemetry;

    public MetricsLogger(TelemetryClient telemetry)
    {
        _telemetry = telemetry;
    }

    public void TrackOrderCost(string orderId, int activities, TimeSpan
    duration)
    {
        var cost = activities * 0.20m / 1_000_000m;

        _telemetry.GetMetric("OrderCostUSD").TrackValue(
            (double)cost,
            "OrderId",
            orderId);
    }
}
```

This kind of calculation is deliberately approximate, and that is fine for the purpose of the chapter. The pattern matters more than the accounting precision. The value is that cost now becomes part of the observability story rather than something discovered much later in a separate billing dashboard.

Once emitted, the metric can be queried like any other telemetry:

```
customMetrics
| where name == "OrderCostUSD"
| summarize avg(value) by tostring(customDimensions.OrderId)
```

That gives the team a way to compare order journeys, highlight unusually expensive processing paths, and reason about whether a given pattern in the workflow is operationally acceptable.

Watching Cold Starts

Cold starts are another important part of the scale story because they connect platform behavior directly to user experience. A system can be inexpensive on paper but still feel slow to the caller if traffic arrives after an idle period and the platform has to warm up execution capacity again. In some systems, that is perfectly acceptable. In others, it may justify a different hosting plan. For `OrderProcessor`, cold starts matter most at the public entry points or time-sensitive workflow edges. If the first request after a quiet period experiences noticeably higher latency, the team should be able to see that pattern in telemetry rather than debating it anecdotally. A simple query might look like this:

```
requests
| extend isCold = iff(customDimensions["ColdStart"] == "true", 1, 0)
| summarize coldCount = sum(isCold), total = count() by name
```

This does not by itself decide whether Consumption or Premium is the right plan. What it does is turn a subjective complaint about slowness into something measurable.

Queue Depth and Backpressure

Queue-triggered workloads introduce another kind of scale signal: backlog. In a healthy system, queue consumers keep up with incoming work. When that stops happening, the queue length begins to rise, which is often one of the first signs that the workflow is under pressure. That pressure may come from high demand, slow downstream dependencies, insufficient concurrency, or repeated failure and retry behavior.

For OrderProcessor, queue depth is especially important because it gives the team an early warning that scaling is not matching workload. A representative query:

```
AzureDiagnostics
| where ResourceProvider == "MICROSOFT.WEB"
| where Category == "FunctionAppLogs"
| summarize avg(QueueLength_s) by bin(TimeGenerated, 5m)
```

When queue length rises faster than Functions consume it, the system is telling the team something useful. Either the scale model needs help, or something further downstream is slowing the flow enough to create backpressure. In both cases, the metric becomes an operational clue rather than just another number.

Applying Scale and Cost Monitoring to OrderProcessor

For OrderProcessor, this section adds a new layer to observability. Traces and structured logs already explain what happened to a request and where it failed. Cost and scale telemetry now explains how much work the platform is actually doing to produce that result. That is a different but equally important kind of visibility.

Once execution counts, retries, queue depth, cold starts, and cost-related custom metrics are visible, the team can start to reason about the operational shape of the workflow. A fraud check that retries too often is no longer just a reliability issue. It is a scale and cost issue as well. A fan-out pattern that works correctly but multiplies executions dramatically is no longer just a design choice. It is a measurable workload characteristic. This is what makes the chapter feel complete. The system is not only traceable and loggable now. It is economically and operationally visible too.

Project Addition: Cost and Scale Visibility for OrderProcessor

This section introduces the first real cost and scale monitoring foundation for `OrderProcessor`. The Functions host now emits richer durable runtime telemetry, Application Insights queries can be used to understand execution volume and retry behavior, and custom metrics can approximate the cost of processing an order rather than leaving all financial visibility outside the application. From this point on, the team is no longer limited to asking whether orders succeeded or failed. It can also ask how heavily the platform had to work, where scale pressure is building, and which workflow paths are becoming unexpectedly expensive.

Alerts and Dashboards

Telemetry only becomes operationally useful when someone can see it at the right moment and in the right form. Traces, logs, and metrics are all valuable, but they do not help much if they stay buried in a backend that nobody checks until after customers have already noticed a problem. That is where alerts and dashboards come in. Alerts turn telemetry into immediate signals that demand attention, while dashboards turn the same telemetry into a continuous view of how the system is behaving over time.

For `OrderProcessor`, both are essential. The workflow now stretches across HTTP boundaries, orchestrations, activity functions, queues, and downstream dependencies. A failure in one part of that path may not break the entire system immediately. It may simply introduce delay, create backlog, or increase the error rate gradually until customers begin to feel it. A useful alerting and dashboard model helps the team notice those signals before they turn into incidents that are much harder to contain.

Why Alerts Are Important

Distributed systems rarely fail in simple or dramatic ways. A downstream API may begin timing out intermittently. Queue length may start growing because consumption has slowed slightly rather than stopped completely. An orchestration may remain technically alive while being stalled on an external event for far too long. Retrying dependencies may push up cost and execution volume long before anyone realizes the workflow is looping inefficiently. That makes alerts important because they shorten the time between problem and awareness. The point of an alert is not merely to say that something is wrong. It is to make the right kind of wrongness visible quickly enough that the team can act before the effect becomes customer-visible or operationally expensive. In a system like `OrderProcessor`, that means alerts should be tied to conditions that actually matter to workflow health rather than to every possible metric fluctuation.

Why Dashboards Are Important

Alerts answer the question of what needs attention now. Dashboards answer a different question, which is what the system looks like as a whole. A team operating `OrderProcessor` needs to be able to see whether orders are flowing through the main stages; whether one stage has become the bottleneck, whether approvals are accumulating; whether dependency latency is drifting upwards; and whether cost-related metrics are moving outside the expected range.

That broader view matters because not every important problem will fire an alert immediately. Some issues develop gradually. A dashboard makes those slower changes visible by turning the telemetry into an operational narrative rather than a collection of disconnected charts. In practice, it allows an engineer or operator to understand the state of the platform quickly without needing to run half a dozen ad hoc queries every time something feels wrong.

The Right Alert Signals for `OrderProcessor`

A useful alerting model for `OrderProcessor` begins with the places where failures actually matter to the business workflow. One important category is failure rate. If a significant percentage of orders are failing over a short window, the team should know quickly. Another is queue backlog, because a rising message count often means that the workflow can no longer keep up with demand or that a downstream dependency is slowing the system enough to create pressure.

External dependency failures deserve their own attention because services such as Fraud, Tax, or ERP may degrade independently of the core application. ERP registration errors are especially important because they often sit near the end of the process and can block successful completion even after the rest of the workflow has behaved correctly. Cost anomalies belong here as well. A sudden spike in execution count or retry volume may indicate a fan-out storm or runaway orchestration pattern that needs intervention even if customer-facing errors are still low.

The common principle is that alerts should be tied to meaningful conditions in the workflow, not to every possible telemetry point. If the team cannot act on an alert when it fires, that alert probably should not exist in its current form.

Building Alerts with Azure Monitor

Azure Monitor and Application Insights together provide a straightforward way to turn telemetry into alert rules. Some alerts are naturally metric-based, such as queue depth, execution failures, or dependency count. Others are better expressed as log queries, especially when the threshold depends on business context such as failed outcomes or a particular stage in the workflow.

A KQL-style alert query for workflow failures could look like this:

```
traces
| where customDimensions.Outcome == "Failure"
| summarize count() by bin(timestamp, 5m)
| where count_ > 10
```

The real value of an alert like this is not just that it can send an email or a notification into Teams or Slack. It is that it turns a growing problem into a visible operational event. Depending on the team's maturity, alerts can also trigger automated responses such as opening tickets, invoking a remediation Function, or activating a protective pattern such as a circuit breaker.

Designing Dashboards for `OrderProcessor`

If alerts are the fast reaction layer, dashboards are the continuous visibility layer. For `OrderProcessor`, a good dashboard should help someone understand the workflow state in a matter of seconds. That usually means focusing on the movement of orders through the key stages rather than trying to visualize every metric the platform emits.

One of the most useful views is the order flow itself. A count of orders by stage makes it easy to see where work is progressing normally and where it is beginning to accumulate. Failures by stage or by reason can then explain where the friction is occurring. Latency views show which dependency calls are consuming the most time. Queue depth adds pressure information. Cost-related charts from the previous section can show whether execution or retry volume is drifting upwards. Pending human approvals matter too, because bottlenecks in an approval step are operationally important even if the rest of the platform is healthy.

The aim is not to create a decorative dashboard full of charts. It is to make the state of the workflow visible enough that an engineer can explain system health quickly and confidently.

Example Dashboard Queries

Once telemetry is structured properly, dashboards become much easier to build because the underlying questions are already reflected in the data. A view of orders by stage might use a query like this:

```
traces
| where customDimensions.Stage != ""
| summarize count() by tostring(customDimensions.Stage)
```

A view of failures by reason might look like this:

```
traces
| where customDimensions.Outcome == "Failure"
| summarize count() by tostring(customDimensions.Reason)
```

A latency view for dependencies might use

```
dependencies
| summarize avg(duration) by target, name
```

And a view of pending supplier approvals might use custom events or orchestration state information such as:

```
customEvents
| where name == "DurableTaskOrchestration"
| where customDimensions.Stage == "AwaitingSupplierApproval"
| summarize count()
```

These are representative rather than exhaustive, but they show the pattern clearly. Because the telemetry is already structured around business stages and outcomes, the dashboard can reflect the workflow rather than just the infrastructure.

Operational Best Practices

A dashboard becomes less useful as it becomes more cluttered. For `OrderProcessor`, that means the dashboard should remain focused on flow, latency, failures, backlog, and cost pressure. Those are the views that help the team understand the platform. Everything else should earn its place.

Alerts also need discipline. A warning alert should inform without causing panic. A critical alert should fire only when the team genuinely needs to act. Routing matters too. Dependency-specific failures may need to go to the application team, while queue or hosting pressure may belong with whoever owns the operational platform. In a mature setup, some alerts may also trigger automated remediation, but that should be done carefully so the response is predictable and well understood.

Most importantly, dashboards should not be treated as something to check only during outages. Their value is highest when the team uses them regularly enough to know what normal looks like. That way, drift and degradation are easier to recognize before they become incidents.

Applying Alerts and Dashboards to `OrderProcessor`

For `OrderProcessor`, this section adds the operational visibility layer that sits on top of the traces, logs, and metrics introduced earlier in the chapter. Tracing shows the path of a request. Structured logging explains what happened at each stage. Cost and scale metrics show how the platform is behaving under load. Alerts and dashboards now turn all of that telemetry into something the team can use actively rather than retrospectively.

This is an important transition in the chapter because it moves observability from collection into operation. The system is no longer just emitting useful signals. The team can now see those signals in near real time, react when thresholds are crossed, and build a shared understanding of workflow health.

Project Addition: Operational Visibility for `OrderProcessor`

This section introduces the first real alerts-and-dashboards foundation for `OrderProcessor`. The telemetry already collected through tracing, logging, and metrics can now be turned into Azure Monitor alert rules and shared dashboards that show order flow, stage bottlenecks, dependency latency, queue pressure, pending approvals, and cost-related behavior. From this point on, `OrderProcessor` is no longer only observable in the forensic sense of "we can investigate it later." It becomes operationally visible while the system is running, which is the point at which observability starts to support day-to-day production operations rather than post-incident diagnosis alone.

Putting It All Together: Observability Playbook

By this point, `OrderProcessor` has tracing, structured logging, cost and scale telemetry, and an operational model built around dashboards and alerts. Each of those pieces is useful on its own, but the real value appears when they work together. Observability is not one feature, and it is not one tool. It is the combined ability to understand what the system is doing, why it is doing it, how often it is happening, and what should happen next when something goes wrong. That matters because distributed systems rarely fail in one clean, obvious way. A trace may show that an ERP dependency is slow, but the trace alone will not explain whether the failure is isolated or widespread. A log entry may show that a supplier approval failed, but the log alone will not show whether hundreds of approvals are backing up. A metric may show that execution count has surged, but the metric alone will not show which workflow stage is driving the increase. The point of an observability playbook is to connect those views so the team can move from symptoms to explanation quickly and consistently.

The Three Pillars in Practice

Observability is often described through three pillars: traces, logs, and metrics. That language is useful, but in practice the important thing is how those pillars complement each other inside a real system. In `OrderProcessor`, traces show the path an order took across the platform. Logs add contextual detail such as order ID, stage, outcome, and failure reason. Metrics show workload shape over time, including execution volume, queue pressure, cost-related behavior, and latency trends.

Taken together, those three forms of telemetry answer different parts of the same operational question. Traces show where something broke. Logs show why it broke. Metrics show how often it is breaking and whether the situation is getting better or worse. Once dashboards and alerts sit on top of that telemetry, the team gains a practical operating model rather than just a large pile of instrumentation.

Building the Playbook Around `OrderProcessor`

The easiest way to understand the observability playbook is to anchor it to the system itself. In `OrderProcessor`, everything starts at the workflow boundary. A customer submits an order, that request enters the system with or without an existing trace context, and the application either propagates or creates the tracing and correlation information needed to follow the journey. From there, the orchestration, activities, queues, and downstream dependencies all contribute their own telemetry, but they do so in a way that still belongs to the same business transaction.

Figure 7-3 shows how those layers fit together in `OrderProcessor`, from the initial order submission through tracing, structured logs, metrics, dashboards, and alerts.

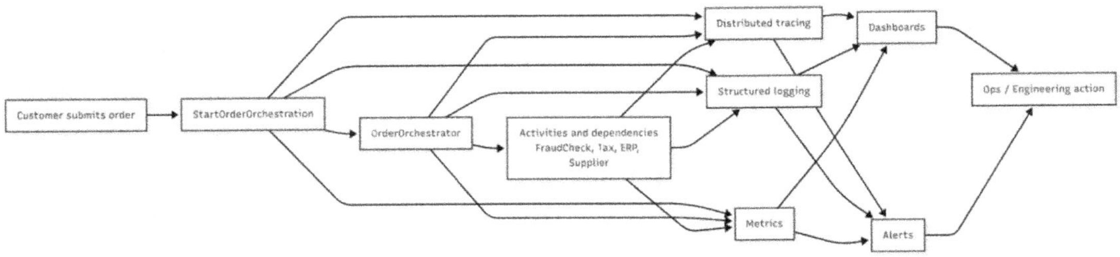

Figure 7-3. *Observability Layers for the Workflow*

Playbook Principles

A useful observability playbook should be simple enough to remember under pressure and concrete enough to apply during real incidents. For `OrderProcessor`, the first principle is that everything starts with traceability. If a request cannot be followed across Functions, orchestrations, dependencies, and events, then the rest of the telemetry becomes much harder to interpret. A request without a usable trace ID is not impossible to debug, but it is needlessly expensive to reason about.

The second principle is that logs must carry business context. A generic exception message may technically describe a problem, but it does not help much if the operator cannot immediately connect it to an order, a workflow stage, or an outcome. Structured logs solve that by keeping the same small set of fields visible across the system. That makes the telemetry useful to both humans and machines.

The third principle is that metrics are the system's behavioral layer. They show whether the problem is isolated, trending, or systemic. In `OrderProcessor`, metrics such as execution count, failure rate by stage, dependency latency, queue depth, and cost per order reveal whether the workflow is merely experiencing one bad request or whether something broader is now wrong.

The fourth principle is that dashboards should tell the story of the platform, not merely display raw charts. An effective dashboard lets an engineer understand the health of `OrderProcessor` quickly by showing flow through the main stages, the points of failure, the slowest dependencies, the amount of work waiting in the system, and the operational pressure building around cost or scale.

The fifth principle is that alerts must lead to action. An alert that cannot be interpreted or acted on is just noise. For `OrderProcessor`, alerts should fire on conditions that matter to workflow health, such as rising failure rate, backlog growth, dependency outage, or execution spikes that suggest runaway behavior. The point of the alert is not simply to inform. It is to shorten the time between signal and response.

The Observability Stack in Action

Once those principles are in place, the observability stack becomes much easier to use in practice. Imagine that ERP starts behaving badly. The trace shows ERP spans slowing or failing. Structured logs show `Outcome=Failure` and a reason such as timeout, linked to the relevant order IDs and trace IDs. Metrics show ERP-related failures increasing over time. The dashboard shows the order funnel shrinking at the ERP stage while pending work rises behind it. Finally, an alert raises the issue directly to the team responsible for responding.

That is the value of the playbook. The system no longer depends on one lucky log line or one engineer remembering a special query under pressure. The telemetry layers support each other. One view leads naturally into the next until the team can understand both the technical cause and the business effect.

Applying the Playbook to `OrderProcessor`

For `OrderProcessor`, this final section turns observability from a collection of techniques into an operating model. The earlier parts of the chapter established the ingredients: trace propagation, correlation middleware, structured logs, runtime and cost telemetry, dashboards, and alerts. What the playbook does is show how those ingredients combine into one response path the team can rely on. This is the point where observability stops being theoretical. A trace is no longer just a developer convenience. A structured log is no longer just a tidier message. A dashboard is no longer just a set of charts. Together, they become the means by which the platform is understood, operated, and improved.

Project Addition: Observability Playbook for `OrderProcessor`

This section completes the Chapter 7 observability foundation for `OrderProcessor`. The platform now has a coherent model in which requests can be traced end to end, business events can be queried through structured logs, workload and cost behavior can be measured through metrics, and dashboards and alerts can turn those signals into day-to-day operational awareness. From this point on, `OrderProcessor` is not just instrumented. It is observable in the fuller sense of the word: understandable while it is running, diagnosable when it fails, and operable with enough confidence that the team can respond quickly instead of guessing.

EXERCISES

1. Submit an order through `StartOrderOrchestration` and inspect the trace in Application Insights. Can you follow the transaction from the HTTP boundary into the orchestration and then into downstream dependency calls?
2. Call the order submission endpoint with your own `traceparent` header. Does the trace ID flow through the workflow and appear consistently in telemetry?
3. Remove the correlation middleware temporarily and submit a new order. What becomes harder to understand in the trace and log output?
4. Add an artificial delay to a downstream dependency such as Tax or ERP. Can distributed tracing show clearly where the extra latency was introduced?
5. Force one downstream API call to fail with a 500 response. Does the trace make it obvious which dependency failed and where the workflow stopped?
6. Add structured logging to one additional activity beyond the examples already shown. Which fields do you consider essential for keeping the logs queryable and useful?
7. Submit three orders and then query logs by `OrderId`. Can you reconstruct what happened to one order without scanning unrelated log entries?
8. Query structured logs grouped by `stage`. Which workflow stage is generating the highest volume of log entries, and does that look expected?

9. Force ERP registration to fail and inspect the structured log output. Is the failure reason easy to query and correlate with the trace?
10. Add a noisy log line inside an orchestrator without guarding it against replay. Run a workflow twice and compare the telemetry before and after adding a replay-safe check.
11. Query Function execution counts over time. Which Functions dominate invocation volume during a burst of orders?
12. Introduce retry behavior in a dependency such as `FraudCheck` and observe the effect on execution count. How much extra work does retrying add to the platform?
13. Record an approximate cost-per-order metric and compare several different orders. Do more complex order journeys produce noticeably different telemetry shapes or cost estimates?
14. Leave the system idle long enough to trigger a cold start, then submit a new order. How does the first request compare with later warm executions?
15. Push a burst of queued work into the system and watch queue depth. Does consumption keep pace, or does backlog begin to build?
16. Create an alert for workflow failures in a short time window and trigger it deliberately. Is the alert actionable, or is it too vague to be useful?
17. Build a dashboard showing order counts by stage. Can someone unfamiliar with the current run explain the workflow state from the dashboard alone?
18. Add a dashboard query for pending approvals or stalled work. Does it help expose business bottlenecks that are not obvious from technical failures alone?
19. Create an alert for a cost or execution spike and then trigger a fan-out-heavy workload. Does the alert surface a meaningful signal rather than just noise?
20. Pick one trace ID from a failed order and use the full observability playbook – trace, structured logs, metrics, dashboard context, and alert history – to diagnose the problem. How quickly can you move from symptom to likely cause?

Summary

Observability in a serverless distributed system begins with visibility across boundaries. In `OrderProcessor`, distributed tracing gives each order journey a coherent path from the HTTP entry point into the orchestration, through activity functions, and out to external dependencies. Instead of treating Functions and APIs as isolated runtime events, tracing turns them into one logical transaction. That gives the team a much better way to understand where time is spent, where failures occur, and how a business action actually moved through the platform. Tracing alone is not enough, which is why structured logging becomes the second essential layer. In this chapter, `OrderProcessor` moved from ad hoc log messages to logs that carry consistent business context, such as `OrderId`, `Stage`, `Outcome`, and `TraceId`. That makes telemetry queryable instead of merely readable. Once those logs are paired with metrics for execution count, queue depth, retry behavior, cold starts, and approximate cost per order, the platform becomes easier to reason about both technically and operationally. The team can now see not just what happened but also how often it is happening and what pressure it is placing on the system.

The final step is turning that telemetry into an operating model. Dashboards make the state of the workflow visible at a glance; alerts shorten the gap between problem and awareness, and the observability playbook ties traces, logs, metrics, and operational response into one coherent approach. For `OrderProcessor`, that means observability is no longer a collection of disconnected tools. It becomes a practical foundation for diagnosing failures, understanding workflow behavior, controlling scale and cost, and running the system with much more confidence.

CHAPTER 8

Security, Identity, and Access Control

Security becomes a different kind of problem once a serverless system starts to grow into a real distributed application. `OrderProcessor` is no longer just a set of Functions reacting to requests and events. It now has multiple entry points, long-running workflows, external integrations, and operational boundaries that all need to be protected consistently. In that sort of system, security cannot sit in one login screen or one shared secret. It has to be carried across the whole platform, from HTTP endpoints and orchestration triggers to downstream API calls, secrets, network paths, and audit evidence.

This chapter brings those concerns into the `OrderProcessor` codebase directly. It begins with identity and token validation at the function boundary and then moves through token handling inside activities, hardening Durable Functions, extending RBAC across workflow boundaries, securing external integrations, moving secrets into Key Vault, locking down network paths, and finally capturing durable audit records for sensitive actions. The goal is not just to stop unauthorized access. It is to make `OrderProcessor` a serverless system that can authenticate correctly, authorize precisely, protect its integrations and secrets, and produce evidence of what happened when it matters.

Identity Basics in Serverless .NET

Security is the invisible backbone of distributed systems. All the observability in the world won't matter if attackers can spoof requests, exfiltrate data, or escalate privileges. In traditional monoliths, identity and access management often live inside the app itself.

© Patrick Kearns 2026
P. Kearns, *Serverless Distributed Systems in Modern .NET and Azure*,
https://doi.org/10.1007/979-8-8688-2839-3_8

In serverless systems, that responsibility shifts outward; APIs, Functions, queues, and events must each integrate with an external identity provider.

In the Azure world, that provider is typically Microsoft Entra ID (formerly Azure AD) for organizational users, and Azure AD B2C for customer-facing apps. For .NET developers, this means embracing token-based identity, usually OAuth2 + OpenID Connect flows, and validating those tokens at every entry point.

Why Identity Looks Different in Serverless

In serverless systems, identity works differently because the application no longer has a single front door. Instead of one central login boundary, requests can enter through HTTP endpoints, Service Bus queue triggers, Event Grid subscriptions, and Durable Functions orchestrations that call external APIs. That broader entry surface changes the security model. Each boundary must be treated as a potential attack vector and secured individually, while still following a consistent identity strategy across the system. In practice, this makes identity token-centric, with every request carrying a bearer token; decentralizes enforcement because each function or component must validate what it receives; externalizes authentication to providers such as Microsoft Entra ID or Azure AD B2C rather than handling it inside the application; and reinforces least privilege by ensuring tokens grant only the narrow scopes required for the operation being performed.

Token Flow in OrderProcessor

When a client submits a new order to `OrderProcessor`, the flow begins with authentication against Microsoft Entra ID or Azure AD B2C. The frontend application, or another API client, signs in and receives a JWT access token containing claims such as the subject identifier, scopes, roles, and expiry. That token is then sent with the request to the `OrderProcessor` API, for example, on the `/orders/orchestrate` endpoint, using the standard Authorization: Bearer <token> header. When the request reaches the Azure Function, the token is validated at the function boundary, which checks the issuer, audience, signature, and expiry before accepting it. Once validated, the token claims are made available as a `ClaimsPrincipal` so downstream code can use them for authorization decisions. From there, the workflow executes with awareness of the caller's identity, either by operating directly within that context or by recording the relevant identity information at the start of the orchestration, allowing activities to enforce claims-based checks before performing sensitive operations (see Figure 8-1).

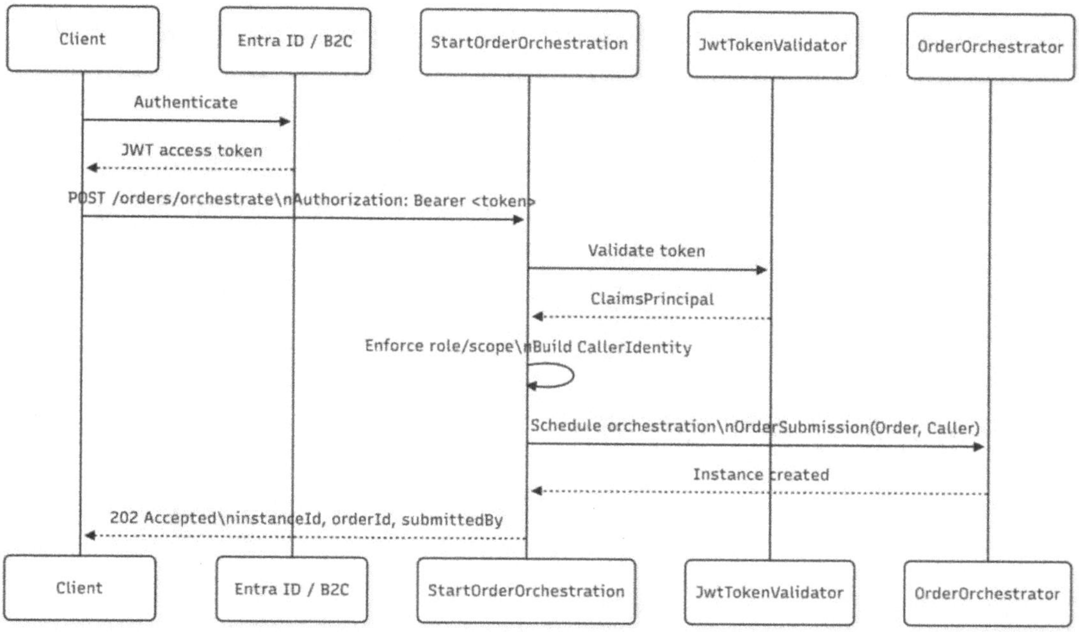

Figure 8-1. *JWT validation and caller identity flow for order submission*

Introducing Identity at the Function Boundary

When you add authentication to an Azure Function, the goal is not to make the function responsible for sign-in, but to ensure that any request reaching it already carries a valid identity. Once that identity has been established, the function can use the caller's claims, roles, or scopes to decide whether the requested operation should be allowed. This keeps authentication at the system boundary and keeps business logic focused on the workflow itself. For this book, that distinction matters, because the aim is to show how identity fits into the overall architecture without introducing an implementation detail that would distract from the codebase being built across the chapters.

The examples in this chapter show JWT validation directly inside the Azure Function so the security flow remains visible in the OrderProcessor codebase. In a production enterprise system, however, the Function App would usually not be exposed directly as the public API surface. Azure API Management would typically sit in front of the Function App and act as the controlled API boundary.

APIM gives the platform a central place to enforce cross-cutting API concerns before requests reach the Functions runtime. That includes validating JWTs, applying rate limits and quotas, checking headers and request shape, enforcing subscription or product-level access rules, routing versions, and producing a consistent API gateway audit trail. It also allows the backend Function App to be protected more tightly, for example, by restricting inbound traffic so only APIM can call it.

This does not remove the need for application-level authorization inside OrderProcessor. APIM can reject obviously invalid or abusive requests at the edge, but the Function still needs to enforce business permissions such as OrderWriter, SupplierApprover, FraudAnalyst, or Admin before changing workflow state. In other words, APIM protects the API boundary, while the Function code protects the workflow boundary.

Understanding JWT Claims

A JWT from Entra ID looks like this (simplified):

```
{
    "aud": "api://orderprocessor",
    "iss": "https://login.microsoftonline.com/{tenantid}/v2.0",
    "iat": 1694800000,
    "exp": 1694803600,
    "sub": "d2f1a0c4-1ab1-4c0b-87e5-d731caa7a1bc",
    "scp": "Orders.ReadWrite",
    "roles": ["OrderWriter"]
}
```

A JWT issued by Microsoft Entra ID carries a set of claims that describe who the caller is, who issued the token, who the token is intended for, and what the caller is allowed to do. The audience claim identifies the API the token was issued for, ensuring that a token meant for one service cannot be reused against another. The issuer claim identifies the authority that created the token, typically the relevant Entra tenant. The subject claim provides a unique identifier for the signed-in user or calling identity. Permission-related claims then describe what access has been granted. A scope claim usually represents delegated permissions, while role claims represent application roles assigned to the caller. In a Function-based system, these claims are what allow the application to move beyond simple authentication and make real authorization decisions. The token is not just proof that the caller has signed in; it is also the basis for deciding whether that caller should be allowed to perform a specific operation.

Project Addition: Securing StartOrderOrchestration

Up to this point, `OrderProcessor` has protected its HTTP functions with function keys. That was enough while the book focused on orchestration patterns, retries, approvals, and workflow structure, but it is not enough for a production-facing order API. A function key proves that the caller knows a shared secret for the endpoint. It does not tell us who the caller is, what role they belong to, or whether they should be allowed to submit orders at all.

The natural place to introduce identity is the existing `StartOrderOrchestration` endpoint, because that is the public entry point into the order workflow. Instead of treating order submission as an anonymous or shared-secret operation, we now move it behind token-based authentication. The Function app is now configured to validate JWT bearer tokens issued by Microsoft Entra ID, ensure they were issued by the expected authority for the expected audience, and expose the resulting claims to the function code.

Once the caller's identity is established, the starter function can enforce authorization rules before any orchestration begins. In practice, that means checking that the user has the right role or scope to submit orders, rejecting unauthorized requests early, and recording the caller's identity in logs and traces. This changes the meaning of the endpoint completely. `POST /orders/orchestrate` is no longer just a function-key-protected trigger. It becomes a real application boundary that accepts orders only from authenticated principals with the correct permissions.

Wiring JWT Validation into OrderProcessor

For this sample, we validate bearer tokens explicitly at the function boundary so the security flow remains visible in the codebase we have built throughout the book.

Program.cs

```
using Microsoft.Azure.Functions.Worker;
using Microsoft.Azure.Functions.Worker.Builder;
using Microsoft.Extensions.DependencyInjection;
```

```
using Microsoft.Extensions.Hosting;
using OrderProcessor.Options;
using OrderProcessor.Security;

var builder = FunctionsApplication.CreateBuilder(args);

builder.ConfigureFunctionsWebApplication();

builder.Services
    .AddApplicationInsightsTelemetryWorkerService()
    .ConfigureFunctionsApplicationInsights();

builder.Services
    .AddOptions<AuthOptions>()
    .BindConfiguration(AuthOptions.SectionName)
    .Validate(options =>
        !string.IsNullOrWhiteSpace(options.Authority) &&
        !string.IsNullOrWhiteSpace(options.Audience),
        "Auth settings are required.");

builder.Services.AddSingleton<ITokenValidator, JwtTokenValidator>();

builder.Build().Run();
```

Options/AuthOptions.cs

```
namespace OrderProcessor.Options;

public sealed class AuthOptions
{
    public const string SectionName = "Auth";
    public string Authority { get; set; } = string.Empty;
    public string Audience { get; set; } = string.Empty;
    public string RequiredRole { get; set; } = "OrderWriter";
    public string RequiredScope { get; set; } = "Orders.ReadWrite";
}
```

Security/ITokenValidator.cs

```
using System.Security.Claims;
namespace OrderProcessor.Security;
```

```
        }

        const string prefix = "Bearer ";

        if (!header.StartsWith(prefix, StringComparison.OrdinalIgnoreCase))
        {
            return null;
        }

        return header[prefix.Length..].Trim();
    }
}
```

Securing the StartOrderOrchestration Endpoint

With token validation in place, the existing StartOrderOrchestration function can now reject unauthenticated callers, enforce the required role or scope, and record who started the workflow.

Earlier development examples used AuthorizationLevel.Anonymous to keep local testing simple and to make the workflow code easier to follow. At this point in the book, the endpoint is being treated as a secured application boundary, so the trigger is changed to AuthorizationLevel.Function. This adds a Function key requirement at the Azure Functions boundary.

The Function key should not be confused with user authentication. It only protects access to the Function endpoint itself. The JWT validation and RBAC checks in this example still provide the real application-level security by proving who the caller is and whether they are allowed to start an order workflow. In production, this endpoint would typically sit behind Azure API Management, with APIM enforcing gateway-level policies and forwarding authorized traffic to the Function backend.

Functions/StartOrderOrchestration.cs

```
using System;
using System.Net;
using Microsoft.Azure.Functions.Worker;
using Microsoft.Azure.Functions.Worker.Http;
using Microsoft.DurableTask.Client;
using Microsoft.Extensions.Logging;
```

```
using Microsoft.Extensions.Options;
using OrderProcessor.Options;
using OrderProcessor.Security;

namespace OrderProcessor;

public sealed class StartOrderOrchestration
{
    private readonly ILogger<StartOrderOrchestration> _logger;
    private readonly ITokenValidator _tokenValidator;
    private readonly AuthOptions _authOptions;

    public StartOrderOrchestration(
        ILogger<StartOrderOrchestration> logger,
        ITokenValidator tokenValidator,
        IOptions<AuthOptions> authOptions)
    {
        _logger = logger;
        _tokenValidator = tokenValidator;
        _authOptions = authOptions.Value;
    }

    [Function("StartOrderOrchestration")]
    public async Task<HttpResponseData> Run(
        [HttpTrigger(AuthorizationLevel.Function, "post", Route = "orders/
        orchestrate")]
        HttpRequestData req,
        [DurableClient] DurableTaskClient client,
        CancellationToken stopToken)
    {
        try
        {
            var bearerToken = req.GetBearerToken();

            if (string.IsNullOrWhiteSpace(bearerToken))
            {
                var unauthorized = req.CreateResponse(HttpStatusCode.
                Unauthorized);
```

```
        await unauthorized.WriteStringAsync("Missing bearer
        token.", stopToken);
        return unauthorized;
    }

    var principal = await _tokenValidator.ValidateAsync
    (bearerToken, stopToken);

    if (principal is null)
    {
        var unauthorized = req.CreateResponse(HttpStatusCode.
        Unauthorized);
        await unauthorized.WriteStringAsync("Invalid or expired
        token.", stopToken);
        return unauthorized;
    }

    var isAllowed =
    principal.HasRole(_authOptions.RequiredRole) ||
    principal.HasScope(_authOptions.RequiredScope);

    if (!isAllowed)
    {
        var forbidden = req.CreateResponse(HttpStatusCode.
        Forbidden);
        await forbidden.WriteStringAsync("Caller is not allowed to
        submit orders.", stopToken);
        return forbidden;
    }

   var order = await req.ReadFromJsonAsync<Order>(cancellationToken:
   stopToken);

    if (order is null ||
    string.IsNullOrWhiteSpace(order.Id) ||
    string.IsNullOrWhiteSpace(order.CustomerEmail))
    {
        var bad = req.CreateResponse(HttpStatusCode.BadRequest);
```

```
            await bad.WriteStringAsync("Invalid order payload.",
            stopToken);
            return bad;
        }

        var caller = new CallerIdentity(
            UserId: principal.GetUserId(),
            UserName: principal.GetUserName(),
            Roles: principal.GetRoles());

        var submission = new OrderSubmission(order, caller);

        var instanceId = await client.ScheduleNewOrchestration
        InstanceAsync(
            "OrderOrchestrator",
            submission,
            cancellation: stopToken);

        _logger.LogInformation(
            "User {UserName} started orchestration {InstanceId} for
            order {OrderId}",
            caller.UserName,
            instanceId,
            order.Id);

        var response = req.CreateResponse(HttpStatusCode.Accepted);

        await response.WriteAsJsonAsync(new
        {
            instanceId,
            orderId = order.Id,
            submittedBy = caller.UserName
        }, cancellationToken: stopToken);

        return response;
    }
    catch (OperationCanceledException) when (stopToken.
    IsCancellationRequested)
    {
```

```
            _logger.LogWarning("StartOrderOrchestration request was
            cancelled.");
            throw;
        }
        catch (Exception ex)
        {
            _logger.LogError(ex, "Failed to start order orchestration.");

            var error = req.CreateResponse(HttpStatusCode.
            InternalServerError);
            await error.WriteStringAsync(
                "An unexpected error occurred while starting the order
                workflow.",
                stopToken);

            return error;
        }
    }
}
```

Carrying Caller Identity into the Workflow

The workflow should not persist the raw bearer token. Instead, it carries only the minimum caller metadata needed for traceability and downstream decisions.

Models/CallerIdentity.cs

```
namespace OrderProcessor;

public sealed record CallerIdentity(
    string UserId,
    string UserName,
    IReadOnlyList<string> Roles);
```

Models/OrderSubmission.cs

```
namespace OrderProcessor;

public sealed record OrderSubmission(
    Order Order,
```

```
    CallerIdentity Caller);
```

Orchestrators/OrderOrchestrator.cs

```
using Microsoft.Azure.Functions.Worker;
using Microsoft.DurableTask;

namespace OrderProcessor;

public static class OrderOrchestrator
{
    [Function("OrderOrchestrator")]
    public static async Task Run(
        [OrchestrationTrigger] TaskOrchestrationContext context)
    {
        var submission = context.GetInput<OrderSubmission>()
            ?? throw new InvalidOperationException("Order submission input
            is required.");

        var order = submission.Order;
        var caller = submission.Caller;

        context.SetCustomStatus(new
        {
            Stage = "Started",
            OrderId = order.Id,
            SubmittedBy = caller.UserName
        });

        var paymentOk = await context.CallActivityAsync<bool>(
            "ProcessPaymentActivity",
            order);

        if (!paymentOk)
        {
            await context.CallActivityAsync(
                "NotifyFailureActivity",
                new FailureNotice(order, "Payment failed"));

            return;
```

```
        }

        var warehouseIds = new[] { "W1", "W2", "W3" };

        var inventoryTasks = warehouseIds.Select(warehouseId =>
            context.CallActivityAsync<bool>(
                "CheckWarehouseActivity",
                new WarehouseRequest(order, warehouseId)));

        var inventoryResults = await Task.WhenAll(inventoryTasks);

        if (!inventoryResults.Any(result => result))
        {
            await context.CallActivityAsync("RefundPaymentActivi
            ty", order);

            await context.CallActivityAsync(
                "NotifyFailureActivity",
                new FailureNotice(order, "Out of stock"));

            return;
        }

        await context.CallActivityAsync("ShipOrderActivity", order);
        await context.CallActivityAsync("NotifySuccessActivity", order);
    }
}
```

For local development, add the authentication settings here.

Local.settings.json

```
{
  "IsEncrypted": false,
  "Values": {
    "AzureWebJobsStorage": "UseDevelopmentStorage=true",
    "FUNCTIONS_WORKER_RUNTIME": "dotnet-isolated",
    "Auth:Authority": "https://login.microsoftonline.com/your-tenant-
    id/v2.0",
    "Auth:Audience": "api://orderprocessor",
    "Auth:RequiredRole": "OrderWriter",
```

```
    "Auth:RequiredScope": "Orders.ReadWrite"
  }
}
```

In OrderProcessor, we have now moved the order submission endpoint from simple function-key protection to identity-based security. The Function app validates JWT bearer tokens issued by Microsoft Entra ID; the StartOrderOrchestration endpoint enforces the permissions required to submit an order, and the caller's identity is recorded for traceability. This means the workflow is no longer started by an anonymous or shared-secret caller. Every order submission is now tied to an authenticated principal, and that identity can flow through logs, traces, and audit records across the workflow.

Handling Tokens in Functions

Validating tokens at the entry point is only the start. In real systems, tokens often need to be acquired again beyond that initial boundary. Activity functions may need them to call external APIs, different downstream services may require different scopes, and long-running workflows must deal with tokens expiring well before the overall process completes. In serverless .NET, token handling is one of the trickiest parts of security because it sits at the intersection of identity, workflow design, and determinism. This section explains how to acquire, use, and refresh tokens safely in Functions and Durable Functions without leaking them into orchestration state.

Why Token Handling Is Tricky in Serverless

Token handling is harder in serverless systems because workflows often outlive the tokens they depend on. Durable Functions replay orchestration history to rebuild state, which means anything nondeterministic, including access tokens with expiry timestamps and other time-sensitive values, does not belong in the orchestrator. Fan-out patterns add another layer of complexity, because one orchestration may schedule many activities, each of which may need to call a different downstream system with a different scope or audience. The central rule is simple: raw tokens should not be stored in orchestration state. Instead, they should be acquired at the point of use, kept short-lived, and scoped only to the downstream operation being performed (see Figure 8-2).

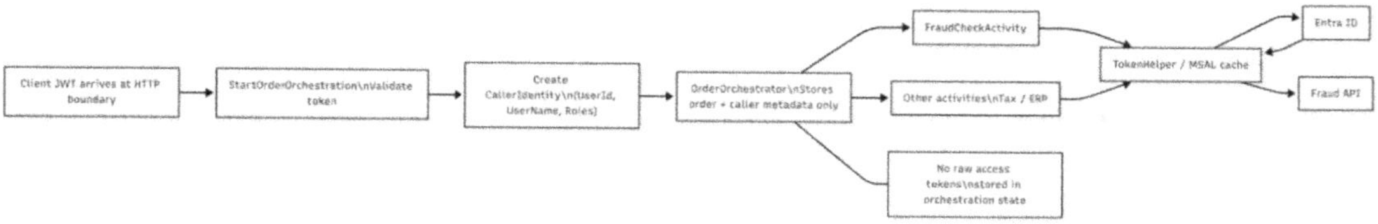

Figure 8-2. *Activity-based token acquisition in a Durable Functions workflow*

Pattern 1: Acquire Tokens Inside Activities

As a general rule, do not pass raw access tokens into orchestrators. The safest place to acquire a token is inside the activity function that needs it. Activities are not replayed like orchestrators, so they can perform nondeterministic work such as fetching tokens, calling Entra ID, and sending HTTP requests. This keeps the orchestrator deterministic and ensures the token is fresh at the moment it is used.

Activities/FraudCheckActivity.cs

```
using System.Net.Http.Headers;
using System.Net.Http.Json;
using Microsoft.Azure.Functions.Worker;
using Microsoft.Extensions.Logging;
using OrderProcessor.Helpers;

public static class FraudCheckActivity
{
    private static readonly HttpClient Http = new();

    [Function("FraudCheckActivity")]
    public static async Task<FraudResult> Run(
        [ActivityTrigger] Order order,
        FunctionContext ctx)
    {
        var logger = ctx.GetLogger("FraudCheckActivity");

        var token = await TokenHelper.GetAccessTokenAsync("api://fraud-
        service/.default");

        using var request = new HttpRequestMessage(
            HttpMethod.Post,
```

```
            "https://fraud-service.contoso.com/api/check")
        {
            Content = JsonContent.Create(order)
        };

        request.Headers.Authorization =
            new AuthenticationHeaderValue("Bearer", token);

        using var response = await Http.SendAsync(request);
        response.EnsureSuccessStatusCode();

        var result = await response.Content.ReadFromJsonAsync<Frau
        dResult>()
            ?? throw new InvalidOperationException("Fraud API returned an
            empty response.");

        logger.LogInformation("Fraud check completed for order {OrderId}",
        order.Id);

        return result;
    }
}
```

Here, the activity calls TokenHelper each time it runs, ensuring the token is fresh and not stored in the orchestrator state.

Pattern 2: Token Caching with Microsoft Authentication Library (MSAL)

When activities request tokens repeatedly, it is important not to call Microsoft Entra ID unnecessarily on every execution. Microsoft Authentication Library (MSAL) is the standard Microsoft library for acquiring tokens in .NET applications, including service-to-service tokens obtained through the client credentials flow.

In this example, OrderProcessor uses MSAL through a small TokenHelper wrapper. The helper creates an IConfidentialClientApplication once and then calls AcquireTokenForClient whenever an activity needs a token for a downstream API. MSAL checks its token cache before going back to Microsoft Entra ID. If a valid token already exists for the requested scope, MSAL can return the cached token. If the token is missing or expired, MSAL requests a fresh one.

The cache shown here is in-memory and belongs to the current Function host instance. That is enough for this sample and keeps the focus on the token-handling pattern. In a high-scale production system, each scaled-out Function instance would have its own in-memory cache, so teams may consider a distributed or persistent MSAL token cache if token acquisition volume becomes significant.

local.settings.json

```
{
  "IsEncrypted": false,
  "Values": {
    "AzureWebJobsStorage": "UseDevelopmentStorage=true",
    "FUNCTIONS_WORKER_RUNTIME": "dotnet-isolated",
    "Auth:Authority": "https://login.microsoftonline.com/your-tenant-
    id/v2.0",
    "Auth:Audience": "api://orderprocessor",
    "Auth:RequiredRole": "OrderWriter",
    "Auth:RequiredScope": "Orders.ReadWrite",
    "DownstreamApis:ClientId": "your-client-id",
    "DownstreamApis:TenantId": "your-tenant-id",
    "DownstreamApis:ClientSecret": "your-client-secret"
  }
}
```

The helper below wraps MSAL so activities do not need to know how the confidential client is created or how token caching works internally.

Helpers/TokenHelper.cs

```
using Microsoft.Identity.Client;

public static class TokenHelper
{
    private static IConfidentialClientApplication? _app;

    public static void Init(string clientId, string tenantId, string
    clientSecret)
    {
        _app = ConfidentialClientApplicationBuilder
            .Create(clientId)
```

```
            .WithTenantId(tenantId)
            .WithClientSecret(clientSecret)
            .Build();
    }

    public static async Task<string> GetAccessTokenAsync(string scope)
    {
        if (_app is null)
        {
            throw new InvalidOperationException("TokenHelper has not been
            initialised.");
        }

        var result = await _app
            .AcquireTokenForClient(new[] { scope })
            .ExecuteAsync();

        return result.AccessToken;
    }
}
```

Program.cs

```
using Microsoft.Azure.Functions.Worker;
using Microsoft.Azure.Functions.Worker.Builder;
using Microsoft.Extensions.DependencyInjection;
using Microsoft.Extensions.Hosting;
using OrderProcessor.Helpers;
using OrderProcessor.Options;
using OrderProcessor.Security;

var builder = FunctionsApplication.CreateBuilder(args);

builder.ConfigureFunctionsWebApplication();

builder.Services
    .AddApplicationInsightsTelemetryWorkerService()
    .ConfigureFunctionsApplicationInsights();

builder.Services
```

```
    .AddOptions<AuthOptions>()
    .BindConfiguration(AuthOptions.SectionName)
    .Validate(options =>
        !string.IsNullOrWhiteSpace(options.Authority) &&
        !string.IsNullOrWhiteSpace(options.Audience),
        "Auth settings are required.");

builder.Services.AddSingleton<ITokenValidator, JwtTokenValidator>();

TokenHelper.Init(
    builder.Configuration["DownstreamApis:ClientId"]
        ?? throw new InvalidOperationException("Missing
        DownstreamApis:ClientId"),
    builder.Configuration["DownstreamApis:TenantId"]
        ?? throw new InvalidOperationException("Missing
        DownstreamApis:TenantId"),
    builder.Configuration["DownstreamApis:ClientSecret"]
        ?? throw new InvalidOperationException("Missing DownstreamApis:
        ClientSecret"));

builder.Build().Run();
```

The remaining patterns are included to show how token handling evolves in more advanced scenarios. They are not applied to `OrderProcessor` at this stage, but they are common approaches in larger serverless systems.

Pattern 3: User Delegation with the On-Behalf-Of Flow

It could be that `OrderProcessor` may need to call a downstream API on behalf of the signed-in user rather than as the application itself. In that case, the OAuth 2.0 On-Behalf-Of flow is used. The incoming user token is exchanged for a new token targeted at the downstream API, allowing that API to evaluate the user's delegated permissions directly.

Flow:

1. The user calls the API with an access token.
2. The function receives that token and exchanges it for a new token targeted at the downstream API.

3. The downstream API sees the call as coming from the user rather than from a service principal.

In code, that exchange looks like this:

```
using Microsoft.Identity.Client;

public static async Task<string> ExchangeTokenAsync(string userToken,
string downstreamScope)
{
    var app = ConfidentialClientApplicationBuilder
        .Create("<clientId>")
        .WithTenantId("<tenantId>")
        .WithClientSecret("<clientSecret>")
        .Build();

    var result = await app
        .AcquireTokenOnBehalfOf(new[] { downstreamScope }, new
        UserAssertion(userToken))
        .ExecuteAsync();

    return result.AccessToken;
}
```

The original user token should be used only at the boundary where the exchange occurs. It should not be stored in the orchestration state or passed through the workflow.

Pattern 4: Long-Running Workflows

Durable workflows may run for hours or days, for example, while waiting for supplier approval or an external callback. Any token captured when the workflow first started is therefore likely to expire before the downstream call is eventually made. The orchestrator should store only stable identifiers such as the order ID, user ID, or correlation ID. When the workflow resumes and an external call is needed, the corresponding activity can acquire a fresh token using either client credentials or the On-Behalf-Of flow. This keeps the workflow independent of token lifetime and avoids persisting sensitive token material in a durable state.

Pattern 5: Least Privilege Tokens

Downstream calls should not all share the same broad token. Each activity should request only the scope it actually needs for the API it is calling. A fraud check activity might request `api://fraud-service/Fraud.ReadWrite`, a tax activity might request `api://tax-service/Tax.Calculate`, and an ERP integration activity might request `api://erp-system/ERP.SubmitOrder`. Keeping scopes narrow reduces the blast radius if a token is exposed and makes it easier to reason about what each integration is allowed to do.

Applying Activity-Based Token Acquisition in OrderProcessor

Of these patterns, `OrderProcessor` applies the first one directly. Rather than passing tokens into the workflow or storing them in orchestration state, `FraudCheckActivity` acquires a fresh token only when it is about to call the downstream fraud API. This keeps token handling close to the point of use, allows token caching to happen behind the acquisition helper, and leaves the orchestrator free of sensitive token data.

Project Addition: Applying Activity-Based Token Acquisition

In `OrderProcessor`, token acquisition now happens inside activity execution rather than inside orchestration state. `FraudCheckActivity` requests a fresh token when it runs; token caching reduces repeated calls to Microsoft Entra ID, and the orchestrator remains free of raw token data so replay and long-running execution do not introduce determinism or expiry problems. The remaining patterns in this section, such as the On-Behalf-Of flow and long-running refresh strategies, become relevant as the system grows to support more complex downstream integrations.

Securing Durable Orchestrations

Durable Functions are the backbone of `OrderProcessor`, they coordinate fraud checks, tax calculations, supplier approvals, and ERP integration. But their flexibility comes with unique security challenges. Unlike stateless Functions, orchestrators maintain long-lived state, wait for external events, and replay execution history. If not secured properly, these features open new attack surfaces. This section explores how to harden orchestrations against replay abuse, state tampering, and untrusted external events, while still keeping workflows resilient and scalable.

The Security Model of Durable Functions

Durable Functions persist workflow state in Azure Storage or SQL, and that persisted state becomes the source of truth for the orchestration. It records scheduled work, received events, and the current progress of the workflow, including any custom status that has been set along the way. That durability is what makes long-running workflows possible, but it also creates a security boundary of its own. If an attacker can inject external events or tamper with orchestration state, they may be able to skip fraud checks, replay sensitive actions such as payment-related operations, or push the workflow into an inconsistent state. Durable workflows, therefore, need protection not only at the HTTP entry point but also around their state store, management endpoints, and event-driven interactions.

Risk 1: Event Injection

Durable orchestrations often use `WaitForExternalEvent<T>` to pause until an external system or human signals back. For example, `OrderProcessor` waits for SupplierApproval.

```
var approval = await
context.WaitForExternalEvent<SupplierDecision>("SupplierApproval");
```

If the event-raising endpoint is left unprotected, a malicious caller could submit a forged approval and advance the workflow without legitimate authorization.

The mitigation is straightforward. Event-raising endpoints should be treated like any other sensitive application boundary. They must validate the caller's token, enforce the correct role, and log the identity responsible for the action. In `OrderProcessor`, that means allowing only callers in the `SupplierApprover` role to raise the `SupplierApproval` event and recording that identity for traceability.

Securing the Supplier Approval Endpoint

In OrderProcessor, the supplier approval endpoint is the boundary through which a paused orchestration can be resumed by an external decision. That makes it one of the most sensitive points in the workflow. If an unauthorized caller can post a forged approval event, they can bypass business controls and advance the workflow incorrectly. For that reason, the event-raising endpoint must validate the caller's identity, enforce the correct role, and record who approved the action.

Models/SupplierDecision.cs

```
namespace OrderProcessor;

public sealed record SupplierDecision(
    string OrderId,
    bool Approved,
    string? Comment);
```

Functions/RaiseSupplierApproval.cs

```
using System.Net;
using Microsoft.Azure.Functions.Worker;
using Microsoft.Azure.Functions.Worker.Http;
using Microsoft.DurableTask.Client;
using Microsoft.Extensions.Logging;
using OrderProcessor.Security;

namespace OrderProcessor;

public sealed class RaiseSupplierApproval
{
    private readonly ILogger<RaiseSupplierApproval> _logger;
    private readonly ITokenValidator _tokenValidator;

    public RaiseSupplierApproval(
        ILogger<RaiseSupplierApproval> logger,
        ITokenValidator tokenValidator)
    {
        _logger = logger;
        _tokenValidator = tokenValidator;
```

```
}

[Function("RaiseSupplierApproval")]
public async Task<HttpResponseData> Run(
    [HttpTrigger(AuthorizationLevel.Anonymous, "post", Route = "orders/
    {instanceId}/supplier-approval")]
    HttpRequestData req,
    string instanceId,
    [DurableClient] DurableTaskClient client,
    CancellationToken stopToken)
{
    var bearerToken = req.GetBearerToken();

    if (string.IsNullOrWhiteSpace(bearerToken))
    {
        var unauthorized = req.CreateResponse(HttpStatusCode.
        Unauthorized);
        await unauthorized.WriteStringAsync("Missing bearer token.",
        stopToken);
        return unauthorized;
    }

    var principal = await _tokenValidator.ValidateAsync(bearerToken,
    stopToken);

    if (principal is null)
    {
        var unauthorized = req.CreateResponse(HttpStatusCode.
        Unauthorized);
        await unauthorized.WriteStringAsync("Invalid or expired
        token.", stopToken);
        return unauthorized;
    }

    if (!principal.HasRole("SupplierApprover"))
    {
        var forbidden = req.CreateResponse(HttpStatusCode.Forbidden);
```

```
            await forbidden.WriteStringAsync("Caller is not allowed to
            approve supplier actions.", stopToken);
            return forbidden;
        }

        var decision = await req.ReadFromJsonAsync<SupplierDecision>(cancel
        lationToken: stopToken);

        if (decision is null || string.IsNullOrWhiteSpace(decision.OrderId))
        {
            var bad = req.CreateResponse(HttpStatusCode.BadRequest);
            await bad.WriteStringAsync("Invalid supplier approval
            payload.", stopToken);
            return bad;
        }

        await client.RaiseEventAsync(instanceId, "SupplierApproval",
        decision, cancellationToken: stopToken);

        _logger.LogInformation(
            "User {UserName} raised SupplierApproval for order {OrderId} on
            instance {InstanceId}",
            principal.GetUserName(),
            decision.OrderId,
            instanceId);

        return req.CreateResponse(HttpStatusCode.OK);
    }
}
```

Now only authorized suppliers can raise the event, and logs record *who* did it.

Risk 2: Replay Abuse

Durable orchestrators replay history to rebuild state, so any side effect placed directly inside the orchestrator risks running more than once. Logging, sending emails, or calling payment APIs from the orchestrator can therefore produce duplicate behavior during replay.

The mitigation is to keep orchestrators deterministic, push side effects into activities, and use `context.IsReplaying` when you need to suppress duplicate log noise during replay.

```
if (!context.IsReplaying)
{
    logger.LogInformation("Resuming orchestrator for order {OrderId}",
    order.Id);
}
```

Risk 3: State Tampering

If an attacker gains access to the storage backing Durable Functions, they may be able to alter orchestration history or inspect sensitive workflow data. The practical response is to restrict access to that storage using managed identities, RBAC, and private endpoints, while also monitoring for anomalies such as unexpected manual edits or unusual access patterns. Durable state should be treated as security-sensitive infrastructure, not just application plumbing.

Risk 4: Long-Lived Identities

Workflows may remain paused for hours or days, especially when waiting for supplier approval or another external decision. If the orchestrator were to store raw access tokens in state, those tokens could later expire, be replayed, or be exposed through durable storage. The safer pattern is the one already introduced in the section "Handling Tokens in Functions": store only stable references such as `OrderId` or `UserId`, and acquire fresh tokens inside activities when an external API call is actually needed.

Risk 5: Orchestrator Endpoints

Durable Functions also expose management operations such as status queries, termination, and event raising. If these are made available without proper protection, they can become an administrative attack surface. Access should therefore be restricted to trusted roles or service principals, and any externally exposed management capability should ideally be wrapped behind a secure application API rather than surfaced directly.

Project Addition: Secure SupplierApproval

In `OrderProcessor`, the supplier approval flow is now protected at the event-raising boundary. The `RaiseSupplierApproval` function validates the caller's token, allows only users in the `SupplierApprover` role to raise the `SupplierApproval` event, and records the caller's identity in logs for traceability. This closes one of the most important attack surfaces in the workflow by ensuring that external approval events cannot be raised anonymously or by the wrong role.

Role-Based Access Control (RBAC) in Serverless APIs

Authentication ensures that only valid, signed-in users can reach your system. But in a real-world application, that's only half the story. Once a user is authenticated, you need to decide, what are they allowed to do? That's where Role-Based Access Control (RBAC) comes in. In serverless systems, RBAC must extend across APIs, Functions, and orchestrations. For `OrderProcessor`, that means different actors, customers, fraud analysts, suppliers, and admins all see different slices of the system, enforced consistently by Azure Functions.

Why RBAC Is Important

Without RBAC, authentication only proves that a caller is signed in. It does not decide what that caller should be allowed to do. In a workflow-driven system such as `OrderProcessor`, that distinction matters immediately. A customer who can submit an order should not also be able to approve supplier actions, override fraud decisions, or terminate orchestrations. RBAC enforces least privilege by ensuring that each actor has only the permissions required for the role they perform.

Defining Roles in Azure AD/B2C

Roles should be defined in the identity provider rather than hardcoded as ad hoc application rules. In Microsoft Entra ID or Azure AD B2C, that typically means creating application roles such as `OrderWriter`, `FraudAnalyst`, `SupplierApprover`, and `Admin`, then assigning them to users, groups, or service principals as appropriate. When a caller authenticates, those assignments flow into the token as role claims. The application can then use those claims to make consistent authorization decisions at the function boundary.

```
{"roles": ["SupplierApprover"]}
```

A role claim like this tells the application that the token holder has been assigned the `SupplierApprover` role and can be authorized accordingly.

A useful way to avoid vague RBAC is to describe permissions as actions against workflow boundaries. OrderProcessor should not simply ask whether a caller is authenticated. It should ask whether the caller can perform this specific action at this specific boundary.

Boundary	Action	Required permission
POST /orders/orchestrate	Start a new order workflow	OrderWriter role or Orders.ReadWrite scope
POST /orders/{instanceId}/supplier-approval	Raise supplier approval event	SupplierApprover role
POST /orders/{instanceId}/fraud-approval	Raise fraud approval event	FraudAnalyst role
POST /orders/{instanceId}/tax-callback	Submit tax callback	TaxService application role
Admin orchestration endpoint	Terminate or retry workflow	Admin role or trusted service principal

Enforcing RBAC in Functions

In `OrderProcessor`, RBAC is enforced at the same boundary where tokens are validated. Once the caller's token has been accepted, the function checks whether the caller has the role required for the operation being performed. Earlier in the chapter, `StartOrderOrchestration` was secured so that only callers with the `OrderWriter` role, or the required submission scope, can begin the workflow. In the section "Securing Durable Orchestrations," `RaiseSupplierApproval` was secured so that only callers in the `SupplierApprover` role can raise the `SupplierApproval` event. Together, those endpoints show the core RBAC pattern for the system: validate the token, check the required role, and reject the request before it can affect workflow state.

Fraud Analyst Approval

Fraud analysts may need a separate endpoint to override or confirm fraud decisions before the workflow continues. That endpoint should follow the same pattern as the other secured boundaries in the system: validate the caller's token, require the `FraudAnalyst` role, and record the identity responsible for the decision.

Models/FraudDecision.cs

```
namespace OrderProcessor;

public sealed record FraudDecision(
    string OrderId,
    bool Approved,
    string? Comment);
```

Functions/ApproveFraudDecision.cs

```
using System.Net;
using Microsoft.Azure.Functions.Worker;
using Microsoft.Azure.Functions.Worker.Http;
using Microsoft.DurableTask.Client;
using Microsoft.Extensions.Logging;
using OrderProcessor.Security;

namespace OrderProcessor;

public sealed class ApproveFraudDecision
{
    private readonly ILogger<ApproveFraudDecision> _logger;
    private readonly ITokenValidator _tokenValidator;

    public ApproveFraudDecision(
        ILogger<ApproveFraudDecision> logger,
        ITokenValidator tokenValidator)
    {
        _logger = logger;
        _tokenValidator = tokenValidator;
    }

    [Function("ApproveFraudDecision")]
```

```
public async Task<HttpResponseData> Run(
    [HttpTrigger(AuthorizationLevel.Anonymous, "post", Route = "orders/
    {instanceId}/fraud-approval")]
    HttpRequestData req,
    string instanceId,
    [DurableClient] DurableTaskClient client,
    CancellationToken stopToken)
{
    var bearerToken = req.GetBearerToken();

    if (string.IsNullOrWhiteSpace(bearerToken))
    {
        var unauthorized = req.CreateResponse(HttpStatusCode.
        Unauthorized);
        await unauthorized.WriteStringAsync("Missing bearer token.",
        stopToken);
        return unauthorized;
    }

    var principal = await _tokenValidator.ValidateAsync(bearerToken,
    stopToken);

    if (principal is null)
    {
        var unauthorized = req.CreateResponse(HttpStatusCode.
        Unauthorized);
        await unauthorized.WriteStringAsync("Invalid or expired
        token.", stopToken);
        return unauthorized;
    }

    if (!principal.HasRole("FraudAnalyst"))
    {
        var forbidden = req.CreateResponse(HttpStatusCode.Forbidden);
        await forbidden.WriteStringAsync("Caller is not allowed to
        approve fraud decisions.", stopToken);
        return forbidden;
    }
```

```
        var decision = await req.ReadFromJsonAsync<FraudDecision>
        (cancellationToken: stopToken);

        if (decision is null || string.IsNullOrWhiteSpace(decision.OrderId))
        {
            var bad = req.CreateResponse(HttpStatusCode.BadRequest);
            await bad.WriteStringAsync("Invalid fraud approval payload.",
            stopToken);
            return bad;
        }

        await client.RaiseEventAsync(instanceId, "FraudApproval", decision,
        cancellationToken: stopToken);

        _logger.LogInformation(
            "User {UserName} raised FraudApproval for order {OrderId} on
            instance {InstanceId}",
            principal.GetUserName(),
            decision.OrderId,
            instanceId);

        return req.CreateResponse(HttpStatusCode.OK);
    }
}
```

Supplier approvals

As implemented in the section "Securing Durable Orchestrations," only SupplierApprover role holders can raise SupplierApproval events.

Administrative Actions

Administrative actions such as terminating an orchestration or triggering a manual retry should be restricted even more tightly. These operations are destructive or highly privileged, so they should be available only to callers in an Admin role or to trusted service principals acting on behalf of an administrative workflow. As with the other endpoints in the system, the check should happen at the function boundary before the operation is allowed to affect orchestration state.

Role Checks Inside Orchestrations

RBAC should be enforced primarily at the function boundary, where the caller's token can be validated and the required role can be checked before any workflow action is taken. The orchestration itself may still use trusted metadata, such as the identity or role recorded by a validated entry point, when applying workflow rules or audit logic. What it should not do is trust arbitrary role claims arriving from an unvalidated external payload. In other words, the boundary establishes trust, and the orchestration consumes the consequences of that trust.

Project Addition: Extending RBAC Across Workflow Boundaries

In `OrderProcessor`, RBAC now spans multiple workflow boundaries rather than stopping at initial authentication. `StartOrderOrchestration` restricts order submission to callers with the correct submission permissions, `RaiseSupplierApproval` limits supplier approval events to the `SupplierApprover` role, and `ApproveFraudDecision` allows only `FraudAnalyst` callers to override fraud outcomes. Together, these boundaries enforce least privilege across the workflow and ensure that each sensitive action is tied to an authenticated identity with the correct role.

Securing External Integrations

So far, the focus has been on protecting `OrderProcessor's` internal APIs and orchestrations. But real-world systems also depend on external services, and those integrations are often where serious security risks emerge. Fraud detection APIs, tax services, ERP systems, and supplier portals all require authentication, trust boundaries, and secure communication. If these integrations are not locked down, attackers can pivot through them, exfiltrate data, or impersonate trusted systems. In this section, we'll explore best practices for securing external integrations in serverless .NET systems, and we'll apply them directly to `OrderProcessor's` Fraud, Tax, and ERP integrations.

The Risks of External Integration

When calling external APIs, several risks appear immediately. Tokens for downstream services may be logged, replayed, or intercepted if they are not handled carefully. If every call uses the same broad token, a single compromise can expose multiple integrations at once. Weak transport security creates man-in-the-middle risk, while hardcoded secrets or connection strings expose credentials through source control, deployments, or logs. Even when your own system is secure, a weaker third-party system can become a stepping stone for attackers. Securing external integrations therefore means protecting credentials, narrowing permissions, enforcing transport security, and treating every partner boundary as untrusted until proven otherwise.

Principle 1: Managed Identities over Secrets

Where the downstream system supports Microsoft Entra ID or Azure-native authentication, `OrderProcessor` can use a managed identity instead of storing client secrets.

Example for Service Bus (similar for other Azure resources):

```
builder.Services.AddAzureClients(clientBuilder =>
{clientBuilder.AddServiceBusClientWithNamespace("orderprocessor-
servicebus").WithCredential(new DefaultAzureCredential());
});
```

Here, the Function App's managed identity is granted access via RBAC. No secret strings are stored in config.

Principle 2: Token Acquisition Per Service

Each downstream system should have its own audience and scope. A fraud API might use `api://fraud-service/Fraud.ReadWrite`, a tax API might use `api://tax-service/Tax.Calculate`, and an ERP integration might use `api://erp-system/Orders.Submit`. Keeping tokens scoped per integration reduces blast radius and makes it easier to reason about what each call is allowed to do.

As introduced in the section "Handling Tokens in Functions," `OrderProcessor` fetches tokens on demand and requests only the scope needed for the integration being called.

```
public static async Task<string> GetFraudTokenAsync()
{
    var cca = ConfidentialClientApplicationBuilder
        .Create("<clientId>")
        .WithTenantId("<tenantId>")
        .WithClientSecret("<secret>")
        .Build();
    var result = await cca.AcquireTokenForClient(
    new[] { "api://fraud-service/.default" }).ExecuteAsync();
    return result.AccessToken;
}
```

Each token is limited to its integration, reducing blast radius.

Principle 3: TLS Everywhere

Always use HTTPS for outbound calls and ensure integration endpoints are configured with secure `https://` URLs.

```
_http.BaseAddress = new Uri("https://fraud-service.contoso.com");
```

On the inbound side, the Function App itself should also reject plain HTTP and require HTTPS at the platform boundary.

Principle 4: Secretless Configuration with Key Vault

For systems that still require API keys (e.g., third-party tax services that don't support Entra ID), store keys in Azure Key Vault, not in `appsettings.json`.

```
builder.Configuration.AddAzureKeyVault(
new Uri($"https://{vaultName}.vault.azure.net/"),
new DefaultAzureCredential());
```

Keys are pulled at runtime, secured by managed identity, and never committed to source control.

Principle 5: Outbound Firewalling

Outbound traffic should also be constrained. In practice, that can mean using VNet integration and private endpoints for internal dependencies, restricting outbound IPs to trusted partners where possible, and introducing Azure Firewall or API Management as a controlled egress layer. The goal is to reduce the blast radius if a Function App is ever compromised and to stop it from freely reaching arbitrary external destinations.

Principle 6: Validate Inbound Integrations

Not all integration risk is outbound. External systems may also call back into `OrderProcessor`, for example, when a tax service returns a calculation result or a partner system confirms an external action. Those inbound calls must be validated just as carefully as user-facing requests. They should carry a valid token, be checked against the expected issuer and audience, be restricted to the correct role where possible, and be logged for auditability.

Models/TaxResult.cs

```
namespace OrderProcessor;

public sealed record TaxResult(
    string OrderId,
    decimal TaxAmount,
    bool Succeeded);
```

Functions/TaxCallback.cs

```
using System.Net;
using Microsoft.Azure.Functions.Worker;
using Microsoft.Azure.Functions.Worker.Http;
using Microsoft.DurableTask.Client;
using Microsoft.Extensions.Logging;
using OrderProcessor.Security;

namespace OrderProcessor;

public sealed class TaxCallback
{
    private readonly ILogger<TaxCallback> _logger;
```

```
private readonly ITokenValidator _tokenValidator;

public TaxCallback(
    ILogger<TaxCallback> logger,
    ITokenValidator tokenValidator)
{
    _logger = logger;
    _tokenValidator = tokenValidator;
}

[Function("TaxCallback")]
public async Task<HttpResponseData> Run(
    [HttpTrigger(AuthorizationLevel.Anonymous, "post", Route = "orders/
    {instanceId}/tax-callback")]
    HttpRequestData req,
    string instanceId,
    [DurableClient] DurableTaskClient client,
    CancellationToken stopToken)
{
    var bearerToken = req.GetBearerToken();

    if (string.IsNullOrWhiteSpace(bearerToken))
    {
        var unauthorized = req.CreateResponse(HttpStatusCode.
        Unauthorized);
        await unauthorized.WriteStringAsync("Missing bearer token.",
        stopToken);
        return unauthorized;
    }

    var principal = await _tokenValidator.ValidateAsync(bearerToken,
    stopToken);

    if (principal is null)
    {
        var unauthorized = req.CreateResponse(HttpStatusCode.
        Unauthorized);
```

```
            await unauthorized.WriteStringAsync("Invalid or expired
            token.", stopToken);
            return unauthorized;
        }

        if (!principal.HasRole("TaxService"))
        {
            var forbidden = req.CreateResponse(HttpStatusCode.Forbidden);
            await forbidden.WriteStringAsync("Caller is not allowed to
            submit tax callbacks.", stopToken);
            return forbidden;
        }

        var payload = await req.ReadFromJsonAsync<TaxResult>(cancellationTo
        ken: stopToken);

        if (payload is null || string.IsNullOrWhiteSpace(payload.OrderId))
        {
            var bad = req.CreateResponse(HttpStatusCode.BadRequest);
            await bad.WriteStringAsync("Invalid tax callback payload.",
            stopToken);
            return bad;
        }

        await client.RaiseEventAsync(instanceId, "TaxCalculated", payload,
        cancellationToken: stopToken);

        _logger.LogInformation(
            "Received tax callback for order {OrderId} on instance
            {InstanceId} from {UserName}",
            payload.OrderId,
            instanceId,
            principal.GetUserName());

        return req.CreateResponse(HttpStatusCode.OK);
    }
}
```

Project Addition: Securing Inbound and Outbound Integrations

In `OrderProcessor`, external integrations are now treated as security boundaries in their own right. Outbound calls acquire tokens per service scope rather than relying on a single broad credential, and inbound callbacks such as `TaxCallback` validate the caller's token and enforce the expected role before affecting workflow state. Together with HTTPS, secret management, and constrained network access, these patterns ensure that partner integrations are protected with the same care as internal APIs.

Secrets, Keys, and Certificates Management

Distributed systems live and die by their secrets. API keys, connection strings, certificates, and encryption keys are the glue that binds components together. But left unmanaged, they become a ticking time bomb: secrets checked into source control, keys that are never rotated, and certificates that expire unnoticed. In serverless .NET, where Functions scale dynamically and run in shared environments, robust secret management isn't optional; it's essential. In this section, we'll explore how to handle secrets, keys, and certificates in `OrderProcessor` using Azure's tooling, Key Vault, App Configuration, and Managed Identities. We'll also cover rotation strategies, audit logging, and integration into CI/CD pipelines.

Managed identity should be the default authentication model for Azure-to-Azure communication. In OrderProcessor, the Function App should use its managed identity when calling Azure services such as Key Vault, Service Bus, Cosmos DB, Storage, and App Configuration. Client secrets and connection strings should be treated as fallback options for systems that cannot participate in Microsoft Entra ID authentication.

That distinction is important. The goal is not simply to move secrets from local.settings.json into Key Vault. The stronger pattern is to remove secrets completely wherever Azure supports identity-based access. Key Vault remains essential for third-party credentials, certificates, and API keys, but internal Azure dependencies should prefer managed identity and RBAC.

Why Secret Management Is Important in Serverless

In monolithic systems, secrets often end up buried in local configuration files or deployment settings. In serverless systems, the problem scales faster. A leaked secret can affect many running instances at once, external integrations may depend on credentials for every call, long-running workflows can outlive short-lived credentials, and frequent deployments increase the chance of accidental exposure through commits, pipelines, or logs. Secret management therefore becomes a core part of system design rather than a deployment afterthought.

Principle 1: Eliminate Secrets with Managed Identities

The safest secret is the one you don't have to manage. Managed identities let Azure services authenticate without keys. Example: `OrderProcessor` calling Service Bus.

```
builder.Services.AddAzureClients(clientBuilder =>
{
clientBuilder.AddServiceBusClient("orderprocessor-
namespace").WithCredential(new DefaultAzureCredential());
});
```

Here, the Function App's managed identity is granted RBAC access to Service Bus. No connection strings in config.

Principle 2: Store Remaining Secrets in Key Vault

Not every system supports managed identities. For external vendors (Fraud API, Tax API), you may still need API keys. Store them in Azure Key Vault.

Add Key Vault integration:

```
builder.Configuration.AddAzureKeyVault(
new Uri($"https://
{builder.Configuration["KeyVaultName"]}.vault.azure.net/"),
new DefaultAzureCredential());
```

Now secrets are pulled at runtime.

Once Key Vault is connected, secret values can be resolved at runtime rather than stored directly in local configuration files or committed to source control.

Principle 3: Certificates in Key Vault

Some integrations (ERP, supplier SFTP) require TLS client certificates. Key Vault manages these too.

Upload certificate:

```
az keyvault certificate import \
--vault-name buy-kv \
--name SupplierCert \
--file suppliercert.pfx
```

Use it in .NET:

```
var client = new HttpClient(new HttpClientHandler
{
    ClientCertificates = { certificateFromKeyVault }
});
```

`OrderProcessor` can load ERP client certificates from Key Vault without exposing `.pfx` files to developers, while certificate lifecycle and rotation remain centrally managed.

Principle 4: Centralize config with Azure App Configuration

Secrets live in Key Vault, but non-secret config (endpoints, feature flags) belongs in Azure App Configuration.

Example:

```
builder.Configuration.AddAzureAppConfiguration(options =>
{
    options.Connect(new Uri("https://buy-
    appconfig.azconfig.io"), new DefaultAzureCredential())
    .ConfigureKeyVault(kv => kv.SetCredential(new
    DefaultAzureCredential()));
});
```

This separates secret values (Key Vault) from feature toggles (App Config). Together, they make the configuration clean and environment-agnostic.

Principle 5: Rotate Secrets Regularly

Stale secrets are dangerous, so rotation should be planned rather than treated as an emergency task. Key Vault supports rotation policies for keys and certificates, and CI/CD workflows can coordinate secret changes with deployments when needed. Where applications authenticate using managed identities instead of stored credentials, rotation pressure is reduced significantly because there are fewer secrets to manage in the first place.

Principle 6: Prevent Leakage in Logs

Never log secrets. Structured logging (from the section "Structured Logging in Serverless Systems" in Chapter 7) should scrub sensitive values.

```
logger.LogInformation("Calling Fraud API at {Url} with key hash {KeyHash}",
fraudUrl, Sha256Hash(apiKey));
```

Only hashes of keys are logged, never raw values.

Principle 7: Secure Access to Key Vault

Key Vault must also be protected as a security boundary in its own right. Access should be controlled through RBAC, private endpoints should be used where possible, audit logs should be enabled through diagnostic settings, and soft delete and purge protection should be turned on to reduce the risk of accidental or malicious deletion.

Applying Key Vault to the Fraud API Integration

For `OrderProcessor`, the most immediate secret management improvement is to remove the Fraud API credential from local configuration and resolve it through Azure Key Vault instead. The Function App can authenticate to Key Vault using its managed identity, while the Fraud API base URL remains in ordinary configuration because it is not itself a secret.

Options/FraudApiOptions.cs

```
namespace OrderProcessor.Options;

public sealed class FraudApiOptions
{
    public const string SectionName = "FraudApi";

    public string BaseUrl { get; set; } = string.Empty;

    public string ApiKey { get; set; } = string.Empty;
}
```

Program.cs

At this point, Program.cs has evolved to include authentication, downstream token setup, Azure App Configuration, and Key Vault integration.

```
using Azure.Identity;
using Microsoft.Azure.Functions.Worker;
using Microsoft.Azure.Functions.Worker.Builder;
using Microsoft.Extensions.DependencyInjection;
using Microsoft.Extensions.Hosting;
using OrderProcessor.Helpers;
using OrderProcessor.Options;
using OrderProcessor.Security;

var builder = FunctionsApplication.CreateBuilder(args);

builder.ConfigureFunctionsWebApplication();

builder.Configuration.AddAzureAppConfiguration(options =>
{
    var endpoint = builder.Configuration["AppConfigEndpoint"];

    if (string.IsNullOrWhiteSpace(endpoint))
    {
        throw new InvalidOperationException("Missing AppConfigEndpoint");
    }

    options.Connect(new Uri(endpoint), new DefaultAzureCredential())
```

```
        .ConfigureKeyVault(kv => kv.SetCredential(new
        DefaultAzureCredential()));
});

var keyVaultName = builder.Configuration["KeyVaultName"];

if (string.IsNullOrWhiteSpace(keyVaultName))
{
    throw new InvalidOperationException("Missing KeyVaultName");
}

builder.Configuration.AddAzureKeyVault(
    new Uri($"https://{keyVaultName}.vault.azure.net/"),
    new DefaultAzureCredential());

builder.Services
    .AddApplicationInsightsTelemetryWorkerService()
    .ConfigureFunctionsApplicationInsights();

builder.Services
    .AddOptions<AuthOptions>()
    .BindConfiguration(AuthOptions.SectionName)
    .Validate(options =>
        !string.IsNullOrWhiteSpace(options.Authority) &&
        !string.IsNullOrWhiteSpace(options.Audience),
        "Auth settings are required.");

builder.Services
    .AddOptions<FraudApiOptions>()
    .BindConfiguration(FraudApiOptions.SectionName)
    .Validate(options =>
        !string.IsNullOrWhiteSpace(options.BaseUrl) &&
        !string.IsNullOrWhiteSpace(options.ApiKey),
        "Fraud API settings are required.");

builder.Services.AddSingleton<ITokenValidator, JwtTokenValidator>();

TokenHelper.Init(
    builder.Configuration["DownstreamApis:ClientId"]
```

```
        ?? throw new InvalidOperationException("Missing
        DownstreamApis:ClientId"),
    builder.Configuration["DownstreamApis:TenantId"]
        ?? throw new InvalidOperationException("Missing
        DownstreamApis:TenantId"),
    builder.Configuration["DownstreamApis:ClientSecret"]
        ?? throw new InvalidOperationException("Missing DownstreamApis:
        ClientSecret"));

builder.Build().Run();
```

local.settings.json

```
{
  "IsEncrypted": false,
  "Values": {
    "AzureWebJobsStorage": "UseDevelopmentStorage=true",
    "FUNCTIONS_WORKER_RUNTIME": "dotnet-isolated",
    "Auth:Authority": "https://login.microsoftonline.com/your-tenant-
    id/v2.0",
    "Auth:Audience": "api://orderprocessor",
    "Auth:RequiredRole": "OrderWriter",
    "Auth:RequiredScope": "Orders.ReadWrite",
    "DownstreamApis:ClientId": "your-client-id",
    "DownstreamApis:TenantId": "your-tenant-id",
    "DownstreamApis:ClientSecret": "your-client-secret",
    "KeyVaultName": "orderprocessor-kv",
    "AppConfigEndpoint": "https://orderprocessor-appconfig.azconfig.io"
  }
}
```

Notice that the local settings file contains only the Key Vault and App Configuration connection points, not the Fraud API key itself.

`FraudApi:BaseUrl` can live in Azure App Configuration, while `FraudApi:ApiKey` should come from Azure Key Vault. The Function App can reach both using its managed identity.

Project Addition: Secretless Fraud API Integration

In `OrderProcessor`, the Fraud API integration now separates ordinary configuration from secret material. The base URL is loaded through Azure App Configuration, while the API key is resolved securely from Azure Key Vault using the Function App's managed identity. This removes the secret from application configuration and keeps credential management centralized, auditable, and easier to rotate.

Secure Networking and Private Endpoints

So far in this chapter, the focus has been on identity, tokens, RBAC, and secrets. But distributed systems do not just exchange tokens; they exchange network traffic. If that traffic crosses the public internet unnecessarily, attackers still have opportunities to intercept, replay, or flood parts of the system. That is why network-level protection forms an important final layer of defense. In Azure, serverless workloads such as Functions can use Virtual Networks and private endpoints to communicate with databases, queues, and other dependencies without exposing those paths publicly. For `OrderProcessor`, that means isolating storage, messaging, and other internal dependencies so workflow traffic stays on trusted network paths wherever possible.

Why Networking Is Important in Serverless

Serverless abstracts servers, but it does not remove networking risk. Function Apps may still depend on publicly reachable services, databases and messaging systems may expose public endpoints, and outbound calls may still leave trusted boundaries unless explicitly constrained. That creates several risks, including traffic interception when transport security is weak, wider exposure to denial-of-service pressure on public endpoints, and the possibility of lateral movement if one publicly reachable resource is compromised. Private networking reduces these risks by shrinking the number of places where traffic can enter or leave the system.

Principle 1: VNet Integration for Functions

For OrderProcessor, the first step is to attach the Function App to a subnet in the application VNet so outbound traffic can flow through controlled network paths.

```
az functionapp vnet-integration add \
  --name orderprocessor-func \
  --resource-group buy-rg \
  --vnet buy-northeurope-ci-vnet \
  --subnet func-subnet
```

Now outbound traffic flows through the VNet. Internal services reachable through private endpoints are resolved inside the VNet rather than over the public internet.

Principle 2: Private Endpoints for Dependencies

Each dependency can then be exposed through a private endpoint inside the VNet. In practice, that often includes services such as Cosmos DB, Service Bus, SQL Database, and Key Vault. Private endpoints ensure those services are reachable over internal network paths rather than through their public endpoints.

Example Service Bus private endpoint

```
az network private-endpoint create \
--name orderprocessor-sb-pe \
--resource-group buy-rg \
--vnet-name buy-northeurope-ci-vnet \
--subnet privateLinkSubnet \
--private-connection-resource-id /subscriptions/<subId>/
resourceGroups/buy-rg/
providers/Microsoft.ServiceBus/namespaces/orderprocessor-sb \
--group-id namespace \
--connection-name orderprocessor-sb-conn
```

DNS updates ensure `orderprocessor-sb.servicebus.windows.net` resolves internally.

Principle 3: Restrict Public Access

Once private endpoints exist, disable public endpoints:

```
az cosmosdb update \
--name orderprocessor-cosmos \
--resource-group buy-rg \
--public-network-access Disabled
```

Once public access is disabled, Cosmos DB accepts connections only through its private network path. The same principle applies to Service Bus, SQL, and Key Vault.

Principle 4: Outbound Firewalling

Even with VNet integration in place, outbound access may still need to be restricted further. Network Security Groups, Azure Firewall, or similar controls can be used to allow only the destinations the Function App actually needs. For `OrderProcessor`, that means permitting only trusted external integrations such as Fraud and Tax services, while blocking unnecessary outbound access. This reduces the blast radius if the Function App is ever compromised.

Principle 5: Isolate Environments

Test, CI, and production should live in separate VNets so lower environments cannot accidentally or deliberately reach production data paths. Where peering is required, it should be tightly limited to specific shared services such as monitoring or central platform components.

Principle 6: Hybrid Integrations

Sometimes external systems such as ERP or supplier APIs do not support Azure private endpoints. In those cases, the alternative is to use controlled private connectivity patterns such as VPN gateways for on-premises integration, ExpressRoute for dedicated private circuits, or API Management as a secured bridge between the Function App and the external system.

`OrderProcessor` ERP, for example, connects over a site-to-site VPN into the supplier's datacenter.

Applying Private Networking to OrderProcessor

For `OrderProcessor`, private networking starts with the Function App joining the application VNet, followed by private endpoints for the core platform services it depends on. The most important first targets are the durable state store and the messaging layer, because they sit directly on the workflow path. Once those dependencies are reachable privately, public access can be disabled, and DNS can be configured so the Function App resolves the internal addresses automatically.

Project Addition: Private Endpoints for Cosmos DB and Service Bus

In `OrderProcessor`, the Function App is now integrated with the application VNet, private endpoints are created for Cosmos DB and Service Bus, public access is disabled for those services, and private DNS resolution ensures the Function App connects to their internal addresses. As a result, workflow state and messaging traffic no longer depend on public network paths, which strengthen the platform against interception, exposure, and lateral movement.

Auditing and Compliance

Security isn't complete until you can prove it. Customers, auditors, and regulators don't just ask, "Is the system secure?" They ask, "Can you show me the evidence?" That evidence comes from auditing (recording what happened) and compliance (demonstrating that what happened meets legal or regulatory requirements). For `OrderProcessor`, this means logging every sensitive action, retaining those logs securely, enforcing access policies, and enabling features like data deletion for GDPR. In this section, we will look at the practical patterns that let a serverless .NET system stand up to audit scrutiny without slowing delivery to a crawl.

Why Auditing Is Different in Serverless

Auditing is not the same as ordinary logging. Logs may be transient, noisy, or duplicated during replay, while audit records need to be durable, selective, and trustworthy. In serverless systems, every Function execution is ephemeral, which makes centralized collection essential. Durable Functions add another wrinkle because replay can generate duplicate log entries unless auditing is designed carefully. Compliance frameworks such as GDPR, SOC 2, and ISO 27001 also require more than simple error tracking. They require evidence of who did what, when they did it, and what the outcome was.

Principle 1: Structured Audit Events

An audit record should capture the minimum set of fields needed to explain the action clearly, including the time, identity, role, action, target, outcome, and trace context.

In .NET, model this as a simple type:

Models/AuditEvent.cs

```
public record AuditEvent(
    DateTime Timestamp,
    string UserId,
    string Role,
    string Action,
    string Target,
    string Outcome,
    string TraceId);
```

This ensures consistency and queryability.

Principle 2: Centralized Storage

Audit events should be written to a durable store that is separate from noisy operational telemetry. Azure Table Storage is cheap and append-friendly, Cosmos DB gives stronger query flexibility by order or user, and Log Analytics is useful for KQL-based investigation. For `OrderProcessor`, Cosmos DB is a good fit because auditors may need to query records by order ID, user, or action (see Figure 8-3).

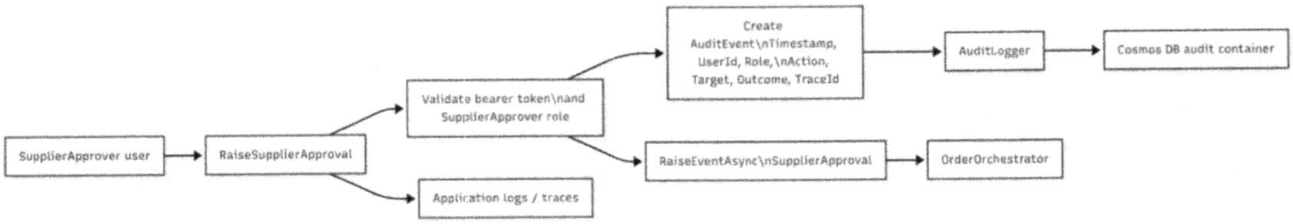

Figure 8-3. *Audit event flow for supplier approvals*

Audit Logger Implementation

Services/AuditLogger.cs

```
public class AuditLogger
{
    private readonly CosmosClient _cosmos;
    private readonly Container _container;
    public AuditLogger(CosmosClient cosmos)
    {
        _cosmos = cosmos;
        _container = _cosmos.GetContainer("orderdb", "audit");
    }

    public async Task LogAsync(AuditEvent ev, CancellationToken stopToken)
    {
        await _container.CreateItemAsync(ev, new PartitionKey(ev.UserId),
        cancellationToken: stopToken);
    }
}
```

Audit events are written as first-class records, separate from debug logs.

Program.cs

```
using Azure.Identity;
using Microsoft.Azure.Cosmos;
using Microsoft.Azure.Functions.Worker;
using Microsoft.Azure.Functions.Worker.Builder;
using Microsoft.Extensions.DependencyInjection;
using Microsoft.Extensions.Hosting;
using OrderProcessor.Helpers;
```

```
using OrderProcessor.Options;
using OrderProcessor.Security;
using OrderProcessor.Services;

var builder = FunctionsApplication.CreateBuilder(args);

builder.ConfigureFunctionsWebApplication();

builder.Configuration.AddAzureAppConfiguration(options =>
{
    var endpoint = builder.Configuration["AppConfigEndpoint"];

    if (string.IsNullOrWhiteSpace(endpoint))
    {
        throw new InvalidOperationException("Missing AppConfigEndpoint");
    }

    options.Connect(new Uri(endpoint), new DefaultAzureCredential())
        .ConfigureKeyVault(kv => kv.SetCredential(new
        DefaultAzureCredential()));
});

var keyVaultName = builder.Configuration["KeyVaultName"];

if (string.IsNullOrWhiteSpace(keyVaultName))
{
    throw new InvalidOperationException("Missing KeyVaultName");
}

builder.Configuration.AddAzureKeyVault(
    new Uri($"https://{keyVaultName}.vault.azure.net/"),
    new DefaultAzureCredential());

builder.Services
    .AddApplicationInsightsTelemetryWorkerService()
    .ConfigureFunctionsApplicationInsights();

builder.Services.AddSingleton<IFunctionsWorkerMiddleware,
CorrelationMiddleware>();
```

```
builder.Services
    .AddOptions<AuthOptions>()
    .BindConfiguration(AuthOptions.SectionName)
    .Validate(options =>
        !string.IsNullOrWhiteSpace(options.Authority) &&
        !string.IsNullOrWhiteSpace(options.Audience),
        "Auth settings are required.");

builder.Services
    .AddOptions<FraudApiOptions>()
    .BindConfiguration(FraudApiOptions.SectionName)
    .Validate(options =>
        !string.IsNullOrWhiteSpace(options.BaseUrl) &&
        !string.IsNullOrWhiteSpace(options.ApiKey),
        "Fraud API settings are required.");

builder.Services.AddSingleton<ITokenValidator, JwtTokenValidator>();

builder.Services.AddSingleton(_ =>
{
    var endpoint = builder.Configuration["CosmosDbEndpoint"]
        ?? throw new InvalidOperationException("Missing CosmosDbEndpoint");

    return new CosmosClient(endpoint, new DefaultAzureCredential());
});

builder.Services.AddSingleton<AuditLogger>();

TokenHelper.Init(
    builder.Configuration["DownstreamApis:ClientId"]
        ?? throw new InvalidOperationException("Missing
        DownstreamApis:ClientId"),
    builder.Configuration["DownstreamApis:TenantId"]
        ?? throw new InvalidOperationException("Missing
        DownstreamApis:TenantId"),
    builder.Configuration["DownstreamApis:ClientSecret"]
        ?? throw new InvalidOperationException("Missing DownstreamApis:
        ClientSecret"));
```

```
builder.Build().Run();
```

Functions/RaiseSupplierApproval.cs

```
using System.Net;
using Microsoft.Azure.Functions.Worker;
using Microsoft.Azure.Functions.Worker.Http;
using Microsoft.DurableTask.Client;
using Microsoft.Extensions.Logging;
using OrderProcessor.Security;
using OrderProcessor.Services;

namespace OrderProcessor;

public sealed class RaiseSupplierApproval
{
    private readonly ILogger<RaiseSupplierApproval> _logger;
    private readonly ITokenValidator _tokenValidator;
    private readonly AuditLogger _auditLogger;

    public RaiseSupplierApproval(
        ILogger<RaiseSupplierApproval> logger,
        ITokenValidator tokenValidator,
        AuditLogger auditLogger)
    {
        _logger = logger;
        _tokenValidator = tokenValidator;
        _auditLogger = auditLogger;
    }

    [Function("RaiseSupplierApproval")]
    public async Task<HttpResponseData> Run(
        [HttpTrigger(AuthorizationLevel.Anonymous, "post", Route = "orders/
        {instanceId}/supplier-approval")]
        HttpRequestData req,
        string instanceId,
        [DurableClient] DurableTaskClient client,
        CancellationToken stopToken)
```

```
{
    var bearerToken = req.GetBearerToken();

    if (string.IsNullOrWhiteSpace(bearerToken))
    {
        var unauthorized = req.CreateResponse(HttpStatusCode.
        Unauthorized);
        await unauthorized.WriteStringAsync("Missing bearer token.",
        stopToken);
        return unauthorized;
    }

    var principal = await _tokenValidator.ValidateAsync(bearerToken,
    stopToken);

    if (principal is null)
    {
        var unauthorized = req.CreateResponse(HttpStatusCode.
        Unauthorized);
        await unauthorized.WriteStringAsync("Invalid or expired
        token.", stopToken);
        return unauthorized;
    }

    if (!principal.HasRole("SupplierApprover"))
    {
        var forbidden = req.CreateResponse(HttpStatusCode.Forbidden);
        await forbidden.WriteStringAsync("Caller is not allowed to
        approve supplier actions.", stopToken);
        return forbidden;
    }

    var decision = await req.ReadFromJsonAsync<SupplierDecision>(cancel
    lationToken: stopToken);

    if (decision is null || string.IsNullOrWhiteSpace(decision.OrderId))
    {
        var bad = req.CreateResponse(HttpStatusCode.BadRequest);
```

```
            await bad.WriteStringAsync("Invalid supplier approval
            payload.", stopToken);
            return bad;
        }

        await client.RaiseEventAsync(
            instanceId,
            "SupplierApproval",
            decision,
            cancellationToken: stopToken);

        await _auditLogger.LogAsync(
            new AuditEvent(
                Timestamp: DateTime.UtcNow,
                    UserId: principal.GetUserId(),
                Role: string.Join(",", principal.GetRoles()),
                Action: "SupplierApproval",
                Target: decision.OrderId,
                Outcome: decision.Approved ? "Approved" : "Rejected",
                TraceId: req.FunctionContext.TraceContext.TraceParent ??
                Guid.NewGuid().ToString()), stopToken);

        _logger.LogInformation(
            "User {UserName} raised SupplierApproval for order {OrderId} on
            instance {InstanceId}",
            principal.GetUserName(),
            decision.OrderId,
            instanceId);

        return req.CreateResponse(HttpStatusCode.OK);
    }
}
```

Local.settings.json

```
{
  "IsEncrypted": false,
```

```
  "Values": {
    "AzureWebJobsStorage": "UseDevelopmentStorage=true",
    "FUNCTIONS_WORKER_RUNTIME": "dotnet-isolated",
    "Auth:Authority": "https://login.microsoftonline.com/your-tenant-
    id/v2.0",
    "Auth:Audience": "api://orderprocessor",
    "Auth:RequiredRole": "OrderWriter",
    "Auth:RequiredScope": "Orders.ReadWrite",
    "DownstreamApis:ClientId": "your-client-id",
    "DownstreamApis:TenantId": "your-tenant-id",
    "DownstreamApis:ClientSecret": "your-client-secret",
    "KeyVaultName": "orderprocessor-kv",
    "AppConfigEndpoint": "https://orderprocessor-appconfig.azconfig.io",
    "CosmosDbEndpoint": "https://orderprocessor-cosmos.documents.azure.
    com:443/"
  }
}
```

Principle 3: Role and Identity Capture

Audits without identity are useless. Every event must capture who acted.

The full `RaiseSupplierApproval` example shown earlier already demonstrates this pattern, capturing the caller identity, role, action, outcome, and trace context in a structured audit record.

Now every supplier action is traceable back to a role and identity.

Principle 4: Replay-Safe Auditing

Durable orchestrations replay, so writing audit events directly from the orchestrator risks recording the same action more than once. Audit writes should therefore happen inside activities or other non-replayed boundaries, while ordinary orchestrator logs should be guarded with `context.IsReplaying` where necessary. Idempotency keys such as `OrderId` plus action name can provide an extra safeguard in the audit store.

Principle 5: Retention and Immutability

Auditors expect records to remain available for a defined retention period, while privacy laws may require personal data to be erasable or anonymized. That balance is easier to manage when audit data is designed with pseudonymization in mind. Instead of storing full email addresses or other directly identifying values, the audit record can store a hash or another irreversible reference. Retention policies in Cosmos DB or Log Analytics can then enforce the required retention window without leaving raw personal data exposed unnecessarily.

Instead of storing full customer emails, log a hash:

```
var emailHash =
Convert.ToHexString(SHA256.HashData(Encoding.UTF8.GetBytes(order.
CustomerEmail)));
```

This way, logs retain uniqueness but don't expose PII. Retention policies in Cosmos or Log Analytics enforce automatic deletion after 7 years.

Principle 6: GDPR Compliance

GDPR introduces a practical separation between business records and personal data. Orders may need to remain for legal or financial reasons, while customer-specific personal data may need to be deleted or anonymized on request. One effective pattern is to store personal data separately, keyed by a stable identifier, while audit records reference only that identifier. When a deletion request arrives, the personal data store can be wiped or anonymized without destroying the audit history.

Principle 7: Continuous Compliance with Azure Policy

Azure Policy can enforce many of the compliance controls that teams otherwise forget to apply consistently. Function Apps can be required to use encryption, Cosmos DB can be prevented from exposing public endpoints, and Key Vault can be forced to use soft delete and purge protection. The value here is not just technical enforcement but continuous visibility, because non-compliant resources appear automatically in compliance reporting.

Applying Audit Logging to Supplier Approvals

`OrderProcessor` applies this pattern directly to supplier approvals. When a supplier approval event is raised, the system writes a structured audit record containing the acting identity, role, action, target, outcome, and trace context. The earlier `AuditEvent` example shows the shape of that record and how it is persisted through `AuditLogger`. This ensures that supplier approvals are not just operationally logged but captured as durable audit evidence.

Project Addition: Auditing Supplier Approvals

In `OrderProcessor`, supplier approvals now produce first-class audit records rather than relying only on ordinary logs. The system records the acting identity, role, action, target, outcome, and trace context in Cosmos DB, while personal data can be pseudonymized to reduce privacy exposure. With retention policies applied, those approval events become durable, queryable, and suitable for both operational investigation and compliance evidence.

Threat Modeling Summary

The security controls in this chapter are easier to understand when they are tied back to the threats they are meant to reduce. OrderProcessor has several important trust boundaries: the public API boundary, the orchestration event boundary, downstream integration boundaries, durable state storage, secrets storage, and audit storage. Each one needs a specific control rather than a general claim that the system is secure.

At the API boundary, the main risks are spoofed callers, token replay, excessive request volume, and malformed payloads. APIM reduces those risks through centralized JWT validation, rate limiting, request validation, and gateway logging, while the Function code still enforces workflow-specific authorization.

At the orchestration boundary, the main risk is unauthorized workflow progression. Supplier approvals, fraud decisions, and external callbacks can change the state of a long-running process, so those endpoints must validate identity, enforce the correct role, and record the action for audit.

At the integration boundary, the risks include over-permissioned credentials, leaked secrets, and untrusted callbacks. Managed identity, least-privilege scopes, HTTPS, Key Vault, and callback validation reduce those risks.

At the state and secrets boundary, the risks are tampering and disclosure. Durable backing stores, Cosmos DB, Service Bus, Storage, and Key Vault should use managed identity, RBAC, private endpoints where possible, diagnostic logging, and restricted public access.

At the audit boundary, the risk is lack of evidence. Sensitive actions need durable audit records that capture who acted, what they did, what target they affected, when it happened, and what the outcome was.

This gives OrderProcessor a practical threat model rather than a generic security checklist. The system authenticates callers, authorizes sensitive workflow actions, protects secrets and network paths, validates integrations, and records evidence for later investigation.

EXERCISES

1. **Missing Token on Order Submission:** Call `/orders/orchestrate` without an `Authorization` header. Confirm the request is rejected with `401 Unauthorized`.
2. **Invalid Token on Order Submission:** Call `/orders/orchestrate` with a malformed or expired bearer token. Confirm the request is rejected with `401 Unauthorized`.
3. **OrderWriter Role Enforcement:** Call `/orders/orchestrate` with a valid token that does not include the `OrderWriter` role and does not include the required scope. Confirm the request is rejected with `403 Forbidden`.
4. **Role vs. Scope Check:** Submit an order using a token that lacks the `OrderWriter` role but includes the `Orders.ReadWrite` scope. Confirm the request is accepted and compare the behaviour with a role-based token.
5. **Identity Traceability:** Submit an order with a valid token and inspect the logs. Confirm that the caller identity is recorded when `StartOrderOrchestration` schedules the workflow.

6. **Token Handling in Activities:** Set a breakpoint or log statement in `FraudCheckActivity` and confirm that the downstream token is acquired inside the activity rather than being passed into the orchestrator.

7. **Token Cache behavior:** Temporarily disable the token cache helper behavior and submit multiple orders in quick succession. Compare latency and token acquisition volume against the cached version.

8. **Least-Privilege Token Check:** Try to call a downstream API with a token intended for a different integration. Confirm the downstream service rejects the request.

9. **Supplier Approval Without Token:** Call `/orders/{instanceId}/supplier-approval` without a bearer token. Confirm the request is rejected with `401 Unauthorized`.

10. **Supplier Approval with Wrong Role:** Call `/orders/{instanceId}/supplier-approval` with a valid token that does not include the `SupplierApprover` role. Confirm the request is rejected with `403 Forbidden`.

11. **Fraud Approval with Wrong Role:** Call `/orders/{instanceId}/fraud-approval` with a valid token that includes `OrderWriter` but not `FraudAnalyst`. Confirm the request is rejected with `403 Forbidden`.

12. **Fraud Approval Success Path:** Call `/orders/{instanceId}/fraud-approval` with a valid `FraudAnalyst` token and a valid payload. Confirm that the `FraudApproval` event is raised and logged.

13. **Replay-Safe Logging:** Add a log statement inside the orchestrator without guarding it with `context.IsReplaying`. Run the workflow and observe duplicate log noise. Then add the replay guard and compare the output.

14. **Durable State Access Check:** Attempt to access the durable backing store directly with a user identity that should not have access. Confirm that access is denied.

15. **Inbound Callback Validation:** Call `/orders/{instanceId}/tax-callback` without a bearer token, then with a token missing the `TaxService` role. Confirm you received `401 Unauthorized` and `403 Forbidden`, respectively.

16. **Key Vault Secret Resolution:** Move the Fraud API secret into Key Vault, start the Function App, and confirm the application resolves the secret successfully at runtime without placing the raw value in configuration files.

17. **Secret Rotation Drill:** Rotate the Fraud API secret in Key Vault and verify that the application continues working after configuration refresh, without requiring the secret to be reintroduced into code or local files.

18. **Log Scrubbing Check:** Inspect logs related to the Fraud API integration and confirm that no raw secret values appear, only safe derived values such as hashes or non-sensitive configuration.

19. **Private Networking Check:** Disable public access to Cosmos DB or Service Bus after private endpoints are configured. Confirm that the Function App can still reach the service privately while a direct public path is blocked.

20. **Audit Trail Verification:** Submit supplier approvals using two different users and query the audit store. Confirm that each record captures identity, role, action, target, outcome, and trace context.

Summary

Security in serverless .NET starts at the boundary. In `OrderProcessor`, identity is no longer treated as a coarse function-key check but as a first-class application concern. Incoming bearer tokens are validated explicitly, claims are turned into usable caller identity, and the order submission boundary enforces the permissions required to start a workflow. From there, role-based access control continues across other workflow boundaries, including supplier approvals, fraud decisions, and inbound service callbacks, so each sensitive action is tied to an authenticated identity with the correct role.

Token handling then builds on that foundation. Durable orchestrations cannot safely carry raw access tokens in their state because replay, expiry, and long-running execution make that approach fragile and insecure. Instead, `OrderProcessor` acquires tokens at the point of use, inside activity execution, where they can remain short-lived and scoped to the exact downstream service being called. More advanced patterns such as the On-Behalf-Of flow, long-running token refresh, and least-privilege service scopes extend that model for more complex systems, but the central rule remains the same: keep the orchestrator deterministic and keep sensitive token material out of durable state.

The chapter then broadens from identity and token flow into operational hardening. External integrations are treated as security boundaries, with inbound callbacks validated and outbound calls protected through scoped credentials, HTTPS, and secret management. Secrets move out of application configuration and into Azure Key Vault; non-secret settings are centralized in Azure App Configuration, and network-level controls reduce exposure through VNets, private endpoints, and restricted public access. Finally, structured audit records give `OrderProcessor` durable evidence of who performed each sensitive action, making the system not only harder to attack but also easier to investigate, govern, and defend under audit.

PART III

Operations and Advanced Cases

CHAPTER 9

Deployment Models and Operational Strategies in Serverless Systems

So far, `OrderProcessor` has evolved from a simple serverless prototype into a structured distributed system. We have built orchestration with Durable Functions, introduced persistence, added observability, and strengthened the platform with security, identity, access control, and operational safeguards. But none of that matters for long if the system cannot be deployed, operated, and improved safely in the real world. A production serverless system is not defined by code alone. It is also defined by how its infrastructure is created, how releases are controlled, how failures are handled, and how the team keeps the platform healthy over time.

This chapter moves `OrderProcessor` into that next stage of maturity. We will look at how to define the platform with Infrastructure as Code, how to automate delivery through pipelines, how to reduce release risk with zero-downtime deployment strategies, and how to strengthen operations through playbooks, governance, cost visibility, disaster recovery, and continuous improvement. The goal is not simply to get the system deployed. It is to make `OrderProcessor` a serverless platform that can be shipped repeatedly, run responsibly, and evolved with confidence.

Introduction to Deployment Models

Designing and securing a serverless system is only half the battle. To run in production, it also has to be deployed, operated, and updated in a way that is reliable, repeatable, and safe. In serverless systems, that means thinking beyond code alone. The Function App

© Patrick Kearns 2026
P. Kearns, *Serverless Distributed Systems in Modern .NET and Azure*,
https://doi.org/10.1007/979-8-8688-2839-3_9

matters, but so do the queues, databases, secrets, network boundaries, and supporting services that surround it. For `OrderProcessor`, deployment is no longer just a case of publishing from an IDE. It becomes a controlled process that creates and configures the full environment in a predictable way every time.

That shift matters because serverless systems change quickly. Functions scale dynamically, infrastructure evolves as the workflow grows, and environment drift between CI, Test, and Production can cause failures that are difficult to diagnose. In a more traditional application, you might deploy a binary to a long-lived server and leave most of the surrounding environment alone for months. In a serverless system, both the application code and the infrastructure are changing together. The practical answer is to treat infrastructure and application code as part of the same delivery story, versioned together, reviewed together, and deployed together.

Why Deployment Is Different in Serverless

Deployment in a serverless system is different because the code is only one part of what makes the application work. `OrderProcessor` depends on Azure Functions for orchestration and activities, but it also depends on storage for durable state, Service Bus for messaging, Cosmos DB for data and audit records, Key Vault for secrets, and networking rules that control how those services communicate. If any one of those pieces is missing, misconfigured, or out of sync with the others, the application may deploy successfully but still fail as a system. That is why deployment discipline matters more in serverless than it often does in simpler applications. The goal is not just to publish code successfully. The goal is to produce the same environment, with the same security posture and the same dependencies, every time. Once you start thinking about deployment in that way, different deployment models become easier to compare.

Deployment Model 1: Manual Deployment

The simplest deployment model is manual deployment. A developer publishes directly from Visual Studio or from the command line:

```
func azure functionapp publish orderprocessor-func
```

This is perfectly reasonable at the prototype stage. In fact, it is often the fastest way to validate that a Function runs, that bindings are wired correctly, or that an orchestration can start successfully in Azure. `OrderProcessor` began in much the same way, with direct deployment used to test early workflow behavior before the surrounding infrastructure had fully taken shape.

The weakness of manual deployment is that it does not scale with the system. Manual steps are easy to forget, difficult to audit, and hard to reproduce exactly. If one developer deploys a slightly different configuration from another, the system begins to drift. That makes production use risky, especially once security settings, queues, databases, and secrets all need to be aligned correctly.

Deployment Model 2: Infrastructure As Code (IaC)

Infrastructure as Code, usually shortened to IaC, addresses that problem by defining infrastructure in source-controlled files rather than in the portal or through memory. Azure supports several IaC approaches, including ARM templates, Terraform, and Bicep. For OrderProcessor, Bicep is the most natural choice because it is Azure-native, concise, and fits well with the rest of an Azure-first .NET solution.

A Bicep template allows the infrastructure to be described declaratively and deployed repeatedly from the same source definition. A simple example might define a Function App and the app settings it depends on:

```
@secure()
param storageConnectionString string

resource storage 'Microsoft.Storage/storageAccounts@2022-09-01'
existing = {
  name: 'yourstorageacct'
}

var keys = listKeys(storage.id, storage.apiVersion)
var conn = 'DefaultEndpointsProtocol=https;AccountName=${storage.
name};AccountKey=${keys.keys[0].value};EndpointSuffix=${environment().
suffixes.storage}'

resource func 'Microsoft.Web/sites@2022-03-01' = {
  name: 'orderprocessor-func'
```

```
  location: resourceGroup().location
  kind: 'functionapp'
  properties: {
    siteConfig: {
      appSettings: [
        { name: 'AzureWebJobsStorage'; value: conn }
        { name: 'FUNCTIONS_EXTENSION_VERSION'; value: '~4' }
      ]
    }
  }
}
```

Once infrastructure is defined this way, deployments become far more predictable. The template lives alongside the application code, changes are reviewed through the same source control process, and every environment can be created from the same baseline definition instead of by hand.

Deployment Model 3: CI/CD Pipelines

IaC solves repeatability, but something still needs to execute the deployment. That is where CI/CD pipelines come in. A pipeline turns build, test, packaging, and deployment into an automated flow that runs the same way each time code is merged. For `OrderProcessor`, this is the point where deployment becomes a team capability rather than an individual developer action.

A pipeline can build the .NET projects, run unit tests, package the Functions app, deploy infrastructure through Bicep, and then deploy the application code itself. A simplified Azure DevOps step for infrastructure deployment might look like this:

```
- task: AzureCLI@2
  inputs:
    azureSubscription: 'buy-ci'
    scriptType: 'bash'
    scriptLocation: 'inlineScript'
    inlineScript: |
      az deployment group create \
        --resource-group buy-ci-rg \
        --template-file infra/main.bicep
```

The important idea is not the specific pipeline task. It is that deployment is no longer a manual sequence of remembered steps. It becomes a repeatable process that can be audited, rerun, and trusted.

Deployment Model 4: Blue-Green and Canary

For production workloads, deployment is not only about getting new code live. It is also about reducing release risk. That is where Blue-Green and Canary strategies come in. A Blue-Green approach keeps two deployment targets available, one live and one staged, and switches traffic only after the staged environment has been validated. A Canary approach sends only a small percentage of traffic to the new version first, watches for errors, and then expands rollout gradually if the system behaves well. In `OrderProcessor`, this is important because the application is not just serving stateless requests. It is coordinating workflows, handling approvals, and interacting with external dependencies such as ERP and payment systems. A bad release is not just an inconvenience. It can affect in-flight orders, duplicate work, or introduce failure into downstream integrations. That makes controlled rollout strategies far more important than they might be in a simpler application.

Deployment Model 5: GitOps

At the more advanced end of the spectrum is GitOps, where the Git repository becomes the source of truth not just for code but for the desired deployed state of the system. Changes to infrastructure or application definitions are reconciled automatically so that the live environment matches what is declared in source control. This is more common in container-based environments, but the underlying idea still applies to serverless systems: the repository should describe the intended state, and automated processes should bring the platform into line with that state. For `OrderProcessor`, a full GitOps model may be more than is needed at the start, but the principle is still valuable. The closer the project gets to treating source control as the authoritative description of both code and environment, the less room there is for drift, surprise, or undocumented platform changes.

Choosing a Model for OrderProcessor

The right deployment model depends on where the system is in its lifecycle. For experimentation and early prototypes, manual deployment is often enough. For CI and shared development environments, Infrastructure as Code combined with automated pipelines becomes the sensible baseline. For production, that baseline usually needs to be extended with safer release strategies such as staged deployments or Blue-Green slot swaps. The point is not that every environment needs the same level of ceremony. It is that every environment should have the level of discipline appropriate to the risk it carries.

For `OrderProcessor`, that means using a hybrid approach. Early work can still move quickly, but once the workflow, infrastructure, and security posture begin to matter, deployment needs to become repeatable and versioned. That is the foundation for the rest of this chapter.

Preparing OrderProcessor for Infrastructure As Code

At this point, `OrderProcessor` is ready to move from ad hoc deployment toward a repeatable infrastructure model. The next section introduces the first real Bicep templates and shows how the project's Azure resources begin to move into source control. From there, pipelines and safer release strategies can build on a concrete IaC foundation.

Infrastructure As Code with Bicep

In the previous section, we established why deployment in a serverless system has to be treated as more than a code publish. `OrderProcessor` depends on infrastructure just as much as it depends on .NET code, and once that becomes true, the infrastructure needs to be versioned, reviewed, and deployed with the same discipline as the application itself. That is what Infrastructure as Code provides. For an Azure-first system, Bicep is a natural fit. It is concise, readable, and built specifically for Azure resource modeling. It keeps the infrastructure definition close to the way Azure itself thinks about resources, while avoiding the weight and verbosity of raw ARM JSON. For `OrderProcessor`, that means we can define the Function App, storage, messaging, database, secrets, and networking in source control and reproduce those environments consistently across CI, Test, and Production.

Why Bicep Fits OrderProcessor

There are several ways to define cloud infrastructure, but Bicep fits `OrderProcessor` particularly well because the system is already anchored in Azure services. The project uses Azure Functions, Service Bus, Cosmos DB, Key Vault, and VNets, so using Azure's native IaC language keeps the infrastructure model aligned with the platform it is targeting. It also means new Azure capabilities are available immediately, without waiting for a separate provider or abstraction layer to catch up.

Just as importantly, Bicep reads cleanly enough to sit comfortably in a .NET-centric codebase. The earlier chapters of this book already moved `OrderProcessor` toward explicit workflow definitions, clearer boundaries, and reproducible configuration. Bicep extends that same mindset into the platform layer. Instead of creating infrastructure in the portal and hoping it stays consistent, we define it in code and let deployments replay that definition whenever a new environment is needed.

Modeling the OrderProcessor Platform

A minimal infrastructure footprint for `OrderProcessor` includes the Function App that runs the orchestrations and activities, a storage account for Durable Functions state, Service Bus for messaging, Cosmos DB for operational and audit data, Key Vault for secrets and certificates, and virtual networking for private connectivity. The important point is not simply that these resources exist, but that they exist together as one versioned platform definition. A root `main.bicep` file is a good place to start. It becomes the composition point for the infrastructure, wiring together the major resources and passing shared values such as environment name and location into lower-level modules.

Starting with Storage

The storage account is one of the first resources to define because Functions and Durable Functions depend on it for checkpoints and runtime state. A simple Bicep resource might look like this:

infra/modules/storage.bicep

```
param storageAccountName string
param location string
```

```
resource storage 'Microsoft.Storage/storageAccounts@2022-09-01' = {
  name: storageAccountName
  location: location
  sku: {
    name: 'Standard_LRS'
  }
  kind: 'StorageV2'
  properties: {
    minimumTlsVersion: 'TLS1_2'
    supportsHttpsTrafficOnly: true
  }
}

output storageAccountId string = storage.id
output storageAccountName string = storage.name
```

This keeps the definition simple, but it already encodes important platform choices. HTTPS-only access is enforced, TLS is pinned to a modern minimum, and the storage account becomes part of the declared environment rather than something provisioned manually.

Adding Service Bus

`OrderProcessor` relies on messaging, so Service Bus is another core part of the platform definition. By putting it into Bicep, the namespace and its queues become repeatable resources rather than portal-created dependencies that may differ between environments.

infra/modules/servicebus.bicep

```
param namespaceName string
param location string

resource sb 'Microsoft.ServiceBus/namespaces@2022-10-01-preview' = {
  name: namespaceName
  location: location
  sku: {
    name: 'Premium'
    tier: 'Premium'
```

```
    capacity: 1
  }
}

resource ordersQueue 'Microsoft.ServiceBus/namespaces/queues@2022-10-01-
preview' = {
  name: '${sb.name}/orders'
  properties: {
    enablePartitioning: true
  }
}

output serviceBusNamespaceId string = sb.id
output serviceBusNamespaceName string = sb.name
```

This keeps the messaging layer explicit and environment-specific. It also lays the groundwork for later sections in the chapter where messaging and deployment strategy start to interact more directly.

Defining the Function App

The Function App is the runtime heart of `OrderProcessor`, but in IaC terms, it is just one part of a broader platform. It depends on a hosting plan, storage, configuration, and eventually secret resolution through Key Vault. The infrastructure definition should reflect that.

infra/modules/functionapp.bicep

```
param functionAppName string
param planName string
param location string
param storageAccountName string

resource storage 'Microsoft.Storage/storageAccounts@2022-09-01'
existing = {
  name: storageAccountName
}

var storageKeys = listKeys(storage.id, storage.apiVersion)
```

```
var storageConnectionString = 'DefaultEndpointsProtocol=https;AccountName=$
{storage.name};AccountKey=${storageKeys.keys[0].value};EndpointSuffix=${env
ironment().suffixes.storage}'

resource appServicePlan 'Microsoft.Web/serverfarms@2022-03-01' = {
  name: planName
  location: location
  sku: {
    name: 'EP1'
    tier: 'ElasticPremium'
    capacity: 1
  }
}

resource functionApp 'Microsoft.Web/sites@2022-03-01' = {
  name: functionAppName
  location: location
  kind: 'functionapp'
  properties: {
    serverFarmId: appServicePlan.id
    siteConfig: {
      appSettings: [
        {
          name: 'AzureWebJobsStorage'
          value: storageConnectionString
        }
        {
          name: 'FUNCTIONS_WORKER_RUNTIME'
          value: 'dotnet-isolated'
        }
      ]
    }
    httpsOnly: true
  }
}

output functionAppId string = functionApp.id
output functionAppName string = functionApp.name
```

At this stage, the Function App definition does not have to include every production setting. The main goal is to move the runtime shape of the application into source control. Later sections can evolve that definition with additional settings, secrets, slots, and network integration.

Bringing in Cosmos DB

Cosmos DB matters to `OrderProcessor` both as operational storage and, later in the book, as an audit store. It should therefore be part of the platform definition from the beginning.

`infra/modules/cosmos.bicep`

```
param cosmosAccountName string
param location string

resource cosmos 'Microsoft.DocumentDB/databaseAccounts@2022-05-15' = {
  name: cosmosAccountName
  location: location
  kind: 'GlobalDocumentDB'
  properties: {
    databaseAccountOfferType: 'Standard'
    locations: [
      {
        locationName: location
        failoverPriority: 0
      }
    ]
    consistencyPolicy: {
      defaultConsistencyLevel: 'Session'
    }
    publicNetworkAccess: 'Disabled'
  }
}

resource database 'Microsoft.DocumentDB/databaseAccounts/
sqlDatabases@2022-05-15' = {
  name: '${cosmos.name}/orderdb'
```

```
  properties: {
    resource: {
      id: 'orderdb'
    }
  }
}

output cosmosAccountId string = cosmos.id
output cosmosAccountName string = cosmos.name
```

This is one of the places where Chapter 9 should stay connected to Chapter 8. Public access is disabled because that security posture should now be part of the declared infrastructure, not something remembered during portal setup.

Defining Key Vault

Key Vault is another strong example of how infrastructure and security now overlap. Earlier chapters moved secrets out of raw configuration and into safer mechanisms. Bicep lets that decision become part of the environment definition itself.

infra/modules/keyvault.bicep

```
param keyVaultName string
param location string

resource kv 'Microsoft.KeyVault/vaults@2022-07-01' = {
  name: keyVaultName
  location: location
  properties: {
    sku: {
      family: 'A'
      name: 'standard'
    }
    tenantId: subscription().tenantId
    enableSoftDelete: true
    enablePurgeProtection: true
  }
}
```

```
output keyVaultId string = kv.id
output keyVaultName string = kv.name
output vaultUri string = kv.properties.vaultUri
```

Even in this simple version, the definition captures non-trivial security decisions. Soft delete and purge protection are no longer optional settings to be remembered later. They are now part of the baseline environment.

Composing the Platform with Modules

As the infrastructure grows, a single huge Bicep file becomes difficult to reason about. Splitting the platform into modules keeps the system readable and makes it easier to evolve individual areas such as networking, messaging, or secrets without turning the root template into a wall of resources.

A modular `main.bicep` might look like this:

infra/main.bicep

```
param environment string = 'ci'
param location string = resourceGroup().location

var baseName = 'orderproc-${environment}'

module storage './modules/storage.bicep' = {
  name: 'storage'
  params: {
    storageAccountName: '${replace(baseName, '-', '')}storage'
    location: location
  }
}

module serviceBus './modules/servicebus.bicep' = {
  name: 'servicebus'
  params: {
    namespaceName: '${baseName}-sb'
    location: location
  }
}

module cosmos './modules/cosmos.bicep' = {
```

```
  name: 'cosmos'
  params: {
    cosmosAccountName: '${replace(baseName, '-', '')}-cosmos'
    location: location
  }
}

module keyVault './modules/keyvault.bicep' = {
  name: 'keyvault'
  params: {
    keyVaultName: '${baseName}-kv'
    location: location
  }
}

module functionApp './modules/functionapp.bicep' = {
  name: 'functionapp'
  params: {
    functionAppName: '${baseName}-func'
    planName: '${baseName}-plan'
    location: location
    storageAccountName: storage.outputs.storageAccountName
  }
}
```

This is the point where the infrastructure becomes recognisably part of the codebase. Instead of scattered portal-created resources, `OrderProcessor` now has a root platform definition and a set of modules that describe its major building blocks.

Deploying the Bicep Templates

Once the templates exist, deployment becomes straightforward. The Azure CLI can deploy the root template directly:

```
az deployment group create \
  --resource-group buy-ci-rg \
  --template-file infra/main.bicep \
  --parameters environment=ci
```

That command matters because it demonstrates the real change in deployment philosophy. The infrastructure is no longer built by clicking through the portal. It is created from source-controlled definitions that can be replayed whenever the environment needs to be created, updated, or recovered.

Project Addition: OrderProcessor Bicep Foundation

This section introduces the first real Infrastructure as Code foundation for `OrderProcessor`. Add the following files and folders:

- `infra/main.bicep`
- `infra/modules/storage.bicep`
- `infra/modules/servicebus.bicep`
- `infra/modules/functionapp.bicep`
- `infra/modules/cosmos.bicep`
- `infra/modules/keyvault.bicep`

With those in place, `OrderProcessor` now has a reproducible infrastructure shape expressed in source control. The Function App, Service Bus, Cosmos DB, and Key Vault are no longer assumed parts of the environment. They are declared, parameterized, and ready to be deployed consistently across environments. That is the real turning point in this chapter. From here, pipelines and deployment strategies can build on a concrete IaC foundation instead of an implied one.

Infrastructure As Code – Bicep Structure

Figure 9-1 shows the Bicep module structure used to compose and deploy the OrderProcessor infrastructure across environments.

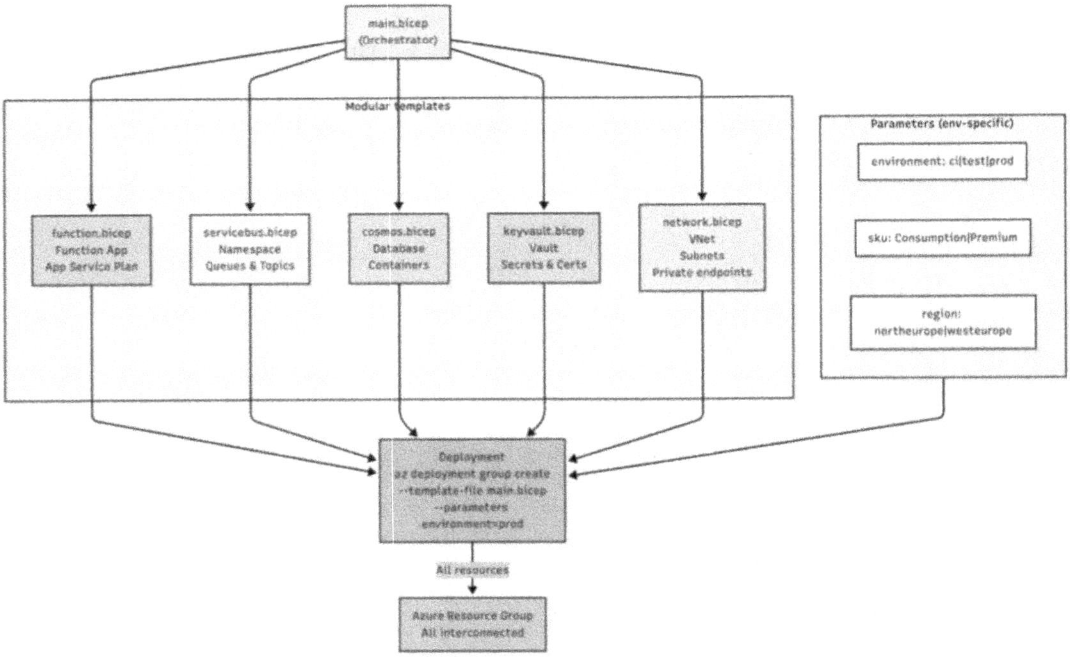

Figure 9-1. *Bicep Module Structure for OrderProcessor Infrastructure*

CI/CD Pipelines for Functions and Event Grid

Infrastructure as Code gives `OrderProcessor` a repeatable way to define the platform, but that is only part of the deployment story. Someone or something still has to run those definitions, build the application, test it, package it, and release it in the right order. In a production system, that job should not depend on a developer remembering the steps or running them manually from a workstation. It should be automated, consistent, and visible. That is where CI/CD pipelines come in.

For `OrderProcessor`, a pipeline becomes the bridge between the source repository and the running system. It restores and builds the .NET solution, runs unit tests, packages the Functions app, deploys the Azure infrastructure defined in Bicep, and then deploys the application code itself. In other words, the pipeline does not just ship binaries. It delivers the full serverless environment in a controlled way, so code and infrastructure evolve together rather than drifting apart.

Why Pipelines Matter in a Serverless System

Without a pipeline, deployment quality depends too heavily on people remembering the exact order of steps. A developer may update the code but forget to apply the matching infrastructure change. Another may publish the Function App before the queue or secret it depends on exists. Problems like that are especially common in serverless systems because the application boundary is broader than the codebase. `OrderProcessor` is not only a Functions project. It is also Service Bus, Cosmos DB, Key Vault, Event Grid, networking, and configuration.

A CI/CD pipeline removes that ambiguity by making build, test, packaging, and deployment part of one repeatable flow. It also improves visibility. Every run has a record, every failure stops the release before it reaches production, and every environment can be updated in the same way. For a system that is expected to change frequently, that consistency is what turns deployment into a reliable engineering practice rather than a fragile release ritual.

Structuring the Pipeline

A good pipeline for `OrderProcessor` should follow the same logic as the system itself. First, validate that the code is buildable and tested. Then package the Functions app so it is ready to deploy. After that, deploy or update the supporting Azure resources through Bicep. Finally, push the application package to the Function App. That ordering matters because the code should land in an environment that already contains the resources and configuration it expects.

A high-level Azure DevOps pipeline definition might begin like this:

```
azure-pipelines.yml
trigger:
  branches:
    include:
      - main

pool:
  vmImage: 'ubuntu-latest'
```

```
variables:
  buildConfiguration: 'Release'
  resourceGroup: 'buy-ci-rg'
  environment: 'ci'
```

This establishes a simple baseline. The pipeline runs on merges to `main`, uses a Linux build agent, and defines reusable variables for the build configuration and target environment. Those details may look small, but they immediately make the pipeline more maintainable because environment-specific values no longer have to be hardcoded throughout the file.

Restoring and Building the Solution

The first job of the pipeline is to prove that the solution can be built in a clean environment. That means installing the right .NET SDK, restoring packages, and compiling the projects in release mode.

```
- task: UseDotNet@2
  inputs:
    packageType: 'sdk'
    version: '10.x'

- task: DotNetCoreCLI@2
  inputs:
    command: 'restore'
    projects: '**/*.csproj'

- task: DotNetCoreCLI@2
  inputs:
    command: 'build'
    projects: '**/*.csproj'
    arguments: '--configuration $(buildConfiguration)'
```

At this stage, the pipeline is doing something more important than just compiling source. It is verifying that the build can be reproduced outside a developer machine. If the solution cannot restore and compile reliably in the pipeline, it is not ready to be trusted in a deployment flow.

Running Tests Before Deployment

Once the solution builds, the next step is to run the automated tests. This matters because deployment should be gated by correctness, not just by successful compilation. In `OrderProcessor`, the pipeline is the right place to stop a broken change before it reaches live infrastructure.

```
- task: DotNetCoreCLI@2
  inputs:
    command: 'test'
    projects: '**/*UnitTests.csproj'
    arguments: '--configuration $(buildConfiguration) --no-build'
```

This keeps the testing step efficient by reusing the earlier build output. More importantly, it establishes the rule that deployment is conditional on the code passing its validation checks. That is one of the key differences between a repeatable CI/CD process and an ad hoc release flow.

Packaging the Functions App

After the code is built and tested, the Functions project needs to be published into a deployable package. In Azure Functions, that usually means producing a published output that can be zipped and deployed to the target Function App.

```
- task: DotNetCoreCLI@2
  inputs:
    command: 'publish'
    publishWebProjects: true
    arguments: '--configuration $(buildConfiguration) --output $(Build.
    ArtifactStagingDirectory)/publish'
    zipAfterPublish: true
```

This is the point where the pipeline turns source code into a release artifact. That artifact can then move through environments in a controlled way, rather than relying on a direct build-and-publish step from a local machine.

Deploying Infrastructure Through Bicep

Before the new code is deployed, the environment itself should be brought into the desired state. Because OrderProcessor now has Bicep templates, the pipeline can do that automatically using the Azure CLI.

```
- task: AzureCLI@2
  inputs:
    azureSubscription: 'buy-ci'
    scriptType: 'bash'
    scriptLocation: 'inlineScript'
    inlineScript: |
      az deployment group create \
        --resource-group $(resourceGroup) \
        --template-file infra/main.bicep \
        --parameters environment=$(environment)
```

This is where the pipeline stops being a code deploy and becomes a full environment deploy. The Function App, Service Bus, Cosmos DB, Key Vault, and related resources can now be created or updated from source-controlled definitions before the application package is pushed. That keeps code and infrastructure aligned and makes environment drift much less likely.

Deploying the Function App

Once the infrastructure is in place, the pipeline can deploy the packaged Functions app itself. In Azure DevOps, that can be done with the Azure Function App deployment task.

```
- task: AzureFunctionApp@2
  inputs:
    azureSubscription: 'buy-ci'
    appType: 'functionAppLinux'
    appName: 'orderprocessor-func'
    package: '$(Build.ArtifactStagingDirectory)/publish.zip'
```

At this point, the application code lands on a Function App that already has the platform resources and configuration it depends on. That sequence is important. It avoids the common release problem where code is deployed into an environment that has not yet caught up with the infrastructure changes required to support it.

Bringing Event Grid into the Deployment Flow

For `OrderProcessor`, infrastructure is not limited to storage, messaging, and hosting. Event-driven connections also matter. If Event Grid is part of the workflow, then subscriptions should be provisioned with the rest of the environment rather than manually after the fact.

A Bicep definition for an Event Grid subscription could look like this:

```
resource eg 'Microsoft.EventGrid/systemTopics@2022-06-15' = {
  name: 'orders-topic'
  location: resourceGroup().location
  properties: {
    source: storage.id
    topicType: 'Microsoft.Storage.StorageAccounts'
  }
}

resource sub 'Microsoft.EventGrid/systemTopics/
eventSubscriptions@2022-06-15' = {
  name: 'orders-topic/order-created-to-function'
  parent: eg
  properties: {
    destination: {
      endpointType: 'AzureFunction'
      properties: {
        resourceId: functionApp.id
        maxEventsPerBatch: 1
      }
    }
    filter: {
      includedEventTypes: [
```

```
          'Microsoft.Storage.StorageAccounts.BlobCreated'
        ]
      }
    }
}
```

That is important because it keeps event wiring inside the same deployment model as the rest of the platform. If a new environment is created, or if the infrastructure is rebuilt, the subscriptions come with it. That makes the deployment more complete and reduces the number of manual follow-up tasks required after release.

The Full Pipeline Flow

Taken together, the pipeline now has a clear shape. It restores packages, builds the solution, runs tests, publishes the Functions artifact, deploys the Bicep templates, and then deploys the Function App package. That flow mirrors the earlier architectural principle in the book that code and infrastructure should move together rather than as disconnected concerns.

For `OrderProcessor`, this is a meaningful change in how the system is operated. The repository no longer contains only application code. It now contains the beginnings of a release mechanism that can recreate and update the system in a consistent way.

Project Addition: CI/CD Foundation

This section adds the first real delivery pipeline for `OrderProcessor`. Add:

- `azure-pipelines.yml`

Update the pipeline so it:

- restores and builds the solution
- runs the unit tests
- publishes the Functions project
- deploys `infra/main.bicep`
- deploys the packaged Functions app

If Event Grid is part of the environment, its subscriptions should also move into the Bicep templates rather than being created manually. With that in place, `OrderProcessor` now has a repeatable build-and-deploy path that covers both application code and infrastructure, which is the real foundation for the rest of the chapter's operational work.

Zero-Downtime Strategies

Once `OrderProcessor` has Infrastructure as Code and a working pipeline, the next question is not whether it can be deployed but how it can be deployed safely while live traffic is still flowing. In production, uptime is not optional. Orders may be entering the system continuously, orchestrations may already be in progress, queue consumers may be processing messages, and downstream integrations such as ERP or fraud checks may be active at the exact moment a deployment starts. That makes release strategy just as important as release automation.

In a serverless system, deployments can look deceptively simple. Upload a new package and Azure Functions updates quickly. But the simplicity of the publish action hides the complexity of what may already be happening inside the system. `OrderProcessor` is not just serving a stateless HTTP endpoint. It is coordinating workflows, waiting on approvals, consuming messages, and reacting to events. A deployment strategy, therefore, has to protect not just availability at the HTTP edge but continuity across the entire workflow.

Why Zero-Downtime Is Important in Serverless Systems

The challenge with zero-downtime deployment in serverless systems is that the platform can change very quickly while business processes remain long-lived. A Durable Functions orchestration may have been running for minutes or hours before the new version is deployed. A Service Bus-triggered Function may restart while messages are still being processed. Event Grid may redeliver events if a handler disappears briefly during an update. All of those behaviors are manageable, but only if they are anticipated.

For `OrderProcessor`, the risk is not theoretical. A careless deployment could duplicate an ERP submission, interrupt a queue consumer at the wrong moment, or introduce a contract mismatch that affects in-flight orders. That is why this section is about more than release speed. It is about making sure new versions can be introduced without dropping requests, corrupting workflow state, or forcing the business process to stop while the platform catches up.

Strategy 1: Deployment Slots and Blue-Green Releases

Azure Functions on the Premium plan supports deployment slots, which makes Blue-Green style releases possible. In practice, that means maintaining a live production slot and a separate staging slot. The new version is deployed to staging first, validated there, and only then swapped into production. If something goes wrong after the swap, rollback is immediate because the previous version is still available in the other slot.

For `OrderProcessor`, that is an especially useful pattern because it allows the release to be tested in a full application environment before live traffic is moved. The staging slot can run the same code, the same configuration shape, and the same supporting dependencies as production, which makes it much safer than pushing directly into the live slot and hoping for the best (see Figure 9-2).

The basic slot creation and deployment flow looks like this:

```
az functionapp deployment slot create \
  --name orderprocessor-func \
  --resource-group buy-prod-rg \
  --slot staging

az functionapp deployment source config-zip \
  --name orderprocessor-func \
  --slot staging \
  --resource-group buy-prod-rg \
  --src publish.zip
```

Once the staging slot has been warmed up and validated, traffic can be switched:

```
az functionapp deployment slot swap \
  --name orderprocessor-func \
  --resource-group buy-prod-rg \
  --slot staging
```

The important point is not just that slots exist. It is that they change the shape of deployment from replacement to cutover. Instead of overwriting the live runtime directly, the new version is introduced beside it and promoted only when it is ready.

Zero-Downtime Deployment – Blue-Green

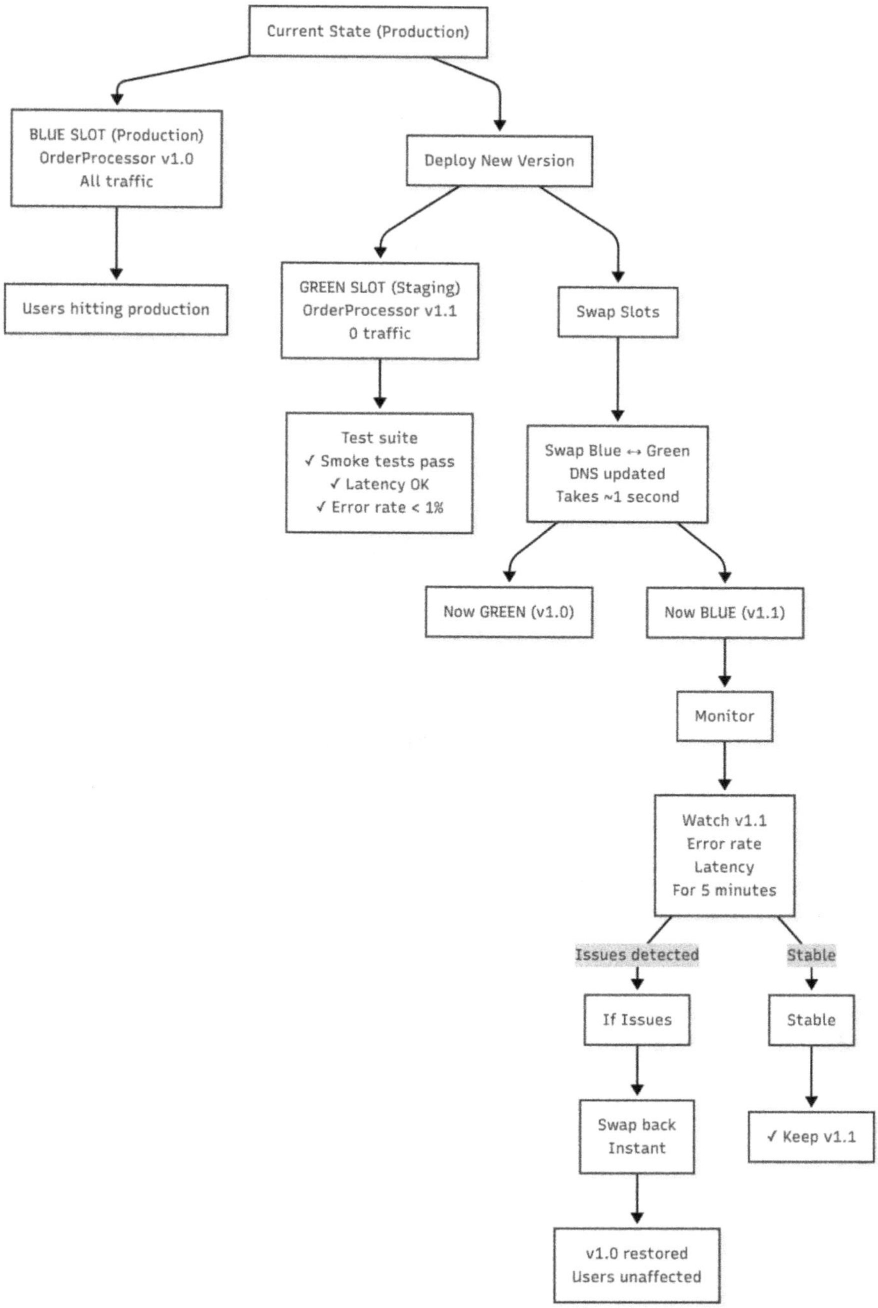

***Figure 9-2.** Blue-Green Deployment and Rollback Flow*

Strategy 2: Canary Releases

Blue-Green deployment gives a clean cutover, but sometimes even that is too large a jump. A Canary release reduces the risk further by exposing only a small percentage of traffic to the new version first. If telemetry remains healthy, the share can be increased gradually until the new version becomes the default.

In `OrderProcessor`, this can be useful when a release touches a sensitive part of the workflow, such as ERP integration, fraud handling, or a changed orchestration path. Rather than sending all live traffic to the new version immediately, a canary slot can receive a small percentage first while the team watches failure rates, latency, and business-level outcomes in telemetry. If the new version behaves well, rollout continues. If not, exposure stays limited, and rollback is straightforward.

The implementation details vary depending on routing strategy, often using Azure Front Door or Application Gateway, but the deployment principle is consistent: reduce the size of the first production step so that a bad release has less impact.

Strategy 3: Event Grid Shadowing and Phased Subscriptions

For event-driven systems, traffic does not arrive only through HTTP. Event Grid subscriptions may still be delivering events while a new version is being deployed. One useful strategy in that scenario is to run the new handler in parallel with the existing one for a period of time, allowing both to receive the same events. This is often called shadowing.

For `OrderProcessor`, that means a new Function version can subscribe alongside the current one while its output is observed in telemetry. The original handler remains responsible for the live path, while the new handler is validated against real event flow. Once confidence is high enough, the old subscription can be removed and the new one can take over.

A simplified Bicep example for a parallel subscription looks like this:

```
resource v2sub 'Microsoft.EventGrid/systemTopics/
eventSubscriptions@2022-06-15' = {
  name: '${eg.name}/orderprocessor-v2'
  properties: {
    destination: {
      endpointType: 'AzureFunction'
```

```
      properties: {
        resourceId: functionV2.id
      }
    }
    eventDeliverySchema: 'EventGridSchema'
  }
}
```

This works well when the goal is to compare behavior without risking a hard cutover too early. It is especially helpful for integrations where correctness matters as much as availability, because the team can validate both the event flow and the downstream effects before retiring the previous version.

Strategy 4: Service Bus Consumer Overlap

Service Bus introduces a slightly different deployment concern. A queue-backed workload is resilient by design, but consumer restarts can still create friction during release. Messages may retry, backlogs may temporarily grow, and changes to consumer behavior may be harder to observe if the old and new versions are not separated clearly.

One useful strategy is to run old and new consumers side by side during a transition period. Instead of forcing all traffic through one updated Function App immediately, a second consumer can be brought online and traffic can be shifted in a controlled way. Depending on the design, this may involve separate Function Apps, routing rules, or controlled forwarding between queues. The key point is that message handling is allowed to overlap rather than being replaced in one abrupt step.

For `OrderProcessor`, this matters when queue consumers are closely tied to fulfillment or downstream integration. A smooth shift between consumer versions reduces the chance of lost throughput, sudden backlogs, or release-time surprises that only appear once all traffic is already on the new path.

Strategy 5: Schema Compatibility During Rollout

Zero-downtime deployment is not only an infrastructure problem. It is also a contract problem. Even with slots, canaries, and phased subscriptions, a deployment can still fail if the new code expects message or event shapes that older parts of the system do not yet understand. That is why backward compatibility is part of release safety.

In practice, `OrderProcessor` should tolerate mixed-version traffic during rollout. If an event contract changes, new fields should be added in a backward-compatible way. Existing fields should not be renamed or removed casually. When a larger change is required, it is usually safer to introduce a versioned contract than to mutate the old one in place. That allows old and new handlers to coexist while the release progresses.

For a workflow-based system, this is particularly important because an orchestration may span a deployment boundary. A version-tolerant contract design helps ensure that in-flight work can complete safely even when parts of the system are moving to a newer release.

Applying Zero-Downtime Deployment to `OrderProcessor`

For `OrderProcessor`, zero-downtime deployment is not a single technique but a combination of them. Slots provide a safe baseline for Blue-Green cutover and rollback. Canary routing adds a more cautious path when a release touches sensitive runtime behavior. Event Grid shadowing makes it possible to validate new event handlers in parallel. Service Bus consumer overlap smooths queue-driven upgrades. Schema compatibility protects in-flight orchestrations and mixed-version event flows from breaking when code changes are introduced.

The common idea across all of these patterns is controlled exposure. A release becomes safer when the new version is introduced beside the old one, validated under realistic conditions, and promoted gradually rather than replacing the live system in a single blind step.

Project Addition: Blue-Green Deployment Foundation for `OrderProcessor`

This section introduces the first real zero-downtime deployment foundation for `OrderProcessor`. Add or update the deployment process so that production releases target a staging slot first, validate the deployed build there, and then swap into production only after checks have passed. If Event Grid subscriptions or queue consumers are part of the release path, plan for parallel validation and phased cutover rather than assuming every deployment can be treated as an instant replacement.

With that in place, `OrderProcessor` moves beyond simple successful deployment and toward safe production rollout. The system can now be updated with much lower risk to live orders, in-flight orchestrations, and downstream integrations.

Operational Playbooks

By the time a serverless system reaches production, it is no longer enough for the architecture to be correct on paper. It also has to be operable under pressure. Pipelines, slots, and failover strategies all improve resilience, but none of them remove the need for clear operational response when something actually goes wrong. If an ERP integration starts failing at 2 a.m., or a queue backlog suddenly surges, the difference between a contained incident and a chaotic outage is often whether the team already knows what to do. That is the role of operational playbooks.

For `OrderProcessor`, playbooks are the practical layer that sits between technical capability and reliable operation. A slot swap only helps if someone knows when to trigger it. Autoscale only helps if the team understands what metrics matter and how to respond when they trend the wrong way. A secure GDPR process only helps if the deletion path is documented, repeatable, and auditable. In that sense, a playbook is not just a document. It is an agreed way of operating the system when normal conditions stop being normal.

Why Playbooks Matter in a Serverless System

Distributed serverless systems rarely fail in one simple, obvious way. A queue consumer may still be healthy while a downstream dependency is failing. A Function App may still be up while an orchestration is stuck waiting on an event that will never arrive. A cost spike may be caused by retries rather than by genuine traffic growth. In that sort of environment, improvised response tends to make incidents worse rather than better, because different people take different actions based on partial information.

A playbook reduces that uncertainty. It turns tribal knowledge into repeatable practice, clarifies which signals should trigger a response, and gives engineers a known sequence of actions to work through under time pressure. Earlier chapters made `OrderProcessor` more secure, more observable, and more deployment-friendly. This section extends that same discipline into operations by making response steps explicit and versioned alongside the rest of the system.

Playbook 1: Incident Response

The first and most obvious playbook is incident response. In `OrderProcessor`, a good example is an ERP integration failure rate rising above an acceptable threshold. The system may still be accepting orders, but downstream fulfillment is now degrading. That is not a theoretical architecture issue. It is an operational event that needs an immediate, consistent response.

The playbook should start with acknowledgement and triage. An alert fires, the incident is acknowledged, dashboards are checked to confirm the trend, and logs are queried to establish whether the issue is isolated or systemic. If the problem began immediately after a deployment, a slot swap rollback becomes a defined response rather than a panicked last resort.

A representative investigation query might look like this:

```
traces
| where customDimensions.Stage == "ERP"
| where customDimensions.Outcome == "Failure"
| summarize Count = count() by bin(timestamp, 5m)
```

If the incident is deployment-related, rollback can be executed with the same slot strategy introduced earlier in the chapter:

```
az functionapp deployment slot swap \
  --name orderprocessor-func \
  --resource-group buy-prod-rg \
  --slot staging
```

The key here is not that rollback exists. It is that the playbook defines when to use it, how to confirm the problem, and how to record the outcome afterwards. That recording step matters because an unresolved incident is not finished simply because the service is stable again. The action taken, the reasoning behind it, and the result should all be captured in the incident record.

Playbook 2: Scaling Surge

A second playbook applies when demand increases sharply. In a serverless system, scale is one of the platform's strengths, but it still needs operational guidance. If Black Friday traffic doubles or an upstream source suddenly pushes a much larger volume of orders than expected, the team needs to know what "healthy scaling" looks like and when intervention is required.

For OrderProcessor, a practical trigger is sustained queue growth. If Active Messages in Service Bus rise past the point where normal processing can catch up, the first task is to confirm whether the increase reflects genuine demand, slow consumers, or a failing downstream integration that is causing retries. Once that has been established, the Function App plan may need to scale.

A direct scaling command:

```
az functionapp plan update \
  --name op-func-plan \
  --resource-group buy-prod-rg \
  --sku EP3
```

That manual response should then be paired with a platform-level rule so the system can respond faster next time. A Bicep autoscaling setting keeps the scaling behavior visible and versioned:

```
resource autoscale 'Microsoft.Insights/autoscalesettings@2015-04-01' = {
  name: 'func-autoscale'
  location: resourceGroup().location
  properties: {
    targetResourceUri: appServicePlan.id
    profiles: [
      {
        name: 'QueueScale'
        capacity: {
          minimum: '1'
          maximum: '10'
          default: '1'
        }
        rules: [
          {
            metricTrigger: {
              metricName: 'ActiveMessages'
              metricResourceUri: sb.id
              operator: 'GreaterThan'
              threshold: 1000
              timeGrain: 'PT1M'
```

```
            statistic: 'Average'
            timeWindow: 'PT5M'
          }
          scaleAction: {
            direction: 'Increase'
            type: 'ChangeCount'
            value: '1'
            cooldown: 'PT5M'
          }
        }
      ]
    }
  ]
 }
}
```

A good playbook does not stop at "scale out." It also defines how to verify that the backlog is draining, when to scale back, and how to capture the event so the team can decide whether a permanent capacity change is needed.

Playbook 3: Poison Queue Recovery

Poison messages are another example where operational discipline matters more than raw technical capability. A queue can continue to function while a subset of bad messages keeps failing and being dead-lettered. If the team has no agreed process for diagnosing and replaying those messages, recovery becomes slow and error-prone.

In `OrderProcessor`, the response should begin by inspecting the poison queue and understanding why the message failed. That may mean deserializing the message locally, identifying whether the error was caused by bad input or by a software defect, and deciding whether the original message is safe to replay once the issue is fixed. The mistake to avoid is pushing poison messages straight back into the main queue without understanding the cause, because that simply recreates the same failure at scale.

The playbook can still use CLI and tooling to support recovery. For example, queue keys or replay tools may be part of the documented path:

```
az servicebus queue authorization-rule keys list \
  --namespace-name opsb \
  --queue-name orders-poison \
  --resource-group buy-prod-rg
```

But the operational value lies in the sequence around the command: inspect first, diagnose second, fix third, replay last. That sequence should be written down and followed consistently.

Playbook 4: GDPR Delete Request

Not every playbook is about outage response. Some are about compliance and controlled operational workflows. A GDPR delete request is a good example. The system needs a repeatable way to verify the request, remove the right personal data, preserve required audit evidence, and produce a verifiable result.

For `OrderProcessor`, that means the deletion process should be an explicit Function-based workflow rather than an ad hoc database task. A dedicated endpoint keeps the process visible and auditable:

```
[Function("GDPRDelete")]
public async Task<HttpResponseData> Run(
    [HttpTrigger(AuthorizationLevel.Function, "post")]
    HttpRequestData req)
{
    var deleteReq = await req.ReadFromJsonAsync<DeleteRequest>();
    await _personalDataStore.DeleteUserAsync(deleteReq.UserId);
    await _audit.LogAsync(new AuditEvent(... "GDPRDelete", "Success"));
    return req.CreateResponse(HttpStatusCode.OK);
}
```

The playbook around that endpoint is just as important as the code itself. It should define how the request is authenticated, how deletion is verified, how the audit trail is checked, and how the response is communicated back to the requester. That turns compliance into an operational process rather than an improvised support task.

Playbook 5: Certificate Expiry

Certificate expiry is a quieter but equally serious operational risk. Nothing may appear wrong until the certificate crosses its expiry threshold, at which point integrations or secure endpoints can begin to fail abruptly. In a system like `OrderProcessor`, where external integrations may depend on certificates managed through Key Vault, expiry needs to be treated as a monitored operational event rather than a calendar reminder.

A practical playbook begins with advanced detection, often through Key Vault events or alerting. It then defines how renewal happens, whether through an automated Key Vault policy or through a controlled manual update, and how downstream consumers are notified or refreshed afterwards. The response should end with verification that the renewed certificate is active and that the dependent integration is healthy.

The point is not merely that certificate rotation can be automated. It is that the team should know what happens if the automation does not work, how to confirm propagation, and how to record the event in the audit trail once it is resolved.

Putting Playbooks into the Repository

For `OrderProcessor`, the most useful thing about playbooks is not that they exist as ideas. It is that they now live beside the code and infrastructure in source control. That means incident response, scaling, poison queue recovery, GDPR workflows, and certificate handling are documented in the same repository that defines the application itself. Engineers do not have to go looking for the "real" operating instructions in someone's notebook or in an out-of-date wiki page.

That also means the playbooks can evolve through the same review process as everything else. If a better incident query is discovered, or a scaling threshold proves too low, the playbook can be updated in the repository, reviewed, and versioned. In that way, the operational model becomes part of the system architecture rather than something external to it.

Project Addition: Playbook Foundation for `OrderProcessor`

This section adds the first operational playbook foundation for `OrderProcessor`. Add a `playbooks` folder to the repository and start documenting the repeatable operational workflows the system now depends on. At a minimum, that should include incident response, surge handling, poison queue recovery, GDPR deletion, and certificate expiry response. Where a playbook depends on executable logic, such as GDPR deletion or automated certificate handling, that logic should be represented in Functions or scripts that are versioned alongside the rest of the solution.

With that in place, `OrderProcessor` becomes easier to operate under real conditions. The system is no longer defined only by its code and infrastructure. It is also defined by the documented, repeatable ways the team responds when something fails, scales unexpectedly, or needs to be governed in production.

Monitoring Costs and Budgets

One of the promises of serverless computing is that you pay only for what you use. That is true, but it can also be misleading if it encourages teams to stop thinking about cost altogether. In a system like `OrderProcessor`, cost does not come from a single VM or a single monthly hosting plan. It emerges from the combined behavior of Functions executions, queue operations, Durable retries, Cosmos DB throughput, storage growth, telemetry ingestion, and whatever external services sit around the workflow. That means financial visibility has to become part of operations in the same way availability, latency, and failures already are.

For `OrderProcessor,` cost discipline is especially important because the architecture is distributed and event-driven. A bug that increases retry volume can raise costs without increasing business value. A poor partitioning decision in Cosmos DB can make the data model more expensive than it needs to be. A premium plan left oversized after a temporary surge can quietly waste money every day. None of those issues are visible if cost is treated as something finance discovers at the end of the month. They become manageable only when the engineering team can observe, explain, and control them while the system is running.

Why Cost Monitoring Is Different in Serverless

Traditional infrastructure often makes cost easier to understand because it is tied to a relatively fixed shape. You provision servers, storage, and network capacity, and your bill is broadly a reflection of that reserved footprint. Serverless platforms behave differently. Cost scales with execution, throughput, storage behavior, and operational mistakes. That elasticity is powerful, but it also means the cost profile of a system can change quickly when usage patterns or workflow behavior change. In `OrderProcessor`, cost is, therefore, not a separate concern from architecture. If Durable Functions retries too aggressively, the bill changes. If Service Bus traffic spikes because messages are replaying or dead-lettering, the bill changes. If Cosmos DB throughput is configured poorly, the bill changes. Monitoring cost in a serverless system is really about monitoring the behaviors that drive cost and making sure those behaviors remain aligned with the business value the system is supposed to deliver.

Using Azure Cost Management and Budgets

The first part of cost control is simply establishing visibility and thresholds. Azure Cost Management and Budgets provides that baseline by allowing spending to be tracked at the subscription, resource group, or resource level. For `OrderProcessor`, this means the production environment can have an explicit monthly budget, with alerts raised before the threshold is fully consumed.

A budget definition could look like this:

```
az consumption budget create \
  --name OrderProcessorBudget \
  --category cost \
  --amount 500 \
  --time-grain monthly \
  --resource-group buy-prod-rg \
  --notifications \
  actual_greater_than_80_percent=true \
  contactEmails="finops@anywebsitename.com"
```

The value of a budget like this is not that it hard-stops cost. It is that it creates an operational signal. Once spend passes a threshold, the team can ask whether the increase reflects real business demand, expected seasonal traffic, or a technical problem such as runaway execution, unnecessary retries, or misconfigured scaling.

Breaking Costs Down by Resource

A total monthly number is useful for governance, but it is not enough to guide engineering decisions. To improve the system, the team needs to understand where the money is actually going. In a serverless architecture, that usually means breaking cost down by service type and looking for the dominant drivers.

For `OrderProcessor`, the likely contributors are Function App execution, Service Bus transactions, Cosmos DB throughput and storage, Key Vault operations, and supporting storage usage. Cost Analysis in the Azure portal can help with that, but the same idea can also be expressed through query tooling so the team can inspect trends programmatically.

```
az costmanagement query \
  --type Usage \
  --timeframe MonthToDate \
  --dataset '{"granularity":"Daily","aggregation":{"totalCost":{"name":
"PreTaxCost","function":"Sum"}},"grouping":[{"type":"Dimension","name":
"ResourceType"}]}'
```

Once the breakdown is visible, cost optimization becomes much more targeted. Instead of asking whether "Azure is expensive," the team can ask whether Cosmos DB is over-provisioned, whether Service Bus traffic is higher than order volume suggests, or whether a specific workflow change increased execution cost disproportionately.

Using Telemetry to Understand Cost Drivers

Cost becomes much easier to reason about when it is linked to telemetry the engineering team is already watching. Application Insights can show execution count, duration, error rate, and throughput patterns, all of which help explain why cost is moving. That makes cost monitoring an extension of observability rather than a separate reporting exercise.

For example, if `OrderProcessor` begins to process more ERP-related orchestration steps than expected, telemetry can show the change before the bill arrives:

```
requests
| where name == "ERPOrchestrator"
| summarize count() by bin(timestamp, 1h)
```

That query does not show cost directly, but it reveals one of the behaviors that contributes to it. When execution count rises, the team can compare that rise to business demand and decide whether the increase is justified. If it is not, the underlying workflow may need attention.

Controlling Cosmos DB Cost

In many Azure-based systems, Cosmos DB becomes one of the most significant cost contributors. That makes it especially important for `OrderProcessor`, because the system already uses Cosmos DB for operational and audit-related storage. Cost control here starts with good modeling, but it also depends on throughput strategy.

One useful approach is autoscale RU/s, which allows the database to respond to spikes without staying permanently provisioned for peak demand. A container definition with autoscale might look like this:

```
resource ordersContainer 'Microsoft.DocumentDB/databaseAccounts/
sqlDatabases/containers@2022-05-15' = {
  name: '${cosmos.name}/orderdb/orders'
  properties: {
    resource: {
      id: 'orders'
      partitionKey: {
        paths: ['/orderId']
        kind: 'Hash'
      }
      autoscaleSettings: {
        maxThroughput: 4000
      }
    }
  }
}
```

That is not a universal answer, but it does align capacity more closely with actual usage. Over time, older or less frequently accessed data can also be archived into cheaper storage tiers where appropriate, which prevents the primary operational database from carrying the full long-term storage burden.

Watching Service Bus Transaction Volume

Service Bus is another place where cost can drift if the team is not watching the right signals. In a messaging-heavy system, transaction count can rise for healthy reasons, such as real order growth, but it can also rise because of retries, poison queue churn, or consumer misbehavior. That makes transaction volume worth monitoring alongside business throughput. For `OrderProcessor`, it is useful to compare message operations against actual order volume. If queue activity rises faster than orders do, something in the system may be producing avoidable churn. A simple telemetry view might look like this:

```
customMetrics
| where name == "ServiceBusRequests"
| summarize sum(value) by bin(timestamp, 1h)
```

Used well, this sort of metric helps the team distinguish normal scale growth from costly inefficiency.

Choosing the Right Hosting Tier

Not every environment should be priced the same way. One of the practical cost controls in a multi-environment system is making sure that CI, Test, and Production are not all running on production-grade capacity when they do not need to be. In `OrderProcessor`, that usually means keeping lower environments lightweight while reserving premium hosting for the production workloads that need slots, stronger scaling guarantees, and safer operational behavior.

This can be made explicit in deployment configuration. Pipeline parameters or Bicep parameters can enforce environment-appropriate hosting choices so that lower environments are not accidentally over-provisioned.

```
parameters:
- name: sku
  values:
    - Consumption
    - EP1
    - EP3
```

The value of this approach is not only cost reduction. It also makes environmental intent visible. CI and Test exist to validate changes efficiently. Production exists to run the live business workload safely. Their hosting choices should reflect that difference.

Forecasting and Planning

Reactive alerts are useful, but mature cost management goes further by trying to forecast future spend from system behavior. In a serverless architecture, that forecast can be grounded in telemetry the team already understands. If the average daily order volume is known and the average number of queue operations, Function executions, and Cosmos reads or writes per order are known, then future spend becomes easier to estimate before usage arrives.

For `OrderProcessor`, this means engineering and finance can work from the same operational data. Dashboards in Power BI, Azure Workbooks, or even spreadsheet models can combine App Insights metrics with Azure billing data to estimate the cost impact of expected growth, traffic spikes, or architectural changes. That helps move the conversation from surprise to planning.

Applying Cost Control to `OrderProcessor`

For `OrderProcessor`, cost monitoring should now be treated as part of normal operations rather than as a separate monthly review. Budgets provide early warning. Cost breakdowns show which services matter most. Application Insights helps explain the technical behaviors behind the bill. Cosmos DB and Service Bus configurations can be tuned with both performance and cost in mind. Environment-level SKU choices prevent lower environments from consuming production-grade budget without good reason.

The important shift is cultural as much as technical. Cost is now another observable property of the system, just like latency, throughput, and failure rate. That means the team can respond to it using the same operational habits it uses elsewhere in the platform.

Project Addition: Cost Visibility Foundation for `OrderProcessor`

This section adds the first real cost visibility foundation for OrderProcessor. Add budget definitions for the shared and production environments, introduce telemetry queries or dashboards that show the major cost drivers across Functions, Service Bus, and Cosmos DB, and update infrastructure and pipeline settings so environment-specific SKU choices are explicit rather than accidental. Where Cosmos containers support it, add autoscale settings that better match capacity to real demand.

With that in place, `OrderProcessor` becomes easier to reason about financially as well as operationally. The team can now see where cost comes from, detect when spend begins to drift, and make architecture or scaling decisions with both technical and financial impact in view.

Deployment Security and Governance

By this point in the chapter, `OrderProcessor` has a deployment path, Infrastructure as Code, safer release strategies, and operational playbooks. But none of that answers a more fundamental production question: who is actually allowed to deploy, under what conditions, and with which controls in place? Automation improves speed and repeatability, but without governance it can also amplify mistakes. A pipeline that can deploy everything quickly is valuable only if the right people, approvals, and policy checks stand between the codebase and production.

That is why deployment security deserves to be treated as part of the architecture rather than as a team process that sits off to the side. In a regulated or business-critical system, the deployment path is itself a security boundary. If a developer can bypass review, push unapproved code into production, or deploy infrastructure that violates security rules, then the system is exposed even if the application code is otherwise well designed. For `OrderProcessor`, governance is what turns deployment from "fast enough" into "safe enough to trust."

Why Deployment Governance Matters

A modern serverless platform makes it very easy to move quickly. That is one of its strengths. The same ease, however, becomes a weakness if the team does not decide how change should be controlled. It is not difficult to imagine a developer accidentally promoting test code into production, or a pipeline deploying a Bicep change that reintroduces public access on a resource that should remain private. The platform will happily do what it is told. Governance is the part that decides what it should be allowed to do.

For OrderProcessor, this becomes especially important because deployment is no longer just about code. A production release may change Function code, queue configuration, network posture, secret handling, monitoring, or failover settings all at once. That means the deployment path must protect not only the runtime behavior of the application but also the security posture of the platform around it. In practice, that brings several concerns together: role-based access, approval gates, policy enforcement, secret handling, auditability, and separation of duties.

Role-Based Access Control for Deployment

The first control is role-based access. The people who write the application should not automatically have the ability to deploy directly into production, and the identity that performs the deployment should not have broader privileges than it actually needs. In Azure, that usually means defining permissions at the subscription, resource group, or resource level so that production deployment rights are tightly scoped.

For OrderProcessor, the clean pattern is for developers to contribute code, but for the pipeline itself to perform the deployment using a service principal or managed identity that has only the permissions required for the target resource group. That immediately improves discipline because production change now flows through the deployment process rather than through direct human access.

A service principal for the pipeline might be created like this:

```
az ad sp create-for-rbac \
  --name orderprocessor-pipeline \
  --role Contributor \
  --scopes /subscriptions/<subId>/resourceGroups/buy-prod-rg
```

The important idea here is not just that a service principal exists. It is that deployment now happens through a purpose-built identity with bounded permissions, instead of through whichever human account happens to be available at release time.

Environment Approvals

Access control by itself is not enough, because a valid pipeline identity can still deploy the wrong thing at the wrong time. That is where approvals come in. Azure DevOps environments support approval gates that can pause a production deployment until designated reviewers have explicitly signed off. That makes release promotion an intentional action rather than a fully automatic consequence of every merge.

A production deployment stage could look like this:

```
stages:
- stage: DeployProd
  jobs:
  - deployment: DeployFunctions
    environment: 'prod'
    strategy:
      runOnce:
        deploy:
          steps:
          - task: AzureFunctionApp@2
            inputs:
              azureSubscription: 'buy-ci'
              appName: 'orderprocessor-func'
              package: '$(Build.ArtifactStagingDirectory)/publish.zip'
```

The YAML is only part of the story. In practice, the real control lives in the environment configuration, where production can be set to require one or more approvers before the stage continues. For `OrderProcessor`, that means a merge to main does not automatically imply a live production cutover. Human review still sits between the artifact and the production environment.

Policy Enforcement at the Platform Boundary

Approvals help control who deploys and when, but they do not guarantee that the deployed infrastructure is safe. That is where Azure Policy becomes valuable. Policy allows the platform itself to reject insecure configurations even if a pipeline tries to deploy them. In other words, governance becomes enforceable rather than advisory. This is important for `OrderProcessor` because many of the security decisions introduced in earlier chapters should now be considered non-negotiable. Public network access on Cosmos DB should not quietly reappear. Key Vault should not be deployed without purge protection. Function Apps should not be allowed to drift away from HTTPS-only enforcement. Those rules are stronger when they live in policy than when they exist only as team conventions.

A simplified policy definition for Key Vault purge protection might look like this:

```
{
  "mode": "All",
  "policyRule": {
    "if": {
      "allOf": [
        { "field": "type", "equals": "Microsoft.KeyVault/vaults" },
        { "field": "Microsoft.KeyVault/vaults/enablePurgeProtection",
        "equals": "false" }
      ]
    },
    "then": {
      "effect": "deny"
    }
  }
}
```

Once attached to the production subscription or management group, a policy like this changes the deployment conversation. The pipeline is no longer trusted simply because it is automated. It is constrained by platform rules that define what a compliant deployment is allowed to look like.

Secrets in the Deployment Pipeline

Pipelines also need governance because they handle secrets and credentials of their own. Service connection details, signing keys, or external integration secrets should not be embedded directly in pipeline files or variable groups if safer alternatives exist. That would simply move the secret sprawl problem from the application into the delivery path. For `OrderProcessor`, the better approach is to let the pipeline retrieve sensitive values from Key Vault at runtime. That keeps the raw secrets out of the repository and reduces the number of places where those values can leak. Azure DevOps supports that pattern directly:

```
- task: AzureKeyVault@2
  inputs:
    azureSubscription: 'buy-ci'
    KeyVaultName: 'op-kv-prod'
    SecretsFilter: '*'
```

This matters because the pipeline is now part of the trusted system boundary. If the application moved to Key Vault for runtime secrets, the delivery path should follow the same principle rather than becoming the weak link.

Auditability and Traceability

A governed deployment process should leave a clear trail behind it. Auditors and engineering leaders alike want to know who approved a release, what commit was deployed, which pipeline executed the change, and which resources were modified. In a mature system, that trace should not have to be reconstructed manually from memory and screenshots.

For `OrderProcessor`, Azure DevOps and Azure Activity Log together provide most of that evidence. Pipeline history records the commit, run, approvers, and task execution. Azure Activity Log records the resource changes made in the subscription. Joined together, they give a much clearer picture of what happened during a release and who was responsible for each part of it.

A simple Azure DevOps query can already begin that chain:

```
az pipelines runs list \
  --org https://dev.azure.com/anywebsitename \
  --project OrderProcessor
```

That kind of traceability matters not only for compliance. It also improves day-to-day diagnosis. When something goes wrong after a release, the team can answer "what changed?" much faster when the deployment path is inherently observable.

Separation of Duties

A final governance concern is separation of duties. In many organizations, especially those with stronger compliance requirements, the same person should not be able to write code, approve it, and deploy it into production entirely on their own. That is not about mistrusting engineers. It is about reducing single-person risk and making the release path more deliberate.

For `OrderProcessor`, this principle maps naturally onto the delivery flow. Developers can write and submit code. Reviewers can approve pull requests. The CI/CD pipeline can validate and deploy to lower environments automatically. Production promotion can then require a separate operational or release approval. Once that structure is in place, production change becomes a controlled team action rather than a unilateral one.

Making Governance Visible

Governance works best when it is visible rather than hidden inside process documentation. If Azure Policy is blocking deployments, the team should be able to see why. If approvals are pending, that should be obvious in the release flow. If production is compliant while a lower environment is drifting, that should show up in reporting rather than waiting for an audit to discover it.

For `OrderProcessor`, that means surfacing deployment governance into dashboards and operational reviews. Compliance state, policy failures, approval flows, and deployment history all become part of how the platform is understood. Governance then stops being seen as a blocker added on top of engineering and starts being understood as part of how safe change is delivered.

Applying Deployment Governance to `OrderProcessor`

Taken together, these controls change the deployment path significantly. `OrderProcessor` is no longer simply something the team can build and publish. It now has a governed release process in which the pipeline deploys with least privilege, production promotion is gated by approval, platform policy prevents insecure infrastructure drift, pipeline secrets are pulled from Key Vault, and deployment actions leave an auditable trail. The release process becomes another designed part of the system.

That is an important architectural step because earlier chapters secured the runtime boundaries of the application itself. This section extends that same thinking into the operational boundary around deployment. In a production environment, both matter.

Project Addition: Deployment Governance Foundation for `OrderProcessor`

This section adds the first real deployment governance foundation for `OrderProcessor`. Update the delivery path so production deployments use a bounded pipeline identity rather than broad human access, production release stages require explicit approval, Azure Policy protects key platform rules such as HTTPS enforcement and restricted public access, and pipeline secrets are resolved from Key Vault rather than stored directly in the release definition. At the same time, make sure pipeline history and Azure activity records are retained in a way that gives the team and auditors a clear chain of evidence for each production deployment. With that in place, `OrderProcessor` moves beyond automated deployment and into governed deployment. The system is now not only easier to ship but also safer to promote, easier to audit, and less vulnerable to accidental or policy-breaking change.

Disaster Recovery and Regional Failover

No matter how carefully a system is designed, deployed, secured, and monitored, there is always the possibility of a failure large enough to overwhelm the normal operating model. In Azure, that might mean a regional outage, a serious platform degradation, an accidental deletion, or corruption in a stateful dependency. At that point, the question is no longer whether `OrderProcessor` is well built. The question becomes whether it can continue operating or recover quickly enough when part of the platform it depends on is no longer available. That is what disaster recovery is really about. It is not simply backup and restore, and it is not just an infrastructure feature you turn on once and forget. In a serverless system, disaster recovery is a combination of architectural design, dependency protection, failover planning, and operational discipline. For `OrderProcessor`, the goal is not that every component remains perfect under regional failure. The goal is that order processing can continue or be restored quickly and predictably without the team inventing a recovery strategy in the middle of the incident.

Why Disaster Recovery Looks Different in Serverless

Disaster recovery in a traditional system often centers on servers, disks, database backups, and restore procedures. Serverless changes that shape. Azure Functions themselves are relatively easy to redeploy because the compute layer is largely stateless. The more difficult problem lies in the stateful services around them. Durable Functions depends on storage for orchestration state. Service Bus and Event Grid are regional services with their own failover characteristics. Cosmos DB can replicate across regions, but only if it has been designed and configured to do so. In other words, the hardest part of disaster recovery is rarely the Function App package. It is protecting and recovering the system state that makes the workflows meaningful.

That is why a serverless DR strategy has to start by separating stateless and stateful concerns. `OrderProcessor` can redeploy Functions into another region relatively quickly. The harder work is making sure that the data, messaging, and integration layers can survive that transition without leaving the workflow in an unrecoverable state. Earlier chapters already laid some of that groundwork by making orchestrations more explicit, retries more controlled, and activities more idempotent. Those choices now matter even more, because failover only becomes credible when the application can tolerate replay and restart safely.

Multi-region Design for `OrderProcessor`

A practical disaster recovery strategy begins with the target shape of the deployed system. For `OrderProcessor`, that means choosing a primary and secondary region and deciding which services are active in both, which ones fail over automatically, and which ones require explicit operational action. A common Azure pairing such as North Europe and West Europe works well for this purpose because it keeps the architecture understandable while still modeling real regional resilience.

In a multi-region design, the Functions application can be deployed to both regions, while stateful dependencies are configured according to their capabilities. Cosmos DB can use multi-region replication and automatic failover. Service Bus can use a geo-disaster recovery alias. Key Vault and application configuration need their own protection and recovery strategies. External integrations such as ERP may require primary and secondary endpoints because they do not necessarily follow Azure's regional model. The key point is that the secondary region is not invented during the outage. It already exists as part of the planned platform (see Figure 9-3).

Regional Failover Design for OrderProcessor

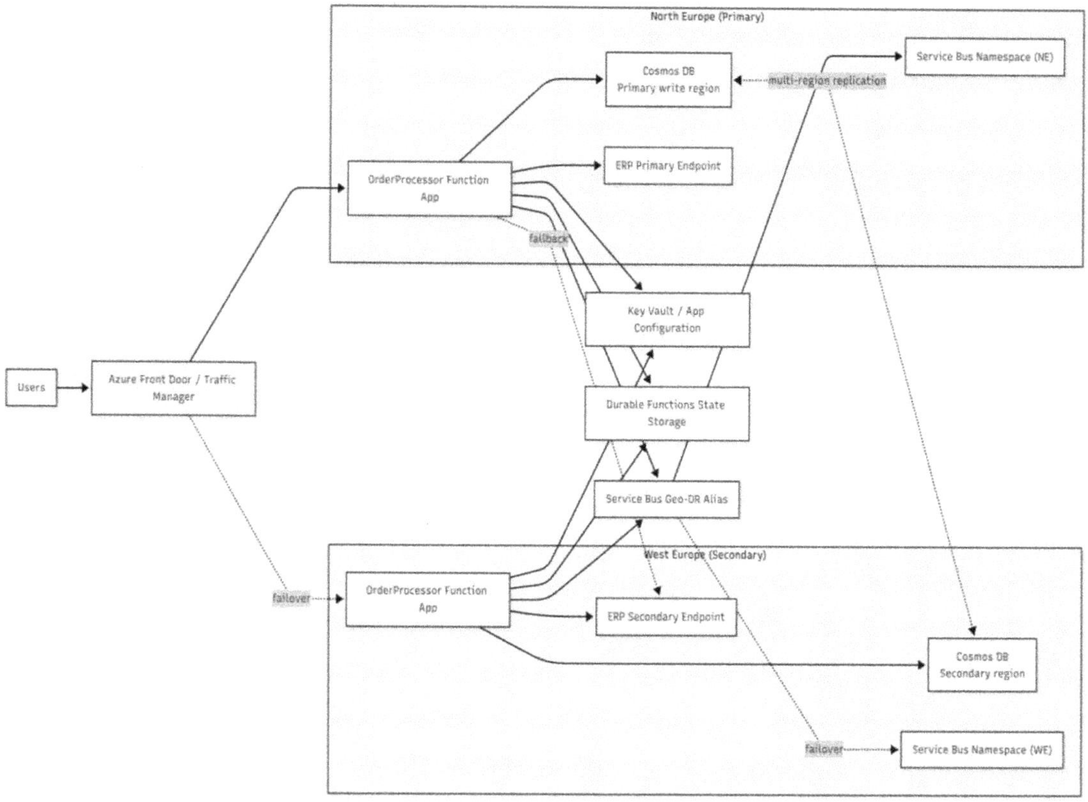

Figure 9-3. *Multi-region Failover Architecture for OrderProcessor*

Protecting Durable Functions State

One of the most important serverless-specific concerns is Durable Functions state. The orchestrator code is easy to redeploy, but the runtime checkpoints and orchestration history live in storage. If that state is lost, the workflow cannot simply resume from where it left off. That is why disaster recovery for a Durable Functions-based system depends heavily on storage design and on the idempotency of the activities that the workflow coordinates. For `OrderProcessor`, the earlier investment in idempotent behavior becomes part of the DR story. If payment, inventory checks, shipping, or ERP submission can tolerate replay safely, then the system is in a much stronger position when recovery requires an orchestration to restart, repeat work, or rebuild its state from durable records. Geo-redundant storage and periodic backup strategies improve the platform side of that story, but the application design still matters. Without replay-safe behavior, failover becomes much riskier because the workflow may recover by duplicating business actions rather than by resuming them safely.

Cosmos DB Multi-region Failover

Cosmos DB is one of the stronger building blocks for regional resilience because it supports multi-region replication natively. For `OrderProcessor`, that makes it a natural place to start when defining failover behavior for operational and audit data. A multi-region configuration can place the primary write region in North Europe and define West Europe as the secondary, with automatic failover enabled.

A Bicep definition for that might look like this:

```
resource cosmos 'Microsoft.DocumentDB/databaseAccounts@2022-05-15' = {
  name: 'opcosmos'
  location: 'northeurope'
  properties: {
    locations: [
      {
        locationName: 'northeurope'
        failoverPriority: 0
        isZoneRedundant: true
      }
      {
        locationName: 'westeurope'
        failoverPriority: 1
        isZoneRedundant: true
      }
    ]
    enableAutomaticFailover: true
  }
}
```

The value of this configuration is not simply that a second region exists. It is that the database account is already prepared to shift responsibility if the primary region becomes unavailable. In operational terms, that reduces the number of manual steps required during failover and makes the state layer more resilient than a single-region deployment ever could be.

Service Bus Geo-Disaster Recovery

Service Bus needs a different approach because it does not replicate queue contents across regions in the same way Cosmos replicates data. Instead, it supports geo-disaster recovery through paired namespaces and aliases. Applications connect to the alias, not directly to one concrete namespace, and the alias can be failed over to the partner region when needed.

For OrderProcessor, that means the messaging layer can be made less region-bound from the application's point of view. A geo-recovery alias can be configured like this:

```
az servicebus georecovery-alias set \
  --resource-group buy-prod-rg \
  --namespace-name opsb-ne \
  --partner-namespace opsb-we \
  --alias opsb-dr
```

The application then targets the alias endpoint rather than a specific regional namespace. That makes the messaging path more flexible during disaster recovery, because the application configuration does not have to be rewritten under pressure just to point at a different namespace. Instead, the alias becomes the stable address, and the regional mapping behind it can change when failover is triggered.

External Integrations and Fallback Endpoints

Not every dependency fits neatly into Azure-native failover patterns. ERP systems, supplier systems, and third-party services may expose regional endpoints of their own or may have no regional failover support at all. That means a realistic DR plan for `OrderProcessor` cannot stop at Azure resources. It also has to consider how external integrations behave when the primary regional path disappears.

One useful pattern is to define explicit primary and secondary endpoints in configuration so that the application can fail over its integration calls more deliberately. A simplified configuration example might look like this:

```
{
  "ERP": {
    "PrimaryUrl": "https://erp.northeurope.anywebsitename.com",
    "SecondaryUrl": "https://erp.westeurope.anywebsitename.com"
  }
}
```

That does not remove the need for retry logic or resilience in the activity code, but it does give the system a more intentional fallback path. If the primary endpoint is unavailable, the application has a known secondary target rather than a vague hope that the original integration will recover in time.

The Failover Playbook

Even with automation, disaster recovery still needs a human-readable sequence of actions. That is particularly true when a regional issue affects several services at once, because the team needs a shared understanding of what order to do things in, how to verify each step, and when the system can be considered healthy again. For `OrderProcessor`, the failover playbook is therefore not optional documentation. It is part of the production readiness of the platform.

A realistic failover sequence begins by confirming the outage through Azure status and internal telemetry. Once the team has established that the issue is real and region-level rather than a local service fault, failover actions can begin. Cosmos DB may need an explicit failover priority change if automatic failover has not already taken effect:

```
az cosmosdb failover-priority-change \
  --name opcosmos \
  --resource-group buy-prod-rg \
  --failover-policies westeurope=0
```

Service Bus alias failover may then be triggered:

```
az servicebus georecovery-alias failover \
  --resource-group buy-prod-rg \
  --namespace-name opsb-ne \
  --alias opsb-dr
```

At the application edge, traffic routing may also need to change so requests are directed to the secondary-region Function App. Once that is done, the team still has to verify end-to-end health. Recovery is not complete when the commands finish. It is complete when new orders can flow, workflows can resume, and dependent services are behaving as expected.

Testing Disaster Recovery

A disaster recovery plan that has never been tested is only a theory. In practice, serverless DR needs to be exercised deliberately, because the first time a team discovers a bad assumption should not be during a live regional outage. Testing does not have to mean destructive chaos all the time, but it does need to include controlled failover drills that prove the plan works under realistic conditions. For `OrderProcessor`, that means running periodic recovery exercises in which the primary region is treated as unavailable and the team walks through the failover playbook. During those drills, two measures matter especially. Recovery Time Objective shows how long it takes to restore normal or acceptable service. The recovery point objective shows how much work is lost or must be replayed. Earlier architectural choices such as idempotent workflows and explicit orchestration state handling directly support those outcomes, because they reduce the chance that recovery produces business duplication or unrecoverable workflow corruption.

Applying Regional Failover to `OrderProcessor`

Taken together, these patterns move `OrderProcessor` from simple regional deployment into planned regional resilience. Functions can exist in both regions. Cosmos DB can replicate and fail over. Service Bus can present a stable alias. ERP integrations can use a fallback path. The team can work from a defined failover sequence instead of inventing one under pressure. The goal is not perfect continuity in every imaginable failure mode. The goal is predictable recovery with a system design that supports it.

That makes disaster recovery a natural continuation of the rest of the chapter. Infrastructure as Code makes the regional platform reproducible. Pipelines make it deployable. Zero-downtime strategies reduce release risk. Governance secures the deployment path. Disaster recovery then completes the operational picture by answering what happens when the problem is no longer a bad release or a local fault but a loss of regional availability.

Project Addition: Disaster Recovery Foundation for `OrderProcessor`

This section adds the first real disaster recovery foundation for `OrderProcessor`. Extend the infrastructure definitions so the system has a clear primary and secondary region model, enable multi-region support where Azure services allow it, introduce geo-disaster recovery aliases or equivalent regional abstractions for the messaging path, and externalize primary and secondary integration endpoints where failover depends on third-party services. In parallel, document the operational failover sequence in a playbook that the team can rehearse rather than inventing recovery steps during a real incident.

With that in place, `OrderProcessor` becomes more than a well-designed single-region serverless system. It becomes a platform that can continue operating or recover in a controlled way when the underlying region it depends on is no longer healthy.

Continuous Improvement and DevOps Culture

By the time `OrderProcessor` reaches this point, the system is no longer defined only by its code. It now has orchestrated workflows, secure boundaries, deployment automation, operational playbooks, cost visibility, governance controls, and disaster recovery planning. But none of those things guarantee a healthy production system on their own. Tools can exist without being used well. Dashboards can exist without being watched. Pipelines can exist without changing how teams actually work. That is why the final section of the chapter needs to move beyond technology and into culture. The earlier chapters already pushed `OrderProcessor` toward clearer workflow ownership, better operational visibility, and more deliberate change. This section takes that one step further. The real goal of DevOps culture is not simply to make development and operations collaborate more politely. It is to shorten feedback loops, turn failures into improvements, reduce manual friction, and make the people responsible for building the system equally responsible for understanding how it behaves in production. That is the point where a technically sound platform becomes a continuously improving one.

Why Culture Matters As Much As Tooling

Modern cloud platforms give teams a powerful toolbox. Azure Functions, Service Bus, Cosmos DB, Key Vault, pipelines, and dashboards all make it easier to build and run a distributed system. But those tools only create value when the team uses them in a disciplined way. A deployment pipeline is only useful if engineers commit often enough for it to become part of the normal delivery path. A failover playbook is only useful if the team actually rehearses it. A cost dashboard is only useful if someone notices when the numbers start to drift in the wrong direction.

For `OrderProcessor`, this matters because the platform is now broad enough that no one person should be carrying all the operational understanding in their head. The system needs shared habits, not just shared tooling. Earlier chapters used explanatory prose and project additions to show how `OrderProcessor` evolved from a simple serverless prototype into a more structured and observable workflow platform. This section completes that progression by making improvement itself part of the system's operating model.

Shared Ownership

One of the strongest shifts in a DevOps culture is the move away from handoff thinking. In a traditional model, developers build the software, and operations teams run it. In a system like `OrderProcessor`, that boundary becomes less useful because the runtime behavior of the application is so tightly connected to architectural and code decisions. Retry behavior affects cost. Queue design affects scaling. Deployment structure affects uptime. Secrets handling affects governance. That means the people writing the code need to care about operational outcomes, and the people managing the platform need to understand the intent behind the code.

For `OrderProcessor`, shared ownership means that developers do not stop at merge time. They also watch telemetry, participate in incident review, and understand the production implications of the changes they make. It also means operational concerns are not left until the end. Infrastructure, deployment, recovery, and monitoring become part of the design conversation much earlier. That makes the system more coherent because responsibility follows the workflow all the way from code to production.

Continuous Feedback Loops

A healthy DevOps culture depends on rapid feedback. The shorter the gap between change and learning, the easier it is to correct mistakes before they become large and expensive. `OrderProcessor` now has several feedback loops built into it. Pull request validation catches problems before the merge. CI/CD pipelines expose broken builds and deployment issues quickly. Telemetry and alerts show how the live system reacts after release. Cost monitoring adds another layer by showing when usage or behavior has changed in a financially significant way.

The value of these loops is cumulative. A developer pushes a change, the build validates it, the deployment promotes it safely, and telemetry shows whether the live behavior matches expectations. If a release begins to increase ERP failures or message volume unexpectedly, the team learns about it quickly enough to respond. This is one of the reasons the earlier chapters leaned so heavily on explicit orchestration, observability, and operational controls. Those technical changes now support a cultural outcome: the team can learn from the system while it is still practical to act.

Blameless Postmortems

Failures are inevitable in distributed systems. What matters most is what the team does after the incident is stabilized. A blame-focused culture makes people defensive and discourages useful learning. A blameless culture does the opposite. It asks what conditions allowed the incident to happen, what assumptions turned out to be wrong, and what should change in the system or process so the same problem is less likely to recur. For `OrderProcessor`, this is especially important because many incidents will not have a single obvious cause. A queue backlog may reflect a scaling rule that was too conservative. A deployment problem may expose a hidden dependency between infrastructure and application code. A failed integration may reveal that retry behavior was too aggressive or too weak. A postmortem is where those lessons become explicit. It is also where the team decides whether the result should be a code change, a pipeline change, a playbook update, a dashboard improvement, or a training gap to address. The point is not just to describe what happened. It is to improve the system because it happened.

Automation As a Default Habit

The operational work introduced earlier in the chapter should not remain manual any longer than necessary. Pipelines already automate deployment. Autoscale rules automate part of the response to surge. Key Vault policies automate parts of rotation and secret handling. Disaster recovery drills can be scripted. Over time, that same mindset should continue to remove fragile manual repetition from the way `OrderProcessor` is run.

For this system, a good rule is simple: if the team has had to do the same manual operational task more than once, it is a candidate for automation. That does not mean every human decision disappears. Production approvals and failover judgment still matter. But the repetitive, mechanical parts of operating the platform should become codified. That keeps the system more reliable and gives the team more time to think about improvement rather than repetition.

Measuring Progress

Continuous improvement only works when the team can see whether things are actually getting better. That means `OrderProcessor` should not measure only technical symptoms such as latency and failures. It should also track delivery and operational metrics that show how the team is performing as a system. Measures such as lead time, change failure rate, mean time to recovery, and error budget consumption help make that visible.

The important thing here is not to turn the platform into a metrics vanity project. It is to make sure the team has enough signal to recognize whether its practices are improving or degrading. If lead time is shrinking without a rise in failure rate, that is good. If deployment frequency is increasing but rollback rate is rising as well, that needs attention. When these measures are treated seriously, they connect the cultural goals of DevOps to observable results in the same way the earlier chapters connected workflow design to observable system behavior.

Documentation and Shared Knowledge

As `OrderProcessor` grows, documentation stops being optional. Earlier chapters already pushed operational knowledge into the repository through Bicep, playbooks, and structured deployment definitions. That should continue here. The goal is that a new engineer should be able to understand the major operational paths of the system by reading the repository rather than relying on tribal knowledge. That means infrastructure remains documented in `infra`, playbooks remain documented in playbooks, and contribution practices become explicit in files such as `CONTRIBUTING.md`. It also means knowledge sharing becomes part of the team rhythm. Cross-review between development and operations perspectives, paired updates to runbooks, and shared ownership of dashboards all reinforce the same thing: the system is understood by the team, not just by the person who built the first version.

Continuous Learning

Serverless platforms do not stand still, and neither should the team running them. Azure evolves, Durable Functions evolves, cost models evolve, and operational practices improve over time. A strong DevOps culture therefore includes deliberate learning. That might be short internal sessions on new Azure features, review of incident learnings, periodic architecture clean-up, or rotating people through on-call and design responsibilities so understanding does not stay isolated. For `OrderProcessor`, the point is not endless experimentation. It is controlled evolution. The team should keep learning enough that the platform continues to improve rather than merely accumulate more components. That is how the system stays healthy over time instead of slowly becoming harder to operate with every new feature.

Applying DevOps Culture to `OrderProcessor`

At this stage, `OrderProcessor` has all the ingredients needed for a stronger operational culture. The workflows are explicit, the infrastructure is reproducible, the deployment path is governed, and the operational model is documented. What this section adds is the expectation that those technical assets are used as part of a living practice. Engineers share ownership, feedback loops are kept short, postmortems improve the platform, repetitive work is automated, and success is measured with more than uptime alone.

That makes this final section a natural conclusion to the chapter. Earlier sections focused on how to deploy and operate a serverless platform safely. This section explains how to make those practices sustainable by embedding them into how the team works.

Project Addition: DevOps Culture Foundation for `OrderProcessor`

This section adds the first explicit culture and improvement layer to `OrderProcessor`. Add a `CONTRIBUTING.md` file that sets expectations for delivery, review, and operational responsibility. Document the key delivery and operational metrics the team intends to track. Add a lightweight blameless postmortem template to the repository, and treat playbook review, deployment review, and periodic resilience drills as part of normal engineering practice rather than exceptional events. If these practices are going to matter, they need to be visible and repeatable, not implied.

With that in place, `OrderProcessor` is no longer just a serverless application with good technical foundations. It becomes a system supported by a team that knows how to improve it continuously, respond to failure without panic, and turn operational lessons into concrete engineering changes. That is the point where platform maturity starts to look like culture rather than just configuration.

EXERCISES

1. Manually publish `OrderProcessor` from the CLI, omit one required setting, and compare the result with a Bicep-driven deployment.
2. Create a simple Bicep template for a Service Bus namespace and deploy it through a pipeline.
3. Break the Bicep template intentionally and confirm the pipeline fails before application code is deployed.
4. Split one infrastructure resource into its own Bicep module and confirm the deployment still works.
5. Deploy the same Bicep stack to CI and Test with different environment parameters and confirm resource names differ correctly.
6. Add a pipeline step that restores, builds, tests, and publishes the Functions project, then verify the package is produced correctly.
7. Add Event Grid subscription provisioning to the deployment flow and confirm the Function receives events after deployment.

8. Deploy to a staging slot and swap it into production. Confirm rollback is possible by swapping back.
9. Route a small percentage of traffic through a canary slot and compare telemetry between old and new versions.
10. Add a backward-compatible field to an event contract and confirm old and new consumers can run together.
11. Create a basic incident playbook for ERP failure, then simulate the incident and follow the documented steps.
12. Trigger a traffic surge and confirm autoscale rules increase Function App capacity appropriately.
13. Push invalid messages into a queue, inspect the poison queue, apply a fix, and replay the messages safely.
14. Run a GDPR delete test and confirm personal data is removed while audit evidence remains intact.
15. Create an Azure budget for one environment and confirm alerts trigger at the chosen threshold.
16. Compare Application Insights execution telemetry with Azure cost data and identify the biggest cost driver.
17. Reduce Cosmos throughput or autoscale settings in a lower environment and confirm cost drops without breaking the test workload.
18. Attempt a deployment that violates Azure Policy, such as enabling public access where it is forbidden, and confirm the deployment is blocked.
19. Simulate regional failover for Cosmos DB or Service Bus and verify that `OrderProcessor` reconnects or recovers as expected.
20. Run a blameless postmortem after a simulated failure and turn at least one lesson into a concrete backlog or automation improvement.

Summary

Chapter 9 moves `OrderProcessor` from a securely designed serverless application into a system that can be deployed, operated, and evolved reliably in production. It begins by establishing that deployment in serverless systems is not just about publishing code. Functions, queues, databases, secrets, networking, and supporting infrastructure must be created and maintained together. That is why Infrastructure as Code, pipelines, and consistent deployment models become first-class parts of the architecture rather than operational afterthoughts.

From there, the chapter shows how operational maturity grows in layers. Bicep turns infrastructure into versioned, reproducible definitions. CI/CD pipelines turn those definitions and the Function code into a repeatable delivery path. Zero-downtime strategies such as slots, canary rollouts, and phased event handling reduce release risk for live workflows. Playbooks, cost monitoring, governance, and failover planning then extend that operational discipline beyond deployment alone, making the system easier to run under stress, easier to govern, and easier to recover when something goes wrong.

Taken together, these practices turn `OrderProcessor` into a more complete production system. It is no longer just secure at the application boundary or resilient inside the workflow. It now has repeatable infrastructure, controlled releases, operational playbooks, budget visibility, deployment governance, and disaster recovery planning. The result is a serverless architecture that is not only functional and secure but also operationally credible, one that can be shipped safely, run responsibly, and improved continuously over time.

CHAPTER 10

Enterprise Case Studies in Serverless Distributed Systems

Earlier chapters introduced the foundations piece by piece: durable orchestrations, messaging patterns, observability, security, deployment, governance, and operational resilience. Those chapters established the building blocks, but real systems rarely present those concerns one at a time. In practice, enterprise systems combine them. A single workflow may involve large file uploads, external partners, tenant-specific rules, regional compliance boundaries, human approvals, and long-running integrations, all while still needing to remain observable, secure, and resilient.

This chapter brings those earlier patterns together through a set of practical case studies built around the evolving `OrderProcessor` platform. Each section takes a real architectural pressure point and shows how the system *can* be extended to handle it without losing the qualities established in the rest of the book. The goal here is not to introduce disconnected examples or add every single example shown to the project. It is to show how a serverless .NET system *can* evolve into a more complete enterprise platform, one that can process files, coordinate multiple services, support multiple tenants and regions, incorporate human decision points, integrate unreliable external APIs, and still remain operable and compliant at scale.

Package Note Code examples in this chapter make use of the Microsoft.Extensions.Http.Resilience NuGet Package.

© Patrick Kearns 2026
P. Kearns, *Serverless Distributed Systems in Modern .NET and Azure*,
https://doi.org/10.1007/979-8-8688-2839-3_10

Case Study: File Streaming and Processing

Throughout the book, `OrderProcessor` has been shaped around durable orchestrations, secure APIs, asynchronous messaging, observability, and operational resilience. Up to this point, most of the examples have dealt with structured payloads such as orders, approvals, and events. Real enterprise systems rarely stay that simple. They also need to deal with files: invoices as PDFs, contracts as Word documents, customer extracts as CSVs, and emails as `.eml` files with nested attachments. Once files enter the picture, the design pressure changes. Payload size increases, content formats vary, processing becomes more stateful, and memory usage matters far more than it did when everything was JSON.

That makes file handling a good case study for the next stage of `OrderProcessor`. The challenge is not simply to accept uploads. It is to accept them in a way that stays consistent with the rest of the architecture already established in the book. Files need to be streamed rather than buffered, persisted durably before deeper processing begins, routed through decoupled event-driven steps, and then handed off into orchestrated workflows when extraction or downstream coordination becomes more complex. The important point is that the file workflow should behave like the rest of the platform: resilient, asynchronous, observable, and scalable.

Why Files Complicate a Serverless System

Text-based business messages are usually small and easy to move through a serverless workflow. Files are different because they put pressure on several parts of the system at once. Size is the most obvious issue. A large PDF or email archive cannot be treated like a normal API payload and safely buffered into memory without risk. Format diversity is another challenge because a file-processing pipeline may need to distinguish between PDFs, Office files, email messages, and attachments, each of which may require different extraction logic. Durability matters too. If an upload fails halfway through or processing crashes after receipt, the platform needs a reliable source of truth for what arrived and what still needs to happen next.

For `OrderProcessor`, that means the platform should separate file receipt from file processing as early as possible. The upload boundary should preserve the raw file quickly and avoid doing too much work inline. Once the raw content is stored durably, the rest of the system can react to its arrival through events and orchestration. That keeps the public entry point lightweight while allowing the heavier processing path to remain asynchronous and resilient.

File Ingestion Architecture for OrderProcessor

A good file ingestion model for `OrderProcessor` follows the same decoupled style used elsewhere in the book. The upload endpoint accepts the file and streams it directly to Blob Storage. The arrival of a new blob then raises an event through Event Grid. A processing Function subscribes to that event, inspects the file type, extracts metadata, and hands off more complex work to orchestration when needed. For example, an email with multiple attachments is better handled as a workflow than as one monolithic processing step. Figure 10-1 shows the end-to-end shape of that pipeline.

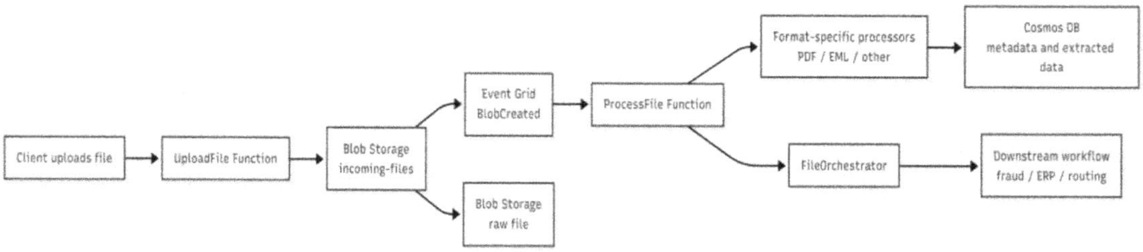

Figure 10-1. *File Ingestion Pipeline*

The value of this model is not only that it scales. It also keeps responsibility boundaries clear. Upload is responsible for accepting and persisting bytes. Event Grid is responsible for signaling arrival. The processor is responsible for file-type routing and extraction. The orchestrator is responsible for coordinating any multi-step downstream work. That separation makes the system easier to reason about and easier to recover when one part fails.

Streaming Uploads into Blob Storage

The first concrete project change is the upload boundary itself. The key pattern is that the HTTP trigger should stream the request body directly into Blob Storage rather than buffering the full file in memory. That keeps the Function lightweight and makes the upload path much more suitable for large files.

Functions/UploadFile.cs

```
using System.Net;
using Azure.Storage.Blobs;
using Microsoft.Azure.Functions.Worker;
using Microsoft.Azure.Functions.Worker.Http;

namespace OrderProcessor;

public sealed class UploadFile
{
    private readonly BlobServiceClient _blobServiceClient;

    public UploadFile(BlobServiceClient blobServiceClient)
    {
        _blobServiceClient = blobServiceClient;
    }

    [Function("UploadFile")]
    public async Task<HttpResponseData> Run(
        [HttpTrigger(AuthorizationLevel.Function, "post", Route = "files/
        upload")]
        HttpRequestData req,
        FunctionContext ctx)
    {
        var fileName = "upload.bin";

        if (req.Headers.TryGetValues("X-File-Name", out var values))
        {
            fileName = values.FirstOrDefault() ?? fileName;
        }

        var extension = Path.GetExtension(fileName);
        var blobName = $"{Guid.NewGuid():N}{extension}";

        var containerClient = _blobServiceClient.GetBlobContainerClient("in
        coming-files");
        await containerClient.CreateIfNotExistsAsync();

        var blobClient = containerClient.GetBlobClient(blobName);
```

```
        await blobClient.UploadAsync(req.Body, overwrite: false);

        var response = req.CreateResponse(HttpStatusCode.Accepted);
        await response.WriteAsJsonAsync(new
        {
            Message = "File uploaded successfully",
            BlobName = blobName
        });
        return response;
    }
}
```

Program.cs addition:

```
builder.Services.AddSingleton(sp =>
{
    var connectionString = builder.Configuration["AzureWebJobsStorage"]
        ?? throw new InvalidOperationException("Missing
        AzureWebJobsStorage");

    return new BlobServiceClient(connectionString);
});
```

Raising Processing Events from Blob Storage

Once the file has landed in Blob Storage, the rest of the platform should react asynchronously. In `OrderProcessor`, that is a natural fit for Event Grid. Blob Storage can raise a `BlobCreated` event whenever a new file appears in the target container, which allows the ingestion path to remain fast while the heavier work starts only after the raw content is safely stored.

infra/eventgrid-file-processing.bicep

```
resource storageEvents 'Microsoft.EventGrid/systemTopics@2022-06-15' = {
  name: 'files-topic'
  location: resourceGroup().location
  properties: {
    source: storage.id
```

```
    topicType: 'Microsoft.Storage.StorageAccounts'
  }
}

resource fileSub 'Microsoft.EventGrid/systemTopics/
eventSubscriptions@2022-06-15' = {
  name: '${storageEvents.name}/fileprocessor'
  properties: {
    destination: {
      endpointType: 'AzureFunction'
      resourceId: fileProcessorFunc.id
    }
    filter: {
      subjectBeginsWith: '/blobServices/default/containers/incoming-files/'
    }
  }
}
```

This is the same architectural principle used elsewhere in the book. The upload path does not immediately perform all processing itself. It emits a durable artifact, in this case a blob, and the rest of the system reacts through asynchronous messaging.

Routing Files to the Correct Processor

Once a blob-created event arrives, the next step is to determine what kind of file the system is dealing with and route accordingly. That is the job of the file processor Function. Its responsibility is not to perform every possible transformation itself. Its job is to inspect the incoming file, establish what kind of content it represents, and invoke the next appropriate stage.

Functions/ProcessFile.cs

```
using Azure.Messaging.EventGrid;
using Azure.Messaging.EventGrid.SystemEvents;
using Azure.Storage.Blobs;
using Microsoft.Azure.Functions.Worker;
using Microsoft.Extensions.Logging;
```

```
namespace OrderProcessor;

public sealed class ProcessFile
{
    private readonly BlobServiceClient _blobServiceClient;

    public ProcessFile(BlobServiceClient blobServiceClient)
    {
        _blobServiceClient = blobServiceClient;
    }

    [Function("ProcessFile")]
    public async Task Run(
        [EventGridTrigger] EventGridEvent ev,
        FunctionContext ctx)
    {
        var logger = ctx.GetLogger("ProcessFile");

        var blobData = ev.Data.ToObjectFromJson<StorageBlobCreatedEve
        ntData>();
        if (blobData is null || string.IsNullOrWhiteSpace(blobData.Url))
        {
            logger.LogWarning("Blob created event did not contain a
            valid URL.");
            return;
        }

        var blobUri = new Uri(blobData.Url);
        var fileName = Path.GetFileName(blobUri.LocalPath);

        var containerClient = _blobServiceClient.GetBlobContainerClient
        ("incoming-files");
        var blobClient = containerClient.GetBlobClient(fileName);

        await using var fileStream = await blobClient.OpenReadAsync();

        if (fileName.EndsWith(".pdf", StringComparison.OrdinalIgnoreCase))
        {
```

```
            logger.LogInformation("Routing {File} to PDF processor",
            fileName);
            await PdfProcessor.ProcessAsync(fileStream);
        }
        else if (fileName.EndsWith(".eml", StringComparison.
        OrdinalIgnoreCase))
        {
            logger.LogInformation("Routing {File} to Email processor",
            fileName);
            await EmailProcessor.ProcessAsync(fileStream);
        }
        else
        {
            logger.LogWarning("Unsupported file type: {File}", fileName);
        }
    }
}
```

Program.cs Addition for Blob Storage:

```
builder.Services.AddSingleton(sp =>
{
    var connectionString = builder.Configuration["AzureWebJobsStorage"]
        ?? throw new InvalidOperationException("Missing
        AzureWebJobsStorage");

    return new BlobServiceClient(connectionString);
});
```

Again, the important pattern here is separation of concerns. The processor is acting as a routing and extraction boundary, not as a giant catch-all Function that knows how to do everything. That keeps the pipeline extensible. Supporting another file type later becomes a matter of adding another processor path rather than redesigning the ingestion model from scratch.

Orchestrating More Complex File Workflows

Some files are simple enough to process in one step. Others are not. An email message with attachments is a good example of where orchestration becomes useful. The raw email may need to be parsed first, each attachment may need to be extracted, and then each extracted attachment may need to be processed independently. That pattern fits naturally into Durable Functions because it gives the system retries, durable progress, and coordination without forcing everything into one Function invocation.

Orchestrations/FileOrchestrator.cs

```
using Microsoft.Azure.Functions.Worker;
using Microsoft.DurableTask;

namespace OrderProcessor;

public static class FileOrchestrator
{
    [Function("FileOrchestrator")]
    public static async Task Run(
        [OrchestrationTrigger] TaskOrchestrationContext context)
    {
        var fileInfo = context.GetInput<FileInfo>()
            ?? throw new InvalidOperationException("File information was
            not provided.");

        var attachments = await context.CallActivityAsync<List<Att
        achment>>(
            "ExtractAttachments",
            fileInfo);

        if (attachments is null || attachments.Count == 0)
        {
            return;
        }

        var processingTasks = attachments
            .Select(attachment =>
                context.CallActivityAsync("ProcessAttachment", attachment))
```

```
            .ToList();

        await Task.WhenAll(processingTasks);
    }
}
```

The orchestrator first extracts the attachments from the uploaded file, then fans out one processing activity per attachment. Each activity is scheduled independently, allowing the Durable Functions runtime to process attachments in parallel where capacity allows. The final Task.WhenAll acts as the fan-in point, ensuring the orchestration does not complete until every attachment has been processed.

One extra point: if a file could contain hundreds or thousands of attachments, do not fan them all out blindly. Use batching:

```
using Microsoft.Azure.Functions.Worker;
using Microsoft.DurableTask;

namespace OrderProcessor;

public static class FileOrchestrator
{
    private const int BatchSize = 10;

    [Function("FileOrchestrator")]
    public static async Task Run(
        [OrchestrationTrigger] TaskOrchestrationContext context)
    {
        var fileInfo = context.GetInput<FileInfo>()
            ?? throw new InvalidOperationException("File information was
            not provided.");

        var attachments = await context.CallActivityAsync<List<Att
        achment>>(
            "ExtractAttachments",
            fileInfo);

        if (attachments is null || attachments.Count == 0)
        {
            return;
        }
```

```
        foreach (var batch in attachments.Chunk(BatchSize))
        {
            var processingTasks = batch
                .Select(attachment =>
                    context.CallActivityAsync("ProcessAttachment",
                    attachment))
                .ToList();

            await Task.WhenAll(processingTasks);
        }
    }
}
```

This is where the chapter starts to tie back into the earlier orchestration patterns. File handling is not separate from the rest of the book's architecture. It is another example of how durable workflows allow the platform to break a complicated task into smaller, resilient steps without losing track of what still needs to happen.

Separating Raw File Storage from Metadata

After processing begins, the system also needs to separate binary content from queryable metadata. Raw files belong in Blob Storage because that is what object storage is designed for. Metadata such as checksums, detected type, extracted text, or processing status belongs in Cosmos DB or another structured store where it can be queried efficiently. Audit information should remain separate again, in line with the earlier audit patterns used in the book.

That division matters because it prevents the structured data store from becoming bloated with binary content while still giving the platform an efficient way to search, query, and monitor what happened to each uploaded file. It also keeps the design consistent with the broader `OrderProcessor` model, where each store has a clear role rather than acting as a dumping ground for every kind of artifact.

Project Addition: File Ingestion Pipeline for OrderProcessor

This section extends `OrderProcessor` with a real file-ingestion path that fits the architecture established in the earlier chapters. The platform now accepts streamed file uploads at the HTTP boundary, persists them immediately to Blob Storage, raises processing events through Event Grid, routes files into format-specific processors, and uses durable orchestration when the processing path becomes multi-step or attachment-driven. Raw files remain in Blob Storage, while metadata and extracted results can be stored separately in Cosmos DB for query and downstream use. From this point on, `OrderProcessor` is no longer limited to structured API payloads alone. It can accept and process unstructured inputs in the same resilient, event-driven style as the rest of the platform.

Case Study: Event-Driven Orchestration Across Services

Up to this point, `OrderProcessor` has mostly been shown as a workflow platform concerned with its own bounded context. Orders arrive, fraud checks run, tax is calculated, ERP is updated, and supporting operational capabilities such as observability, security, and deployment wrap around that core flow. In real enterprise systems, that boundary rarely holds for long. A successful business event inside one service usually matters to several others. Once an order is confirmed, logistics may need to arrange shipment, invoicing may need to generate a document, notifications may need to contact the customer, and reporting systems may need an audit trail. The architectural problem is no longer just how to complete one workflow. It becomes how to let that workflow trigger other services without turning everything into one tightly coupled central process.

That is where event-driven orchestration becomes useful. The system needs a way to keep order-critical steps under strong control while still allowing other services to react independently. For `OrderProcessor`, the right model is a hybrid one. The steps that are central to the correctness of the order itself, such as fraud checks, tax handling, and ERP registration, remain inside a Durable Functions orchestration. Once those have succeeded, the platform publishes an event that other services can consume independently. That preserves the reliability of orchestration where it matters most, while using choreography to scale beyond one bounded context.

Why Cross-Service Orchestration Matters

Enterprise systems do not operate in isolation. Even when each service has a clear ownership boundary, the business process itself still crosses those boundaries constantly. An order that appears complete from the perspective of `OrderProcessor` may only be at the beginning of its wider lifecycle. Downstream teams or systems may care about that order for completely different reasons. The logistics service may care about dispatch. The invoicing service may care about billing. A notifications service may care about customer communication. An analytics or compliance system may care only that the event happened and needs to be recorded.

Without a good event model, those systems often end up polling for changes or relying on brittle direct integrations. That introduces lag, duplication, and unnecessary coupling. A cleaner design lets the core workflow decide when the order has reached a meaningful business milestone, then expresses that milestone as an event. From there, other services can subscribe and react without having to be baked into the original orchestration.

Orchestration and Choreography Working Together

The most useful distinction here is between orchestration and choreography. Orchestration is appropriate when one workflow needs to own the critical path and make explicit decisions step by step. That is exactly what Durable Functions already does well in `OrderProcessor`. Choreography is more appropriate when services should react to business events independently, without one central engine coordinating every detail of their behavior.

For `OrderProcessor`, the right design is not to choose one and reject the other. It is to combine them. The order-critical flow remains orchestrated. Once that flow reaches a stable business outcome, the system emits an event that downstream services can consume in their own way. Figure 10-2 shows how those two models fit together inside the wider platform.

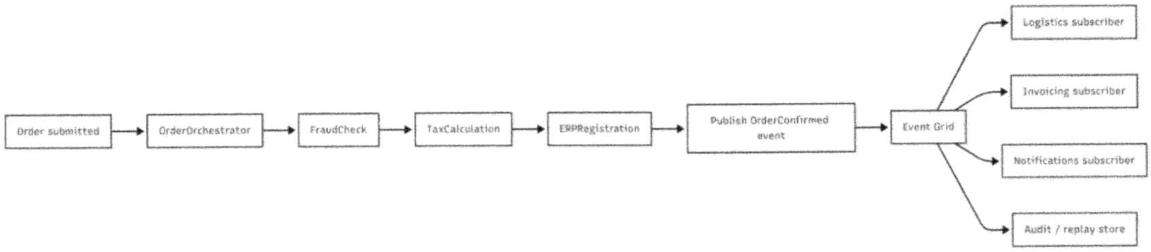

Figure 10-2. *Combining Orchestration and Choreography in OrderProcessor*

This hybrid model is powerful because it preserves discipline where the core transaction needs it while avoiding the trap of turning one orchestration into the owner of every downstream concern. Logistics, invoicing, notifications, and later subscribers can evolve independently as long as they understand the event contract.

Extending the Core Orchestrator

The first concrete project change is to extend the existing orchestrator so that it publishes an `OrderConfirmed` event once the order-critical path has completed successfully. The important thing is that the event is emitted only after the orchestrator has reached a business state that other services are allowed to trust. That keeps the core flow authoritative while still enabling loose coupling outside it.

Orchestrations/OrderOrchestrator.cs

```
using Microsoft.Azure.Functions.Worker;
using Microsoft.DurableTask;

namespace OrderProcessor;

public static class OrderOrchestrator
{
    [Function("OrderOrchestrator")]
    public static async Task Run(
        [OrchestrationTrigger] TaskOrchestrationContext context)
    {
        var order = context.GetInput<Order>()
            ?? throw new InvalidOperationException("Order input is
            required.");

        var retryOptions = TaskOptions.FromRetryPolicy(new RetryPolicy(
```

```
    maxNumberOfAttempts: 3,
    firstRetryInterval: TimeSpan.FromSeconds(5))
{
    BackoffCoefficient = 2,
    MaxRetryInterval = TimeSpan.FromMinutes(1)
});

var fraud = await context.CallActivityAsync<FraudCheckResult>(
    "FraudCheck",
    order,
    retryOptions);

if (!fraud.Approved)
{
    await context.CallActivityAsync(
        "RejectOrder",
        new RejectOrderRequest(order.Id, fraud.Reason),
        retryOptions);

    return;
}

var tax = await context.CallActivityAsync<TaxCalculationResult>(
    "TaxCalculation",
    order,
    retryOptions);

if (!tax.Success)
{
    throw new InvalidOperationException(
        $"Tax calculation failed for order '{order.Id}'.");
}

var erp = await context.CallActivityAsync<ERPRegistrationResult>(
    "ERPRegistration",
    order,
    retryOptions);

if (!erp.Registered)
```

```
        {
            throw new InvalidOperationException(
                $"ERP registration failed for order '{order.Id}'.");
        }

        await context.CallActivityAsync(
            "PublishEvent",
            new OrderConfirmedEvent(order.Id),
            retryOptions);
    }
}

public sealed record FraudCheckResult(
    bool Approved,
    string? Reason);

public sealed record TaxCalculationResult(
    bool Success,
    decimal TaxAmount);

public sealed record ERPRegistrationResult(
    bool Registered,
    string? ErpReference);

public sealed record RejectOrderRequest(
    string OrderId,
    string? Reason);
```

This version keeps the example compact, but it avoids treating the workflow as a blind sequence of calls. Each critical activity returns a business result, and the orchestrator only publishes `OrderConfirmed` after fraud, tax, and ERP registration have all reached an acceptable outcome. Transient failures are handled through activity retry options, while unrecoverable failures are allowed to fail the orchestration visibly. Authentication and authorization should happen before the orchestration is started; the workflow should receive durable business context, not a caller's bearer token.

Publishing the Business Event

Once the orchestrator delegates event publication to an activity, that activity can publish the message into Event Grid. This preserves the pattern used elsewhere in the book, where external or side-effecting operations are pushed into activities rather than sitting directly in the orchestrator.

Functions/PublishEvent.cs

```
using Azure;
using Azure.Messaging.EventGrid;
using Microsoft.Azure.Functions.Worker;

namespace OrderProcessor;

public static class PublishEvent
{
    [Function("PublishEvent")]
    public static async Task Run(
        [ActivityTrigger] Order order,
        FunctionContext ctx)
    {
        var client = new EventGridPublisherClient(
            new Uri(Environment.GetEnvironmentVariable("EventGridEnd
            point")!),
            new AzureKeyCredential(Environment.GetEnvironmentVariable("Even
            tGridKey")!));

        var ev = new EventGridEvent(
            subject: $"orders/{order.Id}",
            eventType: "OrderConfirmed",
            dataVersion: "1.0",
            data: new OrderConfirmedEvent(order.Id));

        await client.SendEventAsync(ev);
    }
}
```

The key pattern here is that the event contract is small and purposeful. Downstream services should receive only the information they need in order to react, rather than being coupled to the full internal shape of the orchestrator's state.

Subscribing from Downstream Services

Once `OrderConfirmed` is being published, downstream services can subscribe independently. A logistics subscriber might start shipping activity, while an invoicing subscriber might generate an invoice or trigger billing workflows. Neither one needs to know how the order reached the confirmed state. They only need a contract they can trust.

Example downstream subscriber: Logistics service

```
using Azure.Messaging.EventGrid;
using Microsoft.Azure.Functions.Worker;

namespace LogisticsService;

public static class StartShipping
{
    [Function("StartShipping")]
    public static async Task Run(
        [EventGridTrigger] EventGridEvent ev,
        FunctionContext ctx)
    {
        var order = ev.Data.ToObjectFromJson<OrderSummary>();
        var logger = ctx.GetLogger("Logistics");

        logger.LogInformation("Shipping started for order {Id}", order.Id);

        await ShippingApi.ScheduleAsync(order.Id, order.CustomerId);
    }
}
```

Example downstream subscriber: Invoicing service

```
using Azure.Messaging.EventGrid;
using Microsoft.Azure.Functions.Worker;
```

```
namespace InvoicingService;

public static class GenerateInvoice
{
    [Function("GenerateInvoice")]
    public static async Task Run(
        [EventGridTrigger] EventGridEvent ev,
        FunctionContext ctx)
    {
        var order = ev.Data.ToObjectFromJson<OrderSummary>();
        var logger = ctx.GetLogger("Invoicing");

        logger.LogInformation("Invoice generated for order {Id}",
        order.Id);

        await InvoiceService.CreatePdfAsync(order.Id, order.Total);
    }
}
```

These examples are intentionally simple because the architectural lesson is more important than any one implementation detail. The important thing is that the subscribers are independent. They do not need to be added as new branches inside the core orchestrator every time the organization wants another downstream reaction to `OrderConfirmed`. They are shown here as downstream service examples rather than as files that must live inside the main `OrderProcessor` codebase.

Wiring Subscriptions Through Infrastructure

The event model also needs to exist in infrastructure, not just in code. Event Grid subscriptions should be part of the platform definition so that downstream routing is created consistently during deployment.

infra/eventgrid-order-confirmed.bicep

```
resource orderConfirmedSub 'Microsoft.EventGrid/
eventSubscriptions@2022-06-15' = {
  name: 'orderConfirmed-sub'
  properties: {
    destination: {
```

```
      endpointType: 'AzureFunction'
      resourceId: logisticsFunc.id
    }
    deadLetterDestination: {
      endpointType: 'AzureStorageBlob'
      properties: {
        resourceId: storage.id
        blobContainerName: 'deadletter'
      }
    }
  }
}
```

This example also introduces an important operational feature: dead-lettering. If one of the subscribers is unavailable or repeatedly failing, the event should not simply disappear. Persisting it to a dead-letter location gives the team a way to inspect, replay, or recover those missed events later.

Audit and Replay

Business events are often valuable beyond their immediate subscribers. In many enterprise systems, an event such as `OrderConfirmed` is both an integration message and an audit artifact. That means it is worth persisting somewhere queryable, especially if the organization may later need to replay downstream actions or analyze business flow historically.

A simple audit write might look like this:

```
await auditContainer.CreateItemAsync(new AuditEvent
{
    OrderId = order.Id,
    EventType = "OrderConfirmed",
    Timestamp = DateTime.UtcNow
});
```

This fits naturally with the earlier audit patterns introduced elsewhere in the book. It also strengthens the choreography model because it gives the system a durable record of what was published, even if one or more downstream consumers experience trouble.

Why the Hybrid Model Works Well

The reason this hybrid architecture fits `OrderProcessor` so well is that it recognizes that not every downstream concern deserves a place in the central orchestrator. Fraud, tax, and ERP are part of the order's correctness and therefore belong in the controlled workflow. Logistics and invoicing are still important, but they do not need to make the orchestrator longer, more brittle, or more tightly coupled than necessary. That balance makes the platform easier to evolve. Adding a new downstream subscriber later, such as customer notifications, fraud analytics, or partner reporting, does not require redesigning the orchestration itself. The core workflow stays stable, and the event model gives the wider organization room to extend the system safely.

Project Addition: Cross-Service Event-Driven Flow for OrderProcessor

This section extends `OrderProcessor` beyond a single bounded workflow and into a broader event-driven service landscape. The core Durable Functions orchestration now publishes an `OrderConfirmed` event once the critical path has succeeded, and downstream services such as logistics and invoicing can subscribe independently through Event Grid. Dead-letter handling and audit persistence strengthen the operational side of the model by ensuring events can be recovered or replayed if a subscriber becomes unavailable.

From this point on, `OrderProcessor` is no longer only an internal workflow engine. It becomes an event source that can coordinate a wider mesh of services while still keeping its own critical path reliable and explicit.

Case Study: Multi-tenant Architectures

Many real-world SaaS systems do not serve just one organization. They serve multiple customers, business units, or partners from a shared platform, while still needing strong boundaries between them. Up to this point, `OrderProcessor` has mostly been described as though it belongs to one organization running one logical environment. That was enough to introduce workflows, orchestration, security, resilience, and operations, but it is not enough to describe how the platform behaves as a shared product. Once multiple tenants enter the picture, the architecture has to answer a different class of question. It is no longer only about whether orders can be processed correctly. It is also about who owns the data, who can see it, which rules apply to it, and how one tenant's activity should be prevented from distorting the experience of another.

That makes multi-tenancy one of the most important architectural case studies in this chapter. A multi-tenant `OrderProcessor` must isolate data, apply tenant-specific configuration, enforce identity boundaries, expose observability by tenant, and still scale economically. The challenge is not simply to add a `TenantId` property somewhere and hope the problem is solved. The platform needs to become tenant-aware across storage, orchestration, configuration, authorization, and operational reporting. The goal of this section is to show how those concerns can be added in a way that remains consistent with the earlier chapters rather than bolting a separate SaaS architecture onto the side.

Why Multi-tenancy Is Difficult

The first challenge in multi-tenancy is isolation. One tenant must never be able to see or influence another tenant's data accidentally. The second is customization. Tenants often need slightly different business rules, such as different fraud thresholds, tax regimes, routing behavior, or ERP endpoints. The third is scale. One tenant may process ten orders a day while another processes hundreds of thousands, and the platform has to absorb that variation without allowing the largest customer to become a noisy neighbor for everyone else.

There are operational and commercial concerns as well. Billing and cost attribution become much more important when the platform is shared. Observability has to break down usage and failure patterns by tenant, not just by service. Compliance may require stronger boundaries for some tenants than for others. In a serverless platform, those concerns are amplified because Functions scale across the shared workload. Without explicit design choices, the runtime will not magically know how to keep customers isolated or fairly treated.

Real Project Update: Make the Order Model Tenant-Aware

The most fundamental multi-tenant boundary is the data model. In `OrderProcessor`, that means the order itself needs to carry tenant identity explicitly, and the rest of the workflow needs to treat that identity as part of the business object rather than as a side note.

Models/Order.cs

```
namespace OrderProcessor;

public sealed record Order(
    string Id,
    string TenantId,
    string CustomerId,
    decimal Total);
```

This is a real project change because the rest of the chapter builds on it. Later sections can extend the model again, but at this stage the key addition is that every order now belongs to a specific tenant.

Real Project Update: Partition Data by Tenant

Once TenantId exists in the model, the write path should enforce it as part of the storage design. Cosmos DB is a natural fit here because logical tenant isolation can align directly with the partition key. That does not magically guarantee total isolation on its own, but it gives the platform a strong structural boundary and lets queries stay tenant-scoped by default.

Infrastructure/OrderRepository.cs

```
using Microsoft.Azure.Cosmos;

namespace OrderProcessor;

public sealed class OrderRepository
{
    private readonly Container _container;

    public OrderRepository(CosmosClient cosmosClient)
    {
        _container = cosmosClient.GetContainer("orderdb", "orders");
    }

    public Task CreateAsync(Order order, CancellationToken stopToken =
    default)
    {
```

```
        return _container.CreateItemAsync(
            order,
            new PartitionKey(order.TenantId),
            cancellationToken: stopToken);
    }

    public async Task<IReadOnlyList<Order>> GetByTenantAsync(
        string tenantId,
        CancellationToken stopToken = default)
    {
        var query = new QueryDefinition(
            "SELECT * FROM c WHERE c.tenantId = @tid")
            .WithParameter("@tid", tenantId);

        var iterator = _container.GetItemQueryIterator<Order>(
            query,
            requestOptions: new QueryRequestOptions
            {
                PartitionKey = new PartitionKey(tenantId)
            });

        var results = new List<Order>();

        while (iterator.HasMoreResults)
        {
            var page = await iterator.ReadNextAsync(stopToken);
            results.AddRange(page);
        }

        return results;
    }
}
```

The key lesson is that tenant identity is now part of both the write path and the read path. The repository does not treat tenant filtering as an optional afterthought.

Tenant-Specific Behavior Through Configuration

Isolation is only one side of multi-tenancy. The other side is controlled variation. Different tenants may need different fraud thresholds, tax rates, ERP endpoints, feature toggles, or notification rules. A clean multi-tenant design keeps that variation in configuration rather than scattering hard-coded tenant checks throughout the workflow.

A representative tenant configuration document might look like this:

Example tenant configuration document

```
{
  "TenantId": "tenant-a",
  "FraudRules": {
    "MaxAmount": 10000
  },
  "TaxRate": 0.21,
  "ERPUrl": "https://erp.tenant-a.com"
}
```

That is the pattern. The actual storage location could be Cosmos DB, Azure App Configuration, or another configuration store. What matters is that tenant-specific behavior becomes data-driven.

Real Project Update: Load Tenant Configuration Inside the Workflow

If tenant rules are going to affect processing, the platform needs a concrete way to retrieve them. In `OrderProcessor`, a small repository plus an activity keeps that logic explicit and reusable.

Models/TenantConfig.cs

```
namespace OrderProcessor;

public sealed record FraudRules(decimal MaxAmount);

public sealed record TenantConfig(
    string TenantId,
    FraudRules FraudRules,
    decimal TaxRate,
    string ERPUrl);
```

Infrastructure/TenantConfigRepository.cs

```
using Microsoft.Azure.Cosmos;

namespace OrderProcessor;

public sealed class TenantConfigRepository
{
    private readonly Container _container;

    public TenantConfigRepository(CosmosClient cosmosClient)
    {
        _container = cosmosClient.GetContainer("orderdb", "tenant-config");
    }

    public async Task<TenantConfig> GetAsync(
        string tenantId,
        CancellationToken stopToken = default)
    {
        var response = await _container.ReadItemAsync<TenantConfig>(
            tenantId,
            new PartitionKey(tenantId),
            cancellationToken: stopToken);

        return response.Resource;
    }
}
```

Functions/LoadTenantConfig.cs

```
using Microsoft.Azure.Functions.Worker;

namespace OrderProcessor;

public sealed class LoadTenantConfig
{
    private readonly TenantConfigRepository _repository;

    public LoadTenantConfig(TenantConfigRepository repository)
```

```
    {
        _repository = repository;
    }

    [Function("LoadTenantConfig")]
    public Task<TenantConfig> Run(
        [ActivityTrigger] string tenantId,
        CancellationToken stopToken)
    {
        return _repository.GetAsync(tenantId, stopToken);
    }
}
```

Program.cs addition

```
builder.Services.AddSingleton<OrderRepository>();
builder.Services.AddSingleton<TenantConfigRepository>();
```

This is a real project addition because it gives the platform a concrete tenant-aware configuration boundary rather than leaving tenant rules implied.

Real Project Update: Make the Orchestration Tenant-Aware

Once orders carry `TenantId` and configuration can be loaded per tenant, the existing orchestration should become tenant-aware too. The point is not to create a completely separate workflow engine for multi-tenancy. The point is to evolve the existing order flow so it applies the right rules for the right tenant.

Inside Orchestrations/OrderOrchestrator.cs

```
var order = context.GetInput<Order>()
    ?? throw new InvalidOperationException("Order input is required.");

var config = await context.CallActivityAsync<TenantConfig>(
    "LoadTenantConfig",
    order.TenantId);
```

```
context.SetCustomStatus(new
{
    Tenant = order.TenantId
});

await context.CallActivityAsync("FraudCheck", (order, config.FraudRules));
await context.CallActivityAsync("TaxCalculation", (order, config.TaxRate));
await context.CallActivityAsync("ERPRegistration", (order, config.ERPUrl));
await context.CallActivityAsync("PublishEvent", new
{
    order.Id,
    order.TenantId
});
```

This is shown as an update inside the existing orchestrator rather than as a brand-new orchestrator file because the architectural point is cumulative evolution. The workflow is still `OrderProcessor`. It is now just operating with tenant-aware rules.

Example Tenant-Scoped Authorization Policy

Authentication also needs to respect tenant boundaries. A caller authenticated for tenant A should not be able to act as tenant B simply by altering a route or header. The exact identity setup may vary depending on whether the platform uses Microsoft Entra ID, B2C, or another model, but the pattern is the same: the request's tenant context should match the caller's tenant claim.

This is best shown as an example boundary pattern rather than as a mandatory drop-in file, because authentication setups will vary between implementations.

```
services.AddAuthorization(options =>
{
    options.AddPolicy("TenantScoped", policy =>
        policy.RequireAssertion(ctx =>
        {
            var tenantClaim = ctx.User.FindFirst("tid")?.Value;
            var httpContext = ctx.Resource as HttpContext;
```

```
            return tenantClaim ==
                   httpContext?.Request.Headers["X-TenantId"];
        }));
});
```

The important point is not this exact code. It is that tenant identity should be enforced at the boundary rather than assumed deep in the workflow.

Tenant-Aware Telemetry and Billing

A shared platform also needs a shared operational model. Once the system serves multiple tenants, telemetry should include tenant identity wherever possible so that the platform can answer operational and commercial questions cleanly. That supports billing, SLA reporting, support diagnosis, and usage analysis without treating the entire system as one undifferentiated stream of work.

A representative logging pattern looks like this:

Example Tenant-Aware Logging

```
logger.LogInformation(
    "Order processed {OrderId} for tenant {TenantId}",
    order.Id,
    order.TenantId);
```

That then enables queries such as

Example Kusto query

```
traces
| summarize Count = count() by customDimensions.TenantId
```

This matters for much more than billing. It also lets the team see whether one tenant is experiencing unusual failures, unusually high load, or unexpected latency compared with the rest of the platform.

Scaling and Noisy-Neighbor Concerns

Multi-tenancy is not only a storage and auth problem. It is also a scaling problem. Cosmos partitioning helps because it gives each tenant a natural data boundary, but Azure Functions still scale against the overall workload. A very active tenant can therefore put pressure on shared execution resources even if the data model is correctly partitioned. That means the shared model needs operational safeguards. In practice, those may include per-tenant quotas through API Management, dedicated Function Apps or isolated plans for premium tenants, or stronger hosting isolation for customers with stricter compliance requirements. Those are architectural options rather than mandatory project additions here, but they are worth mentioning because they show how a shared SaaS platform can evolve as tenant needs diverge.

Applying Multi-tenancy to OrderProcessor

Taken together, these changes turn `OrderProcessor` from a single-organization example into the outline of a real shared SaaS platform. Orders are partitioned by tenant. Workflows carry tenant identity. Configuration varies by tenant without forcing code forks. API boundaries can enforce tenant scope. Telemetry becomes rich enough to support billing and operational reporting per customer.

That is the real architectural value of this section. The platform has not been split into completely separate systems for every customer, but it has gained the structures needed to remain shared without becoming unsafe or unmanageable. That is usually the real balancing act in multi-tenant design. The goal is not to prove that one deployment model solves everything forever. It is to show how a shared platform can remain isolatable, configurable, and observable as it grows.

Project Addition: Multi-tenant Architecture for OrderProcessor

This section extends `OrderProcessor` from a single-organization workflow platform into a multi-tenant design. Orders are now tenant-aware at the data model level, Cosmos DB uses tenant-based partitioning, tenant configuration can be loaded explicitly inside the workflow, and telemetry can be broken down by tenant for operations and billing. Boundary checks can then ensure that authenticated callers act only within the tenant they belong to. From this point on, `OrderProcessor` is no longer just an internal serverless application. It starts to look like a shared SaaS platform, one that can serve multiple organizations while still keeping tenant data, behavior, and operational visibility properly separated.

Case Study: Human-in-the-Loop Workflows

Automation is one of the main strengths of a distributed serverless system, but it is never the whole story. Real business processes often reach points where a human decision is still required. A large order may need approval before it can proceed. A suspicious transaction may need manual review. A compliance rule may require a named person to confirm or reject a step before the workflow can continue. In a platform such as `OrderProcessor`, those cases cannot be treated as exceptions outside the architecture. They have to be designed into the workflow in a way that preserves reliability, traceability, and scale.

That is what makes human-in-the-loop workflows such a useful case study. The challenge is not simply to send an email and wait for someone to reply. The challenge is to pause a distributed workflow safely, persist its state durably, resume it when an approved response arrives, and apply audit and timeout rules without turning the whole system into a fragile synchronous process. This fits naturally with the earlier Durable Functions chapters, because `OrderProcessor` already has a workflow engine capable of waiting, resuming, and coordinating multiple steps. The difference here is that one of those steps now belongs to a person rather than to a service.

Why Human Decisions Still Matter

Earlier versions of `OrderProcessor` already automated fraud checks, tax handling, ERP integration, and event publication. That automation is valuable because most orders should move through the system without manual intervention. But enterprise systems rarely operate with fully uniform risk. A high-value order may exceed a fraud threshold. A supplier-specific rule may require manual confirmation. A compliance policy may demand a human sign-off for flagged transactions before the platform is allowed to proceed.

That means a good architecture should let automation handle the majority of cases while still making room for human judgment when the business rules require it. The important point is that this should happen inside the workflow model rather than beside it. If human approvals are bolted on as an afterthought, the result is often brittle side processes, lost state, unclear ownership, and poor auditability. In `OrderProcessor`, the better approach is to treat human interaction as another kind of durable workflow step.

Waiting Safely for External Input

Durable Functions provides exactly the right primitive for this kind of problem: the ability to wait for an external event. That means an orchestration can reach a decision point, persist its state, and then remain paused until a human response arrives. Crucially, the system does not need to hold compute resources open while it waits. The orchestration state is checkpointed durably and can resume later without turning the approval step into a long-running synchronous process.

This is the real architectural value of Durable Functions in a human-in-the-loop scenario. A paused workflow is not a broken workflow. It is a durable workflow waiting for an external decision.

Real Project Update: Approval-Aware Orchestration

If `OrderProcessor` is being extended to support manual approval for unusually large orders, that should be reflected in the orchestration itself.

Orchestrations/ApprovalOrchestrator.cs

```
using System;
using Microsoft.Azure.Functions.Worker;
using Microsoft.DurableTask;

namespace OrderProcessor;

public static class ApprovalOrchestrator
{
    [Function("ApprovalOrchestrator")]
    public static async Task Run(
        [OrchestrationTrigger] TaskOrchestrationContext ctx)
```

```
    {
        var order = ctx.GetInput<Order>();
        await ctx.CallActivityAsync("FraudCheck", order);

        if (order.Total > 100000m)
        {
            await ctx.CallActivityAsync(
                "NotifyApprover",
                new ApprovalNotificationRequest(order, ctx.InstanceId));

            var approval = await ctx.WaitForExternalEvent<ApprovalResult>("
            ApprovalResult");

            if (!string.Equals(approval.Decision, "Approved",
            StringComparison.OrdinalIgnoreCase))
            {
                throw new InvalidOperationException("Order rejected by
                approver");
            }
        }
        await ctx.CallActivityAsync("ERPRegistration", order);
    }
}
```

Models/ApprovalResult.cs

```
namespace OrderProcessor;

public sealed record ApprovalResult(
    string OrderId,
    string Decision,
    string Approver);
```

Models/ApprovalNotificationRequest.cs

```
namespace OrderProcessor;

public sealed record ApprovalNotificationRequest(
    Order Order,
    string InstanceId);
```

Models/ApprovalAudit.cs

```
namespace OrderProcessor;

public sealed record ApprovalAudit
{
    public string OrderId { get; init; } = string.Empty;
    public string Approver { get; init; } = string.Empty;
    public string Decision { get; init; } = string.Empty;
    public DateTime Timestamp { get; init; }
}
```

Models/ApprovalDecisionRequest.cs

```
namespace OrderProcessor;

public sealed record ApprovalDecisionRequest(
    string OrderId,
    string Decision);
```

This is a real workflow addition because it changes the path an order can take through the system. The orchestration now contains a durable approval checkpoint. Orders below the threshold proceed automatically. Orders above it pause until an explicit decision arrives.

Real Project Update: Notifying the Approver

If the workflow is going to pause for a human decision, the platform also needs a concrete way to notify the person responsible. In `OrderProcessor`, that notification belongs in an activity rather than in the orchestrator itself because it is a side effect and should remain outside orchestration replay logic.

Functions/NotifyApprover.cs

```
using SendGrid;
using SendGrid.Helpers.Mail;
using Microsoft.Azure.Functions.Worker;

namespace OrderProcessor;

public static class NotifyApprover
```

```
{
    [Function("NotifyApprover")]
    public static async Task Run([ActivityTrigger] ApprovalNotification
    Request request)
    {
        var order = request.Order;
        var instanceId = request.InstanceId;

        var client = new SendGridClient(Environment.GetEnvironmentVariable(
        "SendGridApiKey"));

        var msg = new SendGridMessage
        {
            From = new EmailAddress("orders@anywebsitename.com"),
            Subject = $"Approval needed for Order {order.Id}",
            HtmlContent =
                $"<p>Order {order.Id} requires approval.</p>" +
                $"<p><a href='https://orders.approval.com/orders/
                {instanceId}/approval'>Open approval</a></p>"
        };

        msg.AddTo("approver@anywebsitename.com");
        await client.SendEmailAsync(msg);
    }
}
```

This should be treated as a real project update if the chapter is presenting email as the chosen approval channel for the sample system. The important pattern is not SendGrid specifically. The important pattern is that notification is a workflow side effect handled by an activity.

Example Approval Channels

The notification channel does **not** have to be email. Depending on the organization, the approval experience could just as reasonably live in a Teams message, a back-office dashboard, or a dedicated approval portal. The architectural point is the same in every case: the orchestration pauses, and some external channel gives a human a way to respond.

So this part should be read as a **pattern example**, not as a required additional project file. Email is one implementation option. Teams or a custom approval UI would be equally valid choices depending on the system.

Real Project Update: Receiving the Approval Callback

Once the approver acts, the workflow needs an API boundary that can validate and receive that response, then raise the external event back into the orchestration. That callback endpoint is a genuine part of the `OrderProcessor` sample because it closes the loop between the paused workflow and the external human decision.

Functions/ApprovalCallback.cs

```
using System.Net;
using System.Text.Json;
using Microsoft.Azure.Cosmos;
using Microsoft.Azure.Functions.Worker;
using Microsoft.Azure.Functions.Worker.Http;
using Microsoft.DurableTask.Client;
using OrderProcessor.Security;

namespace OrderProcessor;

public sealed class ApprovalCallback
{
    private readonly Container _approvalsContainer;
    private readonly ITokenValidator _tokenValidator;

    public ApprovalCallback(
        CosmosClient cosmosClient,
        ITokenValidator tokenValidator)
    {
        _approvalsContainer = cosmosClient.GetContainer("orderdb", "approvals");
        _tokenValidator = tokenValidator;
    }

    [Function("ApprovalCallback")]
    public async Task<HttpResponseData> Run(
        [HttpTrigger(AuthorizationLevel.Anonymous, "post", Route = "orders/
        {instanceId}/approval")]
```

```
    HttpRequestData req,
    [DurableClient] DurableTaskClient client,
    string instanceId,
    CancellationToken stopToken)
{
    var bearerToken = req.GetBearerToken();

    if (string.IsNullOrWhiteSpace(bearerToken))
    {
        var unauthorized = req.CreateResponse(HttpStatusCode.
        Unauthorized);
        await unauthorized.WriteStringAsync("Missing bearer token.",
        stopToken);
        return unauthorized;
    }

    var principal = await _tokenValidator.ValidateAsync(bearerToken,
    stopToken);

    if (principal is null)
    {
        var unauthorized = req.CreateResponse(HttpStatusCode.
        Unauthorized);
        await unauthorized.WriteStringAsync("Invalid or expired
        token.", stopToken);
        return unauthorized;
    }

    var payload = await JsonSerializer.DeserializeAsync<ApprovalDecisio
    nRequest>(req.Body, cancellationToken: stopToken);

    if (payload is null || string.IsNullOrWhiteSpace(payload.OrderId))
    {
        var bad = req.CreateResponse(HttpStatusCode.BadRequest);
        await bad.WriteStringAsync("Invalid approval payload.",
        stopToken);
        return bad;
    }
```

```
        var result = new ApprovalResult(
            payload.OrderId,
            payload.Decision,
            principal.GetUserName());

        await client.RaiseEventAsync(instanceId, "ApprovalResult", result,
        cancellationToken: stopToken);

        await _approvalsContainer.CreateItemAsync(
            new ApprovalAudit
            {
                OrderId = result.OrderId,
                Approver = result.Approver,
                Decision = result.Decision,
                Timestamp = DateTime.UtcNow
            },
            new PartitionKey(result.OrderId),
            cancellationToken: stopToken);

        return req.CreateResponse(HttpStatusCode.Accepted);
    }
}
```

This is a real project addition because the orchestration cannot resume without a concrete event-raising boundary. It also keeps the architecture consistent with the rest of the book: external interaction arrives through an explicit API surface rather than through hidden state mutation.

Example Timeout and Escalation Pattern

Approvals should not wait forever. In a real business workflow, a manual decision often needs a timeout and an escalation path. Durable Functions supports that naturally through timers and `Task.WhenAny`, which makes it possible to race the approval event against a timeout.

This is best presented as an **example pattern** because different organizations will choose different escalation rules, time windows, and destinations.

Example timeout and escalation pattern

```
using var cts = new CancellationTokenSource();

var approvalTask = context.WaitForExternalEvent<ApprovalResult>
("ApprovalResult");
var timeoutTask = context.CreateTimer(
    context.CurrentUtcDateTime.AddHours(24),
    cts.Token);

var winner = await Task.WhenAny(approvalTask, timeoutTask);

if (winner == timeoutTask)
{
    throw new TimeoutException("Approval not received in time");
}
else
{
    cts.Cancel();
}
```

This should be understood as the pattern, not as "the project must always use 24 hours and throw this exact exception." The architectural lesson is that human-in-the-loop workflows need explicit timeout behavior rather than waiting indefinitely.

Real Project Update: Auditing Approval Decisions

Human decisions are one of the clearest places where audit matters. If a person approves or rejects a workflow step, the platform should be able to answer who acted, what they decided, and when they did it. In `OrderProcessor`, that belongs in the same broader audit story already established earlier in the book.

In the sample, the approval audit is written directly inside `ApprovalCallback.cs` when the callback payload is accepted and the external event is raised back into the orchestration. That keeps the audit write on the same boundary where the human decision enters the system, and it ensures the platform records who acted, what they decided, and when the decision was received.

This is a real project concern, not just an example. If the workflow contains human approvals, those approvals should be auditable.

Why This Scales Well

One of the strongest aspects of this pattern is that it still scales cleanly even though human beings are involved. A paused Durable Functions orchestration does not sit in memory consuming compute the way a naive synchronous design would. Its state is checkpointed in storage, and it can remain paused for minutes, hours, or longer while thousands of other workflows continue independently. That means `OrderProcessor` can support high approval volumes without turning manual review into a platform bottleneck at the compute layer. The true bottleneck becomes the business process itself, which is exactly where it belongs. The platform's job is to wait reliably, resume safely, and record what happened.

Applying Human-in-the-Loop Design to OrderProcessor

Taken together, these changes make `OrderProcessor` more realistic as an enterprise workflow platform. Not every order has to be treated the same way. The system can now distinguish between normal cases that proceed automatically and edge cases that require human judgment. More importantly, it can do that without stepping outside the same durable, event-driven workflow model used elsewhere in the architecture.

That is the central value of this section. Human involvement has not been treated as an exception to automation. It has been absorbed into the workflow design itself. That keeps the system consistent, auditable, and resilient even when a business process cannot be fully automated.

Project Addition: Human-in-the-Loop Flow for OrderProcessor

This section extends `OrderProcessor` with a durable approval flow for high-value or flagged orders. The platform now includes an approval-aware orchestrator, an activity that notifies an approver, a callback endpoint that raises the approval result back into the workflow, and an audit path for recording approval decisions. Timeout and escalation behavior can then be layered on as needed using the same Durable Functions primitives.

From this point on, `OrderProcessor` is no longer limited to fully automated workflows. It can pause for human judgment, resume safely when a decision arrives, and keep a durable audit trail of the interaction without compromising the broader event-driven architecture.

Case Study: Integrating External APIs and Long-Running Tasks

Distributed systems rarely live in isolation. By this point, `OrderProcessor` already depends on external capabilities such as ERP, fraud, and tax services. In many enterprise environments, those integrations do not behave like simple request-response APIs that return in a fraction of a second. They may accept work asynchronously, respond with a job identifier, and complete much later through a callback or status update. Some take minutes. Some take hours. Some are unreliable enough that the platform must assume partial failure from the outset. That shifts the architectural problem from how to call an API to how to integrate with it without breaking the scalability and resilience model of the rest of the system.

That is what makes long-running integrations such a useful case study. A naive design would call the partner API and block while waiting for completion. That works poorly in a serverless platform because it wastes compute, risks timeouts, and couples the platform directly to an external service's behavior. A better design keeps the workflow durable and asynchronous. In `OrderProcessor`, that means starting the external job, persisting enough state to track it, and then letting the orchestration wait for the eventual result. The workflow remains alive, but it does not need to stay actively running while the partner system catches up.

Why Long-Running External APIs Are Difficult

Serverless systems are excellent at short, event-driven units of work. They are much less well suited to holding open long-running synchronous calls. Azure Functions plans have execution limits, external dependencies may be slow or inconsistent, and long waits consume resources that the platform could otherwise use for useful work. Even worse, some external APIs simply do not support immediate completion. They may acknowledge receipt, return a job ID, and expect the caller to poll later or accept a callback when the work is done.

For OrderProcessor, that means the correct architectural unit is not a single long HTTP call. It is a multi-step integration pattern: start the work, persist the tracking state, wait durably, and then resume when the external system has something meaningful to say. That aligns much better with the durable workflow model already established throughout the book. To support callback-based resumption cleanly, the sample also stores a small tracking record that maps the partner job ID to the Durable Functions instance ID. That allows the callback endpoint to look up the correct orchestration instance and raise the completion event against the right workflow.

Choosing the Primary Integration Model for OrderProcessor

There are several valid ways to model long-running integrations. The cleanest option is an asynchronous API with callbacks. In that model, OrderProcessor starts the external job, receives a job identifier immediately, and then waits for the partner system to call back when the work is complete. Durable Functions fits this naturally because the orchestration can pause without consuming active compute and resume only when the callback event arrives.

That is the model this section treats as the real OrderProcessor project update. Polling is still valuable, but it is presented as a fallback pattern for partners that do not support callbacks. You should not think both approaches must be implemented simultaneously in the sample.

Real Project Update: Models for External Job Tracking

Because the workflow needs to pass the Durable instance ID into the start step and later map the partner job ID back to that instance, the sample needs a few small supporting models.

Models/StartExternalJobRequest.cs

```
namespace OrderProcessor;

public sealed record StartExternalJobRequest(
    Order Order,
    string InstanceId);
```

Models/ExternalJobTracking.cs

```
namespace OrderProcessor;

public sealed record ExternalJobTracking
{
    public string Id { get; init; } = string.Empty;
    public string JobId { get; init; } = string.Empty;
    public string InstanceId { get; init; } = string.Empty;
    public string OrderId { get; init; } = string.Empty;
    public DateTime CreatedUtc { get; init; }
}
```

Models/JobResponse.cs

```
namespace OrderProcessor;

public sealed record JobResponse(
    string Id);
```

Models/JobResult.cs

```
namespace OrderProcessor;

public sealed record JobResult(
    string Status);
```

These are small, but they make the callback-based flow explicit and durable rather than leaving the orchestration to guess how partner job state maps back into its own runtime state.

Real Project Update: Orchestration for an Async External Job

The orchestration needs to do three things. It needs to start the external job, wait durably for the result, and then continue the workflow only if the partner reports success.

Orchestrations/ExternalApiOrchestrator.cs

```
using Microsoft.Azure.Functions.Worker;
using Microsoft.DurableTask;
```

```
namespace OrderProcessor;

public static class ExternalApiOrchestrator
{
    [Function("ExternalApiOrchestrator")]
    public static async Task Run(
        [OrchestrationTrigger] TaskOrchestrationContext context)
    {
        var order = context.GetInput<Order>()
            ?? throw new InvalidOperationException("Order input is
            required.");

        var request = new StartExternalJobRequest(order, context.
        InstanceId);

        var jobId = await context.CallActivityAsync<string>(
            "StartExternalJob",
            request);

        var result = await context.WaitForExternalEvent<string>($"JobResu
        lt_{jobId}");

        if (!string.Equals(result, "Success", StringComparison.
        OrdinalIgnoreCase))
        {
            throw new InvalidOperationException("External job failed");
        }

        await context.CallActivityAsync("ContinueWorkflow", order);
    }
}
```

This is a real project change because it gives `OrderProcessor` a durable integration path for partner systems that complete asynchronously. The orchestration is no longer forced to pretend the external service behaves like a fast synchronous dependency.

Real Project Update: Starting the External Job

The orchestration delegates the actual API call to an activity, which keeps the external side effect outside replay-sensitive orchestration code. The activity submits the work, applies retry logic around transient failure, persists the tracking record, and returns the job identifier that the workflow will wait on.

Functions/StartExternalJob.cs

```
using System.Net.Http.Json;
using Microsoft.Azure.Cosmos;
using Microsoft.Azure.Functions.Worker;
using Polly;

namespace OrderProcessor;

public sealed class StartExternalJob
{
    private readonly HttpClient _httpClient;
    private readonly Container _trackingContainer;

    public StartExternalJob(
        IHttpClientFactory httpClientFactory,
        CosmosClient cosmosClient)
    {
        _httpClient = httpClientFactory.CreateClient("PartnerApi");
        _trackingContainer = cosmosClient.GetContainer("orderdb",
        "external-jobs");
    }

    [Function("StartExternalJob")]
    public async Task<string> Run(
        [ActivityTrigger] StartExternalJobRequest request,
        FunctionContext ctx)
    {
        var logger = ctx.GetLogger("StartExternalJob");

        var policy = Policy
            .Handle<HttpRequestException>()
```

```
            .OrResult<HttpResponseMessage>(r => !r.IsSuccessStatusCode)
            .WaitAndRetryAsync(
                3,
                retry => TimeSpan.FromSeconds(Math.Pow(2, retry)));

        var response = await policy.ExecuteAsync(() =>
            _httpClient.PostAsJsonAsync("jobs", request.Order));

        response.EnsureSuccessStatusCode();

        var job = await response.Content.ReadFromJsonAsync<JobResponse>()
            ?? throw new InvalidOperationException("Partner API did not
            return a job response.");

        await _trackingContainer.CreateItemAsync(
            new ExternalJobTracking
            {
                Id = job.Id,
                JobId = job.Id,
                InstanceId = request.InstanceId,
                OrderId = request.Order.Id,
                CreatedUtc = DateTime.UtcNow
            },
            new PartitionKey(job.Id));

        logger.LogInformation(
            "External job {JobId} started for tenant {TenantId} at {Time}",
            job.Id,
            request.Order.TenantId,
            DateTime.UtcNow);

        return job.Id;
    }
}
```

This should be treated as a real project addition because the callback-based model depends on it. It keeps the external submission, retry behavior, tracking, and initial telemetry together at the same integration boundary.

Real Project Update: Receiving the External Callback

If the partner API supports callbacks, `OrderProcessor` needs a concrete API endpoint that can receive the completion notification, look up the matching Durable instance, and raise the correct external event back into the orchestration. That is the other half of the callback pattern.

Functions/ExternalJobCallback.cs

```
using System.Net;
using System.Text.Json;
using Microsoft.Azure.Cosmos;
using Microsoft.Azure.Functions.Worker;
using Microsoft.Azure.Functions.Worker.Http;
using Microsoft.DurableTask.Client;

namespace OrderProcessor;

public sealed class ExternalJobCallback
{
    private readonly Container _trackingContainer;

    public ExternalJobCallback(CosmosClient cosmosClient)
    {
        _trackingContainer = cosmosClient.GetContainer("orderdb",
        "external-jobs");
    }

    [Function("ExternalJobCallback")]
    public async Task<HttpResponseData> Run(
        [HttpTrigger(AuthorizationLevel.Function, "post", Route = "jobs/
        {jobId}/callback")]
        HttpRequestData req,
        [DurableClient] DurableTaskClient client,
        string jobId)
    {
        var payload = await JsonSerializer.
        DeserializeAsync<JobResult>(req.Body);
```

```
        if (payload is null)
        {
            var bad = req.CreateResponse(HttpStatusCode.BadRequest);
            await bad.WriteStringAsync("Invalid callback payload.");
            return bad;
        }

        var tracking = await _trackingContainer.ReadItemAsync<ExternalJob
        Tracking>(
            jobId,
            new PartitionKey(jobId));

        await client.RaiseEventAsync(
            tracking.Resource.InstanceId,
            $"JobResult_{jobId}",
            payload.Status);

        var response = req.CreateResponse(HttpStatusCode.OK);
        await response.WriteStringAsync("Callback received");
        return response;
    }
}
```

This is also a genuine project addition because without it the callback-based workflow cannot resume. It closes the loop between the external system and the paused orchestration.

Program.cs Addition for the Partner API Client

Because `StartExternalJob.cs` now uses `IHttpClientFactory`, the sample also needs a named client registration.

Program.cs addition

```
builder.Services.AddHttpClient("PartnerApi", client =>
{
    client.BaseAddress = new Uri("https://partner.com/");
});
```

Example Fallback Pattern: Polling a Status Endpoint

Not every partner supports callbacks. Some expose only a status endpoint and expect the client to poll for completion. That is still compatible with Durable Functions, but it should be presented as an example fallback pattern, not as a second mandatory integration path for the same sample implementation.

Example polling fallback

```
while (true)
{
    var status = await context.CallActivityAsync<string>("CheckStat
    us", jobId);

    if (status == "Completed")
    {
        break;
    }

    var nextCheck = context.CurrentUtcDateTime.AddHours(1);
    await context.CreateTimer(nextCheck, CancellationToken.None);
}
```

The important lesson is that Durable Functions can wait efficiently between polls instead of spinning or sleeping wastefully. The exact polling interval is a policy decision, not a fixed project rule.

Example Combination Pattern: Human Approval Plus External Processing

Some long-running integrations are not purely technical. A document verification service, for example, may return a manual-review state that requires a person to approve the case before the platform is allowed to continue. That is also a valid pattern, but it should be understood as a design example that combines the section "Case Study: Human-in-the-Loop Workflows" with this section rather than as an additional required file to add right now.

Example human approval plus external processing

```
var approval = await context.WaitForExternalEvent<string>("HumanApproval");

if (approval == "Approved")
{
    await context.CallActivityAsync("NotifyPartner", order);
}
else
{
    throw new InvalidOperationException("Rejected during verification");
}
```

This is useful because it shows how the external integration and human-in-the-loop patterns can be composed without changing the overall workflow model.

Real Project Update: Observability for External Jobs

Because these integrations are asynchronous and potentially long-running, they need to be visible in telemetry. The platform should be able to answer which external jobs started, which are still pending, which have succeeded, and which have failed. That is not optional in practice. Without it, the workflow becomes much harder to operate.

In the sample, job-start telemetry is emitted directly from `StartExternalJob.cs` after the tracking record is written. That keeps the submission, tracking, and observability concerns together at the same integration boundary.

That then enables queries such as

Example Kusto query

```
traces
| where customDimensions.JobId != ""
| summarize count() by customDimensions.Status
```

The query is an example, but the act of emitting telemetry for job start and state is a real project concern.

Example Architectural Option: Decoupling Submission Through a Queue

A further improvement is to decouple `OrderProcessor` from the partner API even more aggressively by introducing a queue between the order workflow and the external submission worker. That way the platform can accept the order, queue the integration work, and let a dedicated worker deal with the partner system later. This is a strong pattern, but in this chapter it is better presented as an architectural option rather than as another mandatory cumulative project change.

Example Decoupling Option

Orders can be written to a Service Bus queue or topic, and then a dedicated worker Function can submit them to the partner API. The orchestration still waits for the callback or status update, but the system is now less tightly coupled to the immediate availability of the partner endpoint.

That option is worth discussing because it shows how the integration can evolve further if the partner becomes especially unreliable or slow.

Applying Long-Running Integration Design to OrderProcessor

Taken together, these changes give `OrderProcessor` a much more realistic model for interacting with partner APIs that do not finish immediately. The workflow can now start external work asynchronously, pause durably while the partner processes it, and resume only when a real completion signal arrives. Retry logic hardens the start path. Telemetry makes job progress visible. Callback endpoints make the orchestration resumable without polling wastefully in the common case.

That is the main architectural value of this section. `OrderProcessor` no longer assumes every dependency behaves like a quick HTTP request. It now treats long-running external work as a first-class workflow concern, which is exactly what large distributed systems have to do in practice.

Project Addition: Long-Running External API Integration for OrderProcessor

This section extends `OrderProcessor` with a durable callback-based model for long-running external integrations. The platform now includes an external API orchestrator, an activity that starts partner jobs asynchronously, a tracking record that maps partner job IDs back to Durable Functions instance IDs, a callback endpoint that resumes the paused workflow when a result arrives, retry logic around the initial API submission, and telemetry that makes job state visible for operations and audits.

From this point on, `OrderProcessor` can integrate with partner systems that complete work minutes, hours, or days later without breaking the event-driven, serverless architecture established in the rest of the book.

Case Study: Advanced Resilience Patterns

Earlier chapters already introduced retries, dead-letter queues, durable orchestration, deployment safety, and operational playbooks. Those patterns give `OrderProcessor` a strong base, but large-scale distributed systems often need more than simple retry logic. When failures ripple across several services, the goal is no longer just to try again and hope the dependency recovers. The platform needs ways to contain failure, isolate stressed parts of the system, undo partial work when consistency matters, and keep useful parts of the workflow moving even when one dependency is unhealthy.

That is what makes advanced resilience patterns worth treating as a case study in their own right. In a real enterprise system, resilience is not measured only by uptime. It is measured by how well the system behaves under stress. If ERP is down, does the whole workflow stop, or does only the ERP-dependent path degrade? If one stage backs up, does it block unrelated work, or is the pressure contained? If a workflow succeeds halfway and then fails, does the system stay consistent? In `OrderProcessor`, these questions push the platform beyond basic retries into patterns such as bulkheads, resilient HTTP boundaries, sagas, dead-letter reprocessing, and graceful degradation.

Why Resilience Matters Beyond Uptime

Availability percentages often make resilience sound binary, as though a system is either up or down. In practice, distributed systems fail more gradually than that. A service may respond, but too slowly. A dependency may fail only for one category of work. A queue may continue to accept messages while one downstream stage can no longer keep up. If the architecture treats every dependency as equally central and every failure as equally global, a localized issue can grow into a system-wide problem far too easily.

For `OrderProcessor`, resilience therefore means keeping failure scoped. A backlog in ERP should not stop fraud checks from continuing. A supplier integration failure should not leave the system in an inconsistent state. A noisy tenant should not drown out everyone else. These are not edge concerns. They are the difference between a system that merely works in the happy path and one that remains usable under real operational pressure.

Isolating Pressure with Bulkheads

One of the most useful resilience ideas is the bulkhead pattern. The idea is simple: do not let every kind of work share exactly the same channel, because a failure or backlog in one area can then spill into all the others. In `OrderProcessor`, a practical version of that pattern is to separate the queues used for different workflow stages. If ERP traffic becomes slow or blocked, fraud and tax processing should still have their own path through the system.

This is a real architectural extension to the sample because it changes how work is partitioned operationally.

infra/servicebus-stage-queues.bicep

```
resource fraudQueue 'Microsoft.ServiceBus/namespaces/queues@2022-10-01-
preview' = {
  name: 'fraud-queue'
  properties: {
    maxDeliveryCount: 5
  }
}

resource taxQueue 'Microsoft.ServiceBus/namespaces/queues@2022-10-01-
preview' = {
  name: 'tax-queue'
  properties: {
```

```
    maxDeliveryCount: 5
  }
}

resource erpQueue 'Microsoft.ServiceBus/namespaces/queues@2022-10-01-
preview' = {
  name: 'erp-queue'
  properties: {
    maxDeliveryCount: 5
  }
}
```

The important lesson is not the exact queue names. It is that stage-specific workloads are no longer sharing one general-purpose path. That gives the platform more control over throughput, retry pressure, and failure isolation.

Real Project Update: Resilient HTTP Boundaries for ERP Integration

Retries are useful when a dependency is suffering short-lived transient failures. They are harmful when the dependency is already struggling and the platform keeps hammering it repeatedly. That is where a circuit breaker becomes valuable. In the sample, the ERP integration now takes the modern .NET approach and configures HTTP resilience at the named `HttpClient` boundary rather than through inline Polly policy code inside the Function itself.

Program.cs addition

```
using Microsoft.Extensions.Http.Resilience;

builder.Services.AddHttpClient("ErpApi", client =>
{
    client.BaseAddress = new Uri("https://erp.anywebsitename.com/");
})
.AddStandardResilienceHandler();
```

This keeps retry, timeout, and circuit-breaker behavior in one place. The ERP registration path itself can then stay focused on business logic.

Inside Functions/ERPRegistration.cs

```
var response = await _httpClient.PostAsJsonAsync("/api/orders", order);
response.EnsureSuccessStatusCode();
```

The architectural lesson is still the same. `OrderProcessor` needs a circuit breaker on the ERP boundary so that repeated downstream failure does not turn into a storm of repeated calls. The difference is that the implementation now follows the current Microsoft `HttpClient` resilience model instead of hand-written Polly policy chains.

Preserving Consistency with Saga Compensation

One of the hardest resilience problems appears when the workflow succeeds partially and then fails later. If fraud passes, tax is calculated, and ERP registration succeeds, but a later supplier step fails, the system may already have changed state in a downstream system that now needs to be undone. That is where saga-style compensation becomes useful. Instead of pretending distributed operations are one transaction, the workflow accepts that they are separate steps and provides compensating actions when later steps fail.

In `OrderProcessor`, that makes sense as a real workflow addition rather than just a theoretical pattern.

Orchestrations/SagaOrchestrator.cs

```
using System;
using Microsoft.Azure.Functions.Worker;
using Microsoft.DurableTask;

namespace OrderProcessor;

public static class SagaOrchestrator
{
    [Function("SagaOrchestrator")]
    public static async Task Run(
        [OrchestrationTrigger] TaskOrchestrationContext context)
    {
        var order = context.GetInput<Order>();

        try
```

```
        {
            await context.CallActivityAsync("FraudCheck", order);
            await context.CallActivityAsync("TaxCalculation", order);
            await context.CallActivityAsync("ERPRegistration", order);
            await context.CallActivityAsync("SupplierIntegration", order);
        }
        catch (Exception)
        {
            await context.CallActivityAsync("CompensateERP", order);
            throw;
        }
    }
}
```

The corresponding compensation action then becomes part of the project too.

Functions/CompensateERP.cs

```
using Microsoft.Azure.Functions.Worker;

namespace OrderProcessor;

public sealed class CompensateERP
{
    private readonly HttpClient _httpClient;

    public CompensateERP(IHttpClientFactory httpClientFactory)
    {
        _httpClient = httpClientFactory.CreateClient("ErpApi");
    }

    [Function("CompensateERP")]
    public async Task Run([ActivityTrigger] Order order)
    {
        await _httpClient.DeleteAsync($"/api/orders/{order.Id}");
    }
}
```

This is a good example of resilience being about correctness, not just availability. The system is not merely trying to keep running. It is trying to keep state across systems consistent even when the later stages of the workflow fail.

Recovering from Dead-Lettered Work

Retries and compensation still will not solve every problem. Some messages will fail repeatedly and end up in a dead-letter queue. At that point, resilience is no longer just about automatic retry. It is about recoverability. The team needs a controlled way to inspect failed work, fix the root cause, and replay the message safely.

That replay path is a real operational addition to `OrderProcessor`, not just an example pattern.

Functions/ReprocessDeadLetters.cs

```
using System.Text.Json;
using Azure.Messaging.ServiceBus;
using Microsoft.Azure.Functions.Worker;

namespace OrderProcessor;

public sealed class ReprocessDeadLetters
{
    private readonly ServiceBusSender _erpQueueSender;

    public ReprocessDeadLetters(ServiceBusClient serviceBusClient)
    {
        _erpQueueSender = serviceBusClient.CreateSender("erp-queue");
    }

    [Function("ReprocessDeadLetters")]
    public async Task Run(
        [ServiceBusTrigger("erp-queue/$DeadLetterQueue", Connection =
        "ServiceBusConnection")]
        string msg)
    {
        var order = JsonSerializer.Deserialize<Order>(msg);

        if (order is null)
```

```
        {
            return;
        }

        await _erpQueueSender.SendMessageAsync(
            new ServiceBusMessage(JsonSerializer.Serialize(order)));
    }
}
```

Program.cs addition required by ReprocessDeadLetters.cs

```
builder.Services.AddSingleton(sp =>
{
    var connectionString = builder.Configuration["ServiceBusConnection"]
        ?? throw new InvalidOperationException("Missing
        ServiceBusConnection");

    return new ServiceBusClient(connectionString);
});
```

The point here is not that every dead-letter message should be replayed automatically without thought. It is that the platform has a deliberate recovery path rather than leaving failed work trapped in a dead-letter queue forever.

Keeping the Workflow Useful Through Graceful Degradation

One of the strongest resilience choices a system can make is not to insist that every dependency must succeed before anything useful can happen. In some cases, the better design is to let the workflow continue partially, mark the missing step clearly, and recover that missing work later. For `OrderProcessor`, ERP is once again a good example. If ERP is unavailable, the system may still be able to continue with customer-facing or downstream steps while recording that the order is pending ERP reconciliation.

This is a second excerpt from the same ERP registration path. Even with a resilient HTTP client and a circuit breaker in place, there will still be cases where ERP cannot be reached successfully. In those cases, the workflow can degrade gracefully by recording the order as pending ERP rather than failing the entire process immediately.

Inside Functions/ERPRegistration.cs

```
if (!await ErpService.TryRegisterAsync(order))
{
    await cosmosContainer.CreateItemAsync(new PendingErpOrder(order));

    logger.LogWarning(
        "Order {Id} marked pending ERP",
        order.Id);
}
```

This changes the business behavior of the platform. Instead of treating an ERP outage as total workflow failure, OrderProcessor can degrade gracefully and recover later.

Example Operational Option: Per-Tenant Rate Limits

Not every resilience control belongs inside the application code. Some belong at the platform boundary. Per-tenant quotas through API Management are a good example. They help stop noisy tenants from overwhelming shared infrastructure, but they are better understood here as an operational design option rather than as a required project file for the sample.

Example API Management rate-limit policy

```
{
  "policies": {
    "inbound": [
      {
        "rate-limit": {
          "calls": 100,
          "renewal-period": 60,
          "key": "tenant-id"
        }
      }
    ]
  }
}
```

Applying Advanced Resilience Patterns to OrderProcessor

Taken together, these patterns make `OrderProcessor` far more robust under stress. Bulkheads stop one overloaded stage from suffocating the rest of the workflow. Resilient HTTP boundaries stop unhealthy downstream services from being hammered repeatedly. Saga compensation keeps cross-system state aligned when later steps fail. Dead-letter reprocessing makes recovery deliberate rather than ad hoc. Graceful degradation allows useful work to continue even when one important dependency is unavailable.

That is the deeper lesson of this section. Resilience is not one pattern, and it is not one retry policy. It is a collection of design choices that make failure smaller, recovery faster, and the system more predictable under real operational pressure.

Project Addition: Advanced Resilience Patterns for OrderProcessor

This section extends `OrderProcessor` with stronger resilience controls across the workflow. Stage-specific queues introduce bulkhead isolation, ERP integration is protected through a resilient named `HttpClient`, saga orchestration adds compensation for partial cross-system failure, dead-lettered ERP work can now be replayed deliberately, and the ERP path can degrade gracefully by marking orders as pending rather than blocking everything outright. Tenant-level throttling remains a useful operational option at the platform boundary rather than a mandatory in-repo implementation.

From this point on, `OrderProcessor` is no longer relying only on retries and durable state to survive trouble. It now has multiple ways to contain, absorb, and recover from failure without turning every dependency issue into a platform-wide incident.

Case Study: Cross-Region Data and Compliance

Modern distributed systems rarely operate in only one geography. As soon as a platform serves customers in multiple regions, the architecture has to balance performance, resilience, and legal constraints at the same time. `OrderProcessor` has already grown into a platform concerned with orchestration, events, multi-tenancy, human approvals, and operational resilience. Expanding that platform across regions introduces another layer of complexity. It is no longer enough to decide where the application runs. The system must also decide where each tenant's data is allowed to live, where it may replicate, where secrets are stored, where logs are retained, and where failover is legally permitted.

That is what makes cross-region design such an important case study. The challenge is not simply to deploy the same app in more than one Azure region. The challenge is to do that without violating data residency requirements or accidentally moving sensitive information into jurisdictions where it should not exist. For `OrderProcessor`, the key idea is that geography must become part of the architecture in the same way that tenant identity became part of the architecture in the previous section. Region is not just deployment metadata. It is an input into storage design, orchestration routing, operational logging, and disaster recovery.

Why Cross-region Compliance Is Difficult

Cross-region architecture introduces pressure from several directions at once. Customers want lower latency and stronger resilience. Regulators may require that personal data never leave a given jurisdiction. Disaster recovery plans may want another region available immediately, while legal policy may restrict which other region is allowed. Replication, failover, audit retention, and analytics all become more complex because the platform cannot assume that "more copies in more places" is always the right answer.

For `OrderProcessor`, that means the platform needs an explicit residency model rather than one implied by default Azure behavior. An EU tenant may be allowed to operate only within EU regions. A US tenant may need to remain inside US-hosted resources. A multinational tenant may require a more complicated arrangement in which sensitive data stays regional but limited metadata is shared more broadly. The architecture has to enforce those rules deliberately, not just document them.

Defining Region-Aware Tenant Boundaries

The most important starting point is to define which geographies each tenant is allowed to use. In practice, that becomes part of the platform contract. An EU tenant may be restricted to North Europe and West Europe. A US tenant may use the East US and

Central US. A global tenant may need a negotiated exception model rather than a shared default. That policy should influence both code and infrastructure. In `OrderProcessor`, it makes sense to include regional identity directly in the order model so that workflows and storage access can make routing decisions explicitly rather than inferring geography indirectly.

Models/Order.cs

```
namespace OrderProcessor;

public record Order(
    string Id,
    string TenantId,
    string Region,
    string CustomerId,
    decimal Total);
```

This is a real project evolution because geography is now part of the business object the workflow operates on. The system is no longer only tenant-aware. It is tenant- and region-aware.

Region-Specific Data Stores

Once a region is explicit in the model, the storage layer should reflect it. A clean approach for `OrderProcessor` is to provision separate Cosmos DB accounts, Blob Storage accounts, and Key Vaults per geography rather than trying to solve all residency concerns inside one global resource. That keeps the compliance boundary visible in infrastructure as well as in application logic.

A representative EU Cosmos deployment:

infra/cosmos-eu.bicep

```
resource cosmos 'Microsoft.DocumentDB/databaseAccounts@2022-05-15' = {
  name: 'opcosmos-eu'
  location: 'northeurope'
  properties: {
    locations: [
      {
        locationName: 'northeurope'
```

```
        failoverPriority: 0
      }
      {
        locationName: 'westeurope'
        failoverPriority: 1
      }
    ]
    enableAutomaticFailover: true
  }
}
```

The architectural lesson is that the legal boundary is embedded in the deployment itself. No US region exists in this EU data-store definition, so cross-jurisdiction replication cannot happen accidentally through a misconfigured failover setting later.

Real Project Update: Region-Aware Storage Routing

Once the infrastructure is separated by region, the application needs a concrete routing rule so that orders are written only to the correct data store. This is a real project concern, not just an example, because the application boundary has to enforce the regional decision the infrastructure makes possible.

Infrastructure/RegionalOrderRepository.cs

```
using Microsoft.Azure.Cosmos;

namespace OrderProcessor;

public sealed class RegionalOrderRepository
{
    private readonly Container _cosmosEuContainer;
    private readonly Container _cosmosUsContainer;

    public RegionalOrderRepository(CosmosClient cosmosEuClient,
    CosmosClient cosmosUsClient)
    {
        _cosmosEuContainer = cosmosEuClient.GetContainer("orderdb",
        "orders");
```

```
        _cosmosUsContainer = cosmosUsClient.GetContainer("orderdb",
        "orders");
    }

    public Task CreateAsync(Order order, CancellationToken stopToken =
    default)
    {
        if (order.Region == "EU")
        {
            return _cosmosEuContainer.CreateItemAsync(
                order,
                new PartitionKey(order.TenantId),
                cancellationToken: stopToken);
        }

        if (order.Region == "US")
        {
            return _cosmosUsContainer.CreateItemAsync(
                order,
                new PartitionKey(order.TenantId),
                cancellationToken: stopToken);
        }

        throw new InvalidOperationException("Unsupported region");
    }
}
```

This is intentionally direct. The important pattern is that region routing is explicit and enforced at the repository boundary. The system does not guess where data should go.

Real Project Update: Region-Aware Orchestration

The orchestration itself should also understand geography. Earlier chapters made the workflow tenant-aware. At this stage, `OrderProcessor` also needs to ensure that processing paths remain region-safe. That can mean invoking region-specific activities, using region-specific stores, or loading region-specific configuration and services.

Orchestrations/RegionAwareOrderOrchestrator.cs

```
using System;
using Microsoft.Azure.Functions.Worker;
using Microsoft.DurableTask;

namespace OrderProcessor;

public static class RegionAwareOrderOrchestrator
{
    [Function("RegionAwareOrderOrchestrator")]
    public static async Task Run(
        [OrchestrationTrigger] TaskOrchestrationContext context)
    {
        var order = context.GetInput<Order>();
        if (order.Region == "EU")
        {
            await context.CallActivityAsync("ProcessInEU", order);
        }
        else if (order.Region == "US")
        {
            await context.CallActivityAsync("ProcessInUS", order);
        }
        else
        {
            throw new InvalidOperationException("Unsupported region");
        }
    }
}
```

This should be treated as a real workflow extension if cross-region routing is part of the evolving sample. The important idea is that geography is not merely an infrastructure deployment concern. It also affects which activities and stores the workflow is allowed to touch.

Region-Specific Storage and Secrets

Residency rules do not apply only to primary business data. They also affect file storage and secrets. If `OrderProcessor` is storing uploaded files, extracted metadata, or tenant-specific credentials, those resources should be region-specific as well. A separate EU storage account and EU Key Vault make the compliance boundary much easier to preserve than a shared cross-region secret store.

A representative storage definition could look like this:

infra/storage-eu.bicep

```
resource euStorage 'Microsoft.Storage/storageAccounts@2022-09-01' = {
  name: 'opstgeu'
  location: 'northeurope'
  sku: {
    name: 'Standard_GRS'
  }
}
```

And the same principle applies to Key Vault, where separate vaults per geography keep secrets inside the same legal boundary as the rest of the tenant's data.

infra/keyvault-eu.bicep or equivalent infrastructure module for the EU jurisdiction

The exact vault definition does not need to be repeated here if the earlier infrastructure chapters already introduced Key Vault patterns. The important point is that `OrderProcessor` should not assume that one global secret store is acceptable once geography becomes a compliance boundary.

Real Project Update: Region-Specific Diagnostics and Audit Paths

Compliance is not only about where transactional data lives. It is also about where access logs and audit records go. If the platform is required to prove who accessed sensitive material in a given region, those audit logs should stay within the same jurisdiction wherever possible.

That makes diagnostic configuration a real project-level infrastructure concern.

infra/diagnostics-eu.bicep

```
resource kvDiagnostics 'Microsoft.Insights/diagnosticSettings@2021-05-01-
preview' = {
  name: 'kv-logs'
  scope: keyVault.id
  properties: {
    workspaceId: euWorkspace.id
    logs: [
      {
        category: 'AuditEvent'
        enabled: true
      }
    ]
  }
}
```

This is a real addition because it extends the compliance boundary into operations. The system is not only storing EU data in EU resources. It is also keeping audit visibility within the same jurisdiction.

Example Architectural Option: Federated Global Workflows

Some tenants will not fit neatly into one geography. A multinational customer may need operations in several regions while still requiring sensitive data to remain local. There are several valid ways to approach that, but they should be presented here as **architectural options**, not as mandatory cumulative code in the sample.

One option is a federated design, in which `OrderProcessor` is deployed separately per region and only non-sensitive metadata moves between them. Another is a data-minimization approach, where personal data stays regional but business events containing limited metadata can be published more broadly. A third option is a hybrid event model where Event Grid topics and subscribers remain region-scoped, and only carefully designed global events are allowed to cross boundaries.

These are important design ideas, but you should not interpret them as "implement all of these in the sample project now." They are there to show how the regional model can evolve for more complex customers.

Disaster Recovery Under Compliance Constraints

Cross-region failover is one of the places where good intentions can accidentally violate policy. A disaster recovery plan that says "fail to any healthy region" may be operationally attractive but legally unacceptable. For `OrderProcessor`, the disaster recovery model needs to be jurisdiction-aware. EU tenants can fail over only to other EU regions. US tenants can fail over only to other US regions. The DR story from earlier chapters still applies, but the permitted targets are now narrower.

That means geography affects not only runtime processing but also the recovery model. The architecture is not fully compliant unless the failover path is compliant too.

Applying Cross-region Compliance to OrderProcessor

Taken together, these changes turn geography into a first-class architectural concern inside `OrderProcessor`. The platform now has region-aware data models, region-specific stores, explicit routing into the correct data resources, region-aware orchestration, and region-specific audit paths. This is what makes the platform feel enterprise-ready rather than merely globally deployed.

The deeper lesson is that compliance cannot sit only in policy documents. It has to be visible in the system's structure. If region matters legally, then region has to matter architecturally too.

Project Addition: Cross-region Data and Compliance for OrderProcessor

This section extends `OrderProcessor` with region-aware data and compliance boundaries. Orders now carry regional identity, storage and secret resources can be separated by geography, repositories route data only into approved regional stores, orchestrations can enforce region-specific processing paths, and diagnostic settings keep audit visibility inside the correct jurisdiction. Broader federation patterns remain valid options for more complex global customers, but the core sample now has a concrete model for region-safe processing.

From this point on, `OrderProcessor` is also capable of respecting regional residency and compliance constraints as part of the workflow and infrastructure model itself.

Case Study: Observability at Scale

By this point, `OrderProcessor` already has the foundations of observability in place. Earlier chapters introduced distributed tracing, structured logging, metrics, dashboards, alerts, and cost awareness. Those patterns work well when the system is relatively contained. As the platform grows into a multi-tenant, multi-region service, the challenge changes. The problem is no longer just collecting telemetry. The problem becomes how to organize it so that the right teams can see the right signals without drowning the platform in cost, query latency, or compliance risk.

That is what makes observability at scale an important case study. A small system can often survive with one Application Insights resource, one dashboard, and a handful of alerts. A larger `OrderProcessor` cannot assume that model will scale cleanly. Different regions may need separate telemetry boundaries. Different tenants may need their own operational visibility. Different teams may care about different slices of the truth. The goal of this section is to show how observability can evolve from a single shared view into a structured model that still feels coherent rather than fragmented.

Why Observability Gets Harder As the Platform Grows

As systems grow, observability tends to become expensive and confusing in two different ways. First, telemetry volume rises sharply. More Functions, more orchestrations, more regions, more tenants, and more integrations all produce more traces, logs, metrics, and alerts. Second, the operational questions become more specific. The platform team wants a global view. A tenant-facing support team wants tenant-specific health and SLA information. Finance wants cost by customer. Regional compliance teams may need to ensure that logs and audit trails stay inside a legal boundary.

If all of that telemetry is dumped into one undifferentiated store, the result is usually poor query performance, unclear ownership, noisy dashboards, and rising cost. For `OrderProcessor`, the answer is not less telemetry. It is better structured. Observability needs to be layered the same way the rest of the system is layered.

A Layered Observability Model

A good large-scale observability design usually has at least three layers. The first is a global layer that shows platform-wide KPIs such as order throughput, system-wide error rate, high-level cost, and broad regional status. The second is a tenant layer that shows metrics and failures per customer, which is essential for SLA reporting, billing, and tenant support. The third is a service layer that focuses on specific parts of the system such as FraudCheck, ERP, invoicing, or logistics.

That layered model fits OrderProcessor well because it mirrors the structure the platform already has. The important thing is that each layer answers a different operational question. Global views are for platform health. Tenant views are for customer experience and cost attribution. Service views are for engineering diagnosis and optimization. Once those layers are recognized explicitly, the telemetry design becomes much easier to reason about.

Region-Aware Telemetry Segregation

Because OrderProcessor is now region-aware, observability needs to respect those same regional boundaries. If EU tenant data stays in EU-hosted data stores, the related telemetry should follow the same rule where possible. That means separate Log Analytics or monitoring workspaces per jurisdiction rather than assuming that all traces and logs can be centralized freely.

This is a real project and infrastructure concern, not just an operational preference, because compliance boundaries apply to telemetry too.

infra/monitoring-eu.bicep

```
resource euWorkspace 'Microsoft.OperationalInsights/
workspaces@2022-10-01' = {
  name: 'orderprocessor-eu-logs'
  location: 'northeurope'
  properties: {
    retentionInDays: 30
  }
}
```

infra/monitoring-us.bicep

```
resource usWorkspace 'Microsoft.OperationalInsights/
workspaces@2022-10-01' = {
  name: 'orderprocessor-us-logs'
  location: 'eastus'
```

```
  properties: {
    retentionInDays: 30
  }
}
```

The point here is not that every environment must look exactly like this. The point is that observability is now aligned with the same regional boundaries that govern the rest of the architecture.

Real Project Update: Tenant and Correlation Tagging in Telemetry

Once telemetry is region-aware, it also needs to remain tenant-aware. Earlier chapters already introduced trace and correlation concepts. At this stage, `OrderProcessor` should make sure that its logs, traces, and metrics consistently carry `TenantId` and a usable correlation or trace identifier. Without that, tenant-level dashboards and diagnosis become much harder.

A representative logging pattern:

Functions or activities handling orders

```
logger.LogInformation(
    "Order {OrderId} processed for tenant {TenantId}",
    order.Id,
    order.TenantId);
```

A correlation middleware pattern may also need to remain visible in the shared code if the platform standardizes around it:

Shared/CorrelationMiddleware.cs

(Already exists from Chapter 7)

```
using Microsoft.Azure.Functions.Worker;
using Microsoft.Extensions.Logging;

namespace OrderProcessor;
public class CorrelationMiddleware : IFunctionsWorkerMiddleware
{
```

```
    Public async Task Invoke(FunctionContext context,
    FunctionExecutionDelegate next)
    {
        var traceId = context.TraceContext.TraceParent ?? Guid.NewGuid().
        ToString();

        context.Items["TraceId"] = traceId;

        context.GetLogger("Correlation")
            .LogInformation("TraceId: {TraceId}", traceId);

        await next(context);
    }
}
```

This should be treated as a real project concern because observability at scale depends on consistent identifiers across services, regions, and tenants. The system cannot build good dashboards or reliable diagnosis paths if the telemetry shape is inconsistent.

Federated Queries Across Regional Workspaces

Once telemetry is split by region, the global operational view still needs a way to see the whole platform. That does not mean moving all telemetry into one jurisdiction. It means querying across approved workspaces in a controlled way. This is a good place to show a representative query pattern rather than another project file, because the principle matters more than one fixed implementation.

Example Federated Query Across Regions

```
union withsource=Region
(workspace("EUWorkspace").traces),
(workspace("USWorkspace").traces)
| summarize count() by Region, customDimensions.TenantId
```

This should be read as an **example operational pattern**, not as a project file to add. The important lesson is that `OrderProcessor` can build global observability views without flattening regional boundaries.

Real Project Update: Observability As Infrastructure

At scale, monitoring resources, alerts, and diagnostic settings should not be created ad hoc through the portal alone. They should become part of the infrastructure definition, just like queues, Function Apps, storage, and databases. That makes observability version-controlled, reviewable, and repeatable.

infra/alerts-order-failures.bicep

```
resource orderFailureAlert 'Microsoft.Insights/metricAlerts@2018-03-01' = {
  name: 'OrderFailureRate'
  location: 'global'
  properties: {
    severity: 2
    enabled: true
    scopes: [
      functionApp.id
    ]
    evaluationFrequency: 'PT5M'
    windowSize: 'PT15M'
    criteria: {
      allOf: [
        {
          name: 'FailureRate'
          metricName: 'FunctionsFailed'
          operator: 'GreaterThan'
          threshold: 5
          timeAggregation: 'Total'
        }
      ]
    }
    actions: [
      {
        actionGroupId: opsTeamActionGroup.id
      }
    ]
  }
}
```

This is a real infrastructure evolution because it makes the monitoring model part of the deployed platform rather than a separate undocumented layer.

Example Persona-Specific Dashboards

Not every dashboard belongs in the codebase as a fixed required artifact, because different organizations will tune them differently. Different stakeholders also need different views. A platform operations team may need throughput, failure rate, latency, and cold start information. Finance may care about cost per tenant and usage growth. Tenant-facing support may care about SLA compliance and per-tenant backlog.

These should be presented as **examples or operational options**, not as mandatory cumulative project files unless you later decide to include workbook JSON in the repo.

A tenant-facing workbook, for example, might include

- Orders per hour
- Error distribution by stage
- A simple SLA widget showing the percentage of orders completed within target latency

A finance dashboard might show

- Tenant usage volume
- Execution trends
- Cost or consumption by tenant over time

These are important to describe because they show how observability becomes targeted as the platform grows, but they do not all need to be implemented literally in the sample for the case study to make sense.

Managing Alert Noise at Scale

One of the first things that breaks in a large observability model is alert discipline. When hundreds of Functions or workflows each produce their own independent alerts, the system becomes noisy enough that teams begin ignoring the signals. For `OrderProcessor`, alerting needs to evolve from per-component noise into something more aggregated and intentional. That usually means alerting on meaningful conditions such as regional error-rate spikes, SLA breaches for a tenant, or large changes in backlog or dependency failure rate. It also means suppressing duplicate notifications during a known incident and being careful about which conditions wake a person up versus which conditions are better suited to dashboards or ticketing systems. These are primarily **operational design choices**, but they are essential to making observability useful rather than exhausting.

Retention and Aggregation

At scale, telemetry volume also creates retention and performance pressure. Keeping every raw event forever is expensive and often unnecessary. A healthier model is to keep detailed raw telemetry for a shorter period and store longer-term aggregates separately for reporting, compliance, or BI use. That way the platform preserves operational visibility without making every dashboard query scan an enormous volume of raw logs.

This is a real architectural concern for `OrderProcessor`, but the exact implementation can vary. Some teams may export aggregates into Cosmos DB or a warehouse for reporting. Others may rely on monitoring platform retention policies and scheduled exports. The key idea is that observability at scale needs storage design just as much as business data does.

Applying Large-Scale Observability to OrderProcessor

Taken together, these changes make the observability story in `OrderProcessor` much more realistic for a growing enterprise platform. Telemetry is now aligned with regional compliance boundaries. Logs and traces remain tagged with tenant and correlation identity. Alerts and monitoring resources become part of infrastructure. Global reporting can be built through controlled federated queries rather than by ignoring residency boundaries. Dashboard design becomes layered by audience rather than assuming one view works for everyone.

That is the central value of this section. Observability is no longer just something the platform emits. It is now something the platform is organized around. As the system grows, the monitoring design grows with it rather than collapsing into noise.

Project Addition: Observability at Scale for OrderProcessor

This section extends `OrderProcessor` with a larger-scale observability model. Monitoring resources can now be separated by region, telemetry remains tagged with tenant and correlation identity, and alerts can be codified as infrastructure rather than treated as portal-only configuration. Federated regional queries and persona-specific dashboards remain important operational patterns, while retention and aggregation strategies help keep the monitoring estate usable as telemetry volume increases.

From this point on, `OrderProcessor` is no longer just observable in one shared environment. It is observable as a growing platform, with enough structure to support regional compliance, tenant-level insight, engineering diagnosis, and platform-wide operational visibility at the same time.

Case Study: Putting It All Together

Throughout this chapter, `OrderProcessor` has been extended in several directions at once. It learned how to ingest and process files without buffering them into memory. It began publishing business events so other services could react without being tightly coupled to the core orchestration. It became tenant-aware, then region-aware, then capable of pausing for human approval, waiting for long-running external integrations, and degrading gracefully when dependencies failed. It also grew a larger-scale observability model so those behaviors could still be understood operationally as the platform became more complex. Each of those case studies solved a specific architectural pressure point, but the real value comes from seeing how they fit together.

That is the purpose of this final section. Rather than introducing one more isolated pattern, it brings the chapter into a single reference architecture for `OrderProcessor`. The important question is no longer "can the platform do file ingestion?" or "can it support multi-tenancy?" The question becomes whether all of those capabilities can coexist in one coherent serverless system without collapsing into a tangled design. The answer is yes, provided the platform keeps the same architectural discipline that has been reinforced throughout the book: durable workflows for critical paths, events for decoupling, explicit identity and tenancy boundaries, region-aware infrastructure, clear resilience controls, and observability that keeps pace with the system's growth.

The End-to-End Architecture

By this point, `OrderProcessor` should be thought of less as a single workflow and more as a platform with several cooperating layers. Orders may arrive either as structured API submissions or as uploaded files. File uploads are streamed directly into Blob Storage and then turned into processing events through Event Grid. The order-critical path remains under orchestration, which means fraud, tax, approval checkpoints, ERP registration, and long-running partner jobs are still coordinated durably rather than left to ad hoc sequencing. Once the order reaches a meaningful business milestone, such as confirmation, the platform emits events that downstream services can subscribe to independently.

Around that workflow core sit the architectural constraints introduced in the rest of the chapter. Tenant identity determines which configuration and operational view applies to the order. Region determines which stores, secrets, and failover targets are legal. Human-in-the-loop decisions can pause the workflow safely. External APIs can be started asynchronously and resumed later through callbacks. Circuit breakers, bulkheads, compensation logic, and graceful degradation stop one failing dependency from turning into a platform-wide outage. Figure 10-3 shows how these pieces combine into one working architecture.

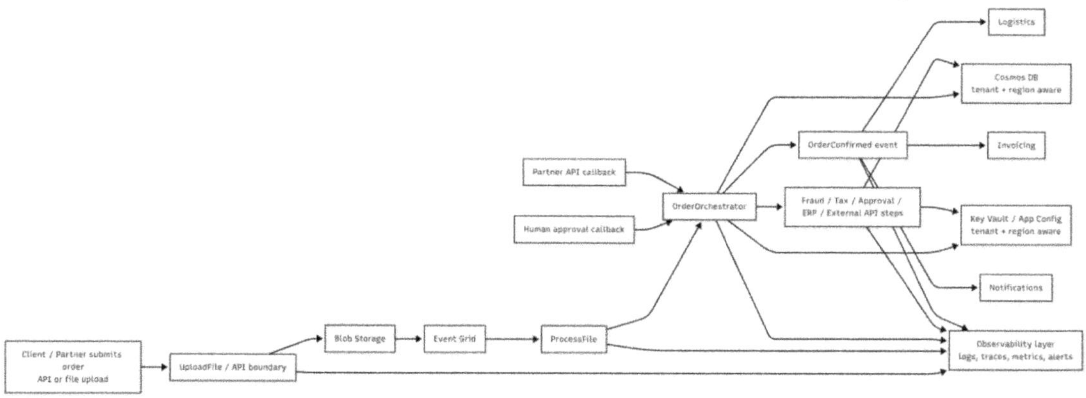

***Figure 10-3.** End-to-End OrderProcessor Architecture Across Ingestion, Orchestration, Events, Approvals, Integrations, and Observability*

The value of this architecture is not just that it contains many patterns. It is that those patterns are not fighting each other. File ingestion still leads into the same workflow model. Human approvals still fit into durable orchestration. Multi-tenancy and regional compliance still shape storage and routing without breaking observability. Downstream services still receive events without forcing the core workflow to become a giant coordinator for everything.

Walking One Order Through the Full System

A useful way to understand the combined architecture is to follow a single order from start to finish. Imagine a high-value EU tenant order arriving as a PDF rather than as JSON. The file upload endpoint streams it into Blob Storage, where Event Grid raises a blob-created event. A file processor extracts metadata and hands the result into the order workflow. From there, the orchestrator begins the order-critical path. Fraud and tax checks run first. Because the order exceeds a configured threshold, the workflow pauses for a human approval event.

Once the approver responds, the orchestration resumes and attempts ERP registration. At the same time, it may need to start a longer-running partner process, such as verification or clearing, using the callback-based integration model from the earlier section. If ERP begins to fail repeatedly, the circuit breaker prevents the system from hammering it indefinitely. If the platform can continue safely without immediate ERP completion, the order may be marked as pending ERP rather than being discarded outright. Once the core path succeeds, `OrderProcessor` emits an `OrderConfirmed` event that downstream services such as logistics, invoicing, or notifications can consume independently.

Throughout this journey, the architectural constraints from the rest of the chapter remain in effect. The tenant identity determines which configuration and reporting view applies. The regional identity keeps data, secrets, logs, and failover targets inside the correct jurisdiction. Observability remains attached at every stage, which means the team can still trace the workflow, query logs by tenant and order, inspect pending approvals, measure dependency failures, and view SLA or cost impact without losing sight of the business flow.

Example Reference Solution Layout

The following reference structure illustrates one way to organize these patterns in a repository.

Example reference solution layout

```
/src
  /OrderProcessor.Api
  /OrderProcessor.Orchestrations
    OrderOrchestrator.cs
    ApprovalOrchestrator.cs
    SagaOrchestrator.cs
    ExternalApiOrchestrator.cs
    FileOrchestrator.cs
    RegionAwareOrderOrchestrator.cs
  /OrderProcessor.Functions
    UploadFile.cs
    ProcessFile.cs
    PublishEvent.cs
    LoadTenantConfig.cs
    NotifyApprover.cs
    ApprovalCallback.cs
    StartExternalJob.cs
    ExternalJobCallback.cs
    CompensateERP.cs
    ReprocessDeadLetters.cs
  /OrderProcessor.Infrastructure
    OrderRepository.cs
    RegionalOrderRepository.cs
    TenantConfigRepository.cs
  /OrderProcessor.Shared
    CorrelationMiddleware.cs
  /OrderProcessor.Models
    Order.cs
    ApprovalResult.cs
    ApprovalAudit.cs
    TenantConfig.cs
    StartExternalJobRequest.cs
    ExternalJobTracking.cs
    JobResponse.cs
```

```
    JobResult.cs

/playbooks
  dr.md
  scaling.md
  postmortems.md

/infra
  cosmos-eu.bicep
  cosmos-us.bicep
  storage-eu.bicep
  storage-us.bicep
  monitoring-eu.bicep
  monitoring-us.bicep
  alerts-order-failures.bicep
  servicebus-stage-queues.bicep
  eventgrid-file-processing.bicep
  eventgrid-order-confirmed.bicep

/dashboards
  global.workbook.json
  tenant.workbook.json

/tests
  UnitTests.cs
  IntegrationTests.cs
```

The reason this type of layout is useful is not that it's the only correct answer. It's that it reflects the separation of concerns established across the chapter. API boundaries, orchestrations, activity-style Functions, infrastructure, shared models, playbooks, and dashboards each have a clear place in the solution.

What the Combined Architecture Achieves

When the chapter's patterns are viewed together, several architectural benefits become clear. The first is resilience. No single dependency owns the fate of the entire platform, because bulkheads, circuit breakers, compensation paths, and graceful degradation all help keep failures contained. The second is scalability. File uploads, external integrations, approvals, and downstream event subscribers all fit the asynchronous design rather than pushing the platform back towards synchronous bottlenecks. The third is compliance. Tenant and regional boundaries are not afterthoughts. They are embedded in the data model, storage layout, routing logic, and operational estate.

The fourth benefit is evolvability. The event-driven parts of the architecture allow new downstream consumers to be added without rewriting the core orchestration every time. The workflow remains authoritative where correctness matters, but the wider system can still grow. The fifth is observability. Because traces, logs, metrics, alerts, and tenant or region tags are already part of the architecture, the platform remains understandable even as its responsibilities widen.

This is why the chapter is important. It shows that serverless .NET is not limited to small APIs or isolated Functions. It can support a serious, distributed, enterprise-grade platform provided the architectural boundaries remain deliberate.

Real Project Evolution Across Chapter 10

Although this chapter has been more case-study driven than some of the earlier ones, there are still several changes that should be understood as genuine evolution of the `OrderProcessor` sample. File ingestion through `UploadFile` and `ProcessFile` is a real platform addition. Publishing `OrderConfirmed` and allowing downstream subscriptions is a real architectural step. Tenant-aware and region-aware models are real changes to the shape of the data and workflow. Approval callbacks, async external job callbacks, circuit breakers, compensation paths, and observability infrastructure also belong to the sample as the platform grows.

At the same time, some material in the chapter was intentionally presented as a pattern choice rather than mandatory cumulative implementation. Polling as a fallback to callbacks, Teams as an alternative to email, persona-specific dashboards, rate-limiting policy variants, and more advanced federation models were shown so you can see the available architectural options. They are part of the design vocabulary, but not every one of them must be added literally to the sample for the chapter to remain coherent.

That distinction matters because it keeps the chapter honest. `OrderProcessor` has grown, but it has not turned into a dumping ground for every possible enterprise feature. It remains a sample platform that demonstrates the right architectural moves.

Project Addition: Reference Architecture for the Complete OrderProcessor Platform

This final section ties together the case studies introduced throughout Chapter 10 into one coherent reference architecture for `OrderProcessor`. File ingestion, orchestration, downstream event publication, tenant-aware and region-aware processing, human approval checkpoints, long-running partner integrations, advanced resilience controls, and larger-scale observability now all fit within the same platform model. The supporting repo structure, infrastructure modules, dashboards, and playbooks reinforce that architecture rather than existing as disconnected artifacts.

From this point on, `OrderProcessor` should be understood not just as a set of isolated serverless examples but as a blueprint for how a distributed .NET platform can evolve towards a more complete enterprise design while remaining event-driven, resilient, compliant, and observable.

EXERCISES

1. Stream a large file through `UploadFile` and confirm that the request body is written directly to Blob Storage without buffering the entire payload in memory.
2. Upload a PDF and verify that the Event Grid subscription triggers `ProcessFile`, routes the file to the PDF processor path, and records metadata for the upload.
3. Upload an `.eml` file with multiple attachments and confirm that the file-processing path hands off to orchestration when attachment handling becomes multi-step.
4. Extend the file-processing pipeline to recognize one additional file type, such as CSV or DOCX, and decide whether it should be handled inline or through orchestration.
5. Trace a file-driven order from upload through Blob Storage, Event Grid, processing, and into the main workflow. Can you follow the end-to-end path in your telemetry?

6. Extend `OrderOrchestrator` so that it publishes `OrderConfirmed`, and then add a new downstream subscriber that reacts without changing the orchestrator again.
7. Stop one downstream subscriber, such as logistics, and verify that dead-lettering preserves failed deliveries for later inspection or replay.
8. Add a simple audit record for each published `OrderConfirmed` event and query those records to reconstruct the last day of business events.
9. Update the order model with `TenantId`, and then confirm that writes and queries are partitioned and filtered by tenant in Cosmos DB.
10. Configure two tenants with different tax or fraud settings and verify that the same core workflow behaves differently without forking the codebase.
11. Test a tenant-boundary rule by trying to submit a request with one tenant identity while targeting another tenant's data. Confirm that the boundary is rejected at the API layer.
12. Add a manual approval threshold and verify that a high-value order pauses durably, waits for `ApprovalResult`, and resumes only after a valid callback is received.
13. Let an approval workflow time out and design the next step. Should the order fail, escalate, or remain pending? Implement one of those choices and explain why.
14. Simulate a long-running partner API that returns a job ID immediately and completes later through a callback. Confirm that the orchestration sleeps durably rather than blocking.
15. Implement the polling fallback for a partner that cannot issue callbacks, then compare the operational trade-offs between the polling and callback models.
16. Force the external partner API to fail intermittently and verify that retry behavior and telemetry make the problem visible without hiding the failure.
17. Introduce a circuit breaker around ERP registration, then trigger repeated ERP failures and confirm that the workflow stops hammering the dependency after the threshold is reached.

18. Simulate a partial workflow failure after ERP registration and verify that the compensation path restores consistency rather than leaving the order half-completed.
19. Route EU and US orders into separate regional stores and confirm that data, secrets, and diagnostics remain inside the intended jurisdictional boundary.
20. Build one global dashboard and one tenant-specific dashboard from the Chapter 10 telemetry model, and then compare the questions each dashboard is actually able to answer.

Summary

Chapter 10 showed how the earlier building blocks of the book can be combined into broader enterprise patterns. `OrderProcessor` moved beyond simple JSON workflows and became capable of streaming and processing files, publishing business events for downstream subscribers, supporting tenant-aware behavior, pausing for human decisions, and coordinating long-running partner integrations. The important point was not that each feature was added separately, but that each one was added in a way that still respected the same architectural style established in the earlier chapters: durable workflows for critical paths, events for decoupling, explicit boundaries for security and tenancy, and asynchronous processing wherever scale or reliability demanded it.

The chapter also showed that enterprise readiness is not just about adding features. It is about making those features coexist without turning the system into a tangled design. Advanced resilience patterns helped contain failure. Region-aware storage and routing made compliance part of the architecture rather than an afterthought. Observability at scale ensured that a multi-tenant, multi-region platform could still be understood and operated clearly. Taken together, these case studies turned `OrderProcessor` from a teaching sample into a reference architecture for how a serverless .NET platform can evolve towards a more realistic enterprise system while remaining resilient, extensible, and operationally manageable.

```
    public static async Task Run(
        [OrchestrationTrigger] TaskOrchestrationContext context)
    {
        var order = context.GetInput<Order>();

        await context.CallActivityAsync("FraudCheck", order);
        await context.CallActivityAsync("TaxCalculation", order);
        await context.CallActivityAsync("ERPRegistration", order);

        await context.CallActivityAsync("PublishOrderConfirmedEve
        nt", order);
    }
}
```

Figure 11-1 shows the difference between an over-coupled orchestrator and a lean orchestrator that publishes events for downstream subscribers.

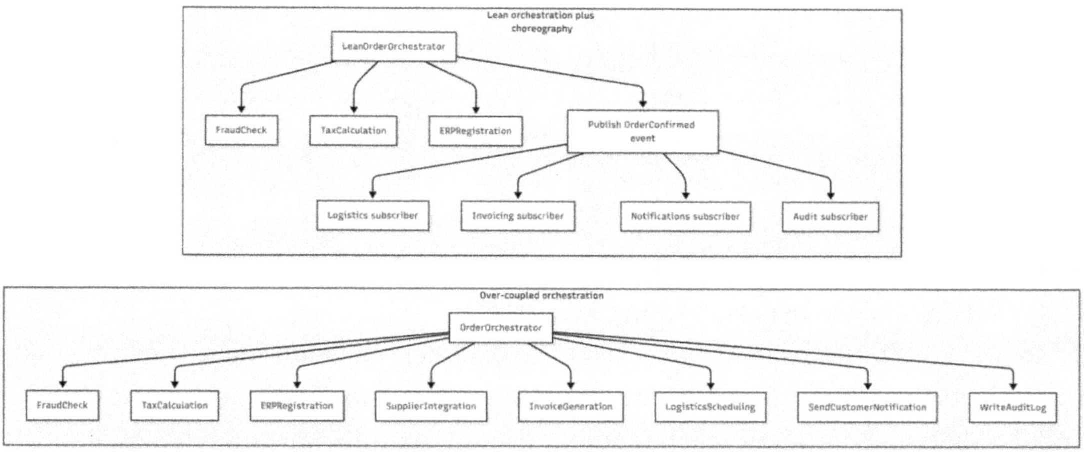

Figure 11-1. *Comparing Lean Orchestration with Over-coupled Orchestration*

This version still uses orchestration where correctness matters, but it stops trying to coordinate everything directly. Logistics, invoicing, notifications, and similar downstream concerns can now react through events rather than becoming hard-coded branches inside the core workflow. That keeps the orchestration authoritative without making it responsible for the entire platform.

Modular Orchestrations Are Still Useful

There are cases where the right answer is not only choreography. Sometimes a workflow really does need another orchestrator, but that orchestrator should still be focused. In `OrderProcessor`, approval handling is a good example. Human approval logic does not belong inside the same unit that coordinates every other concern. Likewise, compensation behavior for sagas, or long-running partner callback flows, often deserves its own orchestration boundary because it solves a different kind of coordination problem.

That is the key discipline. The platform may have multiple orchestrators, but each one should do one job well. An `ApprovalOrchestrator`, a `SagaOrchestrator`, and an `ExternalApiOrchestrator` can coexist quite naturally without creating orchestration bloat, because each one owns a distinct coordination concern. The problem is not having more than one orchestrator. The problem is building one orchestrator that tries to be all of them at once.

A Simple Smell Test for Orchestration Bloat

There is no single perfect line count or dependency count that proves an orchestrator has become over-coupled, but there are useful warning signs. If the orchestration is getting very long, knows about many downstream services directly, or contains business rules from several different domains, it is usually time to pause and ask whether some of that responsibility belongs elsewhere. The same is true if a change to one downstream concern forces a redeployment of the core workflow, or if tests for one path now need to drag several unrelated behaviors along with them.

In practice, these are architectural smell tests rather than hard rules. Their purpose is to make teams stop and examine whether the orchestration is still acting as a focused workflow boundary or whether it has quietly become a central integration monolith.

Why This Matters for Observability As Well

Over-coupled orchestrations also damage observability. A single correlation chain that spans too many unrelated concerns becomes harder to interpret. Instead of showing one clear business path, the trace becomes a crowded tree of loosely related steps. That makes it harder to understand which part of the workflow is truly critical, which part failed, and which downstream concern is simply reacting after the fact. Cleaner orchestration boundaries usually produce cleaner traces, clearer logs, and more useful dashboards.

This is an easy point to miss because teams often think only about maintainability when they discuss orchestration design. In reality, observability suffers too. A focused orchestrator is easier to reason about both in code and in telemetry.

Project Fix: Refactoring OrderProcessor Away from Orchestration Bloat

In `OrderProcessor`, the answer is not to stop using orchestrations. It is to narrow their role. The core order path should stay in orchestration because it coordinates the steps that directly determine whether an order is valid and complete. Downstream concerns such as logistics, invoicing, and notifications should instead react to published events unless they genuinely need to sit inside the core workflow boundary. Separate orchestrators can then handle other coordination-heavy concerns such as approvals, compensation, or long-running partner interactions without overloading the main order flow.

That change matters because it makes the system easier to evolve. A downstream service can change without destabilizing the core order workflow. A new subscriber can be added without extending an already bloated orchestrator. Testing becomes more focused, observability becomes clearer, and the wider architecture stays closer to the event-driven style the rest of the book is building toward.

Risk: Ignoring Eventual Consistency

Developers who come from monoliths and relational databases often inherit a comforting mental model: once a transaction commits, the system is updated, and every reader now sees the same truth. That model works reasonably well inside a single application boundary backed by one strongly consistent store. It does not survive intact once the system becomes distributed. In a platform such as `OrderProcessor`, writes may be replicated across regions, events may arrive asynchronously, caches may lag behind the source of truth, and different services may observe the same business process at different points in time.

That makes eventual consistency one of the most important realities to design for in a serverless distributed system. The danger is not that the platform is inconsistent for a moment. The danger is pretending it is not. When a design assumes a globally immediate, perfectly synchronized state, subtle problems begin to appear. Customers see stale statuses. Retry logic triggers duplicate work because a previous update is not visible yet. Dashboards disagree with operational stores. Support teams struggle to explain what users are seeing. In `OrderProcessor`, the correct response is not to fight eventual consistency everywhere. It is to recognize where it appears and design the workflow, storage, and user experience around it honestly.

The Illusion of Strong Consistency

Inside a monolith, strong consistency feels natural because the same application often performs the write and the next read against the same store in the same logical context. The system appears simple because that boundary is narrow. Once data begins to flow through Functions, queues, regions, caches, and downstream subscribers, that illusion breaks. A write may be accepted and durable while a projection, dashboard, cache, or regional replica still reflects an earlier view of reality.

That is why eventual consistency is so often misunderstood. Developers treat the lag as a bug instead of a property of the architecture. Then they try to "fix" it with brittle workarounds, such as repeated polling, aggressive retries, or unsafe overwrite logic. Those choices often create worse problems than the temporary lag they were trying to hide.

Where Inconsistency Appears in OrderProcessor

In `OrderProcessor`, eventual consistency appears naturally in several places. Regional data replication is one example. If the platform stores order data in one region and reads it in another, there may be a short delay before the latest write becomes visible everywhere. Event-driven updates are another. The core orchestration may publish an `OrderConfirmed` event, but downstream services such as logistics or invoicing may update their own state later, which means different read models can disagree temporarily about where the order currently stands.

Caches introduce another layer of delay. A fast cache can improve performance, but it also creates one more place where yesterday's view of the order may still be present for a short time. Even reporting and dashboards can be affected. Aggregates may refresh on an interval, and late-arriving events may alter totals after a view was already generated. None of this means the system is broken. It means the system is distributed.

Example Inconsistency in a Read Path

A small example makes the problem easier to see. Imagine a read endpoint that consults two different sources, a primary store and a cache. Immediately after an update, those sources may disagree for a while.

Example: inconsistent read across two sources

```
using System.Net;
using Microsoft.Azure.Functions.Worker;
using Microsoft.Azure.Functions.Worker.Http;

namespace OrderProcessor.Examples;

public sealed class ReadOrderStatus
{
    private readonly IOrderStatusStore _primaryStore;
    private readonly IOrderStatusCache _cache;

    public ReadOrderStatus(
        IOrderStatusStore primaryStore,
        IOrderStatusCache cache)
    {
        _primaryStore = primaryStore;
        _cache = cache;
    }

    [Function("ReadOrderStatus")]
    public async Task<HttpResponseData> Run(
        [HttpTrigger(AuthorizationLevel.Function, "get", Route =
        "orders/{id}")]
        HttpRequestData req,
        string id,
        FunctionContext ctx,
        CancellationToken stopToken)
    {
        var logger = ctx.GetLogger("ReadOrderStatus");

        var primaryStatus = await _primaryStore.GetStatusAsync(id,
        stopToken)
```

```
            ?? "Pending";

        var cachedStatus = await _cache.GetStatusAsync(id, stopToken)
            ?? "Unknown";

        logger.LogInformation(
            "Primary store: {PrimaryStatus}, Cache: {CachedStatus}",
            primaryStatus,
            cachedStatus);

        var response = req.CreateResponse(HttpStatusCode.OK);
        await response.WriteAsJsonAsync(
            new OrderStatusReadModel(
                id,
                primaryStatus,
                cachedStatus),
            stopToken);

        return response;
    }
}

public interface IOrderStatusStore
{
    Task<string?> GetStatusAsync(
        string orderId,
        CancellationToken stopToken = default);
}

public interface IOrderStatusCache
{
    Task<string?> GetStatusAsync(
        string orderId,
        CancellationToken stopToken = default);
}
```

```
public sealed record OrderStatusReadModel(
    string OrderId,
    string PrimaryStatus,
    string CachedStatus);
```

This example deliberately reads from two sources to show the visible effect of eventual consistency. The primary store and cache are represented as abstractions, but in a real system these might be backed by Cosmos DB and Redis. Immediately after an update, those sources may temporarily return different answers even though the system is behaving correctly.

Why Ignoring Eventual Consistency Is Dangerous

The first danger is user confusion. A customer completes an order and then immediately sees a status that still says pending. The second danger is duplicate action. If another workflow or a user assumes the first update did not succeed because the new state is not visible yet, the same work may be triggered again. The third danger is a stale overwrite. One component reads an older version of the data and then writes back over a newer version that arrived elsewhere in the meantime. The fourth danger is operational noise. Dashboards and alerts may report "missing" or "late" data when the system is simply still converging.

The important point is that these are not rare edge cases. They are predictable outcomes when a distributed design is treated as though it were a single strongly consistent database. Systems become more robust when they admit that convergence takes time and make that explicit in their behavior.

Designing for Idempotency

One of the most important responses to eventual consistency is idempotency. Events may arrive twice, retries may happen after success, or delayed reads may cause the same operation to be attempted again. If consumers cannot safely handle that, eventual consistency turns quickly into duplicate processing.

A simple pattern looks like this:

Example idempotent consumer logic

```
if (!orderRepo.Exists(order.Id))
{
    await orderRepo.Insert(order);
}
else
{
    logger.LogInformation("Duplicate order {OrderId} ignored.", order.Id);
}
```

That example is deliberately simple, but the principle is essential. When the architecture is distributed, the system should assume duplicate or late-arriving work is possible and make repeated handling safe wherever practical.

Using Versions and Timestamps to Reason About Freshness

Another useful pattern is to make freshness visible in the data itself. If an order carries an update timestamp or version, readers and writers have a better chance of recognizing whether they are dealing with a stale view of the world.

Example version-aware order model

```
namespace OrderProcessor.Examples;

public sealed record VersionedOrder(
    string Id,
    string Status,
    DateTime LastUpdatedUtc);
```

This does not eliminate eventual consistency, but it makes it easier to work with honestly. A reader can see that the data is still processing. A writer can check whether it is overwriting something newer than what it originally read. A dashboard can explain that the displayed value reflects the latest known update time rather than pretending it is globally final.

Using Consistency Levels Where They Actually Help

Eventual consistency does not mean every read must be stale. It means teams should be deliberate about which guarantees matter where. In some parts of OrderProcessor, session consistency may be enough to give a caller a read-your-own-write experience inside one logical interaction even while the wider platform remains eventually consistent overall.

Example session consistency configuration

```
using Microsoft.Azure.Cosmos;

var client = new CosmosClient(
    endpoint,
    key,
    new CosmosClientOptions
    {
        ConsistencyLevel = ConsistencyLevel.Session
    });
```

This is a useful example because it shows the right mindset. The platform is not trying to impose strong consistency on every path globally. It is applying the right consistency guarantee in the places where it improves behavior without fighting the architecture as a whole.

Making the User Experience Honest

One of the easiest ways to make eventual consistency painful is to hide it behind language that sounds stronger than the system can actually guarantee. If the workflow is still processing, the API should not present the state as if every downstream concern has already caught up. In many cases, a more honest transitional state is better for users and safer for the system.

Instead of presenting "Order Confirmed" as though all consequences of that confirmation are already visible, the platform may be better off saying the order is still processing and that downstream updates can take a few seconds. That kind of message reduces confusion and discourages users from retrying actions that already succeeded.

Reconciliation As a Deliberate Design Tool

Some inconsistencies are temporary and acceptable, but the platform should still have mechanisms to converge cleanly over time. That is where reconciliation becomes useful. A nightly or periodic process can compare expected outcomes with recorded outcomes and repair aggregates, delayed projections, or reporting totals that were affected by late-arriving events.

This matters especially for dashboards, billing, and financial views, where small timing delays may be acceptable during the day but must not remain wrong indefinitely. Reconciliation should not be treated as an admission of failure. In distributed systems, it is often a normal and healthy part of the design.

Project Fix: Making Consistency Explicit in OrderProcessor

In `OrderProcessor`, the right answer is not to pretend every part of the platform shares one instantaneously correct state. It is to make consistency boundaries explicit. Orders should carry update timestamps or equivalent freshness signals. Event consumers should remain idempotent. Read models and user-facing APIs should use transitional states when downstream processing has not yet fully converged. Where a stronger local guarantee is useful, such as reading immediately after a write in the same logical interaction, session consistency can be applied deliberately rather than globally.

That changes the system in an important way. Eventual consistency stops being a hidden source of surprise and becomes part of the platform's behavior model. The result is not a weaker system. It is a more honest one - one that handles retries more safely, presents states more clearly, and converges predictably instead of pretending that global synchronization is free.

Risk: Over-reliance on Retries

Retries are often the first resilience tool developers reach for, and for good reason. Many failures in distributed systems are transient. A dependency may be briefly unavailable, a network call may time out, or a downstream service may return an error that disappears a few seconds later. In a system such as `OrderProcessor`, retrying can therefore be useful. The problem begins when retries stop being one resilience technique and start becoming the resilience strategy. At that point, the system is no longer recovering intelligently from failure. It is simply repeating the same action and hoping the environment improves before the platform makes things worse.

That is what makes over-reliance on retries such a serious risk. A retry can help when a service is momentarily slow or unavailable. It becomes harmful when the dependency is already under stress, when the call should not be repeated blindly, or when repeated attempts hide the fact that a deeper problem exists. In a serverless system, that harm is amplified because retries do not just consume time. They also consume executions, create extra load, increase cost, and can turn one failing dependency into a much wider incident. The architectural lesson is not that retries are bad. It is that retries need context, boundaries, and companions such as timeouts, circuit breakers, asynchronous decoupling, and compensation.

Why Retries Feel Safe

Retries are attractive because they are simple to understand. A developer sees an intermittent failure, adds a few repeated attempts, and the immediate problem appears to improve. The code looks small, the change feels local, and the team gains confidence because transient faults really do exist. That is why retry-heavy designs often enter systems gradually. No one starts by deciding to create a retry storm. They start by adding one more retry here, one more loop there, and one more fallback around an unstable dependency.

The danger is that retries often feel safer than they really are. A retry can hide symptoms without resolving the underlying problem. It can increase latency until the user experience becomes worse than a fast, honest failure would have been. It can amplify traffic against a service that is already failing. It can also mask configuration or authentication problems that are not transient at all. When that happens, the platform is not becoming more resilient. It is becoming slower, noisier, and more expensive.

What Retry Abuse Looks Like in Practice

A naive retry design usually appears first at the integration boundary. A Function calls a downstream service, catches any exception, waits briefly, and tries again. If the call still fails, it repeats the pattern several more times. That looks harmless when one request is involved. It looks very different when hundreds or thousands of Function invocations are all doing it at once.

A simple example makes the problem clear.

Example anti-pattern: naive retry loop

```
using System.Text.Json;
using Microsoft.Azure.Functions.Worker;

namespace OrderProcessor.Examples;

public static class ErpCaller
{
    [Function("ErpCaller")]
    public static async Task Run(
        [ServiceBusTrigger("erp-queue", Connection =
        "ServiceBusConnection")]
        string msg)
    {
        var order = JsonSerializer.Deserialize<Order>(msg);

        for (var i = 0; i < 10; i++)
        {
            try
            {
                await httpClient.PostAsJsonAsync(
                    "https://erp.anywebsitename.com/api/orders",
                    order);

                return;
            }
            catch
            {
                await Task.Delay(1000);
            }
        }
    }
}
```

This is intentionally shown as an anti-pattern. The issue is not that the loop retries. The issue is that it retries repeatedly with no real resilience boundary, no timeout, no circuit breaker, and no broader strategy for what should happen when the downstream service is genuinely unavailable.

Why This Is Dangerous

The first risk is the retry storm. If ERP is unavailable and hundreds or thousands of orders all reach the same code path, each invocation begins issuing repeated calls against the already unhealthy dependency. Instead of giving the system time to recover, the platform increases the pressure. The second risk is amplified latency. Even if each retry waits only a short time, several attempts can turn one failing call into a long period of blocked progress. In user-facing paths, that often produces a worse experience than a clear, fast failure.

The third risk is that retries can hide the nature of the real problem. A transient network glitch and a broken authentication configuration do not deserve the same treatment, but a simplistic retry loop treats them identically. The fourth risk is cost. In a serverless platform, every extra execution and delayed processing path contributes to the bill. A retry is not free just because it is small in code. When multiplied across large volumes, it becomes part of the operational shape of the system.

A Better Model: Layered Resilience Instead of Repeated Hope

The right response is not to remove retries from `OrderProcessor`. It is to stop treating retries as a standalone fix. A healthier design puts retries inside a broader resilience model. Calls should fail within a bounded time. Repeated attempts should be limited and spread out rather than fired in tight loops. Downstream boundaries should stop accepting repeated pressure when the service is clearly unhealthy. And in some cases, the best answer is not to retry synchronously at all, but to hand work off asynchronously or compensate later instead of insisting on immediate success.

This is exactly the pattern Chapter 10 moved toward. Rather than wrapping every call in ad hoc retry logic, the platform should configure resilience at the `HttpClient` boundary and let the business code focus on what it is trying to do. The resilience model then becomes consistent across the application rather than being rewritten differently in every Function.

Real Project Update: Resilient HTTP Boundaries Instead of Inline Retry Loops

In the current `OrderProcessor` sample, the better pattern is to configure the downstream client once and allow retry, timeout, and circuit-breaker behavior to live there rather than in handwritten loops spread through the codebase.

Program.cs addition

```
using Microsoft.Extensions.Http.Resilience;

builder.Services.AddHttpClient("ErpApi", client =>
{
    client.BaseAddress = new Uri("https://erp.anywebsitename.com/");
})
.AddStandardResilienceHandler();
```

This is the important architectural shift. Retry behavior is no longer a local improvisation inside each Function. It is part of the HTTP boundary itself. That makes the system easier to reason about and helps avoid a situation where every caller invents its own slightly different retry pattern.

Example: An ERP Call with a Resilient Client Boundary

Once resilience is configured on the named client, the integration code becomes much simpler. The business path no longer has to show every retry step explicitly in order to benefit from resilience.

Inside Functions/ERPRegistration.cs

```
var response = await _httpClient.PostAsJsonAsync("/api/orders", order);
response.EnsureSuccessStatusCode();
```

That simplicity is a strength, not a weakness. It means the call site is focused on business intent while the retry, timeout, and circuit-breaker strategy live in one consistent place.

Timeouts Still Matter

A retry that waits too long to fail is often only a slower failure. That is why resilience also needs clear time boundaries. When a dependency is slow or hanging, the system should not keep an execution open indefinitely while waiting for something that may never arrive. Even if the timeout behavior sits within the configured resilience handler, the architectural principle still matters; failure should happen within a bounded window.

This is one of the reasons retry-heavy code often feels worse in production than in development. In development, a few seconds of extra waiting may seem harmless. In production, those seconds multiply across queues, orchestrations, dashboards, and users. Bounded failure is often healthier than endless optimism.

Asynchronous Design Often Beats Synchronous Retry

Another important lesson is that some work should not be retried inline at all. If a dependency is slow, bursty, or unreliable, the platform may be better off accepting the business event, queuing the work, and letting a background path deal with delivery later. That keeps the user-facing or orchestration-critical path from being held hostage by one unstable service. In `OrderProcessor`, this is especially relevant for downstream integrations such as ERP or partner systems. A durable workflow can move into a waiting state. A queue can absorb pressure more safely than a synchronous API boundary. A replay or compensation path can be clearer and less harmful than a pile of repeated immediate attempts. This is not an argument against retries. It is an argument for using them in the right place and not expecting them to solve every category of failure.

Compensation Is Often Safer Than Endless Retry

There are also situations where retries should stop and a compensating action should begin instead. If a workflow has already partially succeeded and the next step is persistently failing, repeatedly hammering that dependency may simply prolong inconsistency. In those cases, the saga-style compensation patterns from Chapter 10 are often safer than treating every failure as something that one more retry might solve.

This matters because teams sometimes use retries as a substitute for decision-making. A mature resilience design recognizes that some failures call for backoff, some call for waiting, some call for circuit-breaking, and some call for rollback or escalation. The point is not to always keep trying. The point is to respond proportionately.

Observability Should Reveal Retry Pressure

Retries are easy to underestimate when they remain invisible. If the system retries frequently but operators cannot see how often that is happening, retry abuse can continue for a long time before anyone realizes the platform is compensating for a deeper problem. That is why retry behavior should show up in telemetry. The platform should make it possible to spot when a particular dependency is repeatedly hitting resilience boundaries or when retry volume is climbing sharply.

The exact implementation may vary, especially when resilience is configured through `HttpClient` rather than inline loops, but the architectural principle is clear. Retry pressure is an operational signal. If it grows suddenly, that often indicates a systemic issue in a downstream dependency rather than a harmless burst of transient noise.

Project Fix: Smarter Resilience in OrderProcessor

In `OrderProcessor`, the answer is to stop relying on naive repeated attempts and instead treat retries as one part of a broader resilience design. External HTTP boundaries should use configured resilience handlers rather than ad hoc loops. Downstream services should be protected by timeouts and circuit breakers. Async workflows and queues should absorb pressure where synchronous retry would only create contention. Compensation paths should exist for situations where retry is no longer the right answer.

That makes the platform healthier in several ways at once. It reduces the risk of retry storms, shortens the distance between a real failure and a visible diagnosis, lowers the chance of turning one unstable dependency into a wider incident, and keeps cost growth more predictable. The deeper lesson is simple: resilience is not the same thing as repeated effort. A strong serverless design knows when to retry, when to wait, when to stop, and when to recover differently.

Risk: Ignoring Cost Optimization

One of the most attractive promises of serverless architecture is that you pay only for what you use. That promise is real, but it is often misunderstood. Serverless does not remove cost pressure. It changes its shape. Instead of paying for idle servers, teams pay for execution volume, storage, telemetry ingestion, throughput settings, premium hosting, network transfer, and the side effects of design decisions that only become visible at scale. In a system such as `OrderProcessor`, cost problems rarely appear because one service is obviously expensive on its own. They appear because many individually reasonable choices combine into an architecture that is chattier, noisier, and more resource-hungry than the workload really needs.

That is what makes cost optimization a design concern rather than a finance concern that can be deferred until later. A workflow that fans out too aggressively, a telemetry model that logs everything, a database tier set far above real demand, or a premium hosting plan left running for low-value workloads can all distort the economics of the platform. The danger is not simply a higher bill. The danger is that the system becomes harder to justify, harder to scale predictably, and harder to operate responsibly as tenant usage grows. In `OrderProcessor`, cost awareness needs to be part of the architecture from the start, not a late-stage clean-up exercise.

Why Cost Surprises Happen in Serverless Systems

Cost surprises usually happen because serverless hides infrastructure more successfully than it hides architecture. Teams stop thinking about servers, which is helpful, but they can also stop noticing how many invocations, writes, logs, and cross-service interactions their design is actually producing. A Function invocation feels tiny. A queue message feels tiny. A trace event feels tiny. A database request unit feels tiny. The problem appears when those tiny units multiply across thousands or millions of operations and begin reinforcing each other.

In distributed systems, cost also tends to surface indirectly. An orchestration that calls too many activities may look elegant in code but produce unnecessary execution volume. A broad observability strategy may improve visibility but also create telemetry ingestion costs that grow faster than the business workload. Cross-region data movement may support resilience or analytics, but if it is poorly scoped, it can create both compliance and bandwidth problems. The key lesson is that serverless platforms do not automatically optimize design choices for you. They only price them.

Example Anti-pattern: A Chatty Orchestration

A simple example shows how easy it is to create avoidable costs. Suppose an orchestration performs one business action but models every minor audit step as a separate activity call.

Example anti-pattern: chatty orchestration

```
using Microsoft.Azure.Functions.Worker;
using Microsoft.DurableTask;

namespace OrderProcessor.Examples;

public static class ExpensiveOrchestrator
{
    [Function("ExpensiveOrchestrator")]
    public static async Task Run(
        [OrchestrationTrigger] TaskOrchestrationContext context)
    {
        var order = context.GetInput<Order>();

        for (var i = 0; i < 10; i++)
        {
            await context.CallActivityAsync("AuditStep", order);
        }
    }
}
```

This is intentionally exaggerated, but it illustrates the real risk. Ten activity calls per order may not sound dramatic. At high order volume, however, a design like this turns one business event into many billable units of work. Durable Functions remains the right tool, but the way it is used becomes unnecessarily expensive.

Cost Risk Often Begins As Over-chattiness

One of the easiest ways to waste money in a serverless platform is to make the architecture too chatty. That can happen in orchestrations, in event-driven flows, in logging, or in repeated reads and writes against data stores. The issue is not that the platform is distributed. The issue is that the design generates more interactions than the business outcome really requires.

For OrderProcessor, that means the team should keep asking a simple question: does this boundary add useful resilience or separation, or is it just creating extra invocations and storage operations for work that could be batched or handled more simply? This is not an argument for collapsing everything into a monolith. It is an argument for making sure every distributed step has a clear reason to exist.

Cosmos DB and Throughput Waste

Data stores are another common source of unnecessary cost. Cosmos DB is powerful, but it makes cost visible through provisioned throughput, autoscale ceilings, partition design, and query efficiency. A poorly sized deployment can waste money even when the business workload is modest. The most common mistake is provisioning for an imagined peak and then leaving that capacity in place permanently.

That does not mean teams should under-provision the database. It means they should size it deliberately. Autoscale settings should match realistic demand. Partitioning should support the access patterns the system actually uses. Tenant-aware design should not only improve isolation but also help prevent one tenant's usage from distorting the resource profile of everyone else. In a multi-tenant OrderProcessor, throughput design is both a performance concern and a cost concern.

Real Project Update: Using Realistic Autoscale Boundaries

A practical improvement is to express data-store cost control directly in infrastructure. Instead of relying on a large static throughput setting, the sample should move toward autoscale with a sensible upper bound.

Example infrastructure direction: realistic Cosmos autoscale

```
resource ordersContainer 'Microsoft.DocumentDB/databaseAccounts/
sqlDatabases/containers@2022-05-15' = {
  name: '${cosmos.name}/orderdb/orders'
  properties: {
    resource: {
      id: 'orders'
      partitionKey: {
        paths: [
          '/tenantId'
```

```
        ]
        kind: 'Hash'
      }
      autoscaleSettings: {
        maxThroughput: 4000
      }
    }
  }
}
```

This is not about picking one magic throughput number. It is about showing that the platform should encode realistic cost boundaries in infrastructure rather than assuming more capacity is always safer.

Telemetry Can Become a Cost Problem Too

One of the most common ways for serverless systems to become unexpectedly expensive is through telemetry. Teams rightly want visibility, but visibility without discipline turns into ingestion cost, retention cost, and noisy dashboards. If `OrderProcessor` logs every detail of every request, every retry, every successful check, and every intermediate state at high volume, the platform may spend a surprising amount of money telling the team things it does not actually need to know.

This is why observability and cost optimization are connected. Better observability is not the same thing as more observability. A healthier model is to keep raw logs for a shorter period, retain high-value signals, and export or aggregate what needs to live longer. That way, the platform remains diagnosable without turning Application Insights or Log Analytics into a second production bill that nobody planned for.

Real Project Update: Reducing Raw Telemetry Retention

In the sample, a practical step is to shorten raw telemetry retention and move longer-term reporting into cheaper aggregate storage where appropriate.

Example infrastructure direction: shorter raw retention

```
resource appInsights 'Microsoft.Insights/components@2020-02-02' = {
  name: 'orderprocessor-ai'
```

```
  location: 'northeurope'
  properties: {
    Application_Type: 'web'
    RetentionInDays: 30
  }
}
```

This does not mean throwing away operational insight. It means distinguishing between the period in which raw telemetry is actively useful for diagnosis and the longer period in which summaries, aggregates, or compliance-oriented exports are usually enough.

Hosting Plans Matter More Than Teams Expect

Another subtle cost trap is hosting choice. Premium plans are powerful, especially when the system needs always-on behavior, VNet integration, or reduced cold-start sensitivity. But not every part of `OrderProcessor` needs the same hosting characteristics. If low-volume, bursty workloads are left on premium infrastructure without a real reason, the platform may end up paying for reserved capability it is barely using.

That suggests a more selective design. Some paths may belong on premium hosting because their runtime characteristics justify it. Others may be better suited to a consumption-based model. Cost optimization here is not about always choosing the cheapest tier. It is about choosing the tier that actually matches the workload. A platform that treats every Function the same way usually ends up paying either in money or in operational pain.

Cross-region Design Has Cost Consequences Too

Earlier chapters already made the point that cross-region architecture is shaped by resilience and compliance. It is also shaped by cost. Data moving unnecessarily across regions increases bandwidth charges, and a poorly thought-out replication or analytics path can generate expense without creating much business value. In `OrderProcessor`, that means region-aware routing is not only a compliance control. It is also a cost control. Data should stay where it has a reason to stay, and cross-region movement should be deliberate rather than incidental.

This is a useful reminder that optimization is not only about compute. In distributed systems, storage, telemetry, data movement, and hosting decisions often matter just as much.

Observing Cost As Part of the Platform

Cost should be visible in the same way reliability and performance are visible. If teams only discover cost shape at the end of the month, they are reacting too late. The better approach is to treat cost indicators as part of the platform's operating signals. That may mean looking at execution volume, telemetry ingestion, Cosmos throughput patterns, cross-region movement, or per-tenant usage trends. In a multi-tenant platform, it is especially useful to understand which tenants or workflows are driving which kinds of costs.

That does not require turning every engineer into a FinOps specialist. It does require acknowledging that architecture influences cost continuously, not occasionally. A system that can explain latency, failure rate, and tenant usage but cannot explain its own cost profile is only partially observable.

Project Fix: Cost-Aware OrderProcessor

In `OrderProcessor`, the architectural answer is to reduce unnecessary chattiness, size data stores realistically, shorten raw telemetry retention, choose hosting tiers deliberately, and keep data movement aligned with real regional needs. Activity calls should exist because they improve resilience or separation, not because they happen to be easy to add. Cosmos throughput should reflect actual demand rather than a permanent guess at peak scale. Telemetry should be valuable enough to justify its own cost. Premium hosting should be reserved for workloads that genuinely need it.

That changes the platform in an important way. Cost stops being something the team notices only after deployment and becomes part of the design conversation itself. The result is not a "cheap" system in the simplistic sense. It is a system whose operating cost is better understood, more proportional to its workload, and less likely to surprise the people running it.

Risk: Security As an Afterthought

Serverless platforms make it very easy to get working software running quickly. A Function can be deployed in minutes, an event subscription can be added with little ceremony, and a data store can be provisioned with only a few lines of infrastructure code. That speed is useful, but it also creates one of the most dangerous habits in distributed systems: treating security as something that can be tightened later. Teams focus on getting the flow working, promise that authentication, authorization, secret handling, and audit controls will be cleaned up afterwards, and then discover that the insecure version has quietly become the real version.

That is what makes security as an afterthought such a serious architectural risk. In a system such as `OrderProcessor`, security is not a wrapper that sits around the outside once the workflow is already designed. It affects how endpoints are exposed, how approvals are handled, how secrets are loaded, how identities are scoped, how data is encrypted, and how sensitive actions are audited. A workflow can be operationally correct and still be insecure. In fact, that is often what makes the risk so hard to notice. The system appears to work perfectly right up until someone realizes it has been trusting the wrong caller, exposing the wrong boundary, or storing the wrong secret in the wrong place.

Why Security Drifts into "Later"

The drift usually starts with pressure for speed. A team wants to prove that the workflow works, so it opens the endpoint temporarily, hardcodes a connection string for now, or postpones role enforcement until the business flow is stable. Serverless environments encourage this because they reduce the visible setup cost of getting something live. The path from code to deployed endpoint feels short, which makes it easier to believe that security can be layered on once the feature has been demonstrated.

There is also a misleading sense of safety. A Function can feel isolated because it is only one endpoint or one trigger, but that does not make it secure by default. A public HTTP trigger is still public. A key pasted into configuration is still a secret-handling failure even if it only exists for a while. A workflow that accepts human approval decisions still needs strong identity and audit controls even if it began life as a proof of concept. In practice, insecure defaults do not usually arrive through malicious intent. They arrive through convenience.

Example Anti-pattern: An Approval Endpoint with No Meaningful Protection

One of the easiest ways to see this risk is through an intentionally unsafe endpoint. Imagine an approval callback that accepts a sensitive workflow decision but exposes that decision on an anonymous boundary.

Example anti-pattern: insecure approval endpoint

```
using System.Net;
using Microsoft.Azure.Functions.Worker;
using Microsoft.Azure.Functions.Worker.Http;

namespace OrderProcessor.Examples;

public static class PublicApprovalEndpoint
{
    [Function("PublicApprovalEndpoint")]
    public static async Task<HttpResponseData> Run(
        [HttpTrigger(AuthorizationLevel.Anonymous, "post")]
        HttpRequestData req)
    {
        await req.ReadAsStringAsync();
        return req.CreateResponse(HttpStatusCode.OK);
    }
}
```

This is intentionally bad. The problem is not merely that the trigger is anonymous. The deeper problem is that the workflow accepts a security-sensitive decision on a boundary that has no trustworthy notion of who is calling it or whether that caller is allowed to act. In development, this may look harmless because it makes testing easier. In production, it is a serious flaw.

Why This Is Dangerous

The most obvious risk is unauthorized action. If a high-value approval endpoint is exposed without proper identity and role checks, anyone who can reach that endpoint may be able to approve or reject work they should never control. The second risk is secret leakage. Teams under delivery pressure often paste connection strings, account keys, or API secrets into configuration files or source-controlled settings because it is faster than wiring a secure store correctly. The third risk is excessive privilege. A Function identity is granted broad access because it is easier than figuring out the minimum permissions it actually needs.

The fourth risk is weak auditability. A workflow may succeed, but if the platform cannot prove who took the action, when they took it, and under which authority, the system becomes very hard to trust in regulated environments. The final risk is that these weaknesses compound. An open boundary, a copied secret, and an over-permissioned identity are individually bad enough. Together, they create a platform that is much easier to misuse and much harder to investigate.

Security Has to Be Part of the Workflow Design

In `OrderProcessor`, one of the clearest examples is the approval flow. The architecture already established earlier in the book assumes that approval decisions are meaningful business actions. That means the approval boundary is not an ordinary convenience endpoint. It is part of the workflow's trust model. If the wrong caller can trigger it, then the workflow itself cannot be trusted, no matter how correct the orchestration logic may be internally.

That is why the secure answer is not simply to replace `AuthorizationLevel.Anonymous` with another trigger setting and stop thinking about it. The endpoint has to sit behind the authenticated identity model already established elsewhere in the system. The platform should know who the caller is, what tenant context they belong to, and whether they hold the role or claim required to approve that class of work. The approval decision should then be logged as an auditable event, not just accepted as another input payload.

Example Protected Approval Boundary

Because the earlier chapters already established an authenticated API model, the right design here is to treat the approval endpoint as part of that protected boundary. The endpoint should require an authenticated caller, enforce an approval-specific role or claim, and then pass only validated decisions back into the workflow.

Example protected approval boundary

```
using System.Net;
using Microsoft.Azure.Functions.Worker;
using Microsoft.Azure.Functions.Worker.Http;
using OrderProcessor.Security;

namespace OrderProcessor.Examples;

public sealed class SecureApprovalEndpoint
{
    private readonly ITokenValidator _tokenValidator;

    public SecureApprovalEndpoint(ITokenValidator tokenValidator)
    {
        _tokenValidator = tokenValidator;
    }

    [Function("SecureApprovalEndpoint")]
    public async Task<HttpResponseData> Run(
        [HttpTrigger(AuthorizationLevel.Anonymous, "post")]
        HttpRequestData req,
        FunctionContext ctx,
        CancellationToken stopToken)
    {
        var bearerToken = req.GetBearerToken();

        if (string.IsNullOrWhiteSpace(bearerToken))
        {
            var unauthorized = req.CreateResponse(HttpStatusCode.
            Unauthorized);
            await unauthorized.WriteStringAsync("Missing bearer token.",
            stopToken);
            return unauthorized;
        }

        var principal = await _tokenValidator.ValidateAsync(bearerToken,
        stopToken);
```

```
        if (principal is null)
        {
            var unauthorized = req.CreateResponse(HttpStatusCode.
            Unauthorized);
            await unauthorized.WriteStringAsync("Invalid or expired
            token.", stopToken);
            return unauthorized;
        }

        if (!principal.HasRole("Approver"))
        {
            var forbidden = req.CreateResponse(HttpStatusCode.Forbidden);
            await forbidden.WriteStringAsync("Caller is not allowed to
            approve this action.", stopToken);
            return forbidden;
        }

        var response = req.CreateResponse(HttpStatusCode.Accepted);
        return response;
    }
}
```

This example is intentionally schematic. In the evolving `OrderProcessor` sample, approval boundaries should reuse the same bearer-token validation and claims model introduced in Chapter 8 rather than rely on a separate trigger-level security pattern. This is shown deliberately as a boundary example rather than as a full new authentication implementation. The important architectural point is that the approval endpoint must live inside the authenticated and claims-aware model already introduced earlier in the book. It should not create a parallel security model of its own.

Secret Handling Is Part of Application Design

A second recurring problem is secret management. Teams often leave secrets in configuration because the application appears to be working and the hardening task feels administrative rather than architectural. But secrets influence architecture directly.

If the platform depends on Cosmos DB, Service Bus, partner APIs, or certificate-based integration, then secure secret retrieval is part of how the application starts and runs. A secret stored in the wrong place is not just a hygiene issue. It is a trust boundary problem.

That is why `OrderProcessor` should treat secret loading as a first-class platform concern. Secrets belong in a secure store such as Key Vault and should be retrieved through the identity model of the deployed workload rather than copied into files or source control. The earlier chapters already established that direction, and this chapter reinforces it by framing the opposite approach as a risk rather than a convenience.

Least Privilege Matters More in Distributed Systems

The same principle applies to identity scope. In distributed systems, many components talk to many other components. That makes it dangerously easy to grant one broad identity wide access and let several Functions share it simply because that is operationally convenient. In a system such as `OrderProcessor`, that is rarely the right answer. A Function that reads approval data does not automatically need write access to every store in the platform. An ERP integration component does not need broad rights across unrelated parts of the environment. The principle of least privilege matters more, not less, as the system becomes more distributed.

This is another place where teams often confuse speed with simplicity. Broad permissions feel simpler because they avoid access errors during development. In production, they expand blast radius and make mistakes or abuse harder to contain.

Encryption and Audit Are Not Optional Details

Modern cloud services often provide strong defaults for encryption at rest, which is helpful, but regulated systems may still need stronger or more explicit key-management choices. Just as importantly, encryption does not solve the question of accountability. If a sensitive action takes place and the platform cannot show who performed it, which tenant it affected, and when it happened, then the workflow is still weak from a governance and compliance perspective.

That is why approval flows, secrets access, and other sensitive boundaries in `OrderProcessor` should always connect back to the audit model established elsewhere in the book. Security-sensitive actions should produce durable, queryable traces of what happened. That is not separate from observability. It is part of trustworthy observability.

Real Project Fix: Secure Approval and Secret Boundaries in OrderProcessor

In `OrderProcessor`, the architectural answer is to make security part of the workflow design rather than an outer wrapper applied later. Sensitive endpoints such as approval callbacks must sit behind the authenticated model already established earlier in the platform. Caller identity and claims must be validated before workflow decisions are accepted. Secrets should be loaded from secure stores through managed identity or an equivalent trusted mechanism rather than copied into files or deployment settings. Function identities should be scoped narrowly to the resources they actually need.

That changes the platform in an important way. Security stops being a delayed hardening phase and becomes part of how the workflow is defined and trusted. The result is not only a more secure system, but a more understandable one. The platform knows who is allowed to act, which boundary they are acting on, and how that action can be audited later. That is what it means for security to be designed in rather than bolted on.

Risk: Over-logging and Telemetry Noise

Observability is essential in distributed systems. Without logs, traces, and metrics, a platform such as `OrderProcessor` becomes difficult to diagnose, difficult to operate, and difficult to improve. But observability has its own failure mode. Teams often assume that more telemetry automatically means better visibility. In practice, that is not how it works. Excessive logging, duplicated signals, poorly chosen retention, and noisy instrumentation usually create the opposite effect. They make the system harder to understand because the useful signals are buried under a flood of low-value detail.

That is what makes over-logging such an important risk to recognize. In a serverless system, the damage is not only cognitive. It is operational and financial as well. Millions of Function executions multiplied by several low-value log entries each can produce a large ingestion bill, slow down queries, clutter dashboards, and make on-call diagnosis harder instead of easier. `OrderProcessor` needs observability, but it needs observability with discipline. The platform should emit signals that help a human answer a question, not telemetry simply because a line of code was easy to add.

Why Over-logging Happens

Over-logging usually begins with good intentions. A developer is trying to make a workflow diagnosable, so they add a log before and after every step. Then another developer does the same in a different Function. Then a batch path logs every item in a loop, because that helped once in testing. Those logs remain at `Information` level because nothing forced the team to revisit them before production. Over time, the platform accumulates far more telemetry than it actually needs. Serverless environments make this easier to miss because the logging cost is distributed across invocations. A few extra log lines inside one Function do not seem dramatic. At production volume, they become a design choice with real cost and real operational consequences. The same problem appears when teams emit the same signal several ways at once, for example, as a log, a metric, and a trace event, even though only one of those representations is actually needed.

Example Anti-pattern: A Chatty Function

A simple Function makes the problem easy to see. Imagine a fraud-check path that logs every stage of its internal execution, including payload details that are not useful to operators.

Example anti-pattern: chatty fraud check

```
using System.Text.Json;
using Microsoft.Azure.Functions.Worker;

namespace OrderProcessor.Examples;

public static class ChattyFraudCheck
{
    [Function("ChattyFraudCheck")]
    public static async Task Run(
        [ServiceBusTrigger("fraud-queue", Connection =
        "ServiceBusConnection")]
        string orderJson,
        FunctionContext ctx)
    {
        var logger = ctx.GetLogger("FraudCheck");
```

```
        logger.LogInformation("Starting fraud check");
        logger.LogInformation("Received order payload: {OrderJson}",
        orderJson);
        logger.LogInformation("Deserializing order JSON");

        var order = JsonSerializer.Deserialize<Order>(orderJson);

        logger.LogInformation("Checking fraud for order {Id}", order?.Id);

        // ... fraud logic ...

        logger.LogInformation("Completed fraud check for order {Id}",
        order?.Id);
    }
}
```

This is intentionally noisy. The issue is not that each log line is individually impossible to justify. The issue is that together they produce a low signal-to-noise ratio. At scale, this kind of instrumentation creates a large volume of telemetry without giving operators a correspondingly useful view of the business state of the system.

Why This Is Dangerous

The first problem is that when everything is logged at `Information`, nothing stands out. The logs stop telling operators what matters and start narrating everything equally. The second problem is that logs often capture more data than they should. A payload that is convenient to print during development may contain tenant-sensitive or personally identifiable information that should never appear in a production log stream. The third problem is duplication. If the same event is represented redundantly in traces, logs, metrics, and repeated workflow messages, teams may end up counting or reacting to the same issue several times.

The fourth problem is cost. Raw telemetry has a lifecycle cost, not just an ingestion cost. Teams pay to ingest it, store it, query it, and interpret it. A logging strategy that grows without discipline eventually becomes a performance and budget problem as well as an observability problem.

Log Levels Should Express Meaning

One of the simplest corrections is to restore meaning to log levels. Debug should be for highly detailed local or temporary investigation, not production narration. `Information` should mark meaningful lifecycle milestones. `Warning` should highlight recoverable but notable conditions. `Error` should indicate failure that matters. Critical should be reserved for outages or system-level emergencies. When teams use those levels deliberately, the telemetry stream becomes much more useful because operators can distinguish ordinary flow from risk.

This matters particularly in a serverless system because high invocation volume amplifies whatever logging policy the team chooses. A poor choice of level inside one hot path can create large operational noise very quickly.

Sensitive Data Should Not Leak into Telemetry

A second discipline is to log identifiers and context rather than whole payloads wherever possible. For `OrderProcessor`, operators usually need to know which order failed, which tenant was affected, and which stage of the workflow produced the issue. They do not usually need the full raw payload in the log stream. That distinction is important because observability and compliance are closely linked. Logs that contain too much detail can become a second uncontrolled data store.

A healthier pattern looks like this.

Example signal-oriented logging

```
using System.Text.Json;
using Microsoft.Azure.Functions.Worker;

namespace OrderProcessor.Examples;

public static class FraudCheck
{
    [Function("FraudCheck")]
    public static async Task Run(
        [ServiceBusTrigger("fraud-queue", Connection = "Service
        BusConnection")]
        string orderJson,
        FunctionContext ctx)
```

```
    {
        var logger = ctx.GetLogger("FraudCheck");
        var order = JsonSerializer.Deserialize<Order>(orderJson);

        try
        {
            var passed = await FraudService.CheckAsync(order);

            if (!passed)
            {
                logger.LogWarning(
                    "Fraud flagged for order {Id}, tenant {TenantId}",
                    order?.Id,
                    order?.TenantId);
            }
            else
            {
                logger.LogInformation(
                    "Fraud check passed for order {Id}",
                    order?.Id);
            }
        }
        catch (Exception ex)
        {
            logger.LogError(
                ex,
                "Fraud check failed for order {Id}",
                order?.Id);

            throw;
        }
    }
}
```

This version still communicates useful business information, but it avoids dumping the full incoming payload into the telemetry stream. It is also much easier to query because the logs now correspond to meaningful workflow outcomes rather than every internal step.

Not Every Signal Needs to Be a Log

A frequent cause of telemetry noise is forgetting that logs, traces, and metrics serve different purposes. Logs are best for meaningful events that a human may need to read. Metrics are better for quantities and trends, such as retry counts, order volumes, latency distributions, or failure rates. Traces are best for correlation across service boundaries. If the same condition is represented in all three places without thought, dashboards become noisy and teams struggle to decide which signal is authoritative.

For `OrderProcessor`, that means the observability model should remain intentional. If the question is "how many fraud checks failed today?", a metric may be more useful than scanning raw logs. If the question is "which exact order failed and why?", a log is the right tool. If the question is "how did this request move across the system?", the trace is the right tool. Good observability is partly about choosing the right medium for each kind of answer.

Hot Loops Need Especially Careful Logging

Batch-oriented or loop-heavy paths deserve special caution. A Function that logs once per item in a large file or per record in a high-volume queue can produce enormous telemetry very quickly. In those cases, the better pattern is often to log a summary for the batch and reserve per-item logs for exceptional conditions only. This is one of the places where developers often carry development-time habits into production without noticing the scale implications.

That principle is especially relevant for file-driven or tenant-heavy workloads in `OrderProcessor`, where one triggering event may fan out into many smaller pieces of work. The observability design should not grow linearly with every internal step unless the business truly needs that level of raw detail.

Retention Is Part of Observability Design

Retention is another place where telemetry discipline matters. Keeping raw logs for a long period may sound safe, but for most operational scenarios the value of raw detail decays much faster than teams expect. What remains useful in the long term is often aggregate trend data, audit-relevant events, or exported summaries rather than every individual log line. That means observability design should include explicit retention thinking. Raw logs should remain available for an interval that genuinely helps diagnosis.

Longer-lived reporting should rely on aggregates, exported summaries, or other cheaper representations. The point is not to keep less because logs are unimportant. The point is to keep the right form of telemetry for the right length of time.

Sampling Can Improve Signal as well as Cost

Sampling is often treated only as a cost control, but it is also a clarity tool. If the system captures every successful trace at full fidelity while also collecting every failure, the platform may end up overwhelming itself with routine happy-path detail. By contrast, a model that samples a small portion of successful flows while retaining all failures can preserve the most important diagnostic paths without burying them under normal traffic.

This is especially useful in large-volume systems. A sampled success path still gives the team a representative operational picture, while the full set of failures remains available when the system actually needs close attention.

Project Fix: Reducing Telemetry Noise in OrderProcessor

In `OrderProcessor`, the right answer is not to strip observability out of the system. It is to make the observability model more intentional. Functions should emit one or two meaningful logs for a normal path rather than narrating every internal step. Sensitive payload data should be removed or reduced to identifiers. Metrics should carry aggregate questions, traces should carry correlation, and logs should carry the business events that humans may need to understand. High-volume paths should prefer summary logging over per-item chatter. Retention and sampling should be chosen deliberately rather than left as defaults forever.

That changes the platform in a useful way. Observability becomes cheaper, clearer, and more actionable at the same time. Operators can find the important signal more quickly, dashboards become easier to trust, and the telemetry estate is less likely to become a second system that requires its own constant rescue. In a distributed platform, that kind of restraint is not a loss of visibility. It is what makes visibility usable.

Risk: Reinventing the Wheel

Distributed systems force teams to solve difficult problems repeatedly. Messages fail and need replay. Work needs scheduling. The state must survive restarts. Authentication has to be enforced consistently. Logs and traces need to be captured somewhere useful. Because these concerns appear everywhere, developers are often tempted to solve them directly in application code. That temptation is understandable. Familiar tools feel faster than learning a new service, and a custom implementation can look lightweight at first. In practice, however, this is one of the most expensive habits a team can develop. Time is spent rebuilding capabilities that the platform already provides, edge cases are missed, and the application becomes responsible for infrastructure plumbing that should never have been its job.

That is what makes reinventing the wheel such a serious risk in a system such as `OrderProcessor`. The value of the platform is in how it handles orders, approvals, integrations, tenants, and operational constraints. It is not in whether the team can hand-build a retry queue, a timer loop, or a custom token-validation layer. When the system spends too much of its complexity budget on rebuilding commodity platform behavior, it becomes harder to maintain and less reliable under pressure. The architectural lesson is not that every Azure service must always be used. It is that teams should be very cautious before replacing proven platform capabilities with bespoke code that has to be operated, secured, and debugged forever.

Why Teams Reinvent Wheels

Most reinvention starts from a familiar bias rather than a bad intention. Developers know C#, SQL, or EF Core well, so they reach for those tools first. A developer may feel that writing a table-backed retry queue is quicker than learning Service Bus dead-letter handling. Another may believe a `Task.Delay` loop is simpler than understanding Durable timers. Someone else may hand-roll JWT checks because the application only needs "something small for now." Each of those choices feels efficient in the moment because it avoids learning a new platform primitive.

The trouble is that these short-term gains are usually illusions. The custom implementation rarely stops at the first working version. It begins accumulating all the behaviors the underlying platform already solved: retries, ordering, poison-message handling, visibility, persistence, backoff, scaling, observability, and security. Once that happens, the team has not simplified the architecture. It has moved platform complexity into the application codebase, where it is usually harder to test, harder to scale, and easier to get wrong.

Example Anti-pattern: A Hand-Built Retry Queue in SQL

A retry queue is a good example because it is one of the most common things teams try to rebuild themselves. A developer wants failed orders to be retried later, so they write the failed payload into a SQL table and add a background process to poll it.

The example below is deliberately shown as tightly coupled application code. That is the point of the anti-pattern. Wrapping this in a repository would make the code look tidier, but it would not change the architectural problem: the application has started to rebuild messaging infrastructure inside its own database.

Example anti-pattern: SQL-backed retry queue

```
using Microsoft.Data.SqlClient;
using System.Text.Json;

namespace OrderProcessor.Examples;

public sealed class SqlRetryQueueAntiPattern
{
    private readonly string _connectionString;

    public SqlRetryQueueAntiPattern(string connectionString)
    {
        _connectionString = connectionString;
    }

    public async Task SaveFailedOrderAsync(Order order)
    {
        await using var connection = new SqlConnection(_connectionString);
        await connection.OpenAsync();

        var command = new SqlCommand(
            "INSERT INTO RetryOrders (Id, Payload, RetryCount) VALUES (@id,
            @payload, 0)",
```

```
            connection);

        command.Parameters.AddWithValue("@id", order.Id);
        command.Parameters.AddWithValue("@payload", JsonSerializer.
        Serialize(order));

        await command.ExecuteNonQueryAsync();
    }
}
```

On the surface, this looks straightforward. In reality, it is the beginning of a platform feature that now needs a scheduler, retry rules, poison-message handling, visibility, cleanup, and concurrency control. The application has quietly taken ownership of a messaging concern that the cloud platform already knows how to handle.

The Azure-Native Alternative Is Usually Stronger

A healthier design asks whether the platform already provides the capability that the team is starting to rebuild. In this case, Azure Service Bus already supports retries, dead-letter queues, delivery counts, and trigger integration with Functions. Instead of building a queue in SQL and polling it manually, `OrderProcessor` can let failed work land in a dead-letter queue and then reprocess it through a controlled recovery path.

Example platform-native recovery path using Service Bus DLQ

```
using System.Text.Json;
using Azure.Messaging.ServiceBus;
using Microsoft.Azure.Functions.Worker;

namespace OrderProcessor.Examples;

public sealed class ReprocessDlqExample
{
    private readonly ServiceBusSender _sender;

    public ReprocessDlqExample(ServiceBusClient serviceBusClient)
    {
        _sender = serviceBusClient.CreateSender("erp-queue");
    }
```

```
    [Function("ReprocessDlqExample")]
    public async Task Run(
        [ServiceBusTrigger("erp-queue/$DeadLetterQueue", Connection =
        "ServiceBusConnection")]
        string msg)
    {
        var order = JsonSerializer.Deserialize<Order>(msg);

        if (order is null)
        {
            return;
        }

        await _sender.SendMessageAsync(new ServiceBusMessage(msg));
    }
}
```

This is not only shorter than a full custom queuing subsystem. It is also more aligned with how the platform already behaves operationally. The team is using messaging for messaging rather than simulating messaging inside a general-purpose database.

State Management Is Another Common Reinvention Trap

Teams also reinvent durable states surprisingly often. Once a workflow needs to survive restarts or track long-running progress, the instinct is to create state tables, status flags, and homegrown replay logic in SQL or Cosmos DB. That can work in a narrow sense, but it means the application is now responsible for reconstructing workflow progress and restart behavior itself. In a system such as `OrderProcessor`, that is exactly the sort of problem Durable Functions was designed to solve.

This does not mean every stateful process must become a Durable Functions orchestration. It does mean teams should pause before hand-building durable workflow state when the platform already provides checkpointing, timers, resumption, and replay semantics. Custom state management is rarely as simple as it first appears, especially once versioning and failure recovery enter the picture.

Scheduling Is Often Rebuilt Badly

Another classic example is scheduling. Teams often need to run a check later, wait for a timeout, or trigger a recurring process. The simplest code they can imagine is often a loop with `Task.Delay`, a background timer, or a polling worker. That is easy to write and easy to underestimate. A hand-built scheduler is a good example of something that works in development and becomes fragile in production. It can be tied to process lifetime, fail badly across restarts, and create hidden timing assumptions. In `OrderProcessor`, a safer answer is to use the scheduling primitives already provided by the platform.

Example anti-pattern: in-process scheduler

```
while (true)
{
    await Task.Delay(TimeSpan.FromHours(1));
    await CheckOrdersAsync();
}
```

Example platform-native alternative: durable timer

```
using Microsoft.Azure.Functions.Worker;
using Microsoft.DurableTask;

namespace OrderProcessor.Examples;

public static class OrderCheckOrchestrator
{
    [Function("OrderCheckOrchestrator")]
    public static async Task Run(
        [OrchestrationTrigger] TaskOrchestrationContext context)
    {
        await context.CreateTimer(
            context.CurrentUtcDateTime.AddHours(1),
            CancellationToken.None);

        await context.CallActivityAsync("CheckOrders", (object?)null);
    }
}
```

The durable version persists the timer, survives restarts, and fits the same workflow model used elsewhere in the system. The application does not need to invent scheduling reliability for itself.

Authentication and Monitoring Are Often Rebuilt Unnecessarily Too

Security and observability are two more areas where teams frequently create work for themselves. A hand-rolled JWT validation flow may seem manageable at first, but identity is rarely a good place to improvise. The same is true of custom log tables in SQL or homegrown status dashboards assembled from arbitrary storage writes. These solutions tend to start as convenience hacks and end as fragile parallel platforms that duplicate services the cloud already provides more reliably.

For `OrderProcessor`, this is an important reminder. The platform's value is not in proving that it can implement its own authentication middleware, logging store, or scheduling engine from first principles. Its value is in handling business workflows safely on top of strong underlying platform capabilities.

Why Reinvention Hurts the System

The first cost is time. Every custom replacement for a platform primitive demands design, implementation, testing, edge-case handling, deployment, and support. The second cost is fragility. Platform services such as Service Bus, Durable Functions, App Insights, Key Vault, and managed identity exist because these concerns are harder than they look. A simplified in-house version usually works only until scale, failure, or compliance pressure reveals what it never handled properly.

The third cost is focus. Once the codebase starts owning retry queues, schedulers, custom token handling, or bespoke monitoring stores, engineering effort shifts away from business logic and toward infrastructure behavior that should already have been delegated. That leaves the platform with more code, more operational burden, and less clarity about what the system is actually meant to do.

Project Fix: Stop Rebuilding Platform Capabilities in OrderProcessor

In `OrderProcessor`, the right response is to be more disciplined about what belongs in the application and what belongs in the platform. Failed messaging paths should use Service Bus dead-letter queues rather than table-backed retry systems. Long-running workflow state should use Durable Functions rather than hand-built status tables wherever orchestration is the real problem being solved. Timed waits and scheduled workflow steps should rely on durable timers rather than process-bound delay loops. Authentication, secret handling, and observability should continue to build on the platform services already introduced in earlier chapters instead of drifting into custom replacements.

That keeps the application focused on its real job. `OrderProcessor` should spend its complexity on order processing, approvals, integrations, tenancy, compliance, and resilience boundaries - not on recreating infrastructure plumbing the platform already knows how to do better. A strong serverless architecture is not only about what the team builds. It is also about what the team chooses not to rebuild.

Risk: Neglecting Governance and Compliance

Distributed systems are shaped not only by code and architecture but also by rules. Those rules determine where data is allowed to live, who is allowed to deploy, how resources are tagged, how long logs are retained, which boundaries are audited, and what the platform must prove to regulators or internal reviewers. When teams talk about governance and compliance as though they belong to someone else, usually operations, security, or legal, the system starts drifting almost immediately. Resources appear without ownership. Regions are chosen for convenience rather than policy. Audit trails are inconsistent. Retention rules are forgotten. The platform may continue to run, but it does so without the controls that make it trustworthy at scale.

That is what makes governance and compliance such an important design risk in a serverless system such as `OrderProcessor`. Because serverless platforms reduce the visibility of underlying infrastructure, teams can mistakenly feel that governance matters less. In reality, the opposite is true. When resources are easy to create and deploy, they must be governed more deliberately, not less. The goal is not to add paperwork around the outside of the architecture. The goal is to make policy part of the architecture itself so that deployment, storage, retention, and audit behavior all reflect the same rules the organization claims to follow.

Why Governance Is Often Ignored

Governance is frequently deferred because it feels slower and less immediately rewarding than feature delivery. A team under pressure to deliver may see tagging, region policy, retention settings, or audit plumbing as something that can be tidied up later. There is also a recurring ownership problem. Developers may assume governance belongs to operations or security, while operations teams assume developers are already following the required standards. In serverless environments, that confusion is even easier to sustain because much of the infrastructure is abstracted behind services that seem to "just work."

The trouble is that governance gaps do not remain theoretical for long. A resource deployed in the wrong geography can become a compliance issue immediately. A service created without tags can become a cost-allocation problem immediately. Missing diagnostic settings can turn a normal audit request into a scramble to reconstruct history after the fact. Governance is not a separate layer that can be painted on later. It is a set of operating constraints that the platform either encodes or violates.

Example Anti-pattern: An Ungoverned Resource Deployment

A simple infrastructure example shows the problem clearly. Imagine a Cosmos DB account deployed with no meaningful tags, no ownership signal, and in a region that conflicts with the platform's intended jurisdiction model.

Example anti-pattern: ungoverned resource deployment

```
resource cosmos 'Microsoft.DocumentDB/databaseAccounts@2022-05-15' = {
  name: 'randomcosmos123'
  location: 'eastus'
  properties: {
    databaseAccountOfferType: 'Standard'
  }
}
```

The code itself is small, but the implications are large. If the resource belongs to a workload intended for EU-regulated tenants, then the wrong region is now a compliance problem. If the resource has no tags, finance cannot allocate cost cleanly and operations cannot see ownership clearly. If no policy blocks the deployment, then the platform is relying on memory and good intentions rather than enforceable rules.

Governance Failures Usually Begin with Drift

The most dangerous aspect of governance failure is that it often begins quietly. One developer deploys a resource in the wrong place because it is convenient in the moment. Another creates a store without tags because the pipeline does not require them. A team forgets to enable diagnostics on a new component because the system still appears healthy without them. None of these decisions feels catastrophic in isolation, which is exactly why they accumulate. Over time, however, drift becomes operationally expensive. Resources no longer follow naming or ownership standards. Cost analysis becomes harder. Audit evidence becomes incomplete. Regional data boundaries become ambiguous. Teams then discover that governance is not an administrative overhead they avoided but a structural discipline they postponed until it became harder and more expensive to restore.

Region and Jurisdiction Are Architecture, Not Paperwork

For `OrderProcessor`, earlier chapters already established that tenant and regional boundaries matter. Governance is what turns those architectural statements into enforceable rules. If the system is supposed to keep EU-regulated data in approved EU regions, then that must be reflected not only in documentation but also in deployment controls. If a certain class of resource must never be created outside a jurisdiction, then the platform should prevent that rather than merely advising against it.

A policy rule is one direct way to express that intent.

Example policy direction: restrict deployments to approved regions

```
{
  "if": {
    "field": "location",
    "notIn": ["northeurope", "westeurope"]
  },
```

```
  "then": {
    "effect": "deny"
  }
}
```

This example matters because it shows the difference between governance as guidance and governance as enforcement. A policy that can deny a bad deployment is part of the platform. A wiki page telling people to remember the right region is not.

Resource Tagging Is Operational Governance, Not Decoration

Tagging is often treated as a cosmetic concern, but in a distributed system it is one of the simplest ways to make ownership, environment, and compliance intent visible. A Function App, storage account, Cosmos DB account, or monitoring resource without tags is harder to govern because its purpose and owner are not obvious from the platform view. In a growing system such as `OrderProcessor`, that becomes a real operating problem.

A more disciplined deployment should therefore make tagging part of the resource contract rather than leaving it optional.

Example governance direction: tagged resources

```
tags: {
  Environment: 'Prod'
  Owner: 'OrderProcessorTeam'
  Compliance: 'GDPR'
}
```

Again, the exact tags are less important than the principle. A governed platform should make ownership and policy intent visible by default.

Auditability Is Part of Compliance, Not Just Observability

A compliant system must be able to answer questions about what happened, who accessed what, where they accessed it, and which boundary they crossed. This is where governance and observability overlap. A missing audit trail is not only an operational inconvenience. It is often a compliance failure. If `OrderProcessor` cannot show who accessed tenant data, who approved a high-value decision, or whether secrets were accessed unexpectedly, the platform is not merely less observable. It is less trustworthy.

That is why diagnostic settings, audit logs, and retention rules belong in the platform design. Sensitive services such as Key Vault, Cosmos DB, and messaging infrastructure should emit the events needed to support investigation and compliance review. Earlier chapters already established audit patterns inside the application flow. Governance extends that idea to the platform estate itself.

Retention Rules Must Be Deliberate

Retention is another place where teams often create compliance problems through omission. Keeping data forever may feel safe because it reduces the risk of losing something useful, but for many regulated workloads that instinct is wrong. Some logs should exist only for a defined period. Some personally identifiable information should be deleted according to policy. Some raw telemetry should be pruned while aggregates or summaries are retained longer in a cheaper and more appropriate form.

For `OrderProcessor`, this means retention must be part of the operating model rather than a forgotten default. A system cannot claim serious governance if it retains sensitive data indefinitely simply because nobody configured deletion. Retention is not only a storage choice. It is a compliance boundary.

Compliance Should Be Enforced in Delivery, Not Remembered Manually

One of the strongest ways to make governance real is to include it in deployment and delivery paths. If a build can deploy a resource that violates region, tag, or policy requirements, then the platform is still trusting manual attention more than it should. A healthier design makes non-compliant deployment paths fail early, ideally in CI/CD, before drift reaches production.

That is best understood as a delivery pattern rather than as a promise that one exact pipeline task will suit every team. The important point is that policy and deployment should meet in an automated gate. The platform should make the compliant path easier than the non-compliant one.

Example compliance gate in delivery

```
- task: AzurePolicy@1
  inputs:
    Scope: '/subscriptions/xxxx/resourceGroups/OrderProcessor-RG'
    Action: 'evaluate'
```

This is illustrative rather than prescriptive. The core lesson is that compliance checks should live in automated delivery controls, not in memory.

Project Fix: Governance and Compliance Built into OrderProcessor

In `OrderProcessor`, the right answer is to make governance visible in infrastructure, deployment, and operational settings. Resources should carry meaningful tags. Regional restrictions should be enforced through policy rather than left as convention. Diagnostic settings should ensure that sensitive services emit the audit evidence the platform needs. Retention rules should be configured deliberately for logs, telemetry, and regulated data. Delivery pipelines should fail when infrastructure or configuration breaks the platform's stated compliance model. That changes the nature of the system in an important way. Governance stops being something discussed outside the architecture and becomes part of how the architecture is allowed to exist. The result is not a slower platform. It is a platform that is more predictable, easier to operate responsibly, and much less likely to drift into expensive or non-compliant states without anyone noticing.

Risk: Forgetting the Human Factor

Distributed systems are made of code, infrastructure, queues, workflows, APIs, dashboards, and policies - but they are also made of people. Developers have to build and change them. Operators have to run them. Support teams have to explain them. Auditors have to inspect them. Users and approvers have to interact with them. One of the most persistent design mistakes in systems such as `OrderProcessor` is to behave as though all of that human involvement is secondary, or worse, irrelevant. The architecture is treated as a purely technical puzzle, while the people around it are expected to adapt silently to whatever complexity the system happens to expose.

That is what makes the human factor a serious design risk rather than a soft concern. A workflow can be technically correct and still fail socially. A runbook can be complete on paper and still be useless during an incident. An approval flow can be secure and durable yet still confuse the person who is supposed to make the decision. A platform can emit excellent telemetry and still overwhelm operators with noise. In `OrderProcessor`, the architecture does not succeed only when the code runs. It succeeds when developers can change it safely, operators can understand it quickly, users can respond to it sensibly, and the surrounding processes remain aligned with the system that actually exists.

Why Teams Forget the Human Factor

The most common reason is engineering bias. Developers are trained to solve technical problems, so they naturally focus on workflow logic, state, retries, scaling, and correctness. Those concerns matter, but they can crowd out equally important questions. Can someone understand the approval email? Will an operator know what to do when a queue starts backing up? Will a user recognize whether they should retry an action or wait? Will the playbook still match the deployed system six months from now?

Another reason is overconfidence in automation. Serverless platforms scale well and recover from many classes of infrastructure failure automatically, which can create the impression that operational and human workflows no longer need much attention. In reality, automation usually changes human work rather than removing it. Operators still need decision-ready signals. Developers still need safe local feedback loops. Users still need clear messages. If the architecture assumes flawless humans or no humans at all, it will usually fail at the exact moments when clarity matters most.

Example Risk: A Technically Correct but Socially Weak Approval Flow

`OrderProcessor` already introduced durable approval patterns earlier in the book. From a purely technical perspective, the workflow can pause and wait for an external decision.

Example workflow step

```
var result = await context.WaitForExternalEvent<string>("ApprovalResult");
```

There is nothing wrong with that from a workflow perspective. The risk appears when the surrounding human experience is poor. If the approval email lacks the order ID, amount, tenant context, or explanation of why approval is required, the recipient may make the wrong decision or hesitate long enough to create unnecessary delay. The orchestration is still behaving correctly, but the system as a whole is not serving the people inside it very well.

This is the central lesson of the section. Human-facing parts of the architecture are not superficial. They are part of the workflow boundary itself.

Developer Experience Is Part of System Reliability

One of the easiest human-factor risks to underestimate is developer experience. If local testing is painful, developers skip it. If the inner loop is slow, they make bigger, riskier changes less often. If the deployment path is brittle or slow, teams begin to work around it. Over time, these frictions turn into architecture problems because they shape how safely and how often the system changes.

For `OrderProcessor`, that means developer tooling is not a luxury. Emulators, reproducible local environments, reliable CI/CD, and rollback-friendly delivery all reduce the chance that humans introduce avoidable failure. A platform that is difficult to change safely will eventually be changed unsafely.

Operators Need Decision-Ready Signals, Not Raw Machine Output

A second risk appears during operations. Systems often emit plenty of data but very little guidance. A queue fills up, a dependency fails, a circuit breaker opens, or a replay backlog grows - and the dashboards still leave the operator to infer what matters, why it matters, and what should happen next. That is not a telemetry problem in the narrow sense. It is a human-design problem. The system is speaking in machine detail when the operator needs a decision frame.

For `OrderProcessor`, observability should therefore be shaped by human questions. What is broken now? Which workflow stage is affected? Which tenants are affected? Is action required immediately, or is the platform already retrying safely? When telemetry answers those questions directly, operators can act faster and with less error.

User Experience Shapes System Behavior Too

Users are another part of the architecture, whether teams acknowledge that or not. A vague or confusing response can cause users to retry an action that is already in progress, generate duplicate work, or open unnecessary support requests. A harsh raw error can make the platform feel unreliable even when the underlying issue is temporary and already contained. In distributed systems, user messaging is part of control flow because it influences what people do next.

That means `OrderProcessor` should not expose low-level system failures as though they were meaningful user guidance. A better design translates internal complexity into a message that helps the user respond sensibly.

Example user-friendly error response

```
{
  "message": "Your order is still processing. Please try again in a few
minutes.",
  "referenceId": "12345"
}
```

This kind of response is not "just UX." It is part of making the distributed workflow behave safely in the presence of normal human reactions.

Alert Design Must Account for Human Limits

Another common failure mode appears during incidents. The system emits many correct alerts, but the humans receiving them cannot process them at incident speed. Ten Functions all produce warnings. Five downstream services raise related failures. Slack fills with repeated notifications. The monitoring setup is technically thorough, but operationally paralyzing. This is one of the clearest examples of how a system can be correct in instrumentation terms and still poor in human terms.

For `OrderProcessor`, alerting should therefore be shaped by human triage capacity. Alerts should be aggregated where possible, prioritized by severity, and routed to the teams that can actually act on them. A hundred precise alerts are often less useful than one good incident summary.

Documentation Drift Is a Real Systems Risk

Documentation is another place where the human factor often becomes visible too late. Teams write useful playbooks, runbooks, recovery instructions, or approval guidance at one point in time and then continue evolving the system without evolving the documentation alongside it. Months later, the human-facing operational model no longer matches the architecture. During a quiet week that may not matter. During an incident, it matters immediately.

For `OrderProcessor`, this means documentation must be treated as part of the system rather than an afterthought. Playbooks belong close to the code and infrastructure they describe. Changes to the platform should prompt corresponding updates to the human instructions that surround it. The goal is not beautiful documentation. The goal is documentation that still tells the truth when the system is under stress.

Human-Centered Observability Is More Useful Than Raw Detail

A good operational view often says less but means more. Instead of showing a wall of metrics and low-level traces, a human-centered dashboard expresses the system in terms that support action. It summarizes the affected workflow, highlights the dependency causing trouble, shows the next retry or recovery point, and indicates whether someone needs to intervene now.

A useful `OrderProcessor` incident dashboard might therefore answer questions such as these in plain terms: how many orders are blocked right now, which dependency is responsible, whether the circuit breaker is open, when the next recovery attempt is due, and at what point escalation becomes necessary. That kind of view treats the operator as part of the system rather than as a person expected to mentally reconstruct the architecture from raw fragments.

The System Is Socio-Technical Whether Teams Admit It or Not

This is the deeper idea behind the section. Distributed systems are not purely technical artifacts. They are socio-technical systems. Code, infrastructure, automation, operators, users, support teams, auditors, playbooks, and communication paths all interact. If one of those layers is neglected, the platform will still feel the consequences. Serverless architecture does not remove that reality. If anything, it makes it more important, because abstracted infrastructure can make teams underestimate the human complexity that remains.

In `OrderProcessor`, that means workflow design, observability, delivery, documentation, and messaging should all be judged not only by technical correctness but also by whether they support the people who have to live with the platform. Figure 11-2 shows the socio-technical shape of a distributed system, where software, operations, users, and guidance all affect reliability together.

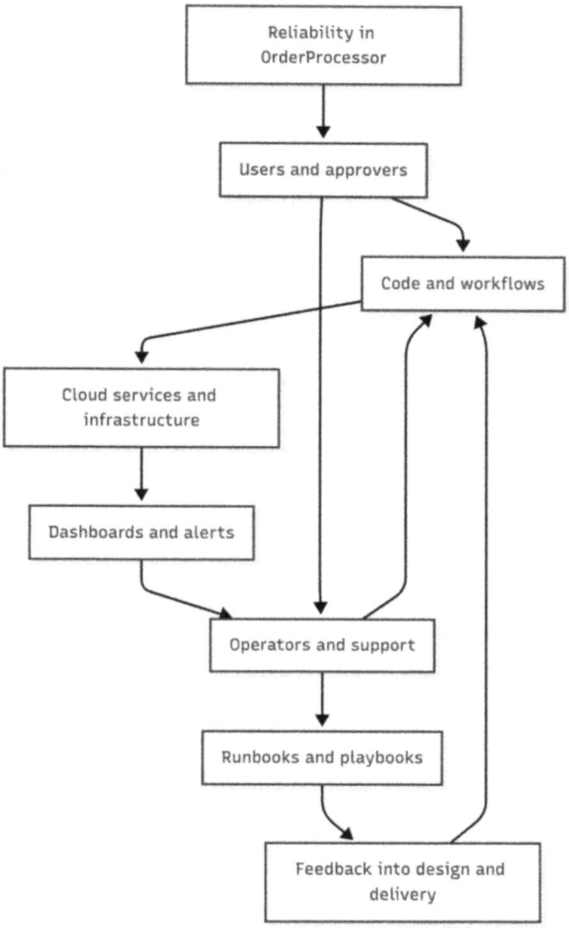

Figure 11-2. *The Socio-Technical Shape of Reliability in OrderProcessor*

Project Fix: Making OrderProcessor Human-Aware

In `OrderProcessor`, the practical answer is to improve the system at the human boundaries as well as the technical ones. Developer workflows should be supported with reliable local tooling and fast, trustworthy delivery paths. Operator dashboards should present what is broken, why it matters, and what to do next rather than simply exposing raw states. User-facing messages should reduce confusion and avoid encouraging harmful retry behavior. Alerts should be aggregated and prioritized so they remain usable during incidents. Playbooks and operational guidance should live close to the system and evolve with it rather than lagging behind it. That makes the platform stronger in a way that pure code changes alone cannot. The system becomes easier to change, easier to run, easier to explain, and easier to trust. In a mature distributed platform, that is not a secondary concern. It is part of what reliability actually means.

EXERCISES

1. Take a deliberately bloated orchestrator that coordinates fraud, tax, ERP, logistics, invoicing, notifications, and audit in one flow. Refactor it so the orchestrator keeps only the critical path and publishes an event for the rest.
2. Compare an over-coupled orchestration trace with a lean orchestration trace. Identify which version makes it easier to see where the business-critical path ends and where downstream reactions begin.
3. Build a small example where two read models for the same order disagree temporarily after an update. Record what the user would see and explain why this is not necessarily a bug.
4. Add idempotency checks to one event subscriber in `OrderProcessor` and then deliver the same event twice. Confirm that the second delivery does not create duplicate business work.
5. Add a `LastUpdatedUtc` field, or a comparable freshness marker, to an order read model. Use it to show how a client or dashboard can detect that a view may still be catching up.
6. Configure a local or sample Cosmos client with session consistency and compare the behavior of a same-session read with a more loosely consistent read path.
7. Replace a naive retry loop around an ERP call with a named resilient `HttpClient` configured in `Program.cs`. Explain what moved out of the business code and why that is an improvement.
8. Simulate a failing downstream dependency and observe the difference between a retry storm and a bounded resilience strategy using timeout, retry limits, and circuit breaking at the client boundary.

9. Identify one workflow in `OrderProcessor` where asynchronous decoupling through a queue would be safer than repeated synchronous retries. Explain the trade-off.

10. Take a chatty orchestration or Function and estimate how many extra billable executions or telemetry events it creates at realistic volume. Then redesign it to reduce unnecessary chatter.

11. Review a Cosmos DB configuration and identify where throughput, autoscale limits, or partitioning choices could create waste for a multi-tenant workload.

12. Reduce raw telemetry retention in a sample monitoring configuration and describe which kinds of data should remain raw, which should become aggregates, and which can be deleted.

13. Start with an insecure approval endpoint and redesign it so that it sits behind the authenticated model established earlier in the book. Describe what claims or roles should be required.

14. Trace one sensitive approval action end to end and define the minimum audit information that should be recorded so the platform can later prove who acted, when they acted, and on which tenant or order.

15. Rewrite a noisy Function so that it logs only meaningful business outcomes, avoids payload dumping, and uses levels deliberately. Compare the old and new versions for signal-to-noise ratio.

16. Take a homegrown retry-queue or scheduler idea and replace it with the Azure-native service that should own that concern instead. Explain what reliability or operational burden is removed by doing so.

17. Write a simple policy rule or governance check that prevents deployment to an unapproved region, and then describe how that rule supports the regional architecture established earlier in the book.

18. Add a required tagging convention to a sample infrastructure deployment and explain how those tags improve ownership, cost allocation, or compliance visibility.

19. Review a user-facing API error message and rewrite it so it helps the user respond safely instead of encouraging retries or confusion during eventual consistency or downstream delay.

20. Take one operator-facing dashboard or playbook and assess whether it answers the questions a human actually needs during an incident. Improve it so it communicates what is broken, why it matters, and what should happen next.

Summary

Chapter 11 reframed serverless distributed architecture through a risk lens. Instead of asking only how to build workflows, integrations, and platform capabilities, it asked how those same designs begin to fail when teams over-couple orchestrations, ignore eventual consistency, rely too heavily on retries, neglect cost, defer security, flood the system with telemetry, rebuild platform features unnecessarily, or treat governance as optional. In each case, the problem was not the technology itself. The problem was a design habit that looked reasonable in isolation but became harmful as the system grew in scale, complexity, and operational pressure.

Taken together, these risks show that robust serverless systems are built as much through restraint as through capability. `OrderProcessor` becomes healthier when orchestrators stay focused, consistency is made explicit, resilience is layered rather than improvised, cost is treated as an architectural signal, security is built into the workflow boundary, observability is designed for signal rather than noise, platform services are used where they should be used, governance is automated, and human operators and users are treated as part of the system rather than as an afterthought. That is the deeper lesson of the chapter: distributed systems fail less often when their technical boundaries, operational boundaries, and human boundaries are all designed deliberately.

CHAPTER 12

The Future of Serverless .NET, Azure, and Distributed Systems

The earlier chapters focused on what it takes to build a modern serverless distributed system in practice. We looked at Functions, messaging, orchestration, consistency, observability, resilience, security, governance, and the human realities of operating a platform once it leaves the whiteboard. By this point, `OrderProcessor` is no longer a simple sample application. It has become a reference architecture for how event-driven .NET systems can be designed on Azure with durable workflows, clear operational boundaries, and cloud-native practices. But distributed systems do not stand still, and neither does the platform beneath them. The final chapter therefore shifts from today's implementation choices to the direction of travel, how .NET has matured for serverless workloads, how Azure's serverless ecosystem continues to expand, and how those changes affect the architectural decisions we make now.

This chapter looks forward without abandoning the lessons of the rest of the book. The goal is not to predict every future feature or chase hype. It is to identify which patterns are becoming more important, which older assumptions are already fading, and how a system like `OrderProcessor` should evolve if it is to remain modern, maintainable, and relevant. That means looking at .NET 10 and the isolated worker model as the current baseline for Azure Functions, examining the growing role of hybrid serverless architectures that combine Functions with container-hosted services, and considering how orchestration, streams, and AI are reshaping what distributed systems can do. The chapter then closes by bringing the entire journey together into a final reference architecture and a set of lessons that should still hold even as the platform continues to change.

© Patrick Kearns 2026
P. Kearns, *Serverless Distributed Systems in Modern .NET and Azure*,
https://doi.org/10.1007/979-8-8688-2839-3_12

The Evolution of .NET for Serverless

The story of .NET in serverless has changed dramatically. What once felt like a constrained or awkward runtime option is now a strong, modern choice for cloud-native workloads. With **.NET 10 now released as an LTS release** and supported through **November 14, 2028,** the discussion is no longer about whether .NET belongs in serverless. It is about how well the modern .NET platform now fits the needs of resilient, observable, high-throughput distributed systems. For `OrderProcessor`, that shift is important because the platform patterns used throughout the book, dependency injection, middleware, resilient HTTP clients, structured logging, async workflows, and streaming, now align much more naturally with mainstream .NET development than they did in the earlier years of Azure Functions.

The most important platform shift is that the **isolated worker model is now the clear path forward for modern .NET Azure Functions.** Microsoft's current guidance is to migrate away from the in-process model; support for the in-process model ends on **November 10, 2026**; and the in-process model currently supports only **.NET 8**, while newer .NET versions require the isolated worker model. That means any forward-looking serverless architecture in .NET should now be framed around isolated workers, standard ASP.NET Core-style startup and dependency injection patterns, and a hosting model that lets the Functions app target .NET independently of the underlying host.

Figure 12-1 shows the shift from the earlier Azure Functions model to the modern isolated-worker, cloud-native .NET model.

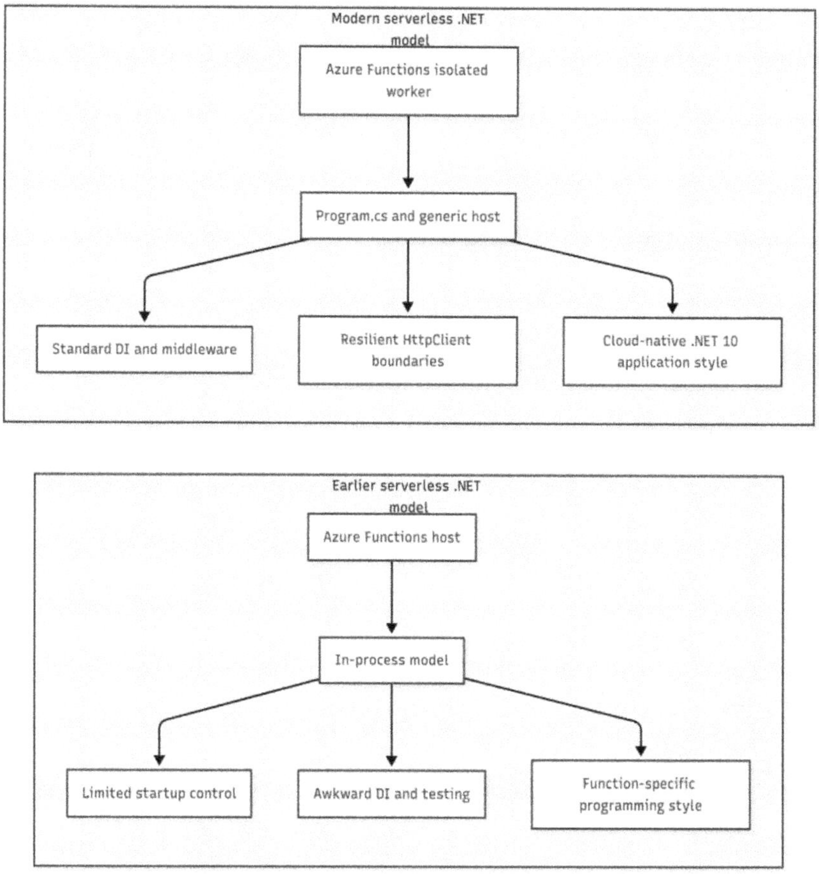

***Figure 12-1.** Comparing Modern Isolated Azure Functions with the Earlier In-Process Serverless .NET Model*

From Specialized Functions Code to Normal .NET Application Structure

One of the biggest practical improvements is that modern Azure Functions development in .NET no longer feels like stepping into a different programming model. In the isolated worker model, the Functions app starts to look much more like a normal .NET application. Startup configuration, dependency injection, middleware, configuration sources, and service registration all follow patterns that are familiar from ASP.NET Core and the generic host. That reduces friction for teams because the same habits they already use in modern .NET applications now carry into serverless code much more cleanly. Microsoft's documentation is explicit that isolated Functions use regular ASP.NET Core dependency injection patterns and can target .NET versions independently of the host.

A modern startup shape for OrderProcessor, therefore, looks less like legacy Functions boilerplate and more like a normal cloud-native .NET host:

Example: modern isolated worker startup

```
using Azure.Storage.Blobs;
using Microsoft.Azure.Functions.Worker;
using Microsoft.Azure.Functions.Worker.Builder;
using Microsoft.Extensions.DependencyInjection;
using Microsoft.Extensions.Hosting;
using Microsoft.Extensions.Http.Resilience;

var builder = FunctionsApplication.CreateBuilder(args);

builder.ConfigureFunctionsWebApplication();

builder.Services.AddSingleton<BlobServiceClient>(sp =>
{
    var connectionString = builder.Configuration["AzureWebJobsStorage"]
        ?? throw new InvalidOperationException("Missing
        AzureWebJobsStorage");

    return new BlobServiceClient(connectionString);
});

builder.Services.AddHttpClient("ErpApi", client =>
{
    client.BaseAddress = new Uri("https://erp.anywebsitename.com/");
})
.AddStandardResilienceHandler();

builder.Services.AddSingleton<ITenantConfigRepository,
TenantConfigRepository>();

builder.Build().Run();
```

The important point is not one exact startup template. It is that modern Functions code now fits naturally into the same hosting and composition style used elsewhere in contemporary .NET.

Async All the Way Is No Longer Optional

Serverless systems live on concurrency, waiting, and efficient I/O. Modern .NET has steadily improved the runtime and library support for that style of application design, which is one of the reasons it now fits serverless much better. The platform's async model is mature, well-understood, and deeply integrated into the networking and hosting stack. For `OrderProcessor`, this means Functions, activities, and downstream service calls can remain non-blocking without fighting the runtime. That translates directly into better throughput and better resource usage when the system is under load.

A simple activity still captures the right shape:

Example: asynchronous activity

```
using Microsoft.Azure.Functions.Worker;

namespace OrderProcessor;

public static class TaxCalculation
{
    [Function("TaxCalculation")]
    public static async Task<decimal> Run([ActivityTrigger] Order order)
    {
        await Task.Delay(100);
        return order.Total * 0.20m;
    }
}
```

This is a small example, but it reflects the wider point. Modern serverless .NET should assume asynchronous, non-blocking work as the default, not as an optional refinement.

Resilience Is Now Configured at the HTTP Boundary

One of the biggest improvements since the older Functions era is that resilient HTTP communication can now be expressed much more cleanly. Instead of scattering retry and circuit-breaker code across individual call sites, Microsoft's current guidance is to use the `Microsoft.Extensions.Http.Resilience` package and configure resilience on named `HttpClient` registrations. That package provides resilience mechanisms specifically for `HttpClient`, and the standard handler can apply retry, timeout, circuit-breaker, and related strategies at the client boundary rather than in handwritten policy code inside every Function.

External calls to ERP systems, partner APIs, and other services no longer need to rely on repeated inline resilience logic. The architecture becomes cleaner because resilience moves to the boundary where it belongs, leaving the Function code focused on business intent rather than plumbing.

Cleaner DI and Modern C# Reduce Friction

The evolution is not only about hosting and libraries. Modern C# also makes service code less verbose. **Primary constructors were added in C# 12**, and Microsoft's own current examples use them in .NET documentation. They are not a serverless feature specifically, but they are exactly the sort of language improvement that makes dependency-heavy cloud code easier to write and maintain. In a Function-heavy system where services frequently depend on logging, HTTP clients, repositories, and configuration, reducing constructor boilerplate is a real quality-of-life improvement.

A service in the current style can therefore look like this:

Example: modern service with a primary constructor

```
namespace OrderProcessor;

public sealed class FraudService(
    ILogger<FraudService> logger,
    IHttpClientFactory httpClientFactory)
{
    public async Task<bool> CheckAsync(Order order)
    {
        var client = httpClientFactory.CreateClient("FraudApi");
        var response = await client.GetAsync($"/api/fraud/{order.Id}");
```

```
        logger.LogInformation(
            "Fraud check returned {StatusCode} for order {OrderId}",
            response.StatusCode,
            order.Id);

        return response.IsSuccessStatusCode;
    }
}
```

The value here is not novelty. It is that modern .NET keeps removing the incidental friction that used to make cloud-native code more cumbersome than it needed to be.

Streaming and Pipelines Are a Better Fit for File-Heavy Workloads

Another area where modern .NET has become more useful for serverless systems is streaming and efficient data handling. The .NET 10 libraries continue that direction, including **new JSON efficiency work such as** `PipeReader` **support** and broader diagnostics and serialization improvements. That matters directly for workloads such as the file-ingestion and email-processing paths discussed earlier in the book. `OrderProcessor` is not limited to tiny JSON payloads. It may need to ingest files, stream attachments, and move data without buffering everything into memory first. Modern .NET is simply better suited to that kind of work than earlier versions were.

A channel-based pipeline remains a good illustration of the direction:

Example: streaming work through channels

```
var channel = Channel.CreateUnbounded<byte[]>();

_ = Task.Run(async () =>
{
    await foreach (var chunk in FileStreamer.ReadAsync("order.eml"))
    {
        await channel.Writer.WriteAsync(chunk);
    }

    channel.Writer.Complete();
});
```

```
await foreach (var chunk in channel.Reader.ReadAllAsync())
{
    await ProcessChunkAsync(chunk);
}
```

This matches the broader serverless principle of streaming and backpressure-aware processing rather than eager buffering.

Hybrid Models Now Feel Normal, Not Unusual

The modern .NET platform also makes it easier to think beyond "Functions only." Serverless systems increasingly combine Azure Functions with other hosted components such as minimal APIs, worker services, or containerized processes, depending on the workload. .NET 10 continues to strengthen the underlying platform with new libraries, diagnostics, serialization improvements, and ongoing SDK/tooling evolution, which makes these mixed architectures feel more natural instead of patched together. For `OrderProcessor`, that means Functions can remain the event-driven glue while other parts of the platform, health endpoints, administrative APIs, CPU-heavy workers, or specialized services can live in adjacent .NET components without forcing a completely different programming model.

The Real Evolution Is Cultural As Much As Technical

The evolution of .NET for serverless is not only a runtime story. It is also a culture story. Modern .NET development has moved strongly toward structured logging, dependency injection, asynchronous programming, local tooling, infrastructure as code, and resilient client boundaries. Those habits now fit serverless development naturally rather than feeling bolted on. That is one of the biggest reasons .NET feels first-class in this space now. The language, runtime, libraries, and ecosystem have all moved closer to the needs of distributed cloud systems.

For `OrderProcessor`, that means the architecture no longer has to choose between using .NET well and using Azure Functions well. The two now fit together far more cleanly than they once did.

Project Tie-In: Updating OrderProcessor for the Modern .NET Model

In practical terms, `OrderProcessor` should now be read as a **.NET 10, isolated-worker, resilient-client** serverless system. The Functions app should use the isolated worker model and standard host configuration patterns. External HTTP integrations should use named `HttpClient` registrations with `Microsoft.Extensions.Http.Resilience` rather than handwritten resilience logic at every call site. Services can take advantage of modern C# patterns such as primary constructors, where that improves clarity. File-heavy paths can lean on channels, streaming, and newer serialization efficiency improvements rather than buffering everything by default. These are not cosmetic updates. They make the platform cleaner, easier to evolve, and more aligned with the current direction of both .NET and Azure Functions.

The Future of Azure Serverless

Azure Functions remain central to serverless .NET, but the broader Azure serverless story is no longer just about Functions in isolation. The platform now includes a wider set of building blocks that are increasingly used together: Azure Functions for event-driven glue, Azure Container Apps for container-based serverless workloads, Event Grid for flexible event routing, Durable Functions for workflow coordination, and a growing set of AI-oriented integrations that let serverless code participate in intelligent application flows. For `OrderProcessor`, that means the future is less about replacing Functions and more about using Functions inside a broader, more hybrid serverless fabric.

The most important shift is that Azure serverless is becoming more composable. Functions still provide event-driven compute, but teams increasingly pair them with other Azure services when the workload calls for different execution shapes. That is especially relevant now that modern .NET Azure Functions are expected to run on the isolated worker model, while some older hosting assumptions are narrowing. For example, Microsoft now states that .NET 9 is the last .NET version supported on the Linux Consumption plan, which means newer .NET versions such as .NET 10 push teams toward supported alternatives such as Flex Consumption and other current hosting choices. In practice, this encourages architectures that are explicit about workload shape instead of assuming one hosting model fits everything forever.

Figure 12-2 shows how Azure Functions now sit inside a broader serverless architecture that also includes containers, events, durable workflows, and AI services.

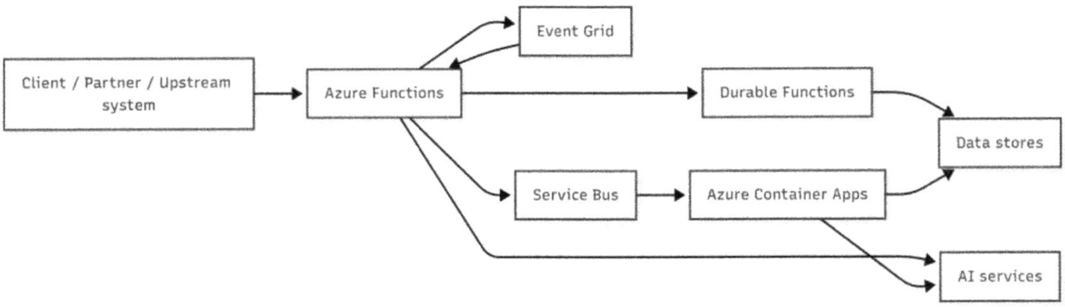

Figure 12-2. *A Modern Serverless .NET Architecture Using Azure Functions, Durable Functions, Service Bus, Container Apps, Data Stores, and AI Services*

Azure Functions Are Still the Event-Driven Core

Azure Functions should still be understood as the event-driven core of many serverless .NET systems. They remain well suited to HTTP APIs, queue-triggered processing, durable workflows, timer-based automation, and glue code that connects services together. The point is not that Functions are becoming less important. The point is that they are now more often used as the coordination and integration layer inside a wider serverless architecture. For `OrderProcessor`, that means Functions can continue to own ingress, orchestration triggers, approval callbacks, event handlers, and API-style endpoints without being forced to host every kind of workload directly. That distinction matters because serverless systems now span more than one execution pattern. Some work is highly event-driven and short-lived. Some is long-running, CPU-heavy, or container-specific. Some are workflow-oriented. Some are stream-oriented. Azure's direction is not to collapse all of those needs into one runtime. It is to make those runtimes work together more naturally.

Azure Container Apps Make Hybrid Serverless Designs More Practical

One of the clearest examples of that broader direction is Azure Container Apps. Microsoft describes Container Apps as a serverless platform for running containerized applications while maintaining less infrastructure, and its jobs model supports manual, scheduled, and event-driven executions. Event-driven jobs and apps use KEDA-based scaling rules, which is particularly useful for workloads that are better expressed as containerized workers than as Functions alone.

For `OrderProcessor`, that makes Container Apps a practical companion rather than a competing idea. Functions can keep handling event ingress and orchestration, while specialized workers in Container Apps can own CPU-heavy document processing, batch-style ERP work, fraud scoring services, or partner integration shims that need a custom runtime or longer-lived execution pattern. That kind of split is increasingly normal because it lets each workload run in an environment that matches its actual behavior instead of forcing every concern into the same host.

A simple illustration of that direction looks like this:

Example: event-driven Container Apps job

```
name: erp-worker
image: anywebsitename.azurecr.io/erp-worker:latest
scale:
  minReplicas: 0
  maxReplicas: 10
  rules:
    - name: sb-scale
      type: azure-servicebus
      metadata:
        queueName: erp-batch
        queueLength: "100"
```

This is not a prediction about one exact future deployment shape. It is a good example of the architectural trend. Some workloads that were once awkward in Functions fit naturally in serverless containers that still scale from events.

Event Routing Is Becoming Richer and More Flexible

Eventing is also getting broader. Azure Event Grid is now more than a simple push-only event router. Microsoft describes Event Grid as a highly scalable managed publish-subscribe service that supports both push and pull delivery patterns and supports the CloudEvents 1.0 specification. Event subscriptions also support dead-letter destinations, which strengthens reliability for event-driven architectures that need explicit recovery behavior.

For `OrderProcessor`, that matters because the platform increasingly depends on events not only to notify downstream services, but also to express tenant boundaries, workflow milestones, and future expansion points. A richer eventing model means the architecture can stay event-driven while becoming more explicit about which consumers should see which events and how failed deliveries should be recovered. The core design principle from earlier chapters still holds: keep the critical path explicit, and then let the rest of the platform react through well-shaped event boundaries. Azure's eventing stack is simply giving teams more ways to do that cleanly.

Durable Functions Continue to Matter, and Entities Remain Useful

Durable Functions are still one of the most important orchestration tools in Azure serverless, and the isolated worker model keeps them aligned with the modern .NET Functions direction. Microsoft's current Durable Functions documentation for .NET isolated explicitly positions the model as a way to run Durable workloads on .NET versions independent of the Functions host. Durable entities also remain part of that story, and Microsoft documents durable entities as being supported in both .NET in-process and .NET isolated workers.

That means the future of serverless orchestration in Azure is not only about long-running workflows. It is also about smaller stateful coordination points where entity-style state is a better fit than a full orchestration. In `OrderProcessor`, that could still mean approval state, per-tenant counters, quota tracking, or small pieces of durable workflow state that do not justify a full round trip to a general-purpose store on every interaction. The important point is not that every problem should become a durable entity. It is that the Azure serverless model now includes both workflow orchestration and lightweight durable state as first-class patterns.

A representative entity example still looks like this:

Example: durable entity for tenant quota tracking

```
using Microsoft.Azure.Functions.Worker;
using Microsoft.DurableTask.Entities;

namespace OrderProcessor.Examples;

public class TenantQuotaEntity : TaskEntity<int>
{
```

```
    public void AddOrder()
    {
        State++;
    }

    public int GetCount()
    {
        return State;
    }

    [Function(nameof(TenantQuotaEntity))]
    public static Task Run([EntityTrigger] TaskEntityDispatcher dispatcher)
    {
        return dispatcher.DispatchAsync<TenantQuotaEntity>();
    }
}
```

AI Integration Is Becoming a Normal Serverless Concern

Another important shift is that AI is no longer something bolted awkwardly onto the side of cloud workloads. Microsoft's Azure Functions documentation now explicitly covers AI-enabled application scenarios, and Azure Functions also has an Azure OpenAI extension for triggers and bindings, although that extension is currently still in preview. This means Functions can increasingly act as the orchestration and integration layer around AI capabilities rather than only being a generic compute endpoint that happens to call a model API.

For `OrderProcessor`, that makes AI a practical extension of existing workflows rather than a separate architecture entirely. Approval emails can be enriched with clearer summaries. Inbound communications can be classified or normalized before entering the workflow. Suspicious patterns can be scored and routed into human review paths. The platform does not need to become "an AI system" to benefit from AI. It simply needs clean workflow boundaries where AI can add value without taking over the architecture.

Governance Is Also Becoming More Automated

The future of Azure serverless is not only about richer execution models. It is also about stronger operational guardrails. The pressure points discussed in Chapter 11, region restrictions, telemetry growth, tenant-aware deployment discipline, and delivery controls, increasingly point toward policy-driven and automation-driven governance. Even where one specific service or feature changes over time, the broader direction is clear: serverless platforms are easier to scale safely when policy is expressed in deployment, configuration, and delivery paths instead of left to memory or convention.

A future-facing `OrderProcessor` is not only more hybrid and more event-driven. It is also more governable. As the platform becomes more capable, the surrounding controls have to become more explicit, not less.

Project Tie-In: The Near Future of OrderProcessor

If `OrderProcessor` is projected forward a short distance, the most likely future is not a total architectural rewrite. It is a cleaner hybrid architecture built from the same principles already established in the book. Core workflows can remain in Durable Functions. Event-driven ingress and reaction paths can remain in Functions. CPU-heavy or long-running components can move into Container Apps where that better matches the workload. Event Grid can continue to serve as the routing fabric around workflow milestones. Durable entities can support narrow stateful coordination concerns. AI can enrich selected points in the process without displacing the core workflow model.

That is the key takeaway from the current Azure serverless direction. The future is not about replacing Functions. It is about composing Functions, container-based serverless compute, event routing, durable workflow state, and intelligent services more deliberately. For `OrderProcessor`, that means less custom plumbing, more workload-specific hosting choices, and a platform that can keep evolving without abandoning the architectural foundations laid down in the rest of the book.

Beyond Functions: Orchestration, Streams, and AI

Azure Functions will remain an important part of serverless .NET, but the future shape of distributed systems is wider than Functions alone. The stronger architectural trend is toward systems that combine several complementary models: orchestration for long-running and stateful coordination, streaming for high-volume and near-real-time event flow, and AI for enrichment, classification, summarization, and decision support. In other words, the platform is moving from simple event handlers toward systems that can coordinate work across time, react continuously to live data, and add intelligent processing where it creates real value. That does not make Functions less relevant. It makes them part of a richer serverless toolkit.

For `OrderProcessor`, this matters because the next stage of maturity is not just "more Functions." It is a better combination of patterns. Durable workflows are still useful for approval paths, sagas, and long-running partner interactions. Streaming platforms become useful when the system needs to observe or react to sustained event flow rather than isolated discrete triggers. AI becomes useful when the workflow benefits from enriched context, natural-language summaries, anomaly detection, or agent-assisted decision support. The architectural question is no longer which single Azure service does everything. It is how these patterns fit together cleanly without turning the platform into a tangle.

Orchestration Is Expanding Beyond One Runtime Boundary

Earlier chapters already showed why explicit orchestration is valuable. Durable Functions makes long-running, fault-tolerant workflows much easier to reason about than scattered retries, timers, and callback state. That remains true. But in a growing distributed system, orchestration does not have to stop at one workflow runtime or one Function App. Some teams will continue to use Durable Functions as the internal workflow engine while also integrating with external orchestration or workflow fabrics where cross-service coordination needs to span several independently deployed components. Dapr workflow is one example of this broader direction. Dapr documents its workflow capability as a reliable way to write long-running, fault-tolerant, stateful workflows that coordinate business logic and integrations across microservices, and it is designed to work alongside Dapr pub/sub, bindings, and state management.

For `OrderProcessor`, that means orchestration should be understood as an architectural capability rather than as a single product choice. Durable Functions can continue to own the internal workflow paths that fit naturally inside the Azure Functions estate. At the same time, external eventing or workflow fabrics can be used where the coordination boundary becomes broader than one app should reasonably own. The important principle is the same one established earlier in the book: use orchestration to make long-running coordination explicit. The implementation boundary can vary depending on how widely that coordination has to span.

A small illustrative example of that externalized direction might look like this:

Example architectural option: external pub/sub boundary with Dapr

```
using Dapr.Client;
using Microsoft.AspNetCore.Mvc;

namespace OrderProcessor.Examples;

[ApiController]
[Route("orders")]
public sealed class OrdersController : ControllerBase
{
    [HttpPost]
    public async Task<IActionResult> SubmitOrder(
        [FromBody] Order order,
        [FromServices] DaprClient dapr)
    {
        await dapr.PublishEventAsync("orders-pubsub", "orders.
        created", order);
        return Accepted();
    }
}
```

This should be read as an architectural option, not as a required cumulative project change. The point is that OrderProcessor can keep its internal Durable workflows while still participating in a broader event- and workflow-oriented environment.

Streaming Becomes Important When Events Stop Being Isolated

Events and streams are related, but they are not the same thing. Event-driven systems often focus on discrete business occurrences: an order was submitted, an approval arrived, and a document was uploaded. Streaming systems are more useful when the architecture needs to process sustained flows of data, observe trends in near real time, or push large volumes of messages through a continuous backbone. Azure Event Hubs is Microsoft's managed real-time data streaming platform, and Microsoft describes it as capable of ingesting millions of events per second with low latency. It also supports Capture, which lets teams work with both real-time and batch-oriented paths on the same event stream.

That makes streaming relevant for the future shape of `OrderProcessor`. A single order confirmation event may still travel well through Event Grid. But if the platform starts needing real-time fraud scoring across large volumes of transaction flow, continuous live operational dashboards, or a stream-based analytical backbone for downstream detection and reporting, then a streaming fabric becomes a more natural fit. The point is not to replace every event with a stream. It is to recognize that some workloads are fundamentally stream-shaped and should be designed that way rather than forced into one-off trigger semantics.

A representative example still fits naturally into Functions:

Example: consuming a stream with Azure Functions

```
using Microsoft.Azure.Functions.Worker;

namespace OrderProcessor.Examples;

public static class StreamOrders
{
    [Function("StreamOrders")]
    public static void Run(
        [EventHubTrigger("orders-hub", Connection = "EventHubConn")]
        string[] events,
        FunctionContext ctx)
    {
        var logger = ctx.GetLogger("StreamOrders");

        foreach (var item in events)
        {
            logger.LogInformation("Order event: {Event}", item);
        }
    }
}
```

Again, the point is not that this exact Function must become part of the final sample. It is that Functions and streaming are complementary. Functions can remain the processing boundary while Event Hubs becomes the continuous transport layer.

AI Is Moving from Optional Add-On to Workflow Participant

Another clear architectural direction is that AI is no longer something separate from serverless systems. Microsoft's current Azure Functions guidance explicitly covers AI-enabled applications, including LLMs, RAG patterns, agentic workflows, and AI framework integration. In other words, Functions are increasingly positioned as a natural place to host triggers, tools, connectors, and lightweight workflow logic around AI capabilities rather than only as general-purpose compute endpoints that happen to call an AI API.

For `OrderProcessor`, that means AI should be treated neither as magic nor as an afterthought. It is most useful when it augments an already well-designed workflow. Approval flows can benefit from summarized context rather than raw JSON. Fraud pipelines can benefit from model-assisted scoring rather than fixed thresholds alone. Inbound documents or emails can be classified, tagged, or summarized before they enter the rest of the workflow. None of that requires the whole platform to become "an AI architecture." It simply means some workflow boundaries can become more intelligent if the value is clear and the integration is controlled.

A small example illustrates the pattern:

Example architectural option: AI enrichment for approvals

```
namespace OrderProcessor.Examples;

public sealed class ApprovalContextEnricher(HttpClient client)
{
    public async Task<string> EnrichAsync(Order order, CancellationToken
    stopToken = default)
    {
        var prompt = $"Summarise order {order.Id} for approval and
        highlight any risk indicators.";

        using var response = await client.PostAsJsonAsync(
            "/ai/summarise",
```

```
            new { prompt },
            stopToken);

        response.EnsureSuccessStatusCode();

        return await response.Content.ReadAsStringAsync(stopToken);
    }
}
```

This is shown as an architectural direction, not a required final project file. The important idea is that AI sits inside a bounded workflow step and produces a useful output for a human or downstream decision-maker.

These Three Directions Work Best Together, Not Separately

The interesting part is not that orchestration, streaming, and AI are each growing. It is that they combine well. A workflow can begin in a Durable Functions orchestration, publish to a stream for real-time detection or analytics, and then enrich a later approval step with AI-generated context. A stream can surface suspicious patterns that route into a human approval workflow. A broad event fabric can let external systems participate without taking ownership away from the core business orchestration. The future architecture is not one huge engine that does everything. It is a composition of clearer, narrower capabilities that work together.

That is a useful way to think about `OrderProcessor's` next stage. The platform does not need to choose between workflows, streams, and AI. It needs to be deliberate about where each pattern adds value and where it does not. Orchestration is best when coordination and durable progress matter. Streaming is best when continuous high-volume flow matters. AI is best when the workflow benefits from interpretation, enrichment, or model-assisted judgement. Putting the right concern on the right backbone is what keeps the architecture understandable.

Project Tie-In: The Next Architectural Layer for OrderProcessor

If `OrderProcessor` evolves beyond its current shape, the most likely next step is not to stop being event-driven. It is to become more explicit about which parts of the platform are workflow-oriented, which are stream-oriented, and which benefit from AI augmentation. Durable orchestrations can continue to own the multi-step business flows that need durable state and explicit control. Event Hubs or another streaming backbone can support real-time analytical or fraud-oriented paths where continuous ingestion matters more than discrete triggers. AI can enrich selected human-facing or decision-heavy stages without displacing the core workflow design.

That is the real lesson of this section. Beyond Functions, the future is not a rejection of serverless Functions architecture. It is a broader composition model in which Functions, durable orchestration, streaming platforms, and AI-enabled services each take the part of the problem they are best suited to solve. `OrderProcessor` remains event-driven at its core, but it becomes more capable by letting those neighboring patterns participate where they genuinely improve the system.

Final Reference Architecture and Lessons Learned

We have travelled a long way through this book. The journey began with the fundamentals of distributed systems and moved through Azure Functions, messaging, consistency, Durable Functions, security, observability, resilience, deployment, governance, case studies, risk analysis, and the evolving direction of both .NET and Azure. Along the way, `OrderProcessor` stopped being a simple teaching sample and became something more useful: reference architecture for how a serverless distributed system can be designed, evolved, and operated in the real world. By this point, the question is no longer whether the platform can process orders. The question is what the complete system looks like when the patterns from the rest of the book are assembled into one coherent whole.

That is the purpose of this final section. It brings the architecture together in its production-minded form and, just as importantly, clarifies the lessons that should survive even as the underlying platform continues to evolve. Azure services will continue to improve. .NET will continue to move forward. New hosting models, integrations, and tooling will continue to appear. But the deeper architectural lessons should remain steady. A good serverless distributed system still needs clear workflow boundaries, durable state where coordination matters, event-driven decoupling where independence matters, disciplined observability, strong security boundaries, explicit governance, and designs that respect both operational failure and human limits.

The Final OrderProcessor Architecture

At the center of the final `OrderProcessor` architecture sits a set of durable workflows that coordinate the business-critical path of order processing. Orders enter the platform through a controlled ingress boundary, either as HTTP submissions or as file-driven inputs. The platform validates those requests, applies authentication and tenant context, and routes them into the event-driven and orchestration layers that own the real business flow. Fraud checks, tax handling, approval checkpoints, ERP integration, external partner callbacks, and selected compensating actions all remain explicit, durable parts of the system rather than being scattered across ad hoc retry logic and hidden callbacks.

Around that workflow core sits a wider event-driven fabric. Business milestones are published so that downstream services such as logistics, invoicing, notifications, analytics, or tenant-facing reporting can react without becoming tightly coupled to the core orchestrator. Some of those downstream paths remain well suited to Azure Functions. Others may fit more naturally into container-hosted serverless workers, stream-processing backbones, or AI-enriched side paths. The important point is that the platform has a center of gravity without becoming a monolith. The core path remains explicit, while the surrounding system remains loosely coupled and able to evolve.

Reading Architecture As a Set of Layers

A useful way to understand the finished platform is to think of it in layers rather than as one large diagram of connected services. The first layer is ingress. Orders arrive through controlled API or upload boundaries and are immediately placed onto reliable paths that can survive failure. The second layer is orchestration. Durable workflows coordinate the long-running business steps that need durable state, retries, timers, human approvals, or external events. The third layer is event distribution. Once key business milestones occur, the wider system reacts through events rather than being hard-coded into the core workflow. The fourth layer is data. Operational data, files, projections, and audit records live in stores chosen according to their access and consistency needs rather than because one store is being forced to do everything.

The fifth layer is cross-cutting control. Observability, resilience, security, and governance surround the system instead of being applied as a finishing pass at the end. The platform emits useful traces, logs, and metrics. External HTTP boundaries are resilient by design. Sensitive boundaries are authenticated and auditable. Region, tenancy, retention, and deployment policies are enforced through infrastructure and delivery controls. Once viewed this way, the architecture becomes easier to reason about. It is not a random collection of Azure services. It is a layered system in which each part has a clear responsibility.

The Role of Orchestration in the Final Design

One of the strongest lessons from the book is that orchestration is most valuable when it is focused. `OrderProcessor` uses durable workflows for the parts of the system that genuinely benefit from durable coordination: approval loops, multi-step order progression, partner callbacks, compensation, and other long-running business processes. What it does not do, at least in the healthier final design, is turn one orchestrator into the owner of every possible side effect in the system. That lesson matters because it separates a robust workflow architecture from an over-coupled one.

This final architecture therefore treats orchestration as the backbone of the critical path, not as the destination for every piece of business logic. Downstream services remain event-driven, which gives them more independence. Narrow stateful concerns can be handled by appropriate data or entity-style models where that is a better fit. The result is a system that remains explicit without becoming centralized in the wrong places.

The Role of Data in the Final Design

The final architecture also reflects the fact that no single data model solves every problem well. Operational order data may live in a tenant-aware and region-aware store such as Cosmos DB. File content belongs in Blob Storage rather than being stuffed into an operational store. Some reporting or strongly consistent read requirements may justify a different persistence model or projection path. Audit records must be queryable and durable. Caches may exist, but the architecture does not pretend they are the primary truth. This is one of the most important ways the finished `OrderProcessor` differs from simpler sample systems. It no longer behaves as if one data store can cleanly satisfy every runtime, analytical, and operational need at once.

Just as importantly, the system now treats consistency honestly. Some read paths are eventually consistent. Some boundaries require stronger guarantees within a narrower scope. The architecture does not pretend that all parts of the platform will converge instantly, and it does not hide that reality behind misleading user messages. That honesty is one of the marks of a mature distributed design.

The Role of Operations and Governance in the Final Design

A production-minded serverless system is not defined only by its runtime behavior. It is also defined by how it is operated and governed. That is why the final reference architecture for `OrderProcessor` includes monitoring, audit, deployment controls, tagging, policy enforcement, retention rules, and region-aware boundaries as integral parts of the design. Without those controls, the platform may still function technically, but it will be much harder to trust, explain, or scale responsibly. This is one of the deeper lessons of the book. Governance is not bureaucracy wrapped around architecture. It is part of architecture. Observability is not a debugging luxury. It is part of architecture. Security is not a later hardening phase. It is part of architecture. Once a system is truly distributed, the operational estate around the workflow becomes as important as the workflow itself.

What the Architecture Achieves

Taken together, the final `OrderProcessor` architecture achieves several things at once. It remains resilient because failures are bounded, workflows are durable, and downstream dependencies do not all sit inside one fragile synchronous path. It remains scalable because the platform is built around events, asynchronous processing, workload-specific hosting choices, and stores that match the nature of the data they hold. It remains governable because region, tenancy, security, and retention are all enforced rather than merely documented. It remains observable because the system is designed to expose meaningful signals rather than raw noise. And it remains evolvable because new downstream behavior can be added without rewriting the core workflow every time.

That combination is what turns a serverless application into a platform. A platform is not simply an app that got bigger. It is a system whose technical, operational, and governance boundaries are deliberate enough that new behavior can be added without collapsing what already exists.

Lessons Learned from the Full Journey

The first major lesson is that distributed systems never become simple just because infrastructure becomes abstracted. Serverless removes many hosting concerns, and that is a genuine advantage, but it does not remove latency, partial failure, eventual consistency, operational complexity, or human error. Those concerns still exist. The win is that Azure and modern .NET provide stronger building blocks for handling them than teams used to have.

The second lesson is that serverless does not mean Functions alone. Functions are important, but they work best as part of a wider architecture that may also include messaging, orchestration, data stores, event routing, secure secret management, policy enforcement, and increasingly hybrid container-hosted workloads. Treating Functions as the whole platform usually produces brittle designs. Treating them as one core part of a broader event-driven system produces better ones.

The third lesson is that explicit coordination is almost always better than hidden coordination. Durable workflows, clear event boundaries, named HTTP clients, visible retry and timeout strategies, and policy-driven deployment controls all help because they make important behavior legible. What breaks systems most often is not that they coordinate too much. It is that they coordinate invisibly and inconsistently.

The fourth lesson is that operational quality is not separate from design quality. A system that is hard to trace, hard to secure, hard to govern, hard to explain, or hard to recover is not a mature system even if its happy path works beautifully. Architecture has to be judged by how it behaves under strain, under change, and under scrutiny, not only by how it behaves on a whiteboard.

The fifth lesson is that humans remain part of the architecture. Developers need safe and productive ways to work. Operators need signals that help them decide what to do. Users need messages that make sense in the face of distributed delay and partial failure. Approvers need context, not raw payloads. Auditors need evidence. A system that ignores these human realities is not complete, no matter how elegant the code may be.

What Readers Should Carry Forward

By the end of this book, the most valuable takeaway should not be a memorized list of Azure services or .NET APIs. It should be a mental model. Start with clear business boundaries. Use durable coordination where long-running progress matters. Use events to decouple where independent evolution matters. Choose data stores according to access and consistency needs rather than convenience. Make resilience visible and bounded. Treat observability, security, and governance as design concerns from the start. Be careful with complexity that accumulates quietly. And always remember that the final system is lived in by people as well as processes.

If you carry that model forward, you will be able to adapt even as the underlying tools continue to change. That is the real value of `OrderProcessor` as a reference architecture. It is not meant to be copied line for line forever. It is meant to show how to think about serverless distributed systems so that the same core ideas remain useful even when the services, runtimes, and libraries evolve.

Final Perspective

The final form of `OrderProcessor` is not "finished" in the sense that no more change will ever come. That is not how living distributed systems work. New platform capabilities will arrive. Hosting choices will evolve. AI will become more deeply integrated into normal workflows. Governance and compliance requirements will continue to tighten. Workloads will shift. Tenants will grow. But the architectural core remains stable. Use events well. Coordinate explicitly. Respect failure. Keep boundaries clear. Design for observability, security, and human use from the beginning.

That is the real lesson learned from the whole book. Modern serverless distributed systems in .NET and Azure are powerful, but they reward discipline more than novelty. They work best when developers combine strong platform primitives with clear workflow design, honest operational thinking, and a willingness to let the architecture evolve without abandoning its foundations.

Index

A

B

C

© Patrick Kearns 2026
P. Kearns, *Serverless Distributed Systems in Modern .NET and Azure*,
https://doi.org/10.1007/979-8-8688-2839-3

E

F, G

H

I

J, K

L

M

N

O, P

T

U

V

W, X, Y

Z

GPSR Compliance
The European Union's (EU) General Product Safety Regulation (GPSR) is a set of rules that requires consumer products to be safe and our obligations to ensure this.

If you have any concerns about our products, you can contact us on

ProductSafety@springernature.com

In case Publisher is established outside the EU, the EU authorized representative is:

Springer Nature Customer Service Center GmbH
Europaplatz 3
69115 Heidelberg, Germany

www.ingramcontent.com/pod-product-compliance
Lightning Source LLC
Chambersburg PA
CBHW060137090926
51106CB00030B/1260
* 9 7 9 8 8 6 8 8 2 8 3 8 6 *